MR AND MRS
JINNAH

MR AND MRS JINNAH

THE MARRIAGE THAT SHOOK INDIA

Sheela Reddy

PENGUIN
VIKING

VIKING

USA | Canada | UK | Ireland | Australia
New Zealand | India | South Africa | China

Viking is part of the Penguin Random House group of companies
whose addresses can be found at global.penguinrandomhouse.com

Published by Penguin Random House India Pvt. Ltd
7th Floor, Infinity Tower C, DLF Cyber City,
Gurgaon 122 002, Haryana, India

First published in Viking by Penguin Random House India 2017

10 9 8 7 6 5 4 3 2 1

ISBN 9780670086436

For sale in the Indian Subcontinent only

Typeset in Sabon by Manipal Digital Systems, Manipal
Printed at Thomson Press India Ltd, New Delhi

www.penguin.co.in

To Mr and Mrs C.N. Reddy

CONTENTS

~

Chapter One

~

After keeping the world guessing for two years, on a hot April evening in the year 1918, Mohammed Ali Jinnah married Ruttie Petit, the only daughter of a rich Parsi baronet. He was a cold, reserved man of nearly forty-two and had so far lived according to his own carefully laid plan, arriving after two decades of exertion exactly where he had intended to be: one of the best-paid lawyers in the country, an elected member of the viceroy's Imperial Legislative Council; the tallest leader in Muslim politics and well on his way to becoming the most important Congress leader. Until now, marriage had not figured in his plans, especially not to a rich, society girl less than half his age. But once he made up his mind to marry Ruttie, he set about it with his usual stoic resolve, unflinching in the face of the innumerable little humiliations and ridicule, skilfully dodging the traps set in his path and planning every step of the way in his diligent, thorough manner.

He began straightforwardly enough, taking his marriage proposal directly to Ruttie's father, with whom he was staying as a guest during that holiday. Ruttie's father, Sir Dinshaw Petit, was a stout, plump-faced, amiable man around Jinnah's age who had inherited a vast fortune. He usually took his family abroad for holidays, either to London or France, where he owned an estate on the French Riviera almost as large as the Prince of Monaco's and the King of Belgium's. But since the War had started, the Petits had been unable to travel abroad and instead moved to the hills whenever they needed a break, travelling with their four children—Ruttie, followed by three boys—and their army of cooks, table boys, maids, governess, tutors, nurses, horses and dogs and any house guests they could assemble.

Sir Dinshaw was a genial host and liked to collect eminent people around him; neither his palatial sea-facing mansion on Malabar Hill nor his hill estates in Poona and Matheran were ever short of guests. He had known Jinnah since before Ruttie was born and was very fond of him, as was the elegant Lady Petit, so invitations to visit them were never lacking. But this was probably the first time that Jinnah had accepted the Petits' invitation—and certainly the last time he ever stayed with them.

Sir Dinshaw admired Jinnah, who was very popular among his contemporaries because of his 'impressive personality and stout-hearted nationalism'. It is unlikely that Jinnah returned the compliment. Sir Dinshaw belonged to a family of Parsi merchants well known for their business acumen and philanthropy. His grandfather was a self-made millionaire, pioneer of Bombay's cloth industry, and a leading benefactor of Parsis; his father ran a colossal business empire, including nearly a dozen cloth mills, and with such a thorough, practical knowledge of the spinning and weaving industry that he wrote a two-volume tome on the subject. When Sir Dinshaw was only twenty-two, his father died leaving him to fill his shoes as best as he could. Six years later, he inherited his grandfather's title as well, although his father had not been the eldest son, thereby cutting out of the succession several cousins who considered themselves more deserving. It gave him, besides his vast fortune, a deep sense of his own importance as well as a lasting insecurity. He was quick to take offence and, according to the British, vain. They refused to take him seriously, with a high-ranking official even pointing out during a cross-examination in court by Jinnah—in a case involving rigging in a municipal election by British officials to keep out an anti-government candidate—that it was really Sir Dinshaw's vanity that drove him rather than any strong political conviction, and implying that the baronet would fall in line with any British-inspired scheme so long as they pandered to his conceit and sense of self-importance. It was an opinion shared by the nationalists as well, with the Parsi firebrand Sir Dinshaw Edulji Wacha deploring his nomination to the viceregal council because, as he later wrote to Dadabhai Naoroji, Sir Dinshaw Petit 'was totally ignorant of public affairs' and the British should have shown 'some balance of the aristocracy of wealth and intellect'.

In his bid to outshine the other fabulous homes rising up on Malabar Hill, he poured lakhs of rupees into renovating Petit Hall, the sea-facing marble mansion that he inherited from his grandfather at the bottom of Malabar Hill. Petit Hall was already an imposing palace, with its Grecian pillars and fountains, and sweeping stairways made of the most expensive imported marble, built by his grandfather as a second home to host his grander receptions. But once Sir Dinshaw took over, he rebuilt it on an even more ambitious scale, adding new wings with suites of bedrooms overlooking the sea, tall shade trees and lawns which almost touched the waves. The gardens were filled with imported French flowers and all of this was on land he reclaimed from the sea, and surrounded by a vast park. Inside were dozens of crystal chandeliers, Louis XV tables and chairs, ancient Ming vases, ceramic potted palms and Persian carpets, 'all in such good taste that one remembers only the beauty and forgets the cost', as poet and nationalist orator Sarojini Naidu, a frequent house guest at Petit Hall, wrote home to say. But he probably could not resist boasting of the cost of such understated elegance, if we can presume that Sarojini got her figures on the cost of furnishing a single room in Petit Hall from her host: 'The day drawing room alone, that is used only for receiving grain merchants and students and stray poets, cost 80,000 rupees to furnish. The tapestry alone used to cover a set of eight chairs in this room cost 20,000 rupees.'

He also entertained lavishly, keeping one of the best tables in Bombay, with his chefs providing the finest of four different cuisines. His annual Polo Ball was the highlight of the Bombay season, and the size and scale of his garden parties were the envy and delight of Bombay's high society. To be fair, in this Sir Dinshaw was only following in the footsteps of his grandfather. The old baronet had famously hosted a fancy dress ball at Petit Hall for the Duke of Edinburgh, turning out for his own party in the costume of the Persian king, Shapurji. But being an astute old man, the previous baronet was able to use his grand receptions as stepping stones to a successful political career. Unlike his grandson, Sir Dinshaw the First was able to extract rich dividends from his extravagant entertaining, earning himself through them a string of public honours, including the office of Sheriff of Bombay and a knighthood, followed three years later by a baronetcy. The first baronet, also called Sir Dinshaw Petit, was an unashamed and energetic British-pleaser—serving on committees to organize public festivities in honour of the marriage of the Prince of Wales, delivering farewell addresses to departing officials and erecting statues in their memory, even organizing on one occasion when the Prince of Wales was seriously ill, a solemn ceremony in all the fire temples to pray for his recovery—without ever losing his clout and eminence within the Parsi community.

He led Parsi delegations to the government, drafted memorandums for them, was chairman of the Bombay Association—a forum to discuss public ideas that was a precursor to the Bombay Presidency Association—steered legislation to codify Parsi personal law relating to marriage, divorce and succession, and was one of the five trustees of the Parsi Panchayat Funds, an honorary but nonetheless the most prestigious position in the community, in charge of all its public funds and charities. But his grandson, despite emulating him in most things and working doubly hard to ensure the same honours for himself, was somehow never able to lift his public career above the ordinary.

The friendship between Sir Dinshaw and Jinnah—if it can be described as such—was unequal from the start. The baronet, despite running a dozen cloth mills and a string of family charities including hospitals, schools and libraries, was an under-confident man, aspiring to a career in public life without being able to win a place for himself beside the many overpowering Parsi leaders of his time, teetering between his sense of what was due to him and his admiration for men of stronger character than him. Jinnah, on the other hand, even when he was a struggling young lawyer, unemployed and living in a small hotel room in Bombay, had a surplus of confidence. The result was that Jinnah, three years younger than the baronet and nowhere close to him in wealth, had always been the more patronizing of the two. This was all the more curious considering that in those first few years of his legal career, between 1896 and 1900, when Jinnah needed work, Sir Dinshaw was in an ideal position to provide it. The baronet was regarded by most lawyers as a walking goldmine for briefs because of his habit of taking all his disputes, no matter how trivial, to court, never counting the costs in legal fee. In fact, Sir Dinshaw did provide Jinnah with his first appearance in high court, but indirectly: it was a case in which Sir Dinshaw had clapped a charge of blackmail against several important persons, and Jinnah was part of the group of lawyers hired by the defendants. The case, which appeared in the Bombay High Court in October 1898, brought Jinnah into the limelight, and after that, on 1 May 1900, Jinnah was appointed a presidency magistrate, when he had work chasing him, rather than the other way round, so that moment was gone when Jinnah needed briefs from Sir Dinshaw, leaving him to bask, undisturbed by lucre, in the baronet's and his lady wife's admiration.

To add to his natural sense of superiority, there was the way Jinnah had forged ahead of Sir Dinshaw in public life, despite the latter's head start over him. Sir Dinshaw was already a Justice of Peace when Jinnah arrived in Bombay as a young man of twenty, but there was no comparison now in their public career. The famous 1916 session when the Muslim League and the Congress held a joint session in Lucknow where he would emerge as the unchallenged leader of Muslims and, as a consequence, of the Congress as well, was still some months away, he was almost there already, preparing to be re-elected the following month as a member of the Imperial Legislative Council. His name was in the papers almost daily, speaking either on behalf of the Congress or the Muslim League, the voice of reason and progress, having overcome conservative forces within both organizations. For Sir Dinshaw, whose public career still languished at the stage where he held grand receptions to celebrate other people's public appointments, never his own, to have Jinnah staying as a guest with him would have been the next best thing to becoming an influential political leader; the reflected glory equivalent almost to brandishing a flag above his castle declaring that in the ongoing battle between the two sides, he was on the side of modernity and progress, and against the orthodox Parsis.

And certainly, Sir Dinshaw was a smart, modern man, at least outwardly. His education, though limited, had been in English. He had received what a journal of his time described unenthusiastically as 'a fair English and general education' at the Fort High School, where boys from the best families were sent to learn English and mix with the sons of rich men from other communities. But he dropped out and instead of passing his matriculation and getting a college degree like so many of his Parsi peers, was tutored at home by an Englishman who, we are told, was a Cambridge graduate. In appearance, he was as British as any of the Parsis who had gone abroad to study. In fact, he was counted, at least by the orthodox, as one of the 'smart set'—one of those anglicized 'bowler-hatted' and 'cheroot-smoking' Parsis whom they regarded with increasing suspicion. There is a photograph of him while his grandfather was still alive, posing outside his uncle's home with a group of his Parsi associates—a stout young man of average height, standing stiffly erect with his chin thrust out, his wispy facial hair in sharp contrast to the thick walrus moustaches of the rest of the men, and lacking their air of easy confidence and style. These Parsi mill owners are much older than the future baronet and appear to be setting off on a cycling trip—all the rage then—with each man standing with his hands holding the bars of his bicycle, dressed identically in stiff white collar and cravat, blazer, knee-length boots, short trousers and bowler hat. The future baronet's uncle is standing next to him, a head shorter but the more flamboyant figure of the two. Clearly, English dress and manners have passed down in the Petit family for at least two generations, so it's puzzling why he should have been stuck with the label of 'smart set' while his uncle escaped unscathed. This may have had something to do with the fact that they were raised by different parents.

Sir Dinshaw's grandfather—his name was also Sir Dinshaw Petit as by the rules of succession to the baronetcy, Ruttie's father had to assume his grandfather's name although he started life as Jeejeebhoy Framjee Petit. But being two generations removed, and considerably embarrassed with the unwieldy name he had been saddled with, he allowed his nearest friends and relatives to address him as 'DP' after coming into his title. The first Sir Dinshaw, like his grandson after him, had been sent to a school run by an Englishman for a few years. It was a far-sighted move on his great-grandfather's part: it helped DP's grandfather to network better with the British. But despite speaking in English when required, the old Sir Dinshaw made no pretence of being anglicized. He was an orthodox Zoroastrian of the old school, married at fourteen to a girl from an aristocratic Parsi family, but strictly brought up. She, in turn, raised her fourteen children to be comfortable with who they were: as cosmopolitan as they pleased outside the home, but strictly Parsi within. Both grandparents were very religious, and the old baronet's idea of charity was usually about building fire temples and making donations connected with religious ceremonies. He was so resistant to any change in tradition within the community that on one occasion when a Parsi with a mechanical bent wanted to introduce an automated corpse-bearer to replace the men who carried the dead into the Tower of Silence, he had the scheme shot down. His sons changed some of that, with both DP's father and his father's brother after him handing out funds for institutions that had nothing whatsoever to do with Zoroastrianism, including a 1000-pound donation to the Northbrook Club in London to start a library, which won DP's father the honour of a special dinner hosted for him at the club during his only trip abroad.

His father walked that dangerous line, between being a socially progressive Parsi and toppling over on to the other side as a pucca Englishman, with consummate ease. He sent both his son and daughter to English-medium schools, entertained men and women of other communities at his home in an age when intercommunity dining was still taboo, and took the leading role in establishing the Masonic Lodge in India. But he also arranged his son's marriage in the orthodox way, marrying him off in 1894 at the relatively early age (for a Parsi male) of twenty-one into the first family among the Parsis. The bride, Dinbai, was the elder daughter of Sir Jamsetjee Jeejeebhoy, grandson of the legendary Parsi philanthropist and rags-to-riches merchant (quite literally, for he started his business career by selling used bottles). She was around his age and almost blind in one eye because of glaucoma, but it was considered a brilliant match, an alliance that cemented ties between the two families that went back several generations. The marriage was a conventional one, and although their temperaments were very different, with Dinbai coming from the most fashionable and Europeanized Parsi families in Bombay, where the women had been out of purdah for several generations before the other Parsis. They led their separate lives tranquilly for the most part, leaving the four children in the hands of well-trained staff, mostly European, as was the fashion then among the rich. But marrying into the first family of Parsi plutocrats seems to have added considerably to the future baronet's confusion over his English and Parsi halves.

At a time when men aspiring to high society were dragging their wives out of purdah, buying them new clothes and high heels so that they would fit into the new world, Lady Dinbai was a rare asset.

The daughter of a baronet herself, she was accustomed to ruling the social world. Several generations ago, girls in her family had to be smuggled to school to receive an English education. But since then the family had acquired an unchallenged status as the first family among the Parsis, and the Jeejeebhoys no longer bothered to hide their modernity. Dinbai's grandmother and aunt were among the first Indian women to be introduced to the Prince of Wales (later, George IV) when he visited India in 1875, with the heir to the British crown later calling on them at Mazagon Castle. As the eldest of the three children of the highest-ranking Parsi in the country, Dinbai was denied no privilege granted to her brother: English nannies, French maids, going to the best school, an English governess, holidays in Europe, and the confidence to go out into society, equipped with an English education. Her brother died young, and the baronetcy passed on to her uncle and his sons, but while Dinbai's father was alive his two daughters ruled high society, even going to the horse shows with their father who won many prizes there, and attending the royal durbars with their father. Ruttie's aunt even attended Queen Victoria's Diamond Jubilee celebrations in London with her father (Dinbai was already married by then) and was received by the queen at an audience in Buckingham Palace.

Dinbai brought to her marriage, besides her fabulous jewels, her cosmopolitan habits and taste as well—more French than English, thanks to her European travel. The elegant luxury of the new Petit Hall was undoubtedly her contribution. Her father-in-law had died within a year of their marriage, and although the title was still six years away, Petit Hall was already theirs to do what they willed with it. The future baronet had also inherited one of his two vast fortunes, this one from his maternal grandfather; so, money was never a constraint. Sarojini Naidu—the same house guest who had been so overwhelmed by Petit Hall's understated extravagance—also accompanied the Petits when they went shopping for Persian carpets; they looked at these rolls of 'woven dreams' and bought twenty at a go. They joined the best clubs—Ripon, Elphinstone, Orient, Asian, Bombay; and became within a year or two of their marriage, one of the most prominent couples in Bombay society, popular not only among the Parsis but also a wider circle that included eminent men from other communities and their wives if they were out of purdah.

Their photographs appeared regularly in English journals, especially the one that specialized in 'native' celebrities called *Men and Women of India*. And there, among the prominent Parsi couples of Bombay, they invariably are: Lady Petit, seated amidst the leading wives of Bombay, a member of the working committee (women's section) of the industrial exhibition held in Bombay in December 1904. And again, when the Prince and Princess of Wales (later, King George V and Queen Mary) visited Bombay in 1905, she was part of the 'reception committee of Indian ladies', chosen to open the ceremony organized for the Princess of Wales in the town hall. There she stood on the steps, dressed in her English lace blouse and French chiffon sari and sporting a single string of pearls, stockinged and shoed, her diaphanous sari pallu draped minimally over her permed black hair and held with a diamond pin, a perfect blend of the East and the West, showing her mastery in the art of adapting her Parsi dress to suit their modern, English tastes. And she had that same flexibility with Parsi ritual as well, judging by her role in the ceremonies that day. She waved an Indian sweet around her royal highness's head three times, performing the Parsi ritual of welcome for the princess, explaining in English what it signified: 'seeking for her life to be filled with sweetness'; then broke a coconut at the royal feet, 'with a prayer that all difficulties may so part and fall away from her'. There is Sir Dinshaw too, dressed if a little less picturesquely, chin downwards, an English gentleman in his stiff collar and cravat, the neck and cut of his coat English, but on his head, the loaf-shaped Parsi hat, and the whiskers neither here nor there—a mere shadow on his face. Both figure in the Royal Visit Souvenir: he as one of the six members of a committee in charge of building the Prince of Wales Museum, present as the prince plastered with a golden trowel the foundation stone of the new building; and she with the ladies' reception committee.

Sometimes the children appear too—a studio portrait of the older three, for example, where Ruttie is perched in the centre with a bold, impish look in her six-year-old eyes, her two little brothers clinging to her on either side. And it is here, for all to see, how far the Petits have travelled from their orthodox Parsi community. Gone are the little Persian caps on the boys' heads and the Parsi coat with its closed neck; gone too the tinselled and gem-embroidered coat that Lady Petit's ancestress wore several generations ago, covered with gold and diamonds from head to chest, or even the ghastly 'frocks' that little girls in Sir Dinshaw's family still wore until they graduated to saris. These could be the viceroy's children, so flawlessly English do they look in their dress and manner—Ruttie in a long dress of exquisite lace, with a matching lace flower in her flowing black hair, her brother Framji, heir to Sir Dinshaw's title, in a dark velvet coat with a lace bib and knee-length trousers, stockings and brass-buckled shoes, his long, black mop of curls parted on one side and bare of any headgear, and the younger one, Manek, a toddler dressed in the English fashion in an infant's long dress, his curls left uncropped. Their last child, another boy named Jamshed, was still five years away, his birth commemorated with a gift from Sir Dinshaw to his eleven-year-old daughter of the complete collection of Tennyson's poems.

They gave their children the best of everything, and were overprotective about their health, and ambitious for them, but distant. Following the fashion of the times, Lady Petit left her children's upbringing entirely in the hands of foreign professionals. Ruttie, like her brothers, grew up with English nannies, nurses and governesses, and French maids; was taught to ride at an early age, and was sent like her brothers to an English school. And while the children may have heard Gujarati and even spoken it to their only surviving grandparent, Lady Petit's mother, the only language commonly heard in Petit Hall was English. In religion, they were more comfortable with Annie Besant's Theosophy than with the ancient Avestan prayers they recited without understanding. It was a cosmopolitan home in other ways: even the *navroz* for each of their children, the thread ceremony where a child is initiated into Zoroastrian prayers by a Parsi priest, became less a religious occasion than a grand celebration, attended by 800 or more guests, their friends from all communities. They were also, like other rich Parsis in their circle, very liberal parents: no mandatory visits to the fire temple; and at thirteen or fourteen, when most of Ruttie's schoolmates had their marriages arranged by their parents, Ruttie was allowed out of the schoolroom into her parents' social circle. And other than hiring a governess—English, presumably, from her name, Irene—and insisting she get home before dark, and wear saris all the time—unless she was going riding when she could wear a riding habit—there seemed few rules for Ruttie once she left the schoolroom beyond those that apply to a young lady in polite society. That is, rules of polite English society. She was allowed to go out on her own to the exclusive shops on Hornby Road where she could sign for whatever she needed on her father's account; entertain her admirers at home, regardless of which community they belonged to; go dancing in the clubs or at the homes of their friends; accompany them for at-homes, garden parties and the races; volunteer with other ladies of her mother's circle for war relief work and accompany them on their travels, now limited to inside the country because of the War.

It was during one of these holidays that Ruttie and Jinnah fell in love, and following what he thought was the modern custom, Jinnah approached Sir Dinshaw with his marriage proposal, shattering both their friendship and Sir Dinshaw's peace of mind forever. The baronet did not see it coming, although his beautiful daughter had spent the entire summer holiday in Jinnah's company, either riding or reading or dining or talking politics with him. She was, after all, not yet sixteen, an age when modern parents of the new century did not expect their daughters to rush into marriage, although in more conventional homes girls were either betrothed or already married by that age. Sir Dinshaw's only sister, Hamabai, after having gone to a French boarding school in Nice for her baccalaureate, was still single at twenty-nine and not an eyebrow was raised. So, Sir Dinshaw could hardly be blamed for thinking that his daughter was too young to consider marrying.

But it was not her youth that was the most preposterous part of Jinnah's proposal, in Sir Dinshaw's eyes, or indeed the world's. According to the norms of even liberal Indian society, while it was all right to aspire to be English in all ways, whether it was dress or food or manners or speech, one simply did not cross the line by marrying out of one's community. It was the unspoken rule that the older generation understood very well, although younger people were beginning to challenge the establishment. Surprisingly, Sir Dinshaw himself had something of a reputation as a staunch champion of intercommunity marriages. He was not only among the progressive Parsis who had come out publicly in support of Ratan D. Tata ('RD' to his friends) when he brought his French bride to Bombay and insisted on marrying her according to Parsi rites after converting her to Zoroastrianism, but also brought the community's wrath upon his head by dragging the issue into court. RD was the first Parsi to marry out of the community, but as long as he lived outside the country, there was no opposition to the marriage. In fact, he received the blessings of both family and friends. His uncle, the industrialist Jamsetjee Tata, not only readily gave his consent to the marriage but attended the wedding in Paris, and followed it up by hosting a reception for the newly-weds aboard a luxury steamer on the Thames. It was attended by the 'largest gathering' of Parsis west of the Suez Canal, including the Parsi British members of the House of Commons, Sir Muncherjee Bhownageree and Dadabhoy Naoroji, and other towering leaders of the community who hailed the marriage as 'progressive' and a sign of the 'social advancement of the community'. But when RD decided to bring home his French wife, rename her as Soonibai, and marry her according to Parsi rites, after first converting her to the Zoroastrian faith, there was an uproar in the community. There was already mounting disapproval among the more orthodox Parsis against the westernized lifestyle of the richer set, and this attempt to gain sanctity for the marriage by buying over the priests brought the differences between the orthodox and the unorthodox Parsis into a pitched battle. So heated did the controversy become that when the wedding did take place, with a high priest officiating and sixty dasturs in attendance, many of RD's friends stayed away for fear of trouble from the orthodoxy. But Sir Dinshaw, instead of staying out of the firing line as other westernized Parsis had wisely done, deliberately courted trouble by taking the issue to the law courts. The case, questioning the authority of the Parsi panchayat to stop a non-Parsi from converting to the Zoroastrian faith and becoming a Parsi, involved a lengthy trial of two years, from 1906 to 1908 in the high court, costing lakhs of rupees in lawyers' fees. While it was a landmark judgment that defined the rights and identity of the Parsis, Sir Dinshaw personally got nothing out of it except a reputation for unorthodoxy—vastly exaggerated, as it turned out eight years later when Jinnah approached him for his daughter's hand in marriage.

It was not an enviable situation for any suitor to be in. Jinnah was not only twenty-four years older than Ruttie but had known her almost from birth and not shown more than an avuncular interest in his host's lively young daughter until then. To break the news to the unsuspecting Sir Dinshaw was not easy, but Jinnah was not a man to be easily daunted. Realizing that the best way would be to take Sir Dinshaw by surprise, he used his courtroom skills in cross-examining witnesses to try and put his host at a disadvantage. He began by asking Sir Dinshaw innocently what his views were on intercommunity marriages. The unwary Sir Dinshaw walked right into the trap by giving the stock answer that all modern Indians felt was expected of them: intercommunity marriages would, he said glibly, 'considerably help national integration and might ultimately prove to be the final solution to inter-communal antagonism'. Thereupon, we are informed, Jinnah calmly told him that he wanted to marry his daughter. And in what seems like a classic case of understatement, a contemporary described Sir Dinshaw as being 'taken aback'. The baronet had not realized, according to M.C. Chagla, a former chief justice of India who had once worked under Jinnah, 'that his remarks might have personal repercussions. He was most indignant and refused to countenance any such idea which appeared to him absurd and fantastic.'

How true is this account of what transpired between the two men will never be known. Jinnah did not confide in anyone; nor did Sir Dinshaw ever speak of it. But certainly, the story about Jinnah's proposal acquired a life of its own—by the time Jinnah returned to Bombay, it had already spread like the proverbial wildfire. It went on in the years to come to become almost a legend, told and retold, always with the same mix of admiration and glee, surviving almost half a century through word of mouth until it was finally etched in print in Chagla's memoir, Roses in December. For all its dryness, the story evoked in the minds of anyone even slightly acquainted with the two men, a picture of them, so stiff and proper and mature, until they trip and collapse under the weight of their own contradictions—so amusing and yet so resonant of an entire generation torn between their British heads and Indian hearts; unable to bridge the chasm between their progressive, modern ideas and what they really felt.

Chapter Two

~

By the beginning of June, before the rains started to swell the rivers and make the roads impassable, all of Bombay's rich and well-to-do returned home to their city in fashionable flocks; and with them returned the Petits and Jinnah, separately. Almost instantly, the strange and fascinating story of Jinnah's and Ruttie's romance began to do the rounds. Within a fortnight, even a stranger attending a public meeting in Bombay heard about their love story. After being introduced to Jinnah at a public meeting at the Bombay Presidency Association, Kanji Dwarkadas, then a young man of twenty-four, found out the gossip doing the rounds of the city on why the otherwise reserved Jinnah was currently in such unusually high spirits: 'The reasons for Jinnah's cheerfulness at the Association's meeting—I found later. He had spent the two months of summer vacation in Darjeeling with Sir Dinshaw and Lady Dinbai Petit and there he fell in love with their 16-year-old beautiful daughter, Ruttie. As they returned to Bombay in early June, all Bombay heard of their impending marriage but the parents did not like the idea of their daughter marrying a Mohammedan. Ruttie was a minor but she was determined to marry Jinnah.'

Kanji, like every other young man of his circle, had worshipped Ruttie from a distance since his student days. Walking on a cold afternoon two years ago across the Bombay Oval, he had caught sight of Ruttie riding in a small carriage driven by a pony. He could not take his eyes off the fourteen-year-old beauty, and watched the carriage and its occupant till they disappeared from sight. He never forgot her face, and discovered who she was from a photograph that appeared in a newspaper three months later. As for Jinnah, Kanji knew of him as a popular leader, without having ever seen him before. Which is why when Kanji saw a dashing man 'in check trousers, black coat, hair parted on the side and moustache, addressing the meeting with great confidence and everybody listening with rapt attention', Kanji turned to his neighbour to ask who this impressive figure was, earning the retort: 'You don't know Jinnah?'

Clearly, Sir Dinshaw's snub had not cooled Jinnah's ardour, which was again very unlike the Jinnah the world knew. He had never been known before to chase a woman, especially not one as young and enchanting as Ruttie, preferring to avoid them at the few parties he attended, where he hated the dancing and music, choosing instead to retreat to a quiet corner and engage any man who was interested in what was so far his only passion: politics. But now here he was, wherever Ruttie appeared—at the races, at parties and even the fashionable Willingdon Club where everyone went for the dancing and the live music—talking to her openly, oblivious to people's looks and whispers. How much his persistence had to do with Ruttie was a matter of guesswork, because she now seemed to be doing all the chasing, going up to him and looking up at him with such open adoration that it would have been beyond even Jinnah's iron will to resist her had he wanted to. They became the talking point of all Bombay—he for having the audacity to stand up to her father and she for her forwardness. In hindsight, it was hardly surprising that fashionable Bombay was so excited about what could, after all, have fizzled out as a mere teenage crush. But Bombay wanted their love to be something more than a passing fancy. The city with its cotton market and cloth mills had become by then not just the richest in the country but also the most cosmopolitan. Here students and professionals from across the country came to make their fortune and name, confident that doors would open to them, regardless of the old barriers of caste and community.

It was a dynamic, modern city, proud of its sons like Jinnah. He had come to the city penniless from Karachi, the eldest of seven children of a failed businessman of the Khoja Muslim community, and within the span of two decades, had clawed himself upwards as one of Bombay's best-known and wealthiest lawyers. A star politician, he was known for his luxury cars and fashionable clothes, able to hold his own with the best in the court as well as in the Imperial Legislative Council, where he was about to be re-elected for his third term. And for the young men who aspired to be like Jinnah, and others wary of his arrogant confidence, the outcome of Jinnah's matrimonial hopes became a matter of pressing interest. No one, not even in Bombay's mixed society, had dared so far to cross the matrimonial divide among the Hindus, Parsis and Muslims. There were men, of course, usually fresh out of Oxford or Cambridge, who had returned from overseas with French or English wives, but to go as far as Jinnah was intending to go was unheard of. It touched a chord in the English chattering classes, and not just in Bombay. 'I got news today that there was much noise in Bombay about Ruttie Petit wanting to marry Jinnah,' wrote Sarojini Naidu's elder son, Jaisoorya, to his sister, Padmaja, from his student digs in Bangalore.

Jaisoorya had only heard of Ruttie so far. But as the eldest child of liberal, English-educated parents like Sarojini and her doctor husband, who themselves had an inter-caste marriage eighteen years ago and had raised all four of their children in a cosmopolitan home, exposing them from childhood to nationalist ideas and culture, one would have expected Jaisoorya to be on Ruttie's side. And indeed he did not dispute her right to marry a Muslim. His issue was with the age of her suitor. 'What put it into her silly little head to suddenly fall in love with a man old enough to be her father,' Jaisoorya wrote from his room in Bangalore's YMCA, urging Padmaja to stay out of it.

It was a mystery that exercised others besides Jaisoorya. In his student circle, scattered across Bombay and Poona and Hyderabad, even Lucknow, Ruttie had been worshipped from afar for her charm and elegance, with young men exchanging snippets about her doings and movements without ever meeting her. So intimidating was the social distance between the Petits and ordinary people that Jaisoorya felt too shy to call on Ruttie even when he moved to Poona later that year to start his college even though he had heard so much about her from the rest of his family. 'I hear Ruttie Petit is in Poona,' he wrote to Padmaja on 30 December 1917, from Yeravada, Poona, 'but I do not know that young lady and she most probably would not care to see such a poor person as myself. And I do not care to go and see big barons who wish to patronize me.' And to now find that teenaged idol throwing herself away—not because the man was a Muslim, for that was quite besides the point for young men like Jaisoorya Naidu; but on a man who was not only famed for his coldness and reserve, but was also around her father's age. It was more than disappointing—it was baffling.

But to those few who knew him closely—and Jaisoorya's mother, Sarojini, was one of those whose admiration for Jinnah was so great that some even misconstrued it as an infatuation on her part—it was easier to understand why a romantic, impressionable young woman could fall in love with Jinnah. 'Never was there a nature whose outer qualities provided so complete an antithesis of its inner worth,' was how Sarojini felt about Jinnah, drawing an unusual portrait of him in a collection of his speeches published a couple of years later. 'Tall and stately, but thin to the point of emaciation, languid and luxurious of habit, Mohamed Ali Jinnah's attenuated form is the deceptive sheath of a spirit of exceptional vitality and endurance. Somewhat formal and fastidious, and a little aloof and imperious of manner, the calm hauteur of his accustomed reserve but masks, for those who know him, a naïve and eager humanity, an intuition quick and tender as a woman's, a humour gay and winning as a child's. Pre-eminently rational and practical, discreet and dispassionate in his estimate and acceptance of life, the obvious sanity and serenity of his worldly wisdom effectually disguise a shy and splendid idealism which is the very essence of the man.'

And no one thrilled to this hidden side of the real Jinnah more than Ruttie, who had not only known Jinnah well since she was a child but had nursed a calf love for him at least since she was twelve or thirteen. He was only three years younger than her father and, like Sir Dinshaw, belonged wholly to the Victorian era both in his dress and manners—but there the resemblance ended. Unlike the stocky and very middle-aged baronet, it would have occurred to no one to describe Jinnah as an old man. With his slim, graceful five-foot-eleven figure, neatly combed black hair, silvering at the temples, his quick, sharp movements and a classically handsome face with sharply etched features and Grecian profile, he too was a head-turner, like Ruttie. 'If you came across him on the street, you were bound to be mesmerized. It was the way he carried himself, the way he walked, the immaculate manner in which he dressed, his handsome face,' as a young man who met Jinnah years later, K.H. Khurshid, put it. And then there was the personal charm and the dry sense of humour with which he could hold a drawing room captive when he was in the mood. His stories of arriving in England, hopelessly adrift in an alien culture, which he had never shared before, would have especially delighted Ruttie. The story, for instance, of finding a hot water bottle on his bed on his first night in an English boarding house and, when his feet touched it in the dark, how he flung it out of the bed, terrified. 'As he peered at it in the dark, he could see water oozing out of it, which he was quite convinced, was blood. "I have killed it," he screamed."' Others had experienced the hypnotic effect that Jinnah could have in the company of those he liked—that 'stretching of his long legs to the full limits of comfort' as he prepared to launch on an anecdote 'in slow, measured and dramatic tones'; the surprisingly sweet smile, the dry wit and the fund of good stories. And given her sheltered life, Ruttie was even more susceptible than most.

It's harder to tell what spell Ruttie cast on him. She was enchanting, of course, and delightfully informal, lively, high-spirited and full of jokes, and the toast of high society for her beauty and breeding, but she was hardly Jinnah's type. That is, if he had a type at all, for he had so far been immune to feminine charm of any kind, preferring to spend his time at parties talking politics with men. He did not ignore them, of course, paying them elaborate and formal courtesies, especially the older women who seemed to him less threatening. Despite his popularity, with his dashing good looks and elegance of dress, he was never as easy in their company as he was with men, having grown up in an environment where men and women did not mingle with each other unless they were family. Added to that was his habitual coldness and reserve that made even men like his junior Chagla dislike him intensely. 'But these obvious outer qualities are like a crust hiding the real man of which (or should it be whom? Being so impersonal an entity my grammar gets rather mixed in relation to him!) you may never get a glimpse,' Sarojini once wrote to Chagla in Jinnah's defence when the former wrote a newspaper article portraying Jinnah in an unflattering light. 'I think you have done a capital impressionist sketch of him—monocle, audacity and all. Someday I hope you will find yourself being a friend of the "lonely man who habitually breathes the rarefied air of the colder regions". There you will find, as those of us who are fortunate enough to know him intimately have discovered long ago—that the spiritual flower that blossoms within colder regions have [sic] a beauty and charm denied to the flora that flower in the warmer valleys of the common human temperament. But I confess you *do* need a fur coat now and then in the course of your botanical expeditions in these frigid regions!!'

Fortunately for Ruttie, she never felt the need for that fur coat, even in her early girlhood. Sensing perhaps her adoration for him, Jinnah had always let down his guard with his friend's young daughter. No one else in his life could draw Jinnah out as effectively as Ruttie, using her entrancing mix of 'coaxing and teasing' to make him talk, and even laugh at himself. Many of the personal details of his life that were to soon find themselves in the short biography Sarojini wrote as an introduction to his maiden book, a collection of his speeches, was stuff she had got second-hand, from talking to Ruttie, personal details like being raised 'in careless affluence and adored by his family' in Karachi; sent to England as 'a tall thin boy in a funny long yellow coat'; his lack of a university education; his family's financial ruin and how he 'set out to conquer the world equipped with nothing but the charmed missiles of his youth, his courage and his ambition'. He had not shared these with Sarojini, despite her affection and admiration for him. Sarojini, of course, did not reveal how she got to know so much about Jinnah which he had never once talked about to any of his friends, but she did acknowledge that the verse on the opening page of the book, *Mohammad Ali Jinnah: An Ambassador of Unity*, published in the same month that he got married, in 1918, was chosen by Ruttie, and not her. Ruttie felt these five lines by William Morris best described Jinnah, being both his motto and his song, and Sarojini, who admired him almost as much as Ruttie, could not help agreeing:

> *By thine own Soul's law learn to live*
> *And if men thwart thee take no heed,*
> *And if men hate thee have no care,*
> *Sing thou thy song and do thy deed,*
> *Hope thou thy hope and pray thy prayer.*

But the gossips seemed to have got their dates and places a little mixed up. It was true that Jinnah had asked Sir Dinshaw for his daughter's hand in marriage and was rejected most rudely, but it did not happen in the summer of 1916, nor in Darjeeling, as rumour had it. In the summer of 1916, Ruttie was indeed at a hill station with her parents but the place they were at was Mahabaleshwar and not Darjeeling. And Jinnah did spend that summer in her close vicinity but never once tried to meet her or her parents. He was caught up instead in Poona where he spent the bulk of his summer holiday appearing in court on a defamation case filed by his close friend, Benjamin Guy Horniman, the editor of the *Bombay Chronicle*, who had been accused by a rival paper of homosexual relationships with the young lads in his employ at his home. Horniman being an important political associate and close friend since his student days in London—they had, in fact, even worked together once briefly in a drama troupe—Jinnah had readily sacrificed his entire summer vacation to appear in the Poona court on his behalf. But he did not take advantage of being within driving distance of Mahabaleshwar to go meet Ruttie or call on her parents. This was hardly surprising because his friendship with Sir Dinshaw had abruptly terminated over a year ago, following close on the heels of his romance with Ruttie, just as the gossips said.

The romance had, in fact, blossomed in Poona in the Christmas holidays of 1914 when Jinnah spent the winter with his great friend, the Parsi nationalist and lawyer Sir Pherozeshah Mehta, who owned a second home in Poona. Jinnah and Horniman often spent their holidays with Sir Pherozeshah Mehta, who though older than them, enjoyed their company. All three of them being bachelors then, who loved to have a good time drinking and talking, were somewhat envied by those outside their close circle, with one contemporary, K.L. Gauba, even describing them as 'painting the town red' as a threesome. That winter, the Petits also spent the Christmas holidays in their home in Poona, their 'monsoon resort', as Ruttie called it, not as large as Petit Hall but where they entertained equally lavishly. And where Jinnah had plenty of time and opportunity to fall for Ruttie. She was then nearly fifteen, just coming out of her schoolgirl phase and already a celebrated beauty in the exclusive circles her parents moved in. What would have made her even more irresistible to Jinnah was the way she ignored her many young admirers and wanted to spend time only with him. She was unlike any other young lady in their fashionable Parsi circle, with her wide reading, her poetic temperament and passionate interest in politics. And Jinnah undoubtedly was a different man on this holiday, giving Ruttie a chance to see him at his most human and charming. The Petits, being extremely fond of amateur dramatics, would have surely tried to rope Jinnah into their performances, with his talent for dramatic reading, and he would most likely have joined in gladly, giving Ruttie a glimpse of this other side to him which people rarely saw. The Petits were also enthusiastic riders, taking their horses with them on holidays, and this was another area in which Jinnah outshone everyone, horse riding being the only outdoor activity he enjoyed and the only other sport he played besides billiards. All this holiday activity gave them plenty of opportunity to meet both indoors and outdoors, without rousing any suspicions on Ruttie's parents' part. And it is quite possible that it was his older Parsi friend, Sir Pherozeshah, who was a liberal through and through, unwilling to recognize the realities of communal and age divides—he himself married very late, in his fifties, in fact just six months before his death—who may have encouraged Jinnah to approach Sir Dinshaw with his proposal. For, Jinnah, for all his vaunted self-confidence, would probably have not had the temerity to go to Sir Dinshaw on his own, unaccustomed as he was to giving in to his feelings.

Jinnah had known Ruttie from her childhood, of course—on the day she was born, 20 April 1900, he was appointed a magistrate in the Bombay Presidency and at least since then knew the Petits, and moved in the same circles. But so far he had treated her in a strictly avuncular way, winning a large place in her schoolgirl heart with his charm and total lack of condescension when talking to her, as if she was his equal. And even as his fame grew as a lawyer and politician, he continued to engage with her in discussions about politics and national matters that she was passionate about while growing up. And influenced by him no doubt, she preferred to accompany her aunt Hamabai Petit, the famous philanthropist and millionairess and her father's only sibling, to all his public lectures instead of more standard girlish pursuits; she would sit patiently through the hours-long speeches that would have scared away most people her age. It was what made her so fascinatingly unlike any other young lady just out of the schoolroom, with little or no interest in dressing up or flirting with her many admirers. Unaffected by the attentions of a long line of young suitors, Ruttie could laugh at them and put her interest in politics and national developments over them. She read the newspapers carefully and was better informed about the world than most men double her age. 'She was a great nationalist, intensely interested in the political developments in the country and in the personal element of the political life in India,' as her lifelong admirer, Kanji Dwarkadas, was to discover a few years later: 'Ruttie was a great intellectualist, well informed, well read and balanced in her judgement of men and women and events but gifted with the curiosity of a research student.' Jinnah had always been attracted to young persons who stood up to him, and in Ruttie he found a fierce sense of independence matching his own and a charming irreverence all her own, able to take on princes and viceroys as her equals.

The aftermath of that winter holiday seems to have had its impact on Ruttie's health. Nine months after Sir Dinshaw practically kicked Jinnah out of his house, Ruttie was back in Poona, laid up in bed recovering from an unnamed surgery, as her letter to Sarojini's daughter, Padmaja, shows. The letter, datelined—true to Ruttie's characteristic fuzziness about dates—'Eagle's Nest, Poona ??th Sept.15', is evidently Ruttie's belated reply to a letter Padmaja wrote inquiring politely after Ruttie's health, post surgery. It was the sort of thing Sarojini insisted her daughters do—reach out to persons they had never met, especially if they were around the same age. Sarojini had, in fact, tried to encourage the two girls to write to each other regularly because, apart from being the same age, she felt a pen friendship would benefit them both, giving Ruttie someone her own age to talk to instead of constantly being in the company of people who were double her age or older. And giving Padmaja, the most dearly loved of her four children, some much-needed exposure to high society through a friend as cultured and kind as Ruttie, and helping her emerge out of her shell. The two girls were only eight months apart in age but with very different temperaments. Unlike the self-assured and well-travelled Ruttie who felt perfectly at home in her parents' cosmopolitan circle of friends and was accustomed to being treated as an adored beauty with a mind of her own, Padmaja was a shy and retiring girl, attending a boarding school in Panchgani with her little sister, Leilamani. At first, the enchanting heiress from Bombay and the shy, plain schoolgirl exchanged the occasional desultory letter, polite and distant with each other as etiquette demanded. But around the time of Ruttie's surgery, when she was fifteen and a half, Ruttie began to show a little more interest in this unknown daughter of her friend. How much this may have had to do with her being laid up in bed in their monsoon resort in Poona, cut off from the social whirl of Bombay because of the surgery, and how much with Ruttie's yearning to find someone to whom she could confide her heartache, is difficult to guess. She was certainly closer to Sarojini than to her daughter, even though Sarojini was around her mother's age.

Ruttie had taken instantly to Sarojini since the day the poetess came to stay with them as a house guest in Petit Hall when Ruttie was only thirteen. She had never before met anyone like Sarojini: unconventional, with an utter lack of prejudice, and playful and curious, and a famous poetess at that. Overruling her mother, Ruttie insisted that their eminent guest sleep in a bedroom next to hers rather than in one of the suites in an independent wing of Petit Hall where guests were usually put up. Already reaching the height of her fame as a published poet and a fiery public speaker, Sarojini had a lively sense of humour and a deep sympathy for the young. What made her even more fascinating for Ruttie was that Sarojini had also fallen in love at fourteen with a young man who was a doctor in the Nizam's army but whom her parents had disapproved of because he was not a Bengali Brahmin like themselves, but came from a non-Brahmin Telugu family. To understand how mature teenaged Indian girls were compared to their British counterparts, English poet Edmund Gosse had this to say about Sarojini at sixteen: 'She was already marvellous in mental maturity, amazingly well-read and far beyond a Western child in all her acquaintance with the world.' At nineteen, having endured her father's fury, a nervous breakdown and three years' exile in England, Sarojini was finally allowed to marry the man of her own choosing. Whether it was Sarojini's unconventional life story, or the fact that she too was a warm admirer of Jinnah, or her poet's empathy with the young and rebellious, the friendship between the mother of four (then in her thirties) and the thirteen-year-old daughter of the Petits was instant and mutual. On that first trip itself, Sarojini wrote home to her daughters in such high praise of Ruttie that they for quite some time both overawed by and resentful of Ruttie and the special place she had won for herself in their mother's heart. 'God bless her, when does Mother think of coming, I should like to know!!'

exclaims Leilamani in one letter to Padmaja, resenting being left alone in Hyderabad while Sarojini is in Bombay staying with the Petits. 'I suppose she is too taken up with Ruttie's lips—or is it her low necked satin blouse—and her "mummas" and "aunties".'

But in this letter, marking a departure from the polite distance they had kept till then from each other, Ruttie seems eager to reach out to the schoolgirl she had not met yet. Making light of her surgery and the attention being lavished on her post surgery—with several doctors, nurses and a governess dancing attendance on her, but no mention of either parent being there—Ruttie writes: 'I have been having rather a dull time of it owing to *"my operation"*, doesn't it sound swanky, Eh! The old doctors and wise grown-ups with all their experience take very great care I don't strain myself in any way possible. I have quite a number of 'em keeping "an eye" on me, the other is at the owner's disposal.'

Ruttie's mother only crops up in the letter when Ruttie mentions her plans to accompany her to Simla after recovering from her surgery: 'Mamma and I are going with Aunty Bhickai and a friend to Simla. We leave on the 30th and return by the 1st Nov. to Bombay.' So far, Ruttie has shown no disinclination to trail behind her mother, part of Bombay's perpetually partying fashionable circle, travelling in a flock from one fashionable spot to the other, depending on the season. But for the first time, Ruttie seems wistful for a girlfriend her own age. She had her three brothers to whom she was quite close, leading them in boisterous games and playing jokes on the grown-ups, and going riding with them. But now that she was grown up, she felt the need for a confidante and a friend her own age. 'I would really very much like to see you and I hope that you will be with your mother on her next visit to Bombay,' her letter says, adding: 'I wish you would send me a photo.' And then afraid of scaring off her friend by her unconventionality, she asks with a touching eagerness to please: 'Have you a *very very* strong objection to slang? I hope not, for I might shock you.'

'Was it the first time you put on a sari?' Ruttie asks, referring to a fete that Padmaja had attended in her school wearing a sari. It's been over a year or more since Ruttie herself must have graduated from schoolgirl frocks to saris, a rite of passage into adulthood that all girls looked forward to, and by now, she is wearing her sari with a style and sophistication that other young women envied and wanted to copy. But in her eagerness to establish a bond with her new friend, Ruttie says in her letter that she too was at first as awkward and uncomfortable wearing it: 'I am quite accustomed to it [sari] now, but I remember the first few days I felt like a jackdaw in borrowed plumes, as I thought it a dignity I had not quite matured for.'

'Do excuse my laziness and please don't think me very rude because I did not reply to your epistle before,' she further writes. 'I know that I could and should have, but, oh dear, I am such an awful slacker. You will not take your revenge on me by making me wait too long for your letter? As I expect one.' And then, unable to resist a pun that strikes her, she ends: 'Revenge is Sweet, I know, but sweet things make one bilious. I have had *that*—"sweet things make you bilious"—*so much* dinned into me, but this is the first time I make any use of it.' But the pun apart, Ruttie's remark points to a physical ailment that persisted throughout her life, and that was her tendency to biliousness, which she seems to have inherited from her father. Sir Dinshaw suffered quite frequently from gastric attacks brought on, no doubt, by his overindulgence at the table. But in Ruttie's case, her 'biliousness' was not just from her weakness for sweets that her mother or governess or both were trying to curb, or the spicy food she loved, but also because of her tendency to worry too much. Except her English governess, Irene, few people understood what a worry rat Ruttie actually was behind her persona 'so lively and full of jokes and wit and high spirits', as an old Parsi acquaintance once put it. Irene alone of all those who thought they knew Ruttie recognized her charge's hidden temperament and was forever advising her not to worry too much and let things go.

Of course, at this point of time with Padmaja, Ruttie is still a stranger, but working harder than she has done so far to get closer to her new friend, adding as a postscript: 'I have just had an idea. Don't you think it would be rather nice if you were to write me a description of yourself? I have been trying to picture you but have had no satisfaction—you know, a sort of essay on self. It would be rather fun, don't you think so?'

The next letter from Ruttie to Padmaja is in the summer of 1916 when she is in Mahabaleshwar with her parents, claiming to be bored and hot but in fact angry and frustrated. Like everyone else in their set, the Petits owned a villa in Mahabaleshwar but they—or at least Ruttie—were not staying at their own place during this trip. Datelined 'St James Cottage. M'war 3rd May', the letter shows Ruttie in an unusually petulant mood, complaining first of Padmaja writing to her about people she does not know: 'It is no fun talking of people I have not seen and do not know—so enough.' Then demanding that Padmaja come and visit her because she is feeling very dull: 'When are you coming to spend the day with me? I want to see you badly and I shall expect an answer to the question.' And then complaining about the hot weather: 'Write to me soon as I feel very dull. It is so hot! and I am writing you this from my bed as it is much too hot to sit up and write—I am sure the effort of reading such a scrawl will send you to yours.' And finally, venting her anger and frustration: 'If this had not been quite such a polished civilized world, I might have resorted to the sensible means of swearing away the hot hours. Swearing would have relieved my state—and the heat would have justified my swearing.'

Of course, Ruttie won't spell it out but there is the undoubted disappointment of Jinnah spending forty days in nearby Poona while Horniman's defamation case was going on and not coming up even once to see her in Mahabaleshwar. Since that winter holiday, while he was not exactly cold to Ruttie when they met anywhere, she could sense his withdrawal. To the Petits, of course, he gave a wide berth, although there were a few occasions when meeting each other was unavoidable, for instance, the condolence meeting on Gopal Krishna Gokhale's death when Jinnah had to share the platform with Sir Dinshaw—both sat in silence, refusing to acknowledge each other. If Ruttie was hoping it would be different in the hills, and that he would let his feelings for her prevail over the offence that Sir Dinshaw had dealt him by rejecting his proposal so summarily, she was mistaken. He did not come up before leaving Poona, going straight to Bombay six days after her letter to Padmaja, leaving her sad and angry.

In a mood now for any distraction, Ruttie first tried to persuade Padmaja to come and visit her in Mahabaleshwar, and that failing, decided to go herself to Panchgani to spend the day with her. But the thought of her grand friend descending on her in Panchgani left Padmaja panic-stricken. Having heard of her beauty and lifestyle from her mother, she was overwhelmed at the prospect of meeting

Ruttie in person. Already feeling inadequate in comparison to Ruttie, Padmaja did not want to have to confess to her that she was still in school, a far cry from the life that Ruttie led, with her at-homes and receptions, and male suitors by the dozen. She was even more ashamed to admit that she had no car at her disposal, as Ruttie was expecting. It was something Ruttie had taken for granted that Padmaja would have her own means of transport like everyone else Ruttie knew, and Padmaja was overcome with the ignominy of it all. She wrote to her mother, hoping that Sarojini would do the needful, but all Sarojini did was to advise her to tell Ruttie the truth. But Padmaja baulked at it, making out instead that her 'mo' was not air-conditioned and would be unsuitable for Ruttie's use during her trip. 'It was a relief to read that your "mo" is not airconditioned,' begins Ruttie's next letter to Padmaja a fortnight later, on 18 May 1916, and then immediately putting Padmaja in another fix by asking: 'Could you arrange one for Sat 27th? That gives you ten long days in which to arrange and reserve a suitable conveyance.' Padmaja seems to have economized on the truth in other aspects of her situation as well: 'I did not know you were staying at a school,' Ruttie writes, struggling to imagine a nearly sixteen-year-old still in school. 'I do not suppose you are studying, are you? You have come up for your holidays here, is that not so?'

On her part, Ruttie is just as anxious not to leave any impression on her friend that she is anything like her parents, distancing from what according to her are their too conservative attitudes, like getting home early. 'Oh, about that concert you were telling me about—I would very much like to but I can't come because you see it will be in the afternoon at about five o'clock—at least I suppose so and it would end at say 6.30 or 7 pm and would be far too late by the time I reached home—not for me—nothing is *too late* for me, but for my parents.' And questioning her governess's wisdom and making a joke of her trying to coach her into submitting to authority: 'Irene says not to grumble and never to worry and I must "give in" to the supreme wisdom of the sage. All sages are fools, do not you think with me? You could not be a "sage" without being a "fool", but you can jolly soon be a "fool" without being a sage. I am at any rate. I feel quite startled at my own limpid logic, don't you?'

But despite the anxieties on both sides, Ruttie's day trip to Panchgani, less than nineteen kilometres away, seems to have gone off very well. Both Padmaja and her younger sister, Leilamani, also in the same boarding school called The Knowle, run by a Mrs Kimmins, warmed instantly to the young woman from Bombay they had heard so much about and who, despite her surface worldliness and sophistication and intimidatingly beautiful looks, was so friendly and informal and eager to win *their* approval. After that, letters between Ruttie and Sarojini's two schoolgirl daughters flew thick and fast, especially over the following year, all the earlier reserve and stiffness between them seemingly vanishing with that one visit, at least on the Naidu girls' part. Each of the girls confided their heartaches to Ruttie, seeking her advice and trusting her not to betray their confidences even to each other or their mother. And Ruttie, although she never failed to respond promptly to each of their queries—answering their calls for advice on love matters with surprising maturity for a sixteen-year-old—she herself does not do any of the confiding as befitted the elder sister's role they thrust upon her. Whatever she thought or felt about her own confusing love life that was by now the talk of all Bombay, she is silent in these letters over the next fifteen months, unwilling, or perhaps merely unable, to expose her feelings fully to these two young friends, or anyone else for that matter—so deep was her natural reserve, despite the outer openness and friendliness.

The next letter is written on 13 June 1916, twenty days after her trip to Panchgani when she was back in Bombay, exciting so much comment by merely being seen in the same room with Jinnah. The letter, addressed either to Padmaja or Leilamani (it doesn't say who), despite being couched in impersonal generalities and romantic clichés, shows her fierce determination to hang on to her passion despite the impediments, feeling somehow ennobled by the process: 'Your hungry passion for love is a yearning upon which you may build your whole character—your whole life. Make your personality the soul of love and sympathy and let your passionate desire grow into a fair and frequent flower—so beautiful that it shall draw and command love through its own loveliness. Just as the lily and carnation—just as the rose and the lotus. Pour love on the parched, unlighted souls, and through sympathy and understanding make them bright as the myriad lamps of heaven. Wisdom is a digit of Love—Love is the Supreme Wisdom. Love it is that makes the sighing winds balmy. Love it is makes the moon shine and gives warmth to the sun. Love it is makes the flowers blossom and the birds sing and the brook laugh through the forests. Love it is makes Life a span of suffering and a chant of joy. Love it is makes woman beautiful and man brave and noble. I understand your sweet emotion. And I find it as beautiful as a poem, as melodious as a sonata. If ever you are sorrowful, if ever you yearn and thirst for love—come to me, speak to me, write to me. Your friend, Rutty.'

For all its vagueness, the letter appears to have found an answering echo in Padmaja's own romantic heart, judging from Ruttie's next letter to her. Datelined 'Petit Hall, Malabar Hill, Bombay, 4th July 1916', and written on notepaper with the Petit crest on it, Ruttie's letter is ecstatic about Padmaja's finely expressed emotions on love: 'Your letter gave me exquisite pleasure. I wish you would always write me something beautiful like that. But I know that is impossible. You must write as you feel and according to your mood—otherwise it cannot be beautiful. At any rate write to me whenever you get into this wonderful phase, will you?'

Each seems to be encouraging the other in this indulgence of emotion, and drawing each other out to further excess. 'I am no Philistine who would think the outpour[ing] of fine emotions akin to madness,' says Ruttie's letter. 'If it really is madness, why can't all of us be mad! I like letters in that strain and I would very much more have liked to see you in this radiantly happy and inexpressibly sad mood. I can quite understand and appreciate your emotion for I too am somewhat like that. And G[od] it hurts, it hurts terribly! My conflicting emotions make me suffer more than anything. I suppose they do you too!'

And each, or so it seems, prides herself on her utter spontaneity and disregard for conventions or caution. 'Strange isn't it,' Ruttie writes, 'but I also never re-read my letters once they are written. I don't know why but somehow it would be unlike me to do so. There is something too tame and calculative about the idea.'

But the letter having barely been sent off, Ruttie received another letter from Padmaja, panic-stricken that she had said too much. Ruttie reassured her that her 'secret', which she does not spell out, was safe with her. In a letter dated 8 July 1916, again from Petit Hall, she writes: 'I could see that you had written your last letter on the impulse of the moment. Nevertheless that made it more beautiful—more like you. There is nothing "mad" or "stupid" in what you have written and I appreciate the trust you have in me and your sweet emotions shall be my own secret.'

But when it came to *her* secrets, Ruttie was not prepared as yet to trust Padmaja with them. She would have preferred to talk to her mother, but Sarojini was now laid up in bed in Hyderabad, too ill even to read or reply to letters, except to her own girls'. The next sentence in Ruttie's letter suggests how much she must have been missing this wise, older friend at a time when she felt so isolated from her own parents, who simply did not understand her passion for Jinnah. 'Do remind your mother of her promise to send me a photo of herself—a large one. I have only got an amateur postcard with just her face, not even taking the whole of the postcard space.' And goes on: 'How is she at present? I hope her spine is alright. Perhaps it is just weakness through the long illness which has caused this pain in the spine. Let us hope it is nothing more.'

To Ruttie, there could be no wiser counsellor in the world, especially in matters of the heart, than Sarojini. She could not imagine why the two Naidu girls, having such a mother, would seek advice from anyone else, including her. In one letter of which the first two pages seem to be missing, but clearly belonging to this phase, Ruttie writes: '. . . rather tell your mother than anyone else and I sincerely think that *no* one will ever listen to you with the same sympathy that she would. I would not say this to everyone, but your mother has a wonderful sympathy which to my mind is the very light of her being and her soul. Perhaps you do not like to speak to her, owing to her delicate condition of health? Perhaps you think that it might excite her over much. Of course if that is the case I can say nothing, it is best for you to feel your way and act according to the promptings within you.'

And yet, she cannot resist urging: 'Yet as an interested and sincere friend, I ask you to seriously think over what I have suggested. And I vouch for it, that if you do follow the suggestion, you will *never never* repent it.' Then she adds, with her delicate tact that has won over Padmaja: 'I have given you my opinion unasked, but please don't let it give you offence. Write to me whenever you like and I shall always read your letters with interest.'

Ironically, when Ruttie did eventually get the benefit of Sarojini's advice, only a couple of months later, she bristled so much at what

Sarojini had to say to her that they almost ended up quarrelling. 'I have given your mother a light scolding,' Ruttie confesses in her next letter to Padmaja, on 24 October 1916, 'for having made a speech.' It was unimaginable for Ruttie to have done this, to snub the older woman she had always sought out and hero-worshipped; but Sarojini apparently had taken her parents' side on the issue of Jinnah's suitability for someone as young as her. It was not the sort of thing that Sarojini often did, interfering in young people's love lives, but she evidently felt strongly enough about this to say so openly to Ruttie, earning a snub for her pains. Ruttie's put-down was delivered in no uncertain terms, as she says in her letter: 'I am sure she will *not* do it again.' However, she is beginning to feel a bit rueful at her burst of temper, as she indicates with a whole row of exclamation marks (twenty-seven in all) following the last sentence. And then she adds a placatory line, no doubt anxious not to offend Padmaja or her mother: 'I remember your having written that it was very beautiful—I mean your mother's speech. Do tell me where she spoke and on what occasion and all the rest of it.'

From the dateline, Ruttie is back in Mahabaleshwar, staying this time at the Petits' own place, Adorn Villa. She does not say what she is doing at the hill station—probably alone except for the servants—at the height of the Bombay season when her parents are usually busy throwing or attending parties day and night. But this is also a month that Jinnah was forced to spend in Poona, taking time off from his busiest year in his political career to appear before the inquiry committee he had asked the government to set up in order to clear his name after his rival in the recent legislative council election accused him of rigging it. If Ruttie hoped their paths would cross, she was disappointed. Jinnah came and left Poona, once again without making any attempt to meet her. She was left seeking solace from the hills.

'Mahabaleshwar is *very* beautiful all green and fresh and young!' she writes in her letter. 'But I have seen no fireflies as yet. All nature seems to be astir with song birds and little insects and often while you are feasting your soul on the exquisite and fierce grandeur of the ghats, the mist will rapidly and almost suddenly veil the scenery as though it were jealous. A few days ago while returning from Bombay Point, the delicate strains of a shepherd's flute caught my ears. It was so beautiful, so simple that it could not help sounding mystic. Oh, it stirred all the fire of my soul! As such things are wont to do. Whenever I hear or see anything beautiful it invariably saddens me, and I simply cannot restrain from pining over it—but it is a melancholy in which I rejoice for I feel that it always leads me towards greater perfection and sympathy.'

She makes a valiant attempt to cover up her feelings by resorting to her habitual flippancy: 'By the way, who is this young Rajah? I am sure I know nothing whatsoever about him. I never even knew of his existence till Leilamani said something of his wearing the same coloured tie and shirt as my sari and following me about. I wonder whether Fido has been mistaken for a young gallant? He usually has the same coloured ribbon as my sari! Nevertheless whoever he be you are at liberty to send him *your* love (and mine also). I *am* extravagant, aren't I?'

But then, as if she was unable to help herself, she gives in to the restlessness and sense of oppression that was bothering her: 'Do you ever get into a Bohemian mood? I do. Today I feel as though only a mad life of roving irregularity could satisfy me. A life without law, without consistency and doctrine. Though my nature is unacquainted with either, still the life I live adheres to the common code of society. I would *much* rather help a friend than pay a creditor. I feel I could enjoy the excitement of being pursued by bailiffs and marked as "unsteady". And if I only had enough money to pay the garriwala or taxi driver, I would most certainly give it to the hungry beggar in the street—he would have the greater claim! But what is the use of saying these things and dreaming a life I can never fulfill? I might just as well tell you while I am about it, that I have a greater regard for unpunctual persons than the more polite beings who somehow always turn up at the right time in the right dress with the right words. Oh dear they *do* make me feel *so* uncomfortable!'

And this leading to a spurt of rage that she makes no more effort to stifle with polite talk: 'I have just been contemplating the nicest way of murder and suicide—and I have come to the conclusion that stabbing with a jewel-handled dagger is far the best—shooting and bombing is much too civilized for my taste!' She signs off with a 'But don't fret. I intend doing neither' just in case Padmaja should get too alarmed.

There are also two poems she wrote that year and shared with the Naidu girls that are on the same theme—of a lover who seems to have moved on, leaving her either sad or piqued, or both. The first, signed merely '1916':

Why should I weep
Or groan in despair
While the stars still peep
At a world so fair?

Why should I be dull
And living, pine
While life is still full
Of Love's sweet wine?

Why should I be sad
And dim mine young eye,
While others are glad
At the glorious deep sky?

Why should I not play,
And laugh, and sing
While the world is so gay
At the coming of Spring?

The second is also on fleeting love, but less defiant and more despairing:

A flower came to me one day in its natural loveliness and it told
me the secret of its colours and then faded.
A wind blew around me once and it whispered the story of
its travels into my ears and then it ceased.
A wave one day dashed up in its native fierceness and it
touched my feet as they rested on the rocks and then withdrew.
A bird came to me one day in its freedom and it sat upon the
young bough of the green tree o'erhead and it told me its tales of
love from birdland and then flew away.
A dream once came to me in its vaporous beauty and then
I awoke.

Happiness came to me one day in all its exquisite radiance and I danced with it full two days and two nights, and then it tired and left me.

Love came to me once in flower-like sweetness, and I breathed its fragrance till it sickened and satiated.

Sorrow came to me with its black robed beauteous form, but it has not forsaken me. I have drunk deep of its cup of gall and I taste it when I wake and when I sleep; when I smile and when I weep.

Sorrow knows not satiety!

Had Jinnah then cooled off? He was, after all, no fool and could see clearly with his legal experience that without her father's consent, their courtship did not stand a chance of going anywhere—unless he wanted to commit political suicide by running away with her or entangling himself in legal hassles that would take years to untangle. Moreover, he belonged to a generation of Indian men who regarded falling in love as a weakness. 'The moment you suspect that any girl has inspired a feeling of some sort in you, break off at once and do not let it grow,' as his friend Motilal Nehru once advised his son, Jawaharlal, in England. And no one could be better than Jinnah at curing himself of an inconvenient attachment, having used his iron willpower all his life to vanquish his feelings. And at this time, he did not even have to try. In the last six months alone, in between Ruttie's two trips to Mahabaleshwar, he had achieved what no man had ever achieved before in Indian politics: he was re-elected to the legislative council, spending less than three days campaigning for himself but still winning with a margin. He was active as usual in the legislative session in Delhi, speaking on all major issues. He was elected president of the Muslim League for the forthcoming joint session of the League and the Congress in Lucknow, which was going to be the turning point in the country's politics, bringing about a settlement between Hindus and Muslims. He was the prime mover of the pact, the only man to be trusted by both sides; and to reinforce his position as the tallest national leader, he was asked to preside over the Bombay provincial Congress conference in Ahmedabad. In contrast, Ruttie's life was lived either in the drawing rooms of her parents' various homes or in the homes of their friends.

Or she escaped into the realms of her fantasy world, living her life through the books she read. She had always done that, even as a child fleeing from her boisterous games with her three brothers into the world of books; she was the acknowledged bookworm of a large family that indulged her passion for reading without sharing it themselves—her copy of *The Complete Works of Alfred Lord Tennyson*, for example, was a present from her father when she was not yet twelve, inscribed with the words: 'To dear Rati from her loving Papa. 14th December 1911. The date of birth of her little brother Jamshed.' And her copy of Charlotte Bronte's *Shirley* was a present from her second brother, Manek, on the eve of her twelfth birthday, with the inscription: 'To dear Ruttie from Manek Feb. 18 1912.' So far her reading had been limited to English authors and poets or at best European writers translated into English—from the standard Milton and *Silas Marner* and Bernard Shaw prescribed for students preparing for the Senior Cambridge exam to her own reading for pleasure, ranging from poetry to novels (almost all of William Thackeray's novels and Alexander Dumas's in English translation), Ibsen's plays (very fashionable then, with many attempting Indian translations, and staple reading in study circles, along with Browning's poems); a heavily marked and annotated copy of the English suffragist Emmeline Pankhurst's *My Own Story* and Oscar Wilde's *The Happy Prince and Other Tales*, but not his 'De Profundis', from which she loved to quote, possibly for its shock effect. But now, for the first time in her life, she took to an Indian book, Rabindranath Tagore's *Chitra: A Play in One Act* (issued in 1914 in a limited edition 'by the Indian Society') which she seems to have read with even more passion than the Romantic English poets she had so far loved, judging by the number of footnotes and pencil markings alone.

Tagore's fame, although growing among the English educated, possibly had not yet travelled to Petit Hall, for the only 'Indian' book to have found a place in the bookshelves of the baronet's castle so far was *The Garden of Kama and Other Love Lyrics from India*, inscribed with Lady Petit's name and dated 1914. One would guess the Tagore book was 'borrowed', for Ruttie did not sign or mention the date of acquiring it on the first page as she invariably did; she liked to stamp her mark of ownership with bold fountain pen strokes inscribing her name, spelt variously as 'Rutty Petit', 'Rutty D. Petit' or even 'Rutty Din Petit', as if trying them all out for the perfect fit.

But whether the book was borrowed or her own, the enthusiastic pencil markings on this dramatic verse based on the Mahabharata story of Arjun falling in love with Princess Chitrangada clearly belong to no one else, and mirror her budding passion and how it emerged. Beginning on page three and continuing till the very end, the markings consist of vertical lines of two or more strokes to signify the most poignant lines for her, such as Madana, the God of Love, saying: 'That requires no schooling, fair one. The eye does its work untaught, and he knows how well, who is struck in the heart'; or 'then for the first time in my life I felt myself a woman and knew that a man was before me'; or 'Fair Lady, the very sight of you is indeed the highest hospitality . . . to feel his heart struggling to break its bounds urging its passionate cry through the entire body—and then to send him away like a beggar—no, impossible'; or 'I felt like a flower which has but a few fleeting hours to listen to all the humming flatteries and whispered murmurs of the woodlands and then must lower its eyes from the sky, bend its head and at a breath, give itself up to the dust without a cry, thus ending the short story of a perfect moment that has neither a past nor present'; or '. . . a smile about his lips like the crescent moon in the morning'; or '. . . I remembered what I used to be and ran and ran like a deer afraid of her own shadow'. And a big cross over these lines: 'shame slipped to my feet like loosened clothes. I heard his call—"Beloved, my most beloved!" And all my forgotten lives united as one and responded to it. I said, "Take me, take all I am!"'

Interestingly, there is a book Ruttie bought and read just before this second trip to Mahabaleshwar. A long English poem in the Sufi tradition—*The Kasidah of Haji Abdu El Yazdi—A Lay of the Higher Law*, written by the British explorer and orientalist Sir Richard Burton, whom Ruttie admired greatly for his daring adventures and unconventionality that she longed to emulate. The book carries Ruttie's name and the date—9 October 1916, and what makes it interesting is not the poem itself but the short biography of Burton that precedes it in which Ruttie has chosen to pencil-mark these lines: 'As a boy he had a strong imagination and where others might have remained silent on this score, or admitted a weakness for invention, he described himself as "a resolute and unblushing liar. I used to ridicule the idea of my honour being in any way attached to telling the truth; I considered it an impertinence being questioned. I never could understand what moral turpitude there could be in a lie, unless it was told for fear of the consequences of telling the truth, or one that would attach blame to another person." He was once asked by a curate if he had shot a man on his way to Mecca. Burton is said to have replied: "Sir, I am proud to say I have committed every sin in the Decalogue."' Could the pampered, protected heiress possibly be plotting sedition?

Whatever be her secret thoughts and hidden plans, Ruttie certainly returned to Bombay restored to good humour. Her next letter to Padmaja, on 22 November 1916, is so much like the girl she used to be before her love troubles, that her parents must have been reassured that she was now on the road to recovery, if not fully recovered. 'I am so glad you like the photograph,' her letter from Petit Hall begins. 'It is a little more than a year ago since it was taken. Mother wants me to have a fresh lot taken, but I always put it off—it is *such* a bother!' The cumbersome process of having one's photograph taken, involving posing before a camera for hours, was something that fashionable families had taken to, especially the Parsis, and everyone was into exchanging these photos of one another for their albums. '*How* many more times have I to remind you to send me a photo of yourself and Leilamani. And oh! When is your mother going to send one of herself? Do remind her!'

The other reassuring sign was her resuming her old activities, and she goes on in her letter to relate an amusing incident that happened at one of the many fetes that the fashionable ladies of Bombay loved to hold, setting up stalls selling knitted socks and other such stuff for the benefit of soldiers fighting in the War. 'I was on duty at Block D of the Lucky Bag(h) enclosure yesterday and it was great fun. One *very* smart young officer handed me his number, which entitled him to 24 yards of some sort of coarse material. He was very vexed, not knowing what to do with it and quite realizing that it would mar his swank were he to carry it about, he went to the enclosure next door from where he received a dozen Turkish towels. You can imagine his distress as he walked off with a bundle under each arm! How we laughed!!!!'

And she can banter once again about her many admirers that she is unaware of and flirt with the idea of them chasing her: 'I wish I could have seen the too "progressive" follower of Islam with the "burning heart". I think I would have taken to him if he has been kicked out of the Aligarh College for his young and flashing patriotism. I suppose that is what was meant by progressive?'

But her parents would have been less reassured if they had read her next sentence, bristling at Padmaja's use of the words 'old fools' when referring to the national leaders at the forthcoming congress. All her hackles rising, Ruttie writes: 'By the way, how do you mean "won't act"? What would you like the "old fools" to do? The only way they can act at present is to unite.' It was a particularly sore point that Padmaja had touched off with her thoughtless remark, echoing the younger generation's impatience with the way politics was going—leaders arriving at the annual Congress session and giving thundering speeches for four days and falling into coma until the next session. For Ruttie, at the stage when Jinnah was the shining hero who would give India back its freedom, and worshipped the work he was doing towards it, 'old fools' was not the words she wanted anyone, least of all her friend, to associate him with.

Two days later, writing to Leilamani, she was again in an elated mood: 'Am I excited about going to Lucknow?' she writes, responding to Leilamani's query about going to the forthcoming Congress session in Lucknow the following month. 'I should think so. Who wouldn't be [?]' And indeed, the Congress's annual session was something people looked forward to, especially politically minded people, young and old, arriving at the venue—held in a different city each year—putting up with friends and acquaintances, prepared not just to hear the rousing speeches delivered in the pandal but also to dress up and be seen at the many parties and dos that were part of the Congress jamboree. It was a national picnic of sorts, lasting four days and four nights, where one met old friends from across the country and made new ones. 'I am so glad your mother will also be there too,' Ruttie goes on in her letter. 'Is it quite settled about her going? You too must try and come.'

But for Ruttie, the excitement about going to Lucknow was not about the session, as she claimed, or even about the prospect of seeing Jinnah again or glorying in his big moment. She had her own plan that she had been plotting for some time that she had not shared with anyone so far, not even with Jinnah. And Lucknow, with its stirring talks of freedom and how to wrest it from those who denied it to Indians, would be the perfect place to put it into action, safe from her parents' meddling.

Chapter Three

~

That the Petits allowed Ruttie to go to Lucknow, and that too without either of them to keep an eye on her, speaks a lot for the way Ruttie was raised. On the face of it, it seemed foolhardy on their part to let her to go to the one place in the world where her chances of meeting Jinnah were not only certain, but where her admiration for him would be redoubled. They could hardly be unaware of the buzz that Jinnah was to be the hero of this historic political session that would bring Muslims and Hindus together on a common platform and accept a pact for unity that promised an imminent end to British rule in India. Freedom, according to the *Bombay Chronicle*, was right round the corner and Jinnah was to be at the helm of these changes. They would have persuaded themselves, of course, that there was really no danger, especially now that Ruttie seemed to have recovered from her misplaced passion for him. Jinnah too, having been put in his place by Sir Dinshaw, had dropped his suit and was visibly preoccupied with matters that had nothing to do with their daughter—from drafting a memorandum of post-War reforms that was widely discussed to presiding over the Bombay provincial Congress, besides defending B.G. Tilak in a high-profile sedition case. But the truth was there was very little the Petits could have done really to stop her—unless they expressly forbade her to go, which would in any case have only made her more defiant. As modern parents of the new century, they were expected to come up with some sounder reason than that they did not wish her to go, and there simply was none—especially when her Aunt Hamabai, as interested in politics as her niece, decided to go along as well.

Not that Ruttie's parents were the kind to worry overly about Ruttie, preoccupied as they were with their own concerns. Sir Dinshaw, after making sure that his sister and daughter would be comfortably lodged in Lucknow and had their own transport, went about his own work, while Lady Petit left on a holiday to Agra with her friends, leaving Ruttie to set off for Lucknow with her aunt.

Of course, not all parents of the new century, not even those who considered themselves thoroughly modern, treated their sixteen-year-olds with the same degree of laxity. There was Sarojini herself, despite being universally acknowledged as a model of a liberal parent because she encouraged her four children to speak their minds and express their wishes. She would not, for instance, think of getting her daughters betrothed or married at twelve or fourteen as most others were doing despite being educated; but nevertheless laid down strict rules for her daughters which she expected them to obey without question. 'School is much the best place for both of you,' Sarojini wrote to Padmaja who at sixteen was understandably keen to leave her boarding school and return home to Hyderabad, 'where you *have* to obey certain rules and accept certain discipline however much you dislike it . . . but when you are at home you will be put on your *honour* to do what is right and pleasing and good for you without compulsion but because it is right that you should do so. Now think over what I have said.'

But the Petits did not believe in imposing their parental authority on the children, leaving it to the staff they had hired at such expense to do the needful. It was Ruttie's governess's job, as far as they were concerned, to instil what was required in their daughter, expecting no more than that she be groomed into a young lady fit for their society. And now that she was of an age to wear saris and join her mother's social circle, having outgrown her governess, it was really up to Ruttie what she did with herself, provided she observed the bare minimum of rules, such as taking care not to stay out too late according to her parents' standards. There was a time when this very minimal expectation of her by her father, especially when it came to her education, used to incense her. The emphatic pencil lines Ruttie drew, for example, on the margins of the English suffragist Emmeline Pankhurst's memoir where Pankhurst describes her father's indifference to his daughters' education while he spent much thought and effort into sending his sons to college, show this clearly touched a chord. But now, of course, she would have been only too relieved at their casual negligence.

To be fair to the Petits, they were not the only parents who believed in outsourcing parenting to the hired help—it was the fashionable thing to do at that time among those who could afford it. Besides, the Petits also belonged to a Malabar Hill set of rich Parsis where women led unbelievably liberated lives for their time, thanks to the liberal Parsi law of inheritance where women enjoyed a considerable share of the family wealth and property. Ruttie's aunt, Hamabai, was a living example of the single Parsi woman of independent means. Ten years younger than Sir Dinshaw and his only sibling, Hamabai was only twelve years old when their father passed away, and her brother became her legal guardian. But richly endowed by her grandparents on either side, her wealth was not controlled by him but by a trust in her own name, with special staff to run it. She could, therefore, insist on going abroad to a French college in Nice for her baccalaureate, a privilege that Sir Dinshaw either denied or was unable to provide his own daughter two decades later, possibly because of the War. And when their mother died, leaving Hamabai an orphan at the age of twenty-four, there was nothing to stop the adventurous young woman from following her inclinations. She travelled widely—'toured the world and visited its remotest parts', as a Parsi who's who put it. She went skiing on the Swiss Alps, owned a collection of pedigreed dogs that she adored, owned race horses which regularly won prizes and was one of the first ladies in India to own and drive a motor car.

In her letters home, Sarojini described her as 'Ruttie's Amazon aunt', but it's not clear whether by this she meant that Hamabai was a strong, strapping woman or because of her stamina for horse riding—'Her Amazon aunt rides *seven horses a day* and sometimes eleven—just think of it!' In the photographs that survive of her, Hamabai has the broad-jawed, plump-faced look of her brother, with the same finely shaped eyes and eyebrows, but there the resemblance between the two siblings ends. Unlike Sir Dinshaw, who preferred to dress in the conventional attire of an English gentleman with his stiff white collar, vest and tie, Hamabai went in for a more unconventional style—teaming up Benarasi silk waistcoats and long, flowing sleeves with her saris made of clinging silk or chiffon, giving her the appearance of an exotic oriental, her curled hair and strands of pearls emphasizing her Hollywoodesque transformation of the ordinary Gujarati sari-clad lady.

But she was by no means an idle heiress who liked to live it up. When her mother died, being already richly endowed, she sold the jewellery she inherited from her and used the proceeds to set up a Parsi girls' orphanage, earning for herself a reputation as one of the great philanthropists in a community known for its charitable work. Since then, her 'charities, both communal and cosmopolitan, reached a very high figure . . . and by her numerous acts of charity she has added glory to the name of the Parsi community'. She was not zealously Zoroastrian, like her grandfather, but took an interest in the spiritual sciences, and it was undoubtedly she who introduced the theosophist and nationalist Annie Besant to Petit Hall. However, Hamabai's spiritual interests seem to have found little resonance in her brother's family except for Ruttie, as indicated by the book she gifted her brother which eventually found its way to Ruttie's bookshelves. The book, *Clairvoyance* by C.W. Leadbeater, is inscribed: 'presented to D.P. from H.P'. There is one more book Ruttie took away from Petit Hall that originally belonged to her aunt—*Many Thoughts of Many Minds Being a Treasury of Reference*, signed 'Hamabai Framjee Petit, 6 February'.

It was Hamabai's involvement with Annie Besant's Home Rule League that drew her to the public meetings being held in different parts of Bombay 'and at every such meeting came and sat in the first row the little girl Ruttie accompanied by her aunt, Miss Hamabai Petit, the multimillionaire philanthropist', as Kanji Dwarkadas recalls in his memoir of Ruttie. To amuse herself through the hours-long speeches, Ruttie watched 'the pranks being played on the platform'. When Kanji 'saw a speaker talking too long and irrelevantly, I poked a sharp pencil behind his knee as he was addressing the meeting and he lost his chain of thoughts, collapsed and resumed his seat and got wild with me. Ruttie told me later that she enjoyed my pranks.'

But it was not only Besant's Home Rule movement that attracted the two Miss Petits to politics. Hamabai, like her brother, had known and enjoyed Jinnah's company long before her niece was out of the schoolroom. The two were probably introduced to each other when Hamabai was studying in Nice. Sir Dinshaw had written to his sister asking her to go to the railway station to meet Jinnah, who was passing through. Later, they became friends, having at least two interests in common—motor cars and horse riding. In fact, they were good enough friends for Jinnah to agree to take up a land acquisition case on her behalf, one of the rare instances when Jinnah took up a civil suit after he became a 'Rolls Royce lawyer', as he liked to call himself.

Hamabai was far too independent-minded to let her brother dictate her relationship with Jinnah, and even after they became sworn enemies, Hamabai continued to attend Jinnah's public meetings, taking Ruttie along. In fact, at the height of the hostilities between her brother and Jinnah following Sir Dinshaw's angry rejection of Jinnah's marriage proposal, Hamabai refused to take sides and even volunteered her services to work under Jinnah as an honorary vice president of the Bombay branch of the Home Rule League of which Jinnah was then the president. The brother and sister were close but went their own way, particularly when Hamabai decided to marry. Her brother did not approve of her choice because although he was a Parsi from an eminent family, being the nephew of the late eminent barrister and national leader Sir Pherozeshah Mehta, he had little to recommend him other than being as well travelled and as consummate a rider as Hamabai. With Sir Dinshaw's inflated ideas of his own family's status among the Parsis, the match was not to his taste, but his sister was by then already in her thirties and in a position to marry whom she pleased. In the circumstances, Hamabai was possibly the most sympathetic chaperone that Ruttie could hope to find.

Their choice of an escort was equally fortuitous for Ruttie. D.N. Bahadurji was not only a family friend, but as a Parsi who had married a Hindu woman from a Brahmin family, as Kanji noted elsewhere, was likely to have been sympathetic to her cause. Besides, he was a useful person to know in Lucknow where he had a grand mansion. Delegates and guests who poured in for the Congress session that year stayed where they could, crammed into small rooms and tents with no conveniences. Bahadurji was also a good friend of Jinnah's, both being successful barristers, and although Bahadurji was more senior, the two had been in the habit of taking holidays together from as far back as 1906, when Ruttie was only six. Jinnah spent the October vacation in Panchgani with Bahadurji that year, as we learn from a criminal case he filed in Bombay's police court the following month. Apparently, while the two barristers were holidaying in Panchgani, Jinnah's coachman was rude to his friend, and when Jinnah rebuked him, was insolent to him as well, causing Jinnah to dismiss the 'purdesi' (to use the *Bombay Chronicle*'s word for a non-local) coachman and send him back to Bombay by the next train. When the two friends returned to Bombay, the sacked coachman tried to frighten Jinnah into coughing up his wages by seizing the reins of his horse as he was driving from his bungalow to the courthouse, along the 'cooperage', as the football ground was then called in Bombay. But Jinnah, as the coachman discovered, was not be intimidated by such crude tactics. After waiting it out for twenty minutes on the road, Jinnah eventually handed him over to the police and he was sentenced to three weeks of rigorous imprisonment for wrongfully detaining a barrister.

At any rate, Ruttie was spotted in the train on her way to Lucknow with her aunt and their escort. Travelling in the next compartment was Kanji, still a student then, with another eminent barrister, Bhulabhai Desai, and his wife and son. They too were on their way to the Congress session—that was one of the nicer things about going to it during the Christmas holidays: you could bump into people you knew or wanted to know. But Kanji did not dare to go up to Ruttie and talk to her because he had not yet been introduced to her. Instead, he watched her from a distance as she walked along the platform with Bahadurji at every junction. Travelling by train, even in a first-class compartment, could be a bone-rattling experience—'all my bones and teeth seem rather looser than they were!' as Sarojini once described it—but few women stepped out of the train at stations to stretch their legs, possibly because of the crowds outside. It could be overwhelming—'coolies moving about . . . a chorus of voices shouting . . . "Hindu chai, Mussulman chai, Hindu pani, Mussulman pani!". . . rich men . . . followed by servants, their ladies lifting their saris so that they shall not touch the crowd . . . turbans of all colours, caps and a few fezes . . . poor men sitting on their bundles together with their families.' For Ruttie, eager to break out of her sheltered life and experience the world, every station would have been an opportunity she did not want to lose, and old, kind Bahadurji no doubt rose courteously to his role as escort at every junction—it wouldn't have done to let his friend's young and beautiful daughter walk by herself on a crowded platform, stared at by scores of strangers.

Did she perhaps also drag Bahadurji out the next morning to join the crowds at the Lucknow station? It was a hero's welcome that awaited Jinnah when he arrived that morning. Lined up in and outside the railway station were Hindus, Christians and Muslims—both Shia and Sunni—with hundreds more joining the triumphal procession through the streets of Lucknow to Kaiserbagh, the Raja of Mahmudabad's residence where Jinnah was to stay as his guest. 'Only about four hundred were allowed on the platform, while there was a seating crowd outside,' as the *Bombay Chronicle* reported, the 'seating crowd' probably referring to seating space outside in contrast to only standing room for the crowd on the platform. When Jinnah arrived by a special train, he was garlanded by the prominent Muslim leader and nationalist—the Raja of Mahmudabad—and the head of the Congress reception committee, Pandit Jagat Narayan, then he 'was taken in procession in a carriage, splendidly decorated with flowers and buntings, to Kaiserbagh'. Was Ruttie amused at the posters of him in a fez cap, describing him as 'Maulana Mohammed Ali Jinnah'? And was she surprised, like the rest of his friends, to see him discarding his usual sola topi and appearing in public only in his new fez cap? She would have surely heard the story of the fez cap straight from Jinnah's mouth? Told with his characteristic dry wit, of how the Muslim League leaders approached him while he was still in his compartment to explain how the posters had mistakenly described him as a 'maulana', their dismay at finding 'that he looked the reverse of what the posters described him'. It was Jinnah who took control of the situation, as usual, calming down the panic-stricken organizers, asking in his pragmatic way what should then be done, and when one of them suggested he wear a fez, the Turkish cap in vogue among the Muslims in those days, he readily agreed, sending one of the organizers rushing to the market to buy one while he stayed out of sight of the crowds inside his compartment until his cap arrived. Was it perhaps on his instructions that the man returned not with one fez cap but a dozen for him to choose from, or was the Muslim League leader commissioned to shop for him already aware of Jinnah's fastidious tastes? Did Ruttie tease him perhaps about this new maulana look, but let him keep it on for the four days the conference lasted? But at least he stuck to his usual European suits, setting him apart from most of the Muslim delegates, dressed in the long, flowing 'chogas', or robes embroidered with silver, gold and silk thread that added such unusual colour to the Congress session that year.

That she did tease him, this enchanting, beautiful chit of a girl with her impish sense of fun, as no one had ever dared to do, was apparent to all their friends. And that he responded to her teasing with a tender amusement and a meekness he had never shown before, touched the hearts of all who knew and loved either of them or, like Sarojini, both. 'He loves her,' concluded Sarojini, who made it to Lucknow despite her recent illness, appearing on the platform at both the Muslim League and Congress sessions as one of the speakers, after seeing Jinnah and Ruttie together. She shared this with her friend Syed Mahmud only fifteen months later, noting it was 'the one really human and genuine emotion of his reserved and self-centred nature'.

But first, Ruttie had to put her plan to work to get him back to her. She did manage to meet Jinnah according to her plan, despite his pressing schedule. He became immersed the very evening of his arrival in thrashing out the details of the famous Hindu–Muslim Lucknow Pact and since neither the Muslim League nor the Congress leaders could agree on the percentage of seats to be reserved for Muslims, the talks extended for two days until late into the night. But sometime after the contract had been signed, and the Congress session was under way, Jinnah made the time to meet Ruttie for the interview she must have sought with him. He was seen climbing into the Petits' car with her, accompanied by her aunt.

It is difficult to guess what happened between them during that brief, snatched time they could have had by themselves without being discovered. Did Ruttie propose, as the gossip had it, in the spirit of the times—the liberated woman of the new century asserting her freedom of choice regardless of her parents' wishes? And did Jinnah really respond with his usual economy of words, in that dry way she loved: 'It sounds like a good proposition.' If she did, she never once said as much to anyone, claiming the reverse, in fact—that she had laid down the terms for accepting him when he proposed. 'You will perhaps agree how that is possible when it was one of the terms on which I accepted him,' she wrote to Padmaja several years later, complaining to her friend of how Jinnah was now breaking one of the conditions she had set down before accepting his proposal, 'that is, that he couldn't touch his hair without my previous sanction'. But that could just be her girlish pride, not wanting to admit how she had to work on him, instead of being chased by him. But whoever it was who did the initial proposing, Jinnah was a changed man now that he knew she was with him against her father, daring not just to hope, but suddenly supremely confident of his ability to pull off what no one had done so far.

It could have also been the effect of the electric atmosphere in Lucknow. During that historic 'National Week', everything seemed suddenly possible. It was the coming together of a new class of people amongst whom the idea of being an Indian had already taken root, erasing the old ideas of community and caste. 'Lucknow was crowded and cosmopolitan beyond all knowledge,' as the lieutenant governor of the United Provinces, Lord Meston, wrote to the viceroy, giving his impressions of the Congress session. 'I never saw so crowded a concourse of educated middle class Indians, so thoroughly enjoying themselves. The Congress has become a great national anniversary, full of excitement and intellectual amusement.' And this session was especially so, with everyone certain that a breakthrough in forging unity between the Hindus and Muslims had at last been achieved. For the first time since the Congress had been founded, there were Muslims attending the sessions in visibly large numbers. For the first time, Hindus and Muslims spoke in the same voice, they rubbed shoulders in the pandals, dined together and heard their leaders speaking from the same platform. It was two years since the greatest war on earth had begun and no one could as yet foresee when it would end, but change was palpably in the air. No one listening to those rousing speeches, feeling the enthusiasm of those crowds, could doubt for a moment that the end of British rule in the country was imminently close and an era of new possibilities about to dawn. It was not Ruttie alone who felt her doubts and fears being swept away, but Jinnah too allowed himself to dream once again of marrying the woman he'd set his heart on, in spite of what the world—and her father—might say.

Whatever may have transpired between them in Lucknow, Ruttie returned from the Congress recharged. Gone was all the melancholy and despair of the previous months. She was bursting to share her joy with someone and yet afraid of giving away her secret. There was no letter from Padmaja waiting as she had hoped. With her perhaps, she might have been tempted to say too much, but instead, there was a letter waiting from Padmaja's twelve-year-old sister, Leilamani, seeking Ruttie's attention and sympathy, as always. Even Leilamani was better than not having anyone to talk to, after her momentous trip. She got down at once to write her a reply, infusing the letter with her new-found joy and sense of profound hope, and all the poetry within her for which Jinnah had so little use, now bursting out from its repression: 'Little passion flower!' begins the letter on Petit Hall stationery with its embossed seal, dated 3rd January 1917. 'You who glory in dreaming! You who love the sun and moon and dancing stars! When days in dawning remind one of blossoming flowers. Why should you breathe despair?'

Seeing her own intense emotions everywhere, she writes to her little friend: 'I call you a passion flower not after the real flower of religious passion, but because every emotion with you has the intensity of a passion. But why this strange cry for love and sympathy? Does not your mother love you? Do not I love you? And do not we both understand you? Do not the fragrant flowers and rustling trees and warbling birds all understand you? Do not you feel your own fragrance in the rose, your freshness in the tree? Do not the stars reflect but your own limpid eyes? Do not your own sweet songs resound the "full throated ease" and the delicate strain of the birds?'

Her high-flown words of romantic verse, somewhat affected, seem to mean little—'And what is this last song that your spirit has sung? Is it a song of passionate despair or "poignant sorrow"?' And 'Oh who shall satisfy your quenchless thirst, but *yourself*? If ever you desire to realize an ideal, it *must* be within yourself and then you attain what is known as self-realisation. So whenever you want to satisfy and appease your heart do it yourself. Let the bubbling red wine flow from the font of your soul, let it quench the thirsty heart.' But under it all, was there perhaps a wistful longing for something she had yet to find? Why was it about her *giving* all the time, what about receiving? But she will not allow the thought to grow; she is in a hurry: 'I would write more but I'm in haste.'

After waiting another four days for a letter from Padmaja, Ruttie could no longer resist her urge to connect with her friend. 'It will be a week on Tuesday since I returned from Lucknow,' Ruttie wrote, aware suddenly of the exact number of days since she returned from Lucknow, in contrast to her usual vagueness about dates, 'and very much more since you last wrote to me. And if I remember aright it is you who owes me a letter. But nay, there is no such thing as "owing" and "turns" with us. We write to each other when we feel inclined and not when convention demands.'

On the surface, there is nothing much she says in her letter dated 7 January 1917 besides the usual things people said when they returned from a Congress session, even if her language was a little more lyrical than the average Congress attendee's: 'Well, and the great capital of the old nawabs of Oudh has had its Congress and Muslim League. It has listened to the cry of those children whose ancestors belonged to a proud and independent nation. The City of Mosques has welcomed the worshippers of the Lords Krishna and Buddha. It has heard the carefully measured words of the moderates, and the reckless indictments of the Extremists against an alien Government. It has thrilled to the passionate appeal of those nationalists who have sacrificed all at the feet of the Motherland. It has sobbed for the birthright of an Empire to be restored.' There is certainly a new consciousness, inspired no doubt by the stirring speeches she absorbed so eagerly only a week ago and it would have been only natural for her to apply the speeches she heard on fighting for freedom to her own determination to fight for her right to choose her way of life and become an equal partner in the freedom struggle. 'India has not yet realized that if the right of nationality and independence is attained through diplomatic parlance, or as a favour or gift, or as a reward for "the blood of her martyred sons", it will be of no avail. We *must* fight for our liberty and not barter for it, *not* by pen and parchment but sword and dagger. Those men and women who bear the distinction of being the children of India, they must renounce all for the Motherland. Her daughters must devote their souls and glory in the life sacrifice of her sons and even fight side by side with those patriots whose blood shall gain India back her own crown of Freedom.'

But the urge to speak of matters less impersonal suddenly gets the better of her and she changes track quite abruptly, referring to what one can only guess is her latest conquest: 'But enough! I feel inclined to mark a lighter vein ere I close.' She talks, instead, of another admirer of hers. 'Oh yes! About that cockeyed pet, isn't he too killing for words!' But the real struggle is on another front altogether. She wants to talk easily and freely about, of all things, sex, but finds, to her dismay, that she cannot break past her own inhibitions. She begins in a roundabout way: 'I asked your mother about the gentleman in whose house you are staying at present—I forget his name! But does he beat Nabi-ullah in—?' and referring to Padmaja's previous love interest, a prominent barrister and Muslim League leader called Syed Nabiullah, Ruttie verges on asking a question that she has never dared ask anyone before but which nevertheless is now uppermost in her mind—how good he was at . . . kissing perhaps? But she is struck mute with shyness despite herself and is forced instead to end her sentence lamely with: 'I don't know what has happened to me today. I want to write a certain word and I keep on, or rather my pen turns on to another!'

What was it that was bothering her so much that she urgently wanted to share with Padmaja but simply could not pluck up the courage to bring up? Was it the utter lack of physical intimacy between her and Jinnah even after they had got secretly engaged? His temperament, first of all, was against it, being as he was 'a celibate introvert who discouraged intimacy, timid of relationships'. But other men were in the same straits, especially if they led a public life. As someone who prided himself on being a sensualist but was nevertheless forced to remain celibate, Jawaharlal Nehru writes in his autobiography: 'We considered ourselves very sophisticated and talked of sex and morality in a superior way, referring casually to Ivan Block, Havelock Ellis, Kraft Ebbing or Otto Weininger . . . As a matter of fact, in spite of our brave talk, most of us were rather timid where sex was concerned . . . my knowledge for many years after I had left Cambridge remained confined to theory . . . I doubt if any of us attached any idea of sin to it. Certainly I did not; there was no religious inhibition . . . yet a certain shyness kept me away, as well as a distaste for the usual methods adopted.' In a sense, Jinnah was more experienced than either Jawaharlal Nehru or Ruttie, having been married before, albeit briefly, when he was only fifteen and a half; but having been raised in an even more strait-laced age than either of the two, he would hardly venture to take any liberties with Ruttie before they were actually married.

But there is so much else to look forward to, especially now that Jinnah too is back from Lucknow and has at least three weeks in Bombay before he leaves for the legislative session in Delhi. They can, of course, only meet at parties and other social occasions but there is no dearth of those in Bombay. Suddenly, Ruttie loves her social life—'I have O such a gay week before me. I love gaiety, don't you? I mean theatres, weddings, races, not "At Homes" and that type of affair.' Her only anxiety is that her mother, who is about to return from her trip to Agra, might put an end to Ruttie's outings: 'Mother is returning today from Agra. I wonder whether she will find me looking better or worse. I caught chill in the train while journeying to Bombay'—evidently the price for stepping out for a walk on the platform in the freezing winter of north India—'and the doctor has made out quite a formidable table of don'ts. You see it has affected the lungs which is not considered quite as insignificant as I think it. And I do hope Mother will not also think that I should be treated as an invalid!'

Luckily for her, Lady Petit did not notice anything amiss. Ruttie's next fortnightly letter, on 20 January 1917—this time to her 'little friend Leilamani'—is full of the festivities of Bombay's high season: 'Well, little friend, I am going to the races this afternoon—and as I did not go to rest till late last night, I must just see if I cannot manage to snatch a few moments sleep ere I begin my toiletry.' The 'toiletry'— always a serious preoccupation, involving choosing the appropriate dress for the occasion and balancing a carefully put together look with an appearance of careless disregard for what one wore, and adding to it the right degree of eccentricity—must have been extra special that afternoon, considering that the chances of bumping into Jinnah at the races were extremely high. With his passion for horses, the races were one social activity he did not disdain.

Padmaja had not yet returned from her visit to her friend's home, and it is Leilamani's thirteen-year-old neediness and prickliness that she is addressing rather than sharing confidences with the friend her own age. Evidently, her last letter quoting the younger girl's highly poetic language back to her had not gone down well. 'But what is the matter with you? Are you not well—I mean physically? Mentally, I know that you are suffering.

'And, O Leilamani! How can you for a moment, even for a moment, think of me as mocking your letters. But I see that it was only a wayward and passing suspicion—but you mustn't even for a breath of a second let such thoughts enter your mind and torture your heart. It is wrong—very wrong! Truly does Oscar Wilde in his 'De Profundis' say that the great sins of the world are committed in the mind—or something to that effect.

'When you are given a flower you do not think of the thorn. You revel in its beauty and feast in its fragrance. So is the friendship I have offered you like a rose and you must not only think of the thorn—the imaginary thorn in this case!'

Was this philosophizing arising from more personal sentiments than Ruttie cared to admit? In the best of circumstances, Jinnah could not have made a satisfactory fiancé for a protected, sought-after society girl, brought up only for the pursuit of pleasure—the 'Blue Flower', as Sarojini fancifully, but not inaccurately, dubbed Ruttie. But in the three weeks since his triumph in Lucknow, Jinnah was busier than ever—political meetings, including a meeting of the Bombay Political Caucus with the governor, Lionel Curtis, and his own legal work to catch up with—leaving him little time to hang around in parties and clubs in the hope of a brief encounter with Ruttie. Clandestine meetings were, of course, out of the question, considering his political image. Yes, her rose had more thorns than she dared to count—and none of them imaginary.

And when at last Padmaja's letter came, Ruttie could no longer restrain herself from at least hinting at the turmoil and confusion within her. 'Life has been such a medley of wild excitement and cold depression!' she wrote to Padmaja on 27 January 1917. 'And yet it has been *so* full—*so* full because of its hollowness! *So* empty because of its fullness!

'I am joyous and I am sad. But they are the emotions of the soul— and not of the heart! By soul I mean temperament—I long for peace and yet I dread the very idea of it. I revel in the storming passions which burn and tear at the fibres of my being till my very spirit writhes in an agony of excitement. And yet were I asked the cause of all this I could only answer by that one word—temperament! Ay, you may almost call it a form of hysteria.'

A wiser person would have perhaps discerned in Ruttie's infatuation merely a young girl's passionate yearning to break out of her empty, unreal life; that she was already on the brink of a realization that her 'storming passions' had more to do with her craving for experience to set against her imaginary world of romance gleaned from books, that she was reluctantly acknowledging that what she was going through was nothing more than an embarrassing 'form of hysteria'. But her father was neither wise nor experienced in dealing with a daughter he barely understood. Among the last to find out the gossip that was doing the rounds about his daughter and Jinnah, and afraid of her headstrong ways that he could not handle, and knowing that it was too late to start laying down the law with her, Sir Dinshaw tried, instead, to stop Jinnah, but with disastrous consequences.

Chapter Four

~

There were two ways of dealing with this new problem of the nationalist times. One was the sensible, modern way—Motilal Nehru's way. As one of the richest and most successful lawyers in the country, he did not believe in the old, orthodox Hindu tradition of not dining or accepting even a glass of water in a Muslim friend's home, not even a paan, unless it was offered by a Hindu servant. Although raised as a conservative Kashmiri Brahmin and married to an orthodox woman from his own community, he had embraced the modern lifestyle with a vengeance. His sprawling home in Allahabad, Anand Bhavan, was divided into an Indian and Western side, with the latter run by an Anglo-Indian housekeeper assisted by Christian and Muslim servants. In keeping with the times, he hired an English governess for his two daughters, took them to the 'hill stations' for three or four months in summer where they could enjoy the pleasures and company that the English-style resorts offered, encouraged them to go riding, mingle with his guests, and laughed at those who predicted a dire future for raising his daughters 'in the uncouth manner of the English'. He had always been fond of entertaining on a lavish scale, but while his children were still young, he had turned to politics and since then, Anand Bhavan had also become a hub of national politics. Guests, mostly political leaders, came and went but there was one among them living there more or less permanently—Syud Hossain, the personable young editor of his newly established newspaper, *Independent*.

Syud was one of those 'fiery progressives' that Ruttie and her friends often referred to—Oxford-educated, clean-shaven young Muslim men who spoke English with an accent that did not betray their provincial roots and dressed fashionably in the English style. They were not just embarrassed by the old style of Muslim leadership—the spade beard and caps, and religious bigotry—but militantly nationalist. It was Hossain's patriotic fervour that first caught Motilal's attention; and when he was looking for an editor to launch his newspaper, he readily took on the young journalist so highly recommended by his friend, B.G. Horniman, the pro-Indian Englishman and founding editor of the *Bombay Chronicle*. But Syud, being delicately raised, found it difficult to rough it out in bachelor digs in Allahabad, and after a bout of illness, was invited by his employer to shift into Anand Bhavan.

It's hard to imagine that a shrewd man of the world like Motilal, a father who had the foresight to warn his young son not to get involved with any of the English girls he met while he was studying abroad, had so carelessly overlooked the consequences of throwing together a smart, sensitive, very dapper young man with the radiantly beautiful teenaged 'Nan', his older daughter. One reason why he may have been led into a false sense of complacency was that he had taken the precaution of betrothing her to his friend's son while she was still in her early teens. Despite the jokes Motilal made in private on the orthodoxy of his own community, his daughter's engagement was arranged in the traditional way by the two families, with the boy and girl having never met, or perhaps just seeing each other from a distance. But having got her engaged, Motilal was far too modern a father to rush her into marriage at twelve or thirteen, as other parents in his community were doing. It could also be that he relied too much on the women in his large household to instruct his daughter on the limits of her freedom. Nan had always been Daddy's girl, loved and indulged by him, allowed to have her own way; but he was a busy man, combining a top lawyer's practice with political leadership, and had to travel quite a bit. But since his wife and several elderly relatives besides Nan's governess all lived in the house, it perhaps did not occur to him that she might be tempted to cross the line.

But it wasn't easy to keep vigil on the daughters of Anand Bhavan. It was a chaotic household, divided both socially and physically into Indian and Western halves, with trays of food going up to the rooms at odd hours and the family assembling together only at dinner time. Mrs Nehru's domain did not extend beyond the Indian quarters, and whatever misgivings she may have harboured about her daughters' unorthodox upbringing, she did not intervene in their activities. As a result, her elder daughter and their Muslim house guest advanced from friendship to intimacy without anyone in the large household noticing. Fearing perhaps that they could never win her father's approval for the match if Syud went to him directly with a proposal, they decided to present him with a fait accompli. By the time Motilal discovered what was going on under his own roof—or more likely, was informed by the lovers—they had already got secretly married, but 'in an informal way', as Syud later confessed to his good friend and only sympathizer, Sarojini Naidu.

Motilal prided himself, and justifiably so, on his judgement of character; and in this hour of crisis, he revealed an admirable tact and presence of mind. Within days, Syud was out of Allahabad, and within weeks, out of the country, having been sent abroad as a member of a Congress deputation to Europe. With the minimum of fuss and drama, the lovers were persuaded to give up their attachment. As his daughter later explained: 'In an era that proclaimed Hindu–Muslim unity, and belonging to a family that had close Muslim friends, I must have thought it would be perfectly natural to marry outside my religion. But in matters such as marriage the times were deeply traditional, and I was persuaded that this would be wrong.'

Part of the 'persuasion' included packing the two now-separated lovers off to Gandhi's ashram in Ahmedabad. Getting Syud there was the easy part. Although Gandhi was not yet the supreme leader of the Congress that he was soon to become, Syud's admiration for the Mahatma bordered on reverence; but winning over Nan was another matter altogether. It took the combined efforts of Gandhi— who happened to pay a visit to Anand Bhavan around that time and was naturally told of the domestic disaster that had recently erupted—and her parents, for her to take up temporary residence in the ashram.

It was probably the first time that her parents were agreed on a scheme they thought was beneficial for their daughter, and they were right. No one could have done a more thorough job of teaching their daughter on what was expected of her than Gandhi. For the girl reared by an English governess since she was five, the first lesson was the ashram itself: 'My heart sank when I first saw the place. Everything was so utterly drab and so unpleasing to the eye. I wondered how long I could survive there.' Life in the ashram was not what she was accustomed to: 'Rising at 4 am for prayers, we went to the chores of the day, which consisted of sweeping and cleaning our living quarters, washing our clothes in the river . . . There was work to be done in the dairy, and daily spinning.' The food was unlike any she'd eaten in her life—no tea or coffee, and two meals a day which consisted of: 'Several vegetables grown in the garden were thrown together into a steam cooker without salt, spice or butter and eaten with home-ground chapattis or unpolished rice' whose sole purpose seemed to be 'to kill one's desire for food'. The only concession given to the girl accustomed to every luxury was not to clean the latrines which, being of the primitive kind, was 'a task impossible to describe'. After another round of prayers at 6 p.m., with readings from the Gita and the Quran, it was early to bed because 'there were only hurricane lanterns in the ashram, and it was not easy to read by their flickering wicks'. Her 'bed' was a bedding roll placed next to Gandhi's outside his hut, where he talked to her about Hindu culture and tried to fill the gaps in her formal religious training by making her read the Gita and the Ramayana.

There were other alarming aspects to ashram life. A very pretty young woman in the ashram fell in love with a young ashramite, and when Gandhi heard they slept together, he sent for the couple and cut off the girl's long, silky hair, 'which was her great beauty'. He also went on fast for several days to atone for the 'sin' that had been committed, thrusting the whole ashram into a state of fear and strain. But Nan's spirit was unbroken; instead of making her repent, the incident only appeared 'bizarre and primeval' to her.

Part of Nan's cultural reorientation included the one-to-one chats Gandhi had with her: 'He told me when I was at the ashram that this event had shaken his belief in all Mussalmans!' Nan later wrote to Padmaja. 'How could you,' he said to me, 'regard Syud in *any* other light but that of a brother—what right had you to allow yourself, even for a minute, to look with love at a Mussalman.' Then later; 'Out of nearly twenty crores of Hindus couldn't you find a single one who came up to your ideals—but you must needs pass them all over and throw yourself into the arms of a *Mohammedan*!!!' The tirade from the Mahatma left her unimpressed: 'Poor man! To him it is inconceivable for a Hindu and a Mussalman to marry and live happily.'

The lectures did not quite have the salutary effect that her parents were expecting. In the same letter to Padmaja, Nan writes: 'Gandhiji was telling me one day how he would have behaved had he been me. Of course it didn't carry much weight because being Gandhiji it is absolutely impossible for him ever to enter into *my* thoughts or feelings. However, imagine me squatting on a little mat about six inches square opposite the great Mahatmaji, receiving the following lecture. "'Sarup [Nan's given name before her marriage], had I been in your place I would *never* have allowed myself to have any feelings but those of friendliness towards Syud Hossain. Then, supposing Syud had ever attempted to show admiration for me or had professed love for me, I would have told him gently but very firmly—Syud, what you are saying is not right. You are a Mussalman and I am a Hindu. It is not right that there should be anything between us. You shall be my brother but as a husband I cannot ever look at you."'

Instead of submitting to the Mahatma's superior wisdom, Nan's response was: 'Ahem! Isn't that a nice, ladylike speech and worthy of a Hindu girl—the descendant of a thousand Rishis?!!!' Gandhi's other arguments were equally ineffective: 'Another strong objection was the difference of age. He (Gandhi) said he did not consider it right that any girl should marry a man who was more than four years older than herself! But then if I started telling you the good Mahatmaji's objections I should fill a few hundred pages. And though it would make quite amusing reading it would also be taking a great risk!'

Syud, on the other hand, was much more susceptible: 'Talking of sisters reminds me—Gandhiji also asked Syud how he had dared to make love to a Hindu girl whom he ought to have looked upon like a little sister. And that gentleman's lame reply was: '"Well, I did look upon her as a sister in the beginning." "And does a brother after a little start making love to his sister?" At this question, Syud *looked* a great many things but what he said I do not know because I was seized with a wild desire to laugh and making some excuse fled from the room.'

But what did have more impact on her was the discovery that she had turned overnight from a petted daughter to a social outcast. Motilal had handled the affair with his usual discretion, but even he couldn't prevent the scandal from leaking out of Anand Bhavan. The first fallout of the incident was the breaking off of her engagement to his friend Raja Narendra Nath's son. Nath was later to become a prominent Hindu leader elected to the Punjab assembly, but even in those early days, he was an orthodox man. On hearing of what had transpired between Syud and Nan, he called off his son's engagement and got him married elsewhere. And while he may or may not have been the source of the stories that were then spread about the clandestine affair, everyone as far as Lahore seemed to know the details, however fabricated. Writing about it years later, one of Raja Narendra Nath's young colleagues in the Punjab assembly, K.L. Gauba, claimed that the marriage that his daughter had hastily contracted with Syud was dissolved, and that Gandhi had to step in to resolve the crisis.

Back home at Anand Bhavan after serving her term at the ashram, Nan must have realized more fully the price she would have had to pay for daring to even contemplate marrying a Muslim. There were the usual taunts, including from the editor who took over from Syud at the *Independent*. As she confided to Padmaja: 'It [an article written by Gandhi in *Young India* giving his opinion against Hindu–Muslim marriages] was shown to me by the present editor of the "Independent", a man I detest and despise and avoid as much as I can. He was simply gloating over it and I'm positive he only showed it to me because he wished to see what sort of an effect it was going to produce. Of course I wasn't going to tell *him* what my opinions were on the subject so he might as well have spared himself the trouble of coming all the way here when he might have been better employed. He even had the impertinence to tell me he sympathized with me—as if I wanted *his* sympathy! And then promptly goes to my brother and tells him that he had been in Syud's confidence and *mine*(!) from the very beginning!! I have never come across a more filthy, despicable type of humanity than the above mentioned specimen!'

Even Nan's own cousins did not hide their disapproval: 'It shows how little you know of my cousins, my dear Padmaja, that you should even vaguely suggest their marrying Mohammedans. Good gracious! I wonder what would happen if I hinted at such a thing. I never have been popular with any of my girl cousins and that would really put the finishing touch to the whole thing! It is no concern of theirs what a madcap like myself chooses to do but *they* have far too much self-respect to copy *me*!'

In the end it was Motilal who rescued her from her plight by arranging another, and more suitable, husband. He handled it with as much skill and sense of judgement as he had shown in breaking up her previous attachment. The hunt had started immediately after Nan's engagement had broken off, and being well connected, Motilal soon found a suitable match. Ranjit Pandit was a bright young lawyer practising in Calcutta, and more importantly, had a high regard for the Nehru family because of their political work, and considered it a privilege to marry Jawaharlal's sister. He was not a Kashmiri Brahmin, but a Saraswat Brahmin from Maharashtra. But for obvious reasons, Motilal was no longer as particular about marrying his children within his own community as he had been while arranging his son's marriage almost a decade ago. Nor did it bother him that the Kashmiri community was likely to boycott the marriage—as, in fact, they did.

Having found a suitable boy, Motilal's problem was how to convince Nan that he was the right choice. She was a spirited young woman, and her notions of marriage too modern for her to be able to blindly accept any man her father chose. But at that time, as Nan's contemporary, K.L. Gauba, who also defied his father and married a Muslim, put it: 'You hardly had an opportunity of meeting young ladies and you had to depend on your sisters, or your cousins to give you a report on them. The best that you could have was a distant view of them and then you had to make up your mind whether she was good enough as your life partner, and she had to make up her mind whether you were good enough for her.' Motilal's master stroke was to invite the chosen one to Anand Bhavan and leave the young man alone to do his own courting.

It worked. As Nan later recounted: 'Breakfast was served on the verandah outside my father's rooms and I came out to find a strange young man seated at the table. He had evidently been misinformed about the time and was embarrassed at being early. He introduced himself . . . I thought him attractive—there was a serenity in his face that seemed unusual for one of his age. Presently, the family assembled and he was tongue-tied and ill at ease in the midst of the talkative Nehrus. When the family dispersed I lingered on and the young man, who obviously did not know what to do with himself, seemed glad of my presence. "Do you like Sanskrit poetry?" was one of the first questions.

'I admitted that my knowledge of Sanskrit was the school variety. Inwardly, I vowed I would devote myself to the study of Sanskrit immediately. My answer did not seem to disturb him and he said, "You have a lovely voice. Do you sing?"

'Not only did I not sing, I belonged to a family singularly lacking in musical talent. I could have run away, but good manners and the young man's charm kept me in my seat . . . Before I could think of an answer, he went on, "You are very beautiful, and I have come here only to meet you. I suppose you have guessed that."

'This was very pleasing and now I could relax. We spent most of the day together wandering in the garden where Ranjit recited beautiful Sanskrit verses and told me about his home and family. We went out riding. I loved to ride and was proud of my horsemanship, but I saw that my companion was a crack rider himself.

'Three days passed swiftly, and the evening before he was to leave, Ranjit asked if he could speak with me alone . . . "It is only two days since we met," he said, "but I have thought about you for a long time and feel as if I know you. It has taken some courage for me to come from far off Kathiawar to the home of the Nehrus to meet a daughter of Kashmir. But I have travelled with hope. Could you trust me enough to travel hand in hand with me through life?"'

For Nan who had known him for only three days, but open as never before to his 'handsome and sensitive' charm, the answer was an immediate 'Yes'. It was the happiest of outcomes for all concerned, except perhaps for 'poor Syud', as Sarojini began to describe him in her letters home. Nan's mother, who had secretly sent out both their horoscopes to an astrologer, was happy because their stars matched perfectly, and Motilal could now congratulate himself 'for my ability to judge human beings'. And by the time she married him in May 1921, the past was well behind her and she could truthfully assert, 'I love Ranjit,' even vocally championing her right to lead a normal married life with him instead of the celibacy vows that Gandhi tried to force on the newly-weds.

There were other fathers elsewhere whose progressive outlook was being put severely to the test by their children. In Lahore, it was Punjab nationalist and entrepreneur Lala Harkishan Lal, a minister in the Punjab Legislative Council, whose son—Kanhaiya Lal Gauba, better known in his family by the name his governess had given him as a child, 'Wal' or 'Walter'—wanted to marry the daughter of Aziz Ahmad, the Punjab government's advocate, a high-ranking official somewhat like an advocate general of now. Wal had been introduced to the girl, Husna, in his own home when Lala Harkishan invited the official for a dinner party along with his wife and daughter because he knew they were out of purdah. Like Motilal Nehru, Lalaji prided himself on his modernity and lack of communal prejudice. His Muslim friends stayed with him whenever they came to Lahore, and there were special arrangements to cook their food. In fact, he went a step further—when Wal's mother died in his childhood, Lalaji married for the second time out of the community and even region. Although it was an arranged marriage, Wal's stepmother was from Maharashtra and he had to convert to Sikhism in order to marry her, because, according to the law at that time, Hindus could not marry outside their own caste. Her father was looking for a suitable match for his educated daughter and was quite willing to settle for the Punjabi candidate a marriage broker produced because of the widower's English education and liberal opinions. Wal, therefore, did not anticipate his father's response to his own marriage plans. 'I asked my father whether I could marry Miss Aziz Ahmed. He was very annoyed. He said, "No, because she is a Muslim and you are a Hindu. If you marry her, I will not be able to marry [off] any one of my other children. Therefore I refuse my consent."'

It was a lame argument as far as the young people of Wal's generation were concerned. Like Nan, he had never been taught to distinguish people by their religion. Nor had he been given any formal religious training; the only place of worship he'd ever been to was as a child to the church with his governess. As he himself admitted, 'I was really a Hindu only in name. I knew nothing about it.' He had only heard of the Hindu–Muslim differences but never actually felt them in his own life. 'There were newspaper articles and all that sort of thing. But socially, I think, in the upper strata, there was free mixing, even though they did not agree with each other on political views. On the whole, so far as our world was concerned, there was no distinction really between Sikhs, Muslims and Hindus. Everybody was welcome and everybody was treated equally.' Their social world was too small to allow for such differences. Not only were their parents on visiting terms, but her best friend was a Mrs Chaman Lal, whose husband was Wal's friend and colleague. They could meet as often as they liked in the Chaman Lals' home or at the fashionable Cosmopolitan Club that had recently started in Lahore for the families that were out of purdah.

Unlike Motilal Nehru, Lalaji did not feel the need to resolve the issue at once. Instead, after prohibiting his son from getting married to a Muslim girl, Lalaji then set out for Simla on his official duties, leaving his son at liberty to give notice to the Registrar of Civil Marriages. The trend of love marriages among educated Indians had forced the British to pass a Special Marriages Act in 1872, but it was still a complicated business. Under the Act, Hindus and those belonging to allied faiths like Buddhists, Sikhs and Jains could intermarry provided they were not underage (the minimum age for bridegrooms was eighteen and for brides, fourteen) and the marriage also required the bride's father's consent. But if either party did not belong to one of these faiths, by birth or conversion, they had to disown all the leading religions.

Luckily for Wal, although his own father refused to give his consent, Husna Ahmad's parents were more than willing, provided it was a civil marriage. Wal attributes it to their broad-mindedness, but it was a fact that single Muslim women who were educated and out of purdah found it extremely difficult to find suitable partners from their own community. One reason was that there were simply not enough educated Muslim men to go around, and of them, quite a few returned from their studies abroad with foreign wives. It was the done thing for both Hindu and Muslim students, as Wal explains: 'Quite a number had European wives and families. Young boys who went abroad were expected to bring back English wives.' Quite apart from the prestige of having a European wife, even if it was only their former landlady's daughter, opened doors for career advancement as well as to the Europeans-only clubs.

By the time Lala Harkishan woke up to the implications of the Special Marriages Act and the freedom it offered his son to marry whom he chose, it was too late for him to use more persuasive tactics. Not that he did not try—his fellow minister and friend, Sir Fazl-i-Hussain, was requested to try and persuade the Aziz Ahmads to refuse their consent. After that failed, Lalaji then called up Wal's best friend, Jiwan Lal Kapur, begging him to coax Wal into putting off the wedding by a day or two until his father returned from Simla. Kapur went to Wal and said, 'I believe you are getting married this morning?' Wal replied, 'That is correct.' He said, 'Why not put it off for a day or two as your father is coming down and he will discuss the matter with you and settle it with you.' Wal said, 'I am afraid my bride is waiting for me and I cannot put off the marriage whatever be the consequences.' He then added, 'You better come along as my best friend and be my best man at the marriage.' But, according to Wal, his friend 'did not have the courage to do that. He came and left me at the gate and wished me well.'

Faced with the inevitable, Lalaji did the sensible thing. After four or five months, after the noise had died down and with it his reservations, he quietly accepted his Muslim daughter-in-law. As Wal recounts: 'We got married and sat in my two-seater car and fled to Kashmir for the honeymoon, because both the communities were very agitated at that time. There was great tension among the Hindus and Muslims as the news of this union got around and the Muslims were furious at the loss of a girl, and the Hindus distressed at the loss of a boy.' When they returned from Kashmir, they did not go back to his father's house but took a small house on rent, where they pulled along on Wal's scanty earnings as a start-up lawyer. But it was fun—'two young people trying to live on chicken once a week and pudding perhaps twice a week, and she hung up her saris for curtains and so on'. And when Diwali came around, Lalaji decided it was time to forgive the couple. 'Father called us and gave her costly jewellery and presents. So it was all settled.'

Sir Dinshaw, on the other hand, panicked. Either because he was the first of the three celebrity fathers to be handling a crisis of this sort or because he was a Parsi at a time when the community was particularly incensed about their men and women marrying out of the community, or simply because he lacked the parental authority and tact of a Motilal Nehru and the mental strength of a Harkishan Lal. Considered from any angle, Sir Dinshaw's next step made no sense.

Six months after Ruttie returned from Lucknow, he abruptly switched his strategy to deal with his daughter's unsuitable attachment. Suddenly one day, somewhere towards the end of June 1917, without even consulting Lady Petit, he went to court seeking an injunction against Jinnah. According to one version, the panic was triggered by Sir Dinshaw finding out one morning that Ruttie, far from obeying her father's wishes in the docile way expected of young ladies, was still seeing Jinnah—and that too openly. According to the story, Ruttie was caught red-handed with a letter from Jinnah, and there ensued an unseemly scene in Petit Hall, with the portly Sir Dinshaw chasing his daughter around the dining table, trying to snatch the letter from her, screaming that he knew it was from Jinnah. The panic that the letter aroused in Sir Dinshaw had probably less to do with his daughter indulging in a passionate correspondence with Jinnah—whose aversion to letter writing, incidentally, was well known—but his fear that the two were plotting to get married under the Special Marriages Act. Whether there was a letter involved or not, and if Sir Dinshaw ever managed to lay his hands on it, and if it indeed contained anything incriminating, something certainly appears to have pushed Sir Dinshaw over the edge. The injunction was apparently sought on the grounds that Jinnah was intending to abduct his daughter, still a minor according to the law although she was above marriageable age.

In his plea for the court injunction—the records are now lost but contemporaries like Kanji Dwarkadas insist it happened—Sir Dinshaw claimed that since Jinnah was planning to marry Ruttie against her father's wishes with an eye on her fortune, he should be kept away from either meeting or corresponding with her. For Sir Dinshaw, litigation was something of a bad habit—he would resort to the courts even to solve his minor domestic and business problems. There was no one, from top-ranking British officials to his former housekeeper, that he had not taken to court at one time or other. But to go to court against one of the country's top lawyers who had a well-deserved reputation for getting his clients out of the most slippery situations was a foolishness of such mind-boggling dimensions that Bombay could hardly stop itself from talking about it, even if the newspapers kept a discreet silence on the subject. And when this top lawyer also happened to be the country's leading political figure of the moment, tongues wagged even more fiercely.

For a respectable father to seek judicial intervention to prevent his daughter from meeting an unsuitable man was bad enough—more or less publicly admitting that he had lost all control over her—but to ask for a court injunction against Mohammed Ali Jinnah! Following his triumph in Lucknow, Jinnah was now equally sought after by the British government, the Congress party and the Muslim League—not to speak of the two Home Rule Leagues started almost simultaneously by Tilak and Annie Besant. He did not join Besant's Home Rule League until her arrest in Madras in mid-June 1917, but the six months after he returned to Bombay from Lucknow were his most glorious—and busiest—period so far. From the working lunch he had with the United Provinces lieutenant governor at the end of the two political sessions in Lucknow on 1 January 1917 to the day six months later when he received the court injunction forbidding him to go anywhere near Ruttie Petit, he seems to have had hardly a moment to himself, chairing assorted meetings, including one of the Indian Economic Society, and a Bombay Presidency students' convention, besides almost all meetings of the Home Rule League even before he accepted the presidentship. Twenty days after meeting Lord Meston at his residence in Lucknow to give him the low-down on Indian politics, he was in Agra, urging Lionel Curtis, the government official recruited to arrange a round table conference between the British government and Indian leaders in Agra. Following Jinnah's advice, Curtis summoned some seventy members of the caucus, including Tilak, B.G. Horniman and Jinnah, of course. Almost the entire months of February and March went into attending the winter session in Delhi of the Imperial Legislative Council, where Jinnah made his presence felt almost from the first day by joining in the discussion on the rules of conduct, and taking an active role in supporting a bill for recruiting Indians into military service, a subject that touched the public pulse so deeply that the visitors' gallery was overflowing, with Jinnah being the fourth member to speak. In March, Jinnah was busy again, this time discussing the budget that had just been presented in the council. By mid-April, he was the natural choice of both the Congress and the Muslim League to be a member of a small political delegation that the Congress wanted to send to England that summer to do the preliminary spadework on its demand for self-government. In the beginning of June, he was in Calcutta to attend a meeting of the Muslim League Council where he was feted by the members of the Bengal Muslim League at a garden party they hosted for him. June was equally busy, with the court reopening after its summer vacation, and Jinnah deciding to take over the presidentship of the Bombay Home Rule League, a decision hailed by all its members as a 'standing example . . . of a man who had done his duty and would always do it' and who added 'distinction and weight to it [the Home Rule League] by his presence'.

That 'distinction' and 'weight' he brought to public life was not marred even slightly by the court injunction against him. Instead, it only added to his glamour as a public figure, especially among young people. To most educated people, Jinnah was, in fact, putting into practice what Annie Besant was preaching through her political work—to promote inter-dining between men of different castes and communities and to encourage inter-communal marriages. He had enough on his hands—what with his new political mission of bringing the British to the table to negotiate Home Rule, and to use these political negotiations to rouse public consciousness by holding innumerable public meetings and issuing press statements—to react to the court injunction with anything other than sheer disdain. And while Jinnah went about his busy life as stubbornly as he had always done, making no attempt to either meet or avoid Ruttie, it was Sir Dinshaw who succeeded in turning himself into a laughing stock.

At home, of course, Sir Dinshaw had hell to pay. As soon as she heard of it, Ruttie locked herself up in her room and refused to let anyone near her. Unable to bear her daughter's plight—'lying on her face, refusing to see her father or mother'—Lady Petit also collapsed, working herself into a 'dreadful condition', as Sarojini, who was at Petit Hall then, described in a letter home. Whatever he was hoping to achieve by going to court against Jinnah, this was certainly not the outcome he expected of it, and Sir Dinshaw too came near to collapse. All said and done, he was an extremely fond father and the fear that his daughter's brain or her body would give way under so much grief, broke him down. Lady Petit too, usually calm and elegantly unruffled, was now in no condition to console him; in his desperation, he turned to the only woman who seemed to have any influence with his daughter and wife.

Sarojini Naidu was in Bombay for the third or fourth time that year, the first time on official work as head of a women's delegation to see the visiting secretary of state for India, Edwin Montagu, and subsequently to admit Padmaja in a college and to make arrangements for her stay in Bombay. Padmaja's health was always frail, even before she contracted tuberculosis ten years later, and Sarojini was undergoing her own share of maternal anxieties—about her daughter's health, the friends she was to stay with and whether or not she should be sent to college so far from home. After settling her daughter in college, and seeing her younger son off to his school in Poona, Sarojini shifted to Petit Hall for a few days' break before heading home to Hyderabad. This was on 23 May 1917 when all was still presumably well at Petit Hall—at least on the surface. But a month later, on 29 June 1917 when Sarojini returned to Bombay to find new accommodation for Padmaja who had just been forced to vacate the house where she had been staying because of an influx of the landlady's relatives, things had turned critical at Petit Hall. As Sarojini elaborates in a letter to her younger daughter, Leilamani, trying to explain why she's been delayed for so long without giving away the Petits' secrets to her thirteen-year-old:

My darling Papi, I wonder where you are now, at home with father or still at Sardar Saheb's. I was hoping to get home this week but I greatly fear I shall not be able to—the poor Petits are in very grave trouble and both Lady Petit and Ruttie are in a dreadful condition and Sir Dinshaw is begging of me to stay and help him through the next week as his wife clings to me so much and Ruttie will not let anyone else near her. I have not left the place except to go see Biban [Padmaja's pet name] who is now staying with the Lateefs for a few days. She did not like the settlement and Mrs Joshi who would like to have kept her suddenly had a flood of relations to sweep Biban out of her house. I am hoping to settle her comfortably in two or three days but I wish she would make up her mind to come home instead. I *don't think* she ought to be doing any work though she insists on going to college. I am going to have her thoroughly examined by a good doctor in a couple of days. Meanwhile the sea air will do her good. She is right on the sea at Chowpatty.

Mina [pet name of Sarojini's younger son, Ranadheera] is not very well at Poona. He is not eating at all I hear. So I have written to him to see a doctor at once. I hope poor little Bebe [another pet name for Padmaja] is alright. I am devoured by all kinds of anxieties but just now I am most afraid of Ruttie's brain giving way or her body, I don't know which. Write her a funny, cheering letter and don't mention anything about her trouble. She will be very pleased. It is so pitiful to see her lying on her face, refusing to let her mother or father come near her—poor child. But she clings to me.

The relationship between the two women had changed considerably in the eight months since Ruttie had snubbed the well-known poet and orator for giving her unsolicited advice. But after having given Sarojini 'a light scolding for having made a speech', the two were friends again. Since then, Ruttie had had a chance to get to know the older woman a lot better. It was probably in Lucknow that Ruttie really warmed to Sarojini, especially after seeing Sarojini's genuine admiration and affection for Jinnah. It was here, in the liberating environment of the Congress session and the Muslim League session that preceded it, that Ruttie perhaps began to appreciate the bond of mutual respect and trust between Jinnah and Sarojini, and to lean on Sarojini for emotional support and advice rather than her aunt who was accompanying her. Within two months of their returning home from Lucknow, Ruttie was claiming Sarojini as her own special friend, snatching her away from her parents' circle. As Sarojini said in a letter home, 'She [Ruttie] would not let her mother give me a proper guest suite downstairs but a little suite next to hers, beautifully furnished and with a charming view.' Both Ruttie and her mother vied for her company. 'Lady Petit will not allow me to undertake any unnecessary work and she is going to make me idle and loaf about,' Sarojini wrote home to say on yet another visit to Petit Hall three months later.

Ruttie's confidence in Sarojini and her conviction that no one, either from her own generation or her mother's, could understand the problems of the young better than her, was quite justified. Despite the twenty-one years' age gap between them, Sarojini had been through many of the moral and social dilemmas that now confronted

Ruttie and her friends. She too was the daughter of very progressive parents—her father, Aghorenath Chattopadhyaya, who belonged to an East Bengali Brahmin family of Sanskrit scholars, flung his sacred thread into the Ganges at fourteen as a sign of his rebellion against caste and convention. As a young man, he joined a Robin Hood gang of social reformers who rescued girls of his Kulin caste of Brahmins from traditional marriages to old and dying men and took them to a girls' school run by a social reformer. He married a girl of his own choice, admitting her to a Brahmo Samaj school while he went to study abroad in Edinburgh and Bonn. When he returned to India, he took a job as an educationist with the Nizam of Hyderabad, setting up English-medium schools and colleges for boys and girls.

An early nationalist and part of the Swadeshi movement of 1905, he was twice deported from Hyderabad state for his politics. He believed in educating his daughters as well as his sons, and not only sent Sarojini to school but insisted that she learn English. In fact, so determined was he to teach English to his daughter that when she was nine and still refused to learn it, he locked her up for a whole day in her room. After that, she spoke only in English to her parents, though her mother spoke back to her in Hindi. Sarojini was among the first generation of Indian women taught deliberately to ignore their mother tongue and adopt English instead. She was also of the first generation to call itself 'Indian', raised in a home that was self-consciously cosmopolitan—visitors of all castes and creeds and regions were encouraged to drop in, were entertained and fed rich Bengali food; it was, as she later claimed proudly, 'a home of Indians and not of Hindus or Brahmins'.

And yet, when the inevitable happened, Aghorenath was as dumbstruck as any conventional father. At fourteen, being perhaps the only unmarried Indian girl out of purdah in Hyderabad—that is, if you didn't count those who came from families that had converted to Christianity—Sarojini Naidu fell in love with a young man she probably met in her own home. Aghorenath, having campaigned almost single-handedly for the Special Marriages Act to be introduced in Hyderabad, fell into more difficulties than most parents of his time in arguing her out of it. There was really very little to argue against— Dr Govindarajulu Naidu was an eligible young man, a doctor with a medical degree from Edinburgh employed in the Nizam's service, highly regarded both by the Nizam and his aristocrats, and the son of a military doctor, upright and honest. The only thing that Aghorenath could possibly hold against him was that he was a non-Brahmin 'Madrasi'; but considering his well-known views and politics, Aghorenath could hardly voice his prejudice aloud, even to his own daughter. Instead of trying to rationalize his need to prevent the marriage, Aghorenath simply packed his daughter away to study in Sholapur, possibly hoping she would soon forget the attachment and put him out of his dilemma. Instead, at fifteen, she had a nervous breakdown. When she recovered, he was still torn between his principles and prejudices, and sent her away again, this time on a scholarship to England, on what she at least considered as a permanent exile from home. It was only when her health broke down three years later that Sarojini was allowed to return home and marry the man who was still waiting for her.

Once he was able to resolve his inner crisis, Aghorenath Chattopadhyaya turned once again into the model 'Indian' father— he organized the wedding in Madras, where it was hailed by the newspapers as 'marking an epoch in the history of the reform movement'. Reclaiming his position among the leading social reformers in the south, he invited the wife of Brahmo Samaj leader Raja Ram Mohan Roy to be the bridesmaid, and social reformer Veerasalingam Pantulu to preside over a unique ceremony that blended Western with traditional elements. It opened with a prayer and Hindu rituals, after which Veerasalingam officiated as a secular priest, delivering a sermon in English on the responsibilities of a married couple, and the father gave away the bride and 'united the pair in holy wedlock in due form, the marriage being solemnized in the presence of Mr F.D. Bird, the Registrar of Marriages of Madras Town. Rao Bahadur Pandit Veerasalingam Pantulu Garu then pronounced the benediction,' as Padmini Sengupta writes in *Sarojini Naidu: A Biography*.

Unlike a similar marriage conducted eighteen years earlier, when Pandita Ramabai Saraswati, a Konkani Chitpavan Brahmin, married a Bengali Kayasth, Sarojini's marriage to Dr Naidu did not create an uproar among either the Telugu Balija clan to which Dr Naidu belonged or among the Bengali sub-caste of Kulin Brahmins to which Sarojini's family belonged. Instead, the guests invited to attend the wedding in the Brahmo Mandir in Madras raised 'toasts and replies in perfect harmony without any distinction of caste', according to Sengupta, and dispersed after 'refreshments were served and partaken with great cheers', the newly-weds receiving 'the congratulations of all friends present and drove off to Capper House Hotel, where Dr Govindarajulu Naidu had been staying'. Everyone, including the newspapers, considered it a watershed mark in social reform, setting the trend for many more inter-caste and inter-communal marriages in the near future.

Except here were Ruttie and Jinnah nearly two decades later up against the same prejudices, only more entrenched than ever. But she may have saved herself some of the agony she underwent if she had only known the depths of Jinnah's determination to succeed in whatever he undertook. Certainly, Sir Dinshaw would have felt even sorrier for himself than he was feeling right then if he had known how Jinnah really reacted to the court order against him. Under his mask of indifference, Jinnah was hardly likely to shrug off the kind of insults Sir Dinshaw was heaping upon him—first rejecting his marriage proposal so rudely and then compounding that insult by slapping a court order on him, as if he was a common criminal or fortune hunter. If only Sir Dinshaw had had a glimmer of understanding of the man he was setting himself up against!

Chapter Five

~

Jinnah had arrived in Bombay in 1896 with a barrister's degree from Lincoln's Inn and an invincible faith in his future as a great leader. He was then not yet twenty years old. And neither his father's bankruptcy nor the fact that he had no patron or connections in a city overpopulated with struggling lawyers could shake his conviction that he was meant for greatness. The idea was seeded in his head by his mother but took root only after she died. She was a devout, simple woman from a village in Kathiawar, devoted to her husband and six children, but especially to Jinnah, her firstborn. While Jinnah was away in England she never tired of telling her daughters of what a fakir had once predicted about her eldest son: pointing to a birthmark on the sole of his infant foot, the holy man declared that Jinnah would one day be 'a big man'. When Jinnah returned from England, transformed into a sahib with a new name and wardrobe, his mother was already dead. But his sisters were curious to see the mark of his future destiny; they begged him to pull off his socks—he had evidently become too much of an Englishman to be caught barefoot even within his own home. And while Jinnah chided his sisters for their superstition, he did not refuse to oblige them by showing off the birthmark. Whether he took this prophecy seriously to heart or not, he relentlessly groomed himself for it, as if determined to meet his destiny more than halfway. His was a temperament far too active and forceful to leave anything to chance, even his destiny.

Only his father had understood that temperament, but even he could seldom deflect his son from going his own way. Jinnah's father, Jinnahbhai Poonja, a Khoja Muslim of the Ismaili sect, was no weak-willed man himself: at sixteen or seventeen, he escaped a stifling—but not completely poverty-stricken—life in a village in Kathiawar to try his luck as a trader; and by the time he was twenty, he had set up his own trading company in Karachi, pushing ahead of other, more established, traders in the growing port city. A tall, lean, austere man, single-minded in his desire to see his business grow and a strict disciplinarian, Jinnahbhai was a figure of authority both at home and work. But he was a different man with his eldest son whom he treated with the regard and respect accorded to an equal. He handled him with a rare tact, careful never to hurt the child's dignity or talk down to him, invariably appealing to his reason and not his emotions. It was almost as if Jinnahbhai was acutely aware from the start of who would be the natural victor in any direct clash of wills with his son. There was the time, for example, when Jinnah decided to drop out of school and join his father's business. Because, as he informed his father calmly, 'I would do better in your office than at school.' What brought this on was his father's decision to admit him that year to a primary school near their home. So far, his education had consisted of a tutor coming home for an hour to teach him Gujarati and arithmetic, both of which subjects he loathed. The rest of his day was spent in the playground, where his temperament and physique made him a natural leader among the neighbourhood boys, reinforcing his belief that he was born to be a ruler. He went ungrudgingly enough to his new school, and perhaps had even established his primacy over his classmates, when the results of his first school examination were declared. It was a rude shock: boys who had already submitted to his suzerainty, some of them much younger, had outclassed him, scoring higher marks. He did not see the point of submitting to this humiliation, slaving at books he had no interest in; or perhaps he persuaded himself that his destiny was calling him to take another direction. At any rate, he was resolved that he would not waste his time any more by going to school. Jinnahbhai, whose dearest wish was to see his firstborn pass at least his matriculation exam, was sorely disappointed. But instead of using threats or cajoling him, he wisely decided to take another approach with his nine-year-old boy. He tried to reason him out of his decision by pointing out that the working hours would be unbearably long: 'You will have to go with me to office early in the morning at eight, return for lunch from two to four, and then again to office from

four to nine in the night . . . that will give you no time at all for play.'
But Jinnah was undaunted, and for the first but not last time, the
father yielded to the son.

For two months, Jinnah stuck grimly to the bargain he had
made with his father. He uncomplainingly kept the long hours his
new life demanded; did the odd jobs that fell to his lot in the office.
The company that his father had spent more than a decade patiently
building up traded in gum Arabic and isinglass—a fishbone extract
and a key ingredient then in the manufacture of industrial glue. But
Jinnahbhai's entrepreneurial energy spilled out into other directions
as well: he ran an informal banking service for traders from the
hinterland visiting Karachi for their transactions, and possibly also
acted as a subcontractor for the British trading firms in Karachi,
having taught himself to read and write English specifically for this
purpose. For Jinnahbhai, his office was his life and passion; for his
son, it seemed rather pointless drudgery. Making money only in order
to make more money seemed a meaningless pursuit to the passionate
young boy dreaming of his heroic future. According to his sister and
biographer, Fatima Jinnah, it was once again his aversion to being led
rather than leading that got in the way of his self-imposed choice: 'He
soon found he could not do anything in office. Everything depended
on reading and writing, monies received and paid had to be entered
into account-books; and he did not know either to read or write or to
keep accounts. All that he could do in the office was to do little odds
and ends of jobs, which was not to his liking. And then decisions for
buying, selling and regarding other important matters were done by
his father. Nobody bothered to consult him or to obtain his approval.
The most irksome disadvantage was that he was absolutely cut away
from the games, which had such fascination for him.' But during
the two months that he worked for his father, he applied himself
so diligently to the tasks assigned to him that he almost fooled his
father into believing that this may, in fact, be the best course for him.
Jinnahbhai, therefore, was taken completely by surprise when his son
announced suddenly one day that he did not like office work and
would like to go back to school. His father was far too careful to
show his evident relief, but he could not restrain himself from making
a lesson of it for his stubborn son: 'You see, my boy, there are only
two ways of learning in life. One is to trust the wisdom of your

elders and their superior knowledge; to accept their advice; and to do exactly as they suggest.' But his boy was not impressed; he wanted to know what the other way was. 'The other way is to go your own way, and to learn by making mistakes; to learn by hard knocks and kicks in life.' It was advice exactly suited to young Jinnah's temperament, and he listened attentively, apparently never forgetting that lesson in his life.

So had he learnt from his mistakes, had the knocks been hard enough to send young Jinnah, impatient to make his mark, back into the arms of conventionality? Could he school his passionate, imperious nature into becoming one of the herd? It would seem so, at least for a while. 'He was a completely transformed child, no more inattentive, indifferent and lagging behind his classmates. He wanted to make up for the lost time, as boys of his age and even younger than him had gone ahead of him. He took to his lessons with a vengeance, studying into the late hours of the night at home, determined to forge ahead,' writes Fatima in her memoir, *Jinnah, My Brother.* A cousin who lived in the same house with Jinnah while he was in Karachi recounts: 'He was a good boy; a clever boy. We lived, eight of us, in two rooms on the first floor of the house on Newnham Road. At night, when the children were sleeping, he would stand a sheet of cardboard against the oil lamp, to shield the eyes of the children from the light. Then he would read, and read. One night I went to him and said, "You will make yourself ill from so much study," and he answered, "But, you know I cannot achieve anything in life unless I work hard." Watching his son attack his studies with that determination, Jinnahbhai must have allowed his hopes to rise. Once again, a vision began to swim before his eyes, a vision of his son clearing the matriculation examination—the holy grail of aspiring parents of this time—before joining him in the family firm and taking it to new heights, a business empire spreading to other cities, perhaps even other countries. But the father's dreams were dashed in a chance meeting with Jinnah's class teacher. Running into him on the road, Jinnahbhai asked the one question foremost in his mind: how was his son faring at school? 'He is coming up,' the teacher said, giving Jinnah the equivalent of an average rating, adding: 'But I must tell you the boy is horrible in Arithmetic.' 'This completely disappointed my father, who already knew that his son was not a child prodigy, as the boy's mother fondly believed,' writes Fatima Jinnah. 'He had already failed to impress his tutors as a pupil of great promise; they thought with hard work he would manage to pass his examinations, possibly to be devoured in the anonymous ranks of office clerks. But my father wanted him to be good at mathematics, as accounts were the backbone of business, and he wanted the firm of Jinnah Poonja &Co., to keep on forging ahead as a going concern, when his son took over the business from him.'

Jinnahbhai, however, was not ready to give up all hopes of his son doing him proud in the future. Like all self-made men, he was convinced that anything was possible with hard work and willpower. And since his son lacked neither diligence nor resolution, he convinced himself that the problem was not Jinnah but his friends in the locality—a crowded district of bazaars and residences of traders, including the few Khoja Muslims who migrated from Gujarat and Kathiawar. 'He thought it better to put him in a school far from their house,' according to Fatima, 'as his classmates in the primary school at Kharadar had a disturbing influence on his attendance at school, tempting him always to abandon books for marbles, tops, gullidanda and cricket.' The new school, Sind Madrassatul Islam, was the ideal place as far as Jinnahbhai was concerned, offering not only the best English education in an Islamic environment, grooming its students in classic English literature as well as Persian, but also located a safe mile away from their home and from Jinnah's playmates. Jinnah, however, was as unimpressed by his new school as he had been with his local primary school, preferring to socialize as before with his old playmates.

A brief experiment—cut short at Jinnah's mother's insistence—of sending him away to Bombay with his aunt to join a school there, also failed to turn him into the star pupil that Jinnahbhai wanted his son to be. His attempts to separate his son from his unsuitable friends was, however, not as unsuccessful as it then appeared to be. It certainly made a deeper imprint on the young boy's mind than Jinnahbhai suspected. A few years later, when Jinnah had the leisure and maturity to reflect on his future and decided on his own to embark on the self-education that he had so stubbornly denied himself as a boy, his father's methods were to resonate with him unexpectedly. At sixteen or seventeen, while he was studying Cicero's classic collection of letters in London as a means of educating himself into the man he wanted to become, Jinnah found the following sentences significant enough to underline heavily with a lead pencil: 'Whenever you design to break off any friendship or displeasing acquaintance, you should loosen the knot little and little, and not try to cut it asunder all at once.'

Jinnahbhai's methods of improving his son's prospects were not limited to discouraging his association with the wrong sort of boys. He also tried to actively encourage him to cultivate friends who might be useful to him. One of these certainly proved to be the turning point in Jinnah's so far unremarkable life. Strictly speaking, Frederick Leigh Croft, an Englishman and bachelor in his thirties, was more his father's friend or acquaintance than Jinnah's. As the general manager of a major English trading company in Karachi, he had probably known and worked with Jinnahbhai for several years. And Jinnahbhai, concerned about his son's future and anxious perhaps for the boy to improve his English conversational skills— skills this aspiring Khoja trader valued so highly that he not only taught himself to read and write English, but gave all his children lessons at home in his version of broken English—introduced him to Leigh Croft who, uncharacteristically, took to the boy at once. At home in England, Leigh Croft was known to be 'uncomfortable in the presence of children, whom he did not like', according to Jinnah's biographer, Hector Bolitho. But at fourteen or fifteen, Jinnah was hardly a child; he was a tall, slim, attractive boy with the face of an aristocrat and the confidence of a grown man and a charm that was difficult to resist, even for a recluse like Leigh Croft. As Jinnahbhai hoped he would, the general manager of Graham's Trading Company immediately took Jinnah under his wing and it was at his suggestion that Jinnahbhai decided to send his son to London. 'The General Manager of Grahams Trading Co . . . who had now become a great friend of my father, offered to get young Mohammed Ali admitted to his Head office in London as an apprentice for three years, where he would learn practical business administration, which would best qualify him to join his father's business on [his] return from London,' writes Fatima. Jinnahbhai was tempted. The astute trader in him was convinced that the apprenticeship would enable their company to expand and prosper as never before, but he still pondered long and hard—it was an expensive business to send his son abroad and he was not a man to risk throwing his money away, being almost allergic to what he considered unnecessary spending.

In this, Leigh Croft proved a useful ally for Jinnah, using his influence with Jinnahbhai to persuade him that the boy would return from London as 'a great asset to his father, helping him to further expand his business'. He also helped Jinnahbhai work out the total expenses involved. 'My father discreetly asked him what would be the cheapest way of transportation from Karachi to London, and how much he would have to spend each month for the upkeep of his son in England. The figures were worked out in detail and with great care; although the total amount involved for three years was quite substantial, my father decided he could afford to deposit the sum with Grahams in London, in order to ensure continuity to his son's training,' Fatima writes. Jinnahbhai's readiness to part with such a substantial sum of cash is even more remarkable considering his real opinion of his son's abilities. Unlike his wife, he did not share in the rosy vision of their son's future. And when one day, Jinnah came running to tell him what a street-side astrologer had predicted for him—that he would be the uncrowned king of India—he remained silently sceptical, refusing to subscribe to his wife's blind faith in the destiny of their son and her oft-repeated 'My Mohammed Ali is going to be a big man.' Her consolation, in the face of her husband's despair over their son's poor record in school, was ever: 'You wait. My Mohammed Ali will do well, and many people will be jealous of him.'

And yet, it was Jinnah's mother, Mithibai, who nearly came in the way of her son embracing his destiny. Her devotion to her firstborn would not allow him to be separated from her for so long. Once before, when Jinnah was ten and Jinnahbhai had sent him away to Bombay with his sister in the hope that the change would help turn him into a serious scholar, it was the otherwise docile and selfless Mithibai who insisted on bringing her son back to Karachi because she missed him unbearably. But this time, the men had their way, with Jinnahbhai coming to his son's aid: 'My mother was adamant,' Fatima writes. 'How can she allow her darling Mohammed Ali to be away from her for three years? Father explained to her that it was in the best interest of the boy's own future, as also of their family business. And after all, three years would soon be over.' It took days of persuasion to get Mithibai to agree, and when she finally did, it was with a caveat: her Mohammed Ali must be married before he left for England. 'England was a dangerous country to send an unmarried young man to, particularly a young man as handsome as her Mohammed Ali. She was afraid he might get married to an English girl, and that would be a tragedy . . .' The argument was hardly unusual for the times, but what was surprising was that Jinnah actually acceded to his parents' plans.

It was true, as Fatima writes: 'In those days it was the parents that arranged marriages of their children, the boy and girl had no option but to believe in the superior wisdom of their parents.' But Jinnah was no ordinary boy; from the age of six he had been allowed to use his own judgement when it came to decisions that affected his life, and now that he was fifteen, neither he nor his parents considered him to be a child. 'He had a consuming hunger for experience gained through his own efforts and he, therefore, refused to be ordered about by others as to what to do and what not to do, as to what was good for him and what was not,' Fatima points out, relying on her own experience of living with him for twenty-eight years. 'It is probably the only important decision in his life that he allowed to be made by others.' The only explanation she can find for this 'paradox' about her brother is: 'He loved his mother so much, he could not refuse her. He trusted his father's worldly wisdom so much, he was sure that his father could hardly make a mistake.'

But of the two, it was his mother who had the stronger hold on Jinnah, able to push her son, despite a mind and will of his own, to accept almost anything, including her choice of a bride for him. The bride was a young girl distantly related to her family, a village girl of fourteen whom neither she nor Jinnah had ever set eyes upon. Yet, such was Mithibai's sway over her son's heart that his 'objection against marrying a girl he had never seen or spoken to vanished like thin mist in the sunshine of the assurances of his mother, who made her son believe that a mother's blessings in such matters prove propitious and such marriages turn out to be happy and auspicious.' Whether he believed her or not, Jinnah's devotion to his simple, illiterate mother was deep enough for him to sacrifice his stubborn sense of independence, going silently along with whatever she wished to do on his behalf. Apart from her choice of a bride, there were other aspects of the wedding that young Jinnah no doubt found painful—his father playing along to his kinsmen's impression of him as having become a 'multimillionaire' in Karachi, for instance, and squandering his carefully saved money on pleasing a bunch of villagers who Jinnah had never met in his life, not to speak of the time he was willing to waste in the month-long celebrations and idle feasting at their ancestral village, Paneli.

His patience, however, appears to have become strained towards the end of the weeks-long celebrations. The wedding was now over, with its endless processions of gift-bearers led by hired drum-beaters, the firecrackers burst, and community dinners and lunches consumed, and he'd been marched to the home of his father-in-law, decked up in flowers from head to foot, where the village moulvi performed the nikah ceremony marrying him to the fourteen-year-old Emi Bai, whose face he had not yet seen. And now that they had paid village tradition its due, they were impatient to return home to Karachi—his father primarily because of his business, but Jinnah and his mother too were anxious to return with him. But the bride's family held them back, declaring that according to tradition, their newly-wed daughter must remain in her natal home for at least a month, if not three months, before they could agree to her being taken by her bridegroom to Karachi. For days, the two families argued on what was possible and not possible according to tradition, unable to resolve the issue, while the bridegroom stood by, a silent spectator. And then, when he saw that the negotiations between the two families had finally broken down and they had reached an impasse, Jinnah abruptly became himself again, quietly but firmly taking charge of the situation. 'Without informing my father or mother,' Fatima writes, 'Mohammed Ali went to see his father-in-law and mother-in-law. They welcomed their newly married son-in-law with warmth and ceremony . . . but after the formalities were over, Mohammed Ali spoke in a firm tone. He said that his father and mother could no longer stay in Paneli and they must return to Karachi, and that he would go with them. He would like to take his bride with him . . . but if they decided otherwise, in deference to village custom and tradition, they could have their own way. He had come to tell them that in that case they could keep their daughter with them, and send her to Karachi whenever they wished . . . he would be soon leaving Karachi for Europe, and he would be gone for three years. Perhaps they would like to send her to Karachi in his absence, and she would have to wait for three years until his return from England.' That clinched it, of course, with his in-laws calling on his parents the very next day, 'solicitously asking when they would like to take Emi Bai with them to Karachi, so that they could make the necessary arrangements. Cordiality was restored between the two families, dispute and acrimony were forgotten.'

Once home, Jinnah showed the same firmness in dealing with his own parents, insisting that Emi Bai not cover her face as was the custom when she came in the presence of her father-in-law. 'Mohammed Ali had his own views on such matters. His wife was like a daughter of his parents, a full member of the family, and it was unnecessary to cover one's face, just because one's great-grandmother had been doing it.' Once again, Jinnahbhai followed his son's lead and agreed that Emi Bai discard 'the age-old custom, which had been running in the family for generations'.

Was it this ease with which he was able to impose his will on his family even as a boy of fifteen that gave him his extraordinary self-confidence? Certainly, it was the most remarkable quality about him even before he reached England. The combination of his youthful appearance and 'the self-confidence of a person much beyond his years' was striking enough to impress at least one stranger on the ship to England. The unnamed Englishman, on his way home from India for his annual holiday, 'took to him like his own son'. His fellow voyager took it upon himself to coach the young Jinnah on the life ahead of him in England. 'Everyday he would spend much of his time talking to my brother, giving him such information about London as he thought might be useful to him,' writes Fatima, and 'before disembarking at Marseilles, gave my brother his London address and asked him to see him occasionally. During the next four years, whenever this Englishman came back to his native land from India, he would call my brother to his house and ask him to have a meal with his family.' At least one piece of advice his shipmate gave him, Jinnah was never to forget. Congratulating Jinnah on not losing his wallet in Port Said to the pickpockets who operated there, the Englishman made a remark that must have reminded Jinnah strongly of his own father: 'That's it, my boy. It is best to be very careful with everything in life.'

It was advice he was to put to use almost the moment he disembarked in Southampton. He needed a hotel room for the night before catching the train to London the next morning, and asked the cab driver to recommend a suitable place—inexpensive but comfortable. It was not in his nature to betray the nervousness he felt, but when he walked up to the reception desk of the hotel, demanding a modest room, he must have looked awkward enough for the receptionist to ask: 'Young man, will you be able to afford the charges?' But even at sixteen and just off the boat, Jinnah refused to be intimidated by the hotel staff's manner. 'Oh, yes, oh, yes,' he replied firmly. 'But I hope they will be reasonable.' All the fear and loneliness he had to deal with on his first night in England, he kept hidden until he was safely locked within his hotel room. Almost half a century later, when he was able to tell the story, it was with his usual dry humour, taking great care to strip his narration of all the emotions he must have undergone, and it was one of the few funny stories he ever told of himself, although he did pass it off as happening to somebody else: 'He was out late and when he returned and slipped into bed and felt the warm (hot water) bottle near his feet, he thought it was an animal and threw it out. As he peered at it in the dark, he could see water oozing out of it, which he was quite convinced, was blood. "I have killed it,"' he screamed, but there was no one to hear him.

It could not have been easy—so far from home, reaching London alone in the depths of winter and discovering that the only two persons his father had asked him to get in touch with were out of town. But it had ever been a point of honour with Jinnah, even at that youthful age, not to show any outward sign of distress. Besides, there were things that had to be done—find a hotel room for himself and report at the office of Grahams Shipping and Trading Company the next morning, where he was given a small table and chair and asked to join the other office hands. He trudged daily through the damp, chilly London streets to his office, struggling with the cold strangeness of it all. By the time he got through the first few months, the silent stoicism he began to cultivate was on its way to becoming a lifelong habit. And except perhaps for his lasting horror of the London fog, which always reminded him of what he had undergone in those first few months, he was able to shrug off the pain and any trauma he might have felt, as if it were no more than the homesickness of the average boarding school boy. And when, over half a century later, a biographer wrote to ask him if he'd been happy in those early years as a student in Britain, Jinnah was able to condense the whole awful experience in one brisk, no-nonsense sentence which he dictated to his secretary: 'During [the] first few months he found (a) strange country and surroundings, not knowing a soul, and [the] fogs and winter of London upset him a great deal, but he soon settled down and was quite happy.'

It was not really so far from the truth. Jinnah certainly appears to have had an easier time adjusting to the new world than his Indian counterparts, perhaps because he refused to give in to the usual insecurities that made Indian students so miserable when they first set foot in England. He was certainly better prepared for his new life than most of them. His father, for all his parsimony, had deposited sufficient funds in the London office of Grahams Trading Company to ensure that his son could live in modest comfort for at least two years, which Jinnah then prudently managed to stretch to last for an additional year. More than providing him the money, Jinnahbhai equipped his son for this life with his rigorous training in living as frugally as possible, keeping account of every penny he spent. The habit of saving was so strongly ingrained in Jinnah that he had even saved enough money out of his travelling expenses to take care of his initial expenses in London until the first transfer of cash came through. He decided to walk the long distance to work in order to save on cab fare, and searched for paying guest accommodation as soon as he could, because living in a hotel room seemed like an unnecessary expense. His other expenses were minimal: even if his pride had allowed him to go in at once for a sartorial makeover as the other Gujarati young man, Mohandas Karamchand Gandhi, had done when he came to study in London a few years earlier, Jinnah was probably not in as urgent need of it as Gandhi. In fact, despite the myth of him sailing for England in a 'funny long yellow coat', his mentor in Karachi, Leigh Croft, was too much of a dandy—'with a freshly picked carnation in his buttonhole each morning', as Bolitho put it—to send Jinnah away ill-dressed for the occasion.

Nor was Jinnah the type of young man who yearned to impress English girls with his smartness. In fact, it was his stubborn refusal to impress them that was probably the secret of his charm, using the cold hauteur that he could turn on and off at will to squash all unwanted attention from girls. His landlady's daughter, an attractive girl his own age, was particularly persistent, pursuing him at parties she organized in the house, with games that required kissing as a penalty. After standing out of these kissing games for as long as he could, Jinnah was caught unawares under a sprig of mistletoe at a Christmas party, embraced against his will and asked for a kiss. Fed up of trying to keep her at a respectful distance, Jinnah gave her the cold snub that was to become his most effective weapon in later years: 'I reprimanded her and said that this was not done nor was it permissible in our society,' he recounted many years later to Fatima. And although he was rarely discourteous to women, he refused to feel any remorse: 'I am glad I behaved that way with her,' he said. 'For, after that day I was saved the daily embarrassment of her coquettishness.'

Once he settled down, he found that there was little about his new life that he wanted to change. He began to even like it, as he confessed later to Fatima. Far from missing the spicy food that his mother cooked—Gondal, his parents' native state in Gujarat, was famous for its chillies—Jinnah took at once to the bland English food, counting roast beef and fruit tart as the best things about his student days in London. Even the bitter cold of London he began to regard as yet another challenge, forcing himself to take cold baths; sometimes he would fill the tub overnight, just for the pleasure of breaking its frozen surface the next morning, and jump into the icy water. There were other habits of the indulged son that he was glad to drop. As a boy in Karachi, for instance, he was accustomed to throwing his things about the room, knowing that everything would be neatly arranged for him by the time he returned home in the evening. Now with no one to tidy up after him, Jinnah learnt to be orderly, putting things back neatly in their place for the first time in his life.

Even the solitude that he had found unbearably oppressive in the early days, he now began to savour. He found a freedom in it that he had not experienced before. And knowing 'not a soul in London except for some employees at Grahams' proved to be a blessing, forcing him to turn to newspapers for consolation. He soon adopted 'the typically English habit of carefully reading his morning paper as he awoke and to complete reading it before finishing his breakfast'. It was through the newspapers that he discovered a stimulating new world of politics. It was the era of the Liberals in English politics and to make it even more exciting, an Indian was contesting for Parliament for the first time. He may not have reached London in time to take part in Dadabhai Naoroji's election campaign as Fatima claimed in her biography, but his later biographers agree that Jinnah was likely to have participated in the public meeting to celebrate Naoroji's victory in London, in which 'fully two thousands of friends and admirers of India's own number were present'. The public meeting was instrumental in generating Jinnah's first lively interest in the question of freedom for his country: 'Jubilation among Indian students in London was tremendous,' as Jinnah later told his sister. 'As I sat in the galleries, listening to the maiden speech of the Old Man in the Commons, I felt a new thrill within me.'

The public meeting was instrumental in another way: it put Jinnah in touch with the Indian students of law in London who attended the meeting in large numbers. It was after this meeting that Jinnah began to rethink his career prospects: 'Wherever he went, he heard conversation revolve round the utterances of these political leaders, whom the people looked upon as men of destiny . . . And here he was buried under the drudgery of office routine at Grahams from morning to evening, and the only prize that might in the end crown his patience, industriousness and devotion would be to join his father's business and make it more prosperous and flourishing than when he took over. This appeared to him to be such a sordid and narrow prospect.' And 'as he began to waver between two alternatives—to continue to work as an apprentice with Grahams, or to qualify himself for the entrance examination in order to obtain admission to one of the Inns in London and become a barrister', he learnt that this would be the last year when he could get admission without being a matriculate, by passing an entrance examination called the 'Little Go'. The rules were going to change the following year, Jinnah told Fatima, 'and it would take me two additional years to be called to the Bar'. Away from the weight of his parents' expectations, the choice was not hard to make. Jinnah decided to give up his apprenticeship and to devote himself to getting through the 'Little Go' exam, taking care to inform his father only after he had quit Grahams and joined Lincoln's Inn as a student of law.

Was it his fear of parental pressure or of failing the entrance exam that made Jinnah keep his plans a secret from the father he had once adored? Neither fear was unfounded. Passing the 'Little Go' exam was by no means an easy task—the written exam alone consisted of three papers: English language, English history and Latin, after which he would be subjected to a thorough grilling by a board of Masters of the Inn. For someone who was a dropout from a high school in Karachi, never particularly bright academically or very fond of reading, and never having passed a public examination in his life before, Jinnah's confidence seemed foolhardy. Yet, with less than three months to prepare for the exam, Jinnah had no doubts about giving up his apprenticeship. In fact, he was so sure that he could clear the exam by sheer hard work that he even began making advance inquiries on which of the four Inns of London he should join once he passed the 'Little Go'. Even the fact that one of the three papers that he had to pass was Latin, a language he had never studied before and which would take at least two years of intensive study to familiarize himself with, did not daunt him. He managed to plough through half his Latin textbook, making meticulous notes and writing down the meaning of words—and fastidiously correcting one or two typos in the text—before someone told him that he could seek an exemption from Latin on the grounds that, as a native of India, he had never studied the subject before. He was granted the exemption, but there were whole passages of the English translation of the Latin text which evidently etched itself on his mind—passages like 'It is fitting that all men who are eager to excel [over] the rest of living creatures should strive with the utmost energy not to pass through life in obscurity, like cattle, whom nature has made stooping and slaves to the belly.' The words, so laboriously culled from a foreign tongue, appear to have fired Jinnah up like nothing else in his life before. 'A complete transformation seems to have come over him, and he sat glued to his books,' writes Fatima.

The unswerving faith he had in himself—a trait that his peers and colleagues found either the most endearing or exasperating aspect of him—apparently paid off. The selection committee at Lincoln's Inn was certainly favourably impressed by this earnest young man's unusual self-confidence when he appeared before them after clearing the written examination. But beyond his deep conviction that he could not ever fail at anything so long as he worked hard enough, there was a deeper faith that he had inherited from his mother and could not quite shake off, no matter how often or loudly he declared himself to be a rational, modern man with no belief in superstitions. It was a part of him he kept well hidden, admitting it only years later to Fatima. Jinnah confessed to his sister that before clearing the 'Little Go' examination, he visited the various Inns in London and met students studying there in order to make up his mind which Inn he would join when he passed the exam. 'My inquiries and discussions made me decide for another Inn than Lincoln's,' Jinnah told Fatima. 'But then I saw the name of our great Prophet engraved on the main entrance of Lincoln's Inn among the greatest law-givers of the world.' So he did something that his mother would have done—and did, in fact, when he was an infant. He took a *mannat*, or a silent vow, to join Lincoln's Inn if he passed the 'Little Go' exam. And when he did clear the written papers, he took it as a sign that he must join Lincoln's Inn, even though it had not been his first choice of the four Inns of London where students were admitted to prepare for their Bar examination.

It was only after joining Lincoln's Inn, paying a princely sum of 138 pounds and 14 shillings for his admission, that Jinnah informed his father of his decision. There was not much Jinnahbhai could do now to stop him—Jinnah had already withdrawn the 200 pounds that his father had sent through Grahams for his expenses and deposited it in a newly opened savings account in his own name—but he was frantic enough to send his son a 'strongly worded' letter, ordering him to stop wasting his money and time in 'this unprofitable pursuit' and to return home immediately. Unwilling perhaps to offend his father by openly disobeying him, Jinnah tactfully resorted to pleading, using the one argument he knew would work with his father: he would not ask his father to send any more money for him and would somehow manage to stretch his two years' allowance to last for four years. Having watched his son do flip-flops throughout his academic career, Jinnahbhai had no reason to feel reassured, but he knew his son too well to force a confrontation of wills. 'He reconciled himself to the situation and hoped and prayed for the best,' according to Fatima.

As it turned out, Jinnahbhai would have been better off worrying about the state of his own finances instead of his son's. Within a year of his son's departure, Jinnahbhai Poonja's trading company went bankrupt, taking down along with it all his other business ventures.

Clearly, he was in no position to bankroll his son's legal studies even if he had wanted to. But the training he had provided his son in living as frugally as possible now came in most handy. So thoroughly had he indoctrinated his son in his measures of economy that Jinnah not only effortlessly stretched his modest funds to last double the number of years, but even managed to return home four years later with savings of 70 pounds. And this, after paying for his passage to India—around 40 pounds, inclusive of meals. This miracle—certainly a record of sorts—he seems to have accomplished partly by earning some money from odd jobs, but mostly by a careful management of his budget. Thus, with one exception when he drew out an extra 5 pounds from his bank account soon after appearing for his 'Little Go', Jinnah stuck firmly to living within the tight budget of 11 pounds a month he imposed on himself—6 pounds of which he paid for his board and lodging, leaving him 5 pounds for his other expenses. But despite the surface resemblance, Jinnah had little in common with his father when it came to their attitude towards money. For Jinnahbhai, money was everything—or very nearly so; he became a broken man the day he stopped making it. But his son, for all the penny-pinching ways he seemed to have inherited from his father, had no miser's obsession with accumulating money for its own sake. He liked to consider himself above it, and sometimes demonstrated his apparent indifference by throwing away quantities of it without batting an eyelid. The aim evidently was to 'make his packet', but only as a means to meet his ends.

Both the means and the end were beginning to become clearer in the following few months. The first glimpse of the path he would pursue came about through a personal trauma—the death of his mother in Karachi. She died giving birth to her seventh child, possibly some ten months after Jinnah set out for England. Mithibai's death coincided with the collapse of Jinnahbhai's once thriving business, and while it is unclear if Jinnahbhai's sudden bankruptcy was because of his wife's death, it certainly appears to have broken his will to rebuild his business empire. The news of her death had an equally devastating effect on Jinnah. His child-wife had also died a few months earlier, soon after he left for England, but he had taken her death more matter-of-factly, too engrossed in his new life in London to care very much. But now, when he learnt of his mother's death, the sane and practical young man was unusually overcome—he had a violent fit of fainting. Then he wept and sobbed for many hours. 'He suffered intensely,' according to Fatima, and found the shock 'unbearable'. He had loved his mother 'more than anything else in the world'. Only she had been able to penetrate his armour of hard-headed practicality and reach the intensely sensitive boy within, a dreamer and idealist.

Alone with his grief, so far away from home, Jinnah recalled the parting scene with her in Karachi, which he would never forget now: 'She said to him, "My son, I hate to be away from you. But I am sure this visit to England will help you to be a big man. This has been my dream all my life."' Jinnah had listened in silence and she continued, 'Mohammed Ali, you are leaving now on a long journey. I have a feeling I will not live to see you come back from England.' She had cried then, but Jinnah, manfully overcame his 'choking emotion' as he embraced her for the last time. Her farewell words to him had been: 'Mohammed Ali, God will be your protector. He will make my wish come true. You will be a big man. And I will be proud of you.' The words etched themselves so deeply in Jinnah's mind that years later when he came across, in an essay he was reading, a few lines of a poem on a mother's dying prophecy for her son, he was so moved he underlined the verse.

But the grief only strengthened his determination to prove his mother's faith in him had not been in vain. He had already joined Lincoln's Inn, and instead of giving it all up and returning home to help his father cope with his business and personal loss, he became grimly resolved to succeed at any cost. He threw himself fiercely into his law course. It was way above his academic level but he refused to be daunted, even choosing to take an extra course in constitutional law, which he thought would be useful for his future career in India. Nor was he intimidated by the other students, most of them university graduates; he decided he would clear the examination at least a year ahead of most of them. It proved harder than he had bargained for, especially Roman law, the first paper he was required to clear, which needed a working knowledge of Latin. Hard work and willpower and belief in himself had worked for him in the past and he tried it again, gluing himself to his textbooks. But it didn't work; he failed to clear the preliminary paper in his first attempt. But luck came miraculously to his aid, and the rules of the examination suddenly changed, making it no longer a requirement to clear the paper on Roman law before appearing for the general examination. Once more he tried to cram into one term a year's worth of study, but when the exam results were announced, he had cleared only some of the papers. Without losing any time, he appeared for the third time but still failed in some of the papers. Driven and unrelenting, he went at it once again and finally cleared all his papers in his fourth attempt. He was eighteen and a half, making him the youngest of fifty-three candidates who had passed the Bar examination in that year—or for that matter, in any year before or after.

With another year to wait before he was eligible to be called to the Bar, Jinnah could now afford to relax. All that was required of him was to merely attend six out of the twenty-three dinners at the Inn in each of the four remaining terms—a stiff, formal affair with its strict dress code that other students dreaded, but which Jinnah relished. But his driving ambition would not allow him to rest; he was determined to groom himself for the political career he wanted to pursue after first 'making his packet', as he termed it, as a practising lawyer. He had begun working for Dadabhai Naoroji even before passing his Bar examination, making himself useful enough to be elected to the British branch of the Indian National Congress alongside the most eminent national leaders, but that was hardly enough to satisfy his ambition. He was determined to remake himself, grooming himself in the qualities he considered important for the role he was determined to play in the future. He got himself a reading card from the British Museum library and meticulously began to pursue what he described later as 'independent studies', poring over volumes of political philosophers of the past and present. His studies led him to the conclusion that a politician must never be too emotional. He must toughen up, learn to control his feelings and become impervious to flattery because he should expect to be hit and should have the strength to hit back. He got rid of all that he considered sentimental about himself, resolutely becoming a down-to-earth realist. By the time he was ready to return home, some fifteen months later, he had by force of will and his solitary reading, transformed himself from Mohammed Ali—or 'Mamad', as he was called at home—the friendly, sporty boy from Karachi who preferred his playmates to his books, and who was sensitive and quick to respond to love and admiration, into M.A. Jinnah, as he now liked to be addressed, an austere loner who despised wasting time or money and made no secret of the fact that he was very particular about whom he chose to be friends with.

But his sense of duty never changed. He had discovered another hidden aspect of himself during these months of waiting: his flair for acting. The talent had come to light perhaps through a reading circle he joined with an eye to develop his public-speaking skills as preparation for the courtroom. But his dramatic flair for reading aloud was impressive enough for his friends to urge him to audition for a role in a theatre company. He was accustomed by now to consulting no one's wishes but his own—with his months of studying in the British Museum library only bolstering his inclination to think independently—so when he got the part, he signed up at once with the theatre company, writing to his father only as an afterthought to inform him of the money he could now earn. But Jinnahbhai was far from pleased. He wrote back to his son, a long letter, of which one line—'Do not shame the family'—persuaded Jinnah to give up his new job immediately. Aside from this one chink in his armour, the Jinnah who eventually returned from London in 1896, after his law degree, was unrecognizable: he was impeccably attired in clothes of the best quality and cut, projecting a careless affluence but in fact he had carefully picked out both for their bargain price and quality. He had discarded all Indian clothes—even the pyjamas he went to bed in were made of silk, wearing a dressing gown on top of them before getting dressed in the British fashion he had thoroughly adopted. He had also bought himself a monocle during his stay and used it with an actor's flair whenever occasion demanded it. But the dramatic change in his appearance, which others found so striking, was really nothing when compared to the inner transformation he had so deliberately worked upon.

The transformation, both inner and outer, served him well even in the legal profession, although it was cultivated for another, bigger purpose. In a hopelessly overcrowded field where it took a barrister years of knocking on the right doors to be let in, Jinnah climbed up into the ranks of the eminent in less than two years. And he insisted on doing it his way—fiercely refusing to beg for patronage, even when he had no work. He was a figure hard to overlook, even when he was starting out: a stylish, handsome young barrister who strode arrogantly down the corridors of courtrooms without talking to anyone, returning to his cheap hotel room every evening without a rupee in his pocket. Curiously, that attitude of arrogance, so far exclusively a British trait, won him several admirers, especially among the British. The acting advocate general of Bombay, Sir John Molesworth MacPherson, was one of them. MacPherson invited Jinnah to work in his chamber, the first time such a courtesy was extended to an Indian. Even the chief of the municipal corporation, a Scotsman called James MacDonald, was impressed by the spirited young lawyer. They met in a crowded courtroom where MacDonald was seated on a chair reserved for lawyers. Jinnah insisted on MacDonald vacating the chair for him, and when refused, threatened to appeal to the judge, forcing MacDonald to give up his seat to him. But instead of taking offence, MacDonald offered him work. Yet another official who was struck by Jinnah's bearing and confidence was Sir Charles Ollivant, then a member in charge of the judicial department. He was so impressed by the fact that the young Indian barrister approached him directly for a job instead of going through influential contacts, that he not only appointed him as a temporary magistrate but tried to persuade Jinnah to stay on permanently, offering him a princely salary of Rs 600 a month. Jinnah refused, confidently informing Ollivant that he hoped to make that much in a single day. It was no idle boast: he did succeed, and sooner than anyone could have imagined, in making more than double that amount in a day.

But the arrogance, coupled with his single-minded devotion to his career, could hardly have endeared Jinnah to his peers. As a fellow barrister later put it, a figure like Jinnah 'invites criticism, especially in the lazy East, where we find it easier to forgive a man for his faults than his virtues'. What other lawyers found hard to forgive, according to the barrister, was that Jinnah, despite being the only Muslim to have become a notable barrister, felt entitled to set such high standards for himself—and indirectly, for others as well. 'There was no pleasure in Jinnah's life: there were no interests beyond his work. He laboured at his briefs, day and night.' And worse: 'There was never a whisper of gossip about his private habits. He was a hard-working, celibate, and not very gracious young man.'

But by 1916, the year he decided to marry Ruttie and went to her father with his proposal, something softer within him was beginning to awake. Why else, one wonders, would he underline the following passage in a book he'd been gifted that year: 'My heart was dusty,' he underlined with a lead pencil in an autobiography by Richard Jefferies, *The Story of My Heart*—the nearest he ever came to making a journal entry—'parched for want of the rain of deep feeling; my mind arid and dry, for there is a dust which settles on the heart as well as that which falls on a ledge. It is injurious to the mind as well as to the body to be always in one place and always surrounded by the same circumstances. A species of thick clothing slowly grows about the mind, the pores are choked, little habits become a part of existence, and by degrees, the mind is enclosed in a husk.' And if Ruttie had indeed succeeded in shaking him out of his emotional stupor, as she seems to have done, there was no force on earth, certainly none among mankind, who could persuade Jinnah to give her up. Everyone knew that about him.

Having thrown down the gauntlet in the form of the court injunction, there was little else for Sir Dinshaw to do other than wait and watch. But what he seems to have not realized was that by publicly challenging Jinnah in this way, he had ensured that things could now go only one way. Because, even more than his love for Ruttie, Jinnah's pride would not allow him to retreat.

Chapter Six

~

At breakfast, Sir Dinshaw Petit opened his favourite newspaper, the
Bombay Chronicle, and turning to a column on page eight, collapsed
on his own dining table, bringing the meal to a halt mid-course perhaps
for the first time in Petit Hall's proud history of sumptuous dining.
It was a Saturday, 20 April 1918, a time of the year when Petit Hall
was usually under dust covers, when the family took off with all of
Bombay's smart set to the hills for their two months' summer holiday.
But this summer, again for the first time in Petit Hall's history, Sir
Dinshaw chose to keep himself and his family at home in Bombay,
pleading official engagements. They were no more pressing than a
routine municipal corporation meeting and another one of the board
of trustees of the family-owned animal hospital, but in the cloud that
had descended on Petit Hall ever since Ruttie's romance with Jinnah
had become public, no one was in a mood to argue with his decision.
So there was really no one other than his own family and perhaps
one or two visiting mill owners at the table to witness the scene that
erupted in the dining hall that morning. But few acquainted with
the Petits and their castle had trouble visualizing the scene: shrill
voices suddenly cutting through the georgette-sari and pearl-clad
ladies and morning-suited gentlemen, bearers stopping mid-service
while the house manager summoned the maids—'pure European',
according to the current fashion in servants—for questioning. The
house guests, if any, retreating discreetly to their suites; butlers
sent to make inquiries of the grooms and stable boys; drivers of the
family's carriages and motor cars cross-examined, search parties sent
to scout the woods behind Petit Hall where the family went riding;

doctors summoned, then lawyers . . . One imaginative raconteur went so far as to claim that he had gone to pick up the Petits' family friend Sarojini Naidu that morning, and heard her remark as she swept down the ancient marble stairway of the castle: 'The old man has gone off his head and the house is upside down.' Whether the story is true or not—the poetess and national leader was, in fact, on a political lecture tour in northern India that week—people who heard it had no trouble believing it. For, the news that appeared in the newspaper that morning would have shaken a man with the calmest of tempers, let alone someone as excitable as Sir Dinshaw. There, in a column called 'Official and Personal', tucked between news of an 'At Home' hosted by a member of Servants of India Society, and an official notice of a judge rejoining the Madras High Court after serving on the Rowlatt Commission, was a single sentence destined to dominate discussions in drawing rooms and clubs across India in the weeks and months to come: 'The marriage of the Hon. M.A. Jinnah and Miss Ruttie Petit, daughter of the Hon. Sir Dinshaw and Lady Petit, took place last evening.'

That the *Bombay Chronicle*, the only nationalist paper of that time, should choose to underplay the most sensational news of the year, burying it in an inside page, was understandable. The bridegroom, in all likelihood the author of that cautiously worded wedding announcement, was not only on the newspaper's board of trustees, but also a close and intimate friend of its editor, Benjamin G. Horniman. No reporter anxious to keep his job would obviously have dared to say more in the circumstances. That might explain why Jinnah's book of speeches got more play in the paper that Saturday than the wedding announcement. The ad for the first book of Jinnah's speeches compiled by the nationalist publisher Ganesh & Co. with a foreword by the Raja of Mahmudabad and a 'Biographical Appreciation' by Sarojini Naidu, took up almost a whole column as a top spread.

But even the *Times of India*, the leading English newspaper in Bombay and no friend of Indians or their sentiments, puzzlingly limited the story of Jinnah's most unusual marriage to a single-line announcement, burying it at the bottom of page 10, below a listing of the Calcutta sharemarket. Except for a headline, 'Mohamedan-Parsi Wedding', and referring to Ruttie by her formal Parsi name,

Ruttenbai, that no one had ever called her by, the one-liner was no different from the announcement in the *Bombay Chronicle*, giving none of the details usual on such occasions, such as the venue, ceremony and names of eminent guests. Clearly, the reporters of both papers had neither been invited to the wedding nor encouraged to ask any questions from those who had, and relied on what appears to be a press release. Or were they afraid of a defamation case, perhaps? Jinnah certainly was a man the newspapers feared, especially after the defamation case he won against the *Briton* two years earlier for an aspersion made by their columnist about his friend B.G. Horniman, the editor of the *Bombay Chronicle*, suggesting he was indulging in homosexual activities in his home. Even the papers that came two days too late to the news were equally cautious with details, except for one small but important addition to the statement already published. Datelined Bombay, 19, but carried in the following Monday's edition on 22 April of the *Statesman*, the *Pioneer* and the *Civil and Military Gazette*, it said: 'Ruttenbai, the only daughter of the distinguished Parsi baronet, Sir Dinshaw Petit, yesterday underwent conversion to Islam and is today being married to the Hon. Mr. M.A. Jinnah.'

What no one ever figured out, however, was how Ruttie managed to slip out of Petit Hall unnoticed on two consecutive days, first on 18 April to go with Jinnah to the Jama Masjid to be converted to Islam by a renowned maulana; and again the next evening, on 19 April, to escape from the watchful eye of both her parents, walk up the street to Jinnah's bungalow on Mount Pleasant Road, where he awaited her with a moulvi and a dozen male witnesses, then disappear for the night before anyone noticed she was missing from her bed, with even her parents hearing of the marriage only through the newspapers. If she confided to anyone the details of her dramatic exit from Petit Hall, with supposedly only an umbrella tucked under her arm—and her little dog that went everywhere with her—there's no record of it. Her usual confidante and best friend, Padmaja, had moved from Hyderabad to Bombay for college that year, bringing their correspondence to a temporary halt, and although she had by now shifted location to a boarding school in Mussoorie they had not resumed writing to each other as yet. And while she still looked up to Sarojini, and knew that the older woman sympathized with her feelings for Jinnah, it is unlikely that Ruttie would have risked jeopardizing her plan by confiding details to someone who might try to stop her. Although Sarojini's admiration for Jinnah was great—in fact, at one point nearing infatuation—she was not blind to his faults. And only a year earlier, she had tried to caution her impetuous young protégée against doing anything rash, advice that Ruttie did not take too kindly to, admitting to Padmaja that she had given her mother a scolding 'for having made a speech'. But still, there were many in their common circle of acquaintances who were convinced that it was Sarojini who had encouraged Ruttie to elope with Jinnah, even though she appears to have heard the news, like everyone else, through the newspapers: 'So Jinnah has at last plucked the Blue Flower of his desire,' she wrote over a week later to her beloved friend, Syed Mahmud, the young nationalist from Bihar from whom she kept no secrets. 'It was all very sudden and caused terrible agitation and anger among the Parsis: but I think though the child has made far greater sacrifices than she yet realizes, Jinnah is worth it all—he loves her: the one really human and genuine emotion of his reserved and self-centred nature and he will make her happy.'

But although she had turned eighteen only two months before her marriage, Ruttie was not the child that Sarojini imagined her to be. Loving Jinnah with all the passion of her romantic soul did not blind her to the fact that he had grown even more remote in the last eleven months. At the height of their courtship, she had found him elusive, with his unsentimental and silent ways, leaving her with a deep yearning, 'this medley of wild excitement and cold depression', as she described it. And the court injunction had not only ended their casual meetings in clubs or at the races, when they could exchange a few words, even if it was under the public gaze, but he insisted on sticking strictly to the letter of the law, refusing to write to her. He loathed writing letters anyway, keeping them brisk and practical, filling them with bare and unvarnished facts, in answer to her own letters of ardent longing, running into several pages. He was not demonstrative but his heart was, of course, hers. But she could see, not as clearly perhaps as Sarojini that it would not always be easy. She had her moments of self-doubt although she was too deeply in love to want to look deeper: either into that feeling of 'emptiness' and 'hollowness' that he was already evoking, or that 'longing' and 'dread' that she could not rid herself of, despite her trust and her devotion to him.

There were others no doubt, sensible friends and relatives, to advise her to forget a man who was not just unsuitable because of his age and religion, but also because of the mismatched temperaments: he, universally admired but liked by very few; politics his only and ruling passion; and she, with her spirit of freedom and passion, yearning for she knew not what. But she would not hear a word against him. 'When you are given a flower,' as she rather sternly advised Leilamani the previous year, 'you do not think of the thorn. You revel in its beauty and feast on its fragrance.' It was in her temperament to love. And with the English Romantic poets and novelists having formed her only reading from before the age of ten, she exulted in her feelings, as if nothing else mattered: 'I revel in the storming passions which burn and tear the fibres of my being till my very spirit writhes in an agony of excitement,' she proudly confessed to Padmaja when she was still sixteen. And in another letter: '. . . it is a melancholy in which I rejoice for I feel that it always leads me towards greater perfection and finer sympathy'. She was learning, even then, at the height of their courtship, to look inwards at her own passion rather than towards the man she had chosen, at such cost to herself. 'Who shall satisfy your quenchless thirst but *yourself*?' as she wrote to Leilamani the same week. 'If ever you desire to realize an ideal, it must be within yourself and then you attain what is known as self-realisation.'

And who was there to pour her intense, troubled feelings out to, even if she were able to express this inchoate longing for a man she had really glimpsed just once, that summer when they fell in love, when he let down his guard long enough in the holiday spirit, 'told her the secret of his colours and faded', as her poem said, leaving her chasing ever since for that elusive man behind this distant other, almost a stranger? There was only one thing to do: she hid behind her vivacity, with her wit and jokes and smart clothes and daring make-up, hardly daring to examine her mix of emotions, let alone confessing them to anyone. Jinnah, of course, had no suspicion of the state of his beloved's heart. He too was in love for the first time in his life, and almost despite himself. But he had no time for sentiment, and even less patience with anything he considered woolly-headed. With him, one had to be always brief and clear. Perhaps he too didn't want to look too deep, and once he was assured of her adoration, and more importantly, her loyalty, he threw himself into his political activity with more energy and passion than ever. It was his tribute to their love, as was his resolve to marry her, despite all the fuss and trouble it entailed.

But girls her own age, wary of her surface sophistication and brittle vivacity, could make little of the strange passion of this mismatched pair. That a vivacious, witty, sophisticated girl like Ruttie, an icon already for her generation of young women, should choose to fall in love with a Muslim came as no shock to her friends; no English-educated person would ever admit to labelling their friends as Hindu or Muslim or Parsi, that was left to the lower classes. In fact, it was not uncommon for very anglicized girls, including Motilal Nehru's daughter, 'Nan' or Sarup, to regard it as 'perfectly natural to marry outside my religion'. But Jinnah, despite his youthful good looks and perfect manners, was, after all, twenty-four years older and it was that which Ruttie's friends found unpardonable. For them, it was almost as if by choosing to marry a man more than double her age, she was ruining the image of educated Indians in the eyes of the British. There was enough contempt from them already about the shameful disparity of age between a traditional Indian bride and her bridegroom without her adding to that stereotype. There was, too, her sense of entitlement, her casual assumption that she could do what she pleased with her own life—that shocked even the girls educated in the most anglicized of Indian homes.

It was inconceivable, for instance, for Nan, who too had been in love with a Muslim, not to back down when her parents demanded it of her. And although the same age and from the same affluent background as Ruttie, she was convinced that Ruttie could not have ever really been in love with Jinnah and there was some other, hidden motive for her wanting to marry a man so much older than her. As she writes in her memoir, *The Scope of Happiness*, under her married name, Vijaya Lakshmi Pandit: 'Ruttie was a friend of mine. We were the same age but brought up very differently. She was spoiled, very beautiful and used to having her own way. She was much younger than Jinnah and it was certainly not a "love match." But Jinnah was a Muslim, and the Parsis were, in those days, a very conservative group. This in itself seemed reason enough to Ruttie to shock the community—"wake it up", as she was fond of saying. Besides, he had made a name for himself at the Bar, was very much in the news, and a coming political leader. All these things appealed to her. In spite of the opposition of her parents and the Parsi community, she married him.'

Certainly, even for someone with Ruttie's singular lack of personal conceit, to have made a conquest of someone who was not just 'a coming political leader', as her so-called friend rather grudgingly put it, but increasingly regarded by the British and both Hindu and Muslim nationalists as the rising political star, was profoundly flattering. It would have justifiably turned any woman's head, no matter what her age—a man of his charm, powerful, handsome, elegant, with his dry humour and affability; mesmerizing to both men and women; a man who had disdained the attention of every woman who had so far thrown herself at him, to be now so clearly besotted with her. Anyone could see the power she held over him; he made no attempt to conceal it from anyone, not just her. He even changed his face to please her, shaving off his thick walrus moustache and wearing his hair longer, brushed sleekly backwards in the style favoured by the more fashionable young Parsis. She had demanded it playfully as the price of accepting his proposal. It meant giving up the last trace of his Muslim identity—there had always been a sort of visual grading of Muslim-ness by which people placed you: moustache, beard, turban, cap, sherwani. But he complied readily, shaving it off without a second thought, as if her answer depended on it.

But, of course, she would have married him, with or without his moustache. Whatever misgivings she might have had were less to do with his vestigial Muslim-ness but with marriage itself. And how could she not have any doubts, growing up during the War, exposed fully to the new ideas, especially that of marriage no longer being the only mission in a woman's life. Too much had changed with the unending Great War for Ruttie to be comfortable with the idea of immersing herself forever in domesticity or living in Jinnah's reflected glory, as her friends suspected was her real motive in marrying a man more than double her age. There were the suffragists, for one, tilting constantly at the old notions of marriage as the only aspiration for a woman. And if her intensive reading of Emmeline Pankhurst's autobiography failed to impress her sufficiently about the need to find better reasons to marry a man other than running a good home for him, the English novelists of the period were equally bent on disillusioning women about the institution and its ability to fulfil a modern woman's life. Both of Ruttie's favourite English authors, H.G. Wells and George Moore, were among the early writers bringing down the edifices of Victorian marriage and morals, with their novels showing women conflicted between the old ideas of living happily married ever after and searching for meaning in their lives outside the home. Ruttie devoured all their writing, leaving her generous pencil underlinings in her copy of George Moore's short story collection, *Celibates*, with one of its female protagonist rebelling against marriage to the man she was engaged to. But if she ever gave in to her misgivings, she had only to think of the alternative. Her education, wide and impressive though it had been, fitted her for no profession other than a brilliant marriage to someone from her own community, to follow in the footsteps of women like her mother, running a lavish home and throwing fashionable parties for people like themselves while she outsourced her maternal duties to an army of foreign nannies and governesses. The very prospect of settling forever in such a 'polished, civilized world' made her ardent young spirit rebel, longing even more to break away to Jinnah's side, into his world of pure and passionate politics. And how could it ever be a sacrifice to leave behind a home where she was treated like a child, sent to bed at the slightest sign of having caught a chill, for a life where she would be able 'to fight side by side' with the man she loved, to 'gain India back her own crown of Freedom'. Her romantic heart thrilled at the prospect. She yearned for what Jinnah seemed to stand for: an exciting life of intense political discussions extending late into the nights, the camaraderie, the fervour of a shared mission to liberate the country, the sacrifices. It was, in fact, Jinnah's very austerity and loathing for her fashionable world that called to her most deeply, not his celebrity status or political power, as Nan so wrongly assumed.

And the real struggle in her mind was not with the sacrifices involved in renouncing the old life, with its wealth and luxury and the security that her parents provided; it was whether, when it came to the test, she might fail to break free of her shackles. She had always prided herself on her ability to plunge headlong into things, never looking back or heeding the consequences, finding it 'too tame and calculative' to even reread her letters once they were written. It was unlike the Ruttie everyone knew, but she was a secret worrier. 'But what is the use of saying these things and dreaming a life I can never fulfill?' she had admitted wistfully to Padmaja three months before her seventeenth birthday. But now, having given her consent to Jinnah to make plans for her escape, almost begged him to liberate her from that world, she had to muster the courage for it without breathing a word to a soul, least of all to the man to whom she had pledged herself. She needed inspiration and, as usual, she found it in a book she was reading. 'I dare do all that may become a man, who dares do more, is neither more nor less' were the lines she marked out in William Thackeray's *Novels by Eminent Hands*. It was to be her motto in those last few months she spent in Petit Hall, before walking out forever, with only her umbrella under her arm.

And yet her heart must have quailed as she stepped out of the familiar tall gates of Petit Hall, and entered what was now to be her new home. Perched midway up Malabar Hill, Jinnah's bungalow was a mere 100 yards' climb up Malabar Hill from Petit Hall at its bottom. The uphill route she took from Petit Hall to Mount Pleasant Road, with its flowering trees of pluming pink cassias and flaming *gulmohars*, would have been a familiar one for Ruttie, and at this evening hour, with the summer heat lifting and a cool breeze blowing from the Arabian Sea, a pleasant walk of five or ten minutes. She had never entered Jinnah's home before but her aunt, Lady Petit's younger sister and only surviving sibling, Cooverbai 'Coomi' Powallah, lived on the same road, facing Jinnah's house. She had taken that walk countless times, sometimes with one of her three brothers, perhaps even alone—for her parents were more liberal about dispensing with chaperones, especially when she was within the neighbourhood. Malabar Hill in April was a colourful sight even when the temperature was a simmering 72 degrees Fahrenheit, as it had been that morning— 'gulmohars and flame of the forests dyed like life blood . . . crimson oleanders, scarlet lilies, vermilion of the blossoming *dhak* trees, surpassing the splendour of all Nature's pageant of the seasons, April month is an ecstasy of such width and luminous colour, neither red nor rose nor orange but a commingled glory stolen from the land of Poetry and Romance,' as the lyrical Sarojini put it. But for Ruttie, indifferent at the best of times to natural beauty, the chief attraction

MR AND MRS JINNAH 105

of Malabar Hill had always been her aunt's house perched midway on it. For both herself and her siblings, Aunt Coomi's home was almost an extension of Petit Hall. They'd been there at least once or twice a week since early childhood, either to play with their three cousins or call on their grandmother, who lived with Coomi. But now, entering for the first time the house on the opposite side of the road, hidden from view even without the high walls and gates of the Powallahs' imposing mansion, it seemed another world away.

If Ruttie had ever spared a thought from her romantic flights of fancy to consider what her future home would be like, she probably assumed it would be more or less like Aunt Coomi's—not comparable, of course, to Petit Hall in grandeur, but stylish and modern, like all homes on Malabar Hill. Jinnah's bungalow was on the same road, after all, and if the Powallahs were one of the richer landed families among the Parsis, Jinnah was no less affluent or lacking in taste or aspiration to live up to Bombay's most fashionable address. She had never been to Jinnah's home before, having always met him either at one of the clubs or the races, or in her own home or in the homes of others. But this house she was just stepping into had nothing to do with people like herself; it belonged to an earlier time, at least fifty years ago, when Malabar Hill was still a jungle and had not become the fashionable place it now was, when rich people occasionally came up for a weekend of hunting and sea air. It was undoubtedly the most dreary home that Ruttie had ever stepped into. Hector Bolitho, the author from London commissioned to do an official biography of Jinnah three years after his death and long after the old house had been razed and rebuilt, described it as 'a Goanese bungalow'. But whatever it may have originally been, it had served in the last half-century to accommodate British civil servants, one of the last remaining old houses on the street that had yet to give way for the fortress-like white marble mansions of the new century. However, it wasn't so much South Court's austere refusal to conform to the luxurious norms of the neighbourhood that disturbed Ruttie so much as its air of sad, unlived dinginess, so unlike the owner with his youthful energy and taste for motor cars and horse riding and elegant clothing. 'A fun-forsaken house', was how Ruttie later described it to Padmaja.

Not that Jinnah had ever hidden anything from her, but how was she to suspect that his taste for luxury ended at motor cars, clothes and cigars. Few people had ever entered his home. Although he was one of Bombay's top ten leading barristers, he did not believe in entertaining like the other successful lawyers. While he sometimes condescended to attend their extravagant garden parties and at-homes with hundreds of guests, exotic refreshments and live bands, he never felt obliged to return their hospitality, offering at best a cup of tea to a visitor if he turned up at teatime. And the only two receptions he ever threw in his long bachelor life were exclusively for men, and both were held outside his home— in a rented flat in Colaba, not far from Apollo Hotel where he lived when he first moved to Bombay. Jinnah had bought South Court from a departing Scottish civil servant six years earlier as both a wise investment and a good address for a successful barrister, but without any intention of living there. As long as he remained a bachelor, it had suited him to go on living in his rented house, despite its more unfashionable address and size. These things didn't matter to him—'So long as the house did not leak, he did not mind' where he lived, as his architect was to later say about him.

Besides, it was more convenient than moving to Malabar Hill. The house was closer to the high court, where his real life was. His chamber in the high court was, in fact, his real home, one of the two great political centres in Bombay—the other being Lokmanya Tilak's house, Sardar Griha. Jinnah's rooms at the court was not only a place to meet his clients but the centre of political discussions and a gathering place for his young admirers, with Jinnah holding court there sometimes till late into the night. He was popular with young men who admired him both for his dashing appearance with his well-cut suits and monocle and his sense of humour, considering him the only one of his generation with the courage to be himself without counting the consequences. With them, he dropped his guard, all his hauteur gone, letting them come to him with their problems. His Saturdays, especially, were reserved for his young friends from every community when he devoted two or three hours exclusively to talking politics with them, talking to them as equals, allowing them to contradict him and throwing out anyone who came to him with a brief during that time, so precious was this time both for him and them.

At home, his needs were minimal, and his establishment small: a few servants, a valet, certainly, to help with his dressing, and one or two cooks and drivers. What little entertaining he did was limited to throwing stag parties for his close friends, who stayed all night drinking and talking politics. He was a frequent guest, of course, at the homes of his rich friends, but they were the sort of grand persons you went to see but never invited home. Not that Jinnah was intimidated by the grandness of his friends' mansions—he was known to walk into these fabulous palaces by the sea, hurry unseeingly through the galleries of priceless treasures that his host had collected with such zeal and pride, to 'seek a sofa in a corner, where he could ensnare his host and talk politics—at him, rather than with him, late into the night', as Bolitho writes.

But even he could see that the Colaba flat was no place to bring a bride raised in Petit Hall. Neither his sense of her prestige nor his pride would allow that. It would, of course, have been more sensible for him to shift to South Court after his marriage, giving his bride enough time to redecorate the house according to her own taste. And that was probably his intention. But there were practical considerations. He needed a place to hold their wedding ceremony without the risk of Sir Dinshaw discovering their plan before it could take place. And what better place than his own house in Malabar Hill, locked up for so long. Even if Sir Dinshaw were somehow able to stumble upon Jinnah's carefully laid plans for their wedding, the last place he would think of hunting down the lovers would be in a house that was supposedly vacant and barely a stone's throw from Petit Hall.

And that could be why the house looked even bleaker from the inside than outside: preoccupied with making leakproof arrangements for the secret wedding, with no opportunity to consult Ruttie and having just shifted his only female companion of the last ten years—his younger sister, Fatima—out of his household, Jinnah seems to have relied entirely on his trusted old retainers for this last-minute move to South Court. To anyone entering the uncarpeted living room with its single unfashionable sofa set arranged stiffly in the centre of the room, and no pictures on the walls to distract the eye, the room would have appeared cold and unwelcoming, but for Ruttie, it was a shock she never got over. The contrast to her home, of course, was obvious: no marble nymphs and fountains at the entrance vestibule, no potted palms and marble statues at every corner, or chandeliers—at least three in Petit Hall's palatial drawing room alone—no painted

Chinese screens or China vases with fresh-cut flowers and Persian carpets—at least four at each end of the drawing room alone—or dozens of fluted marble pillars in every room, not to speak of the stained-glass windows and the view of the garden and the sea beyond. But without really wanting all that, Ruttie didn't know what she was expecting. She was out on the Bohemian adventure she had wanted to make of her life, but what she was completely unprepared for was the prim conventionality of Jinnah's home. Not to speak of the largely male gathering assembled in the drawing room awaiting her arrival.

It wasn't much of a crowd. On a busy day, Sir Dinshaw probably had more visitors in his day drawing room than Jinnah's wedding party that evening. For Ruttie, never having attended a purdah party before in her life, it was her first encounter with a roomful of hostile bearded men in kurta pyjama, only two of them clean-shaven like Jinnah: the Raja of Mahmudabad, famous for his hospitality and forty-two-course dinners, and Jinnah's energetic young associate from the Home Rule League, Umar Sobhani. But Jinnah had chosen his wedding guests not for their conviviality or social graces but for their trustworthiness as witnesses for their nikah. The only women he had invited for the ceremony were his two younger sisters, Shirin Peerbhoy and Fatima. But if he thought they would help make his bride feel more at home, he couldn't have been more mistaken. Neither of them was in a mood to be hospitable to this georgette-clad and lipsticked Parsi bride with her low-cut satin blouse, blowing smoke rings as she warded off the disapproving stares, making straight towards Jinnah. He, at least, was reassuringly himself, tall and thin and strikingly handsome, impeccably clad as usual in his silk suit and shiny pumps, advancing towards her, his sharp eyes not even noticing that his bride's diaphanous sari and sleeveless, low-cut blouse was hardly appropriate for this sombre circle of wedding guests awaiting her arrival.

It had been a difficult year for him as well. Political activity was at its frenzied height that year—'a seething, boiling, political flood raging across the country', as the secretary of state, Edwin Montagu, put it—with night-long parleys and public meetings and daily drafting of resolutions to send to the government. He could not have possibly chosen a worse time to get married. He had been persuaded to take over the Home Rule League the previous year, soon after the founding president, Annie Besant's arrest in Madras in June 1917. The Home Rule movement had made little headway in Bombay, where seasoned politicians regarded the white-haired sari-clad Irish theosophist with suspicion for her 'impatient idealism'. Nearly every leader she approached turned down her invitation to work with her organization, but her arrest forced political leaders to take her more seriously. Jinnah was among those leaders who had turned her down, pleading leadership duties in the Congress and the Muslim League as an excuse. But when Besant was interned by the government, her young associates in Bombay were able to persuade him to step in until she was released. He had never been a great admirer of the Irish theosophist and socialist, nearly thirty years older than him, considering both her methods and goal too drastic and impractical. And once he agreed to take charge, Jinnah began transforming the movement beyond recognition, appointing his own deputies and roping in his large circle of influential friends in order to displace the theosophists who previously dominated it. It soon became an important channel for his political activities, with Jinnah using it as a launching pad for a series of public meetings for the educated classes, and moulding it in the months leading up to his marriage into the foremost political force in the country. He opened branches of the Home Rule League in different parts of Bombay and across the Bombay Presidency, particularly in Gujarat. He brought almost the entire legal fraternity into its activities, raising huge funds. Thousands of leaflets and pamphlets had to be published and distributed week after week. There were meetings, usually after dinner, extending late into the night, and large public rallies at Shantaram Chawl, the only place in Bombay where such public meetings were permitted. Special permits had to be arranged for the open-air meetings. And to ensure that this vast organization was smoothly administered, he met his deputies in his chamber almost daily for an hour or two.

Nor did he let up on his other work. While the session lasted, he was one of the most active and vocal delegates in the Imperial Legislative Council, rising to speak on almost every issue discussed there and trying almost single-handedly to push through legislation on Indianizing the armed forces. He was a popular speaker in the legislature, able to put across his points so forcefully that he was the most feared among the members by the British rulers. In both the Indian National Congress and the Muslim League he had by now become indispensable, a natural candidate to lead their delegations to the government or to London to lobby members of Parliament. He was not a rousing public speaker, his appeal being to the head rather than the heart, but as a leader of delegations to the government, he was far superior to any other political leader. His biggest asset was that he got on much better with the British rulers than the usual run of politicians, being someone who refused to cringe and crawl, able to meet them on their own ground, in their own language, dressed more impeccably than them in their own clothes. At a time of such intense dialogue and negotiations, both among Indians of different communities and with the British government, Jinnah's star, already rising, reached its zenith. It was taken for granted by everyone, including the British government, that he was the leader of the future after Home Rule was granted, with Jawaharlal Nehru having not arrived on the scene and Gandhi not yet fully ascendant. In fact, he became so overloaded with his political work that for the first time in his legal career of eighteen years, he had to seek the adjournment of a case because he had to go to Delhi as a member of not one but two joint delegations to the viceroy demanding reforms. And as if all this was not enough to take his mind off Ruttie, the Allies tasted their first victory in the War barely a month before his wedding, triggering even more intense political activity to negotiate with the government for some form of self-rule before the War actually ended. Even two days before his wedding, he spent the evening with his Home Rule colleagues, drafting a wire to the British government, addressed to the prime minister, the viceroy and the secretary of state for India, protesting at the last-minute ban on Tilak's trip to London. With such an opportunity and his ambition and drive, Sir Dinshaw wasn't the only one duped into believing that Jinnah had at last given up Ruttie for his real passion—politics.

Even his sister Fatima, the closest companion he'd had so far, could not have suspected what Jinnah was plotting, especially in the preceding months, when he worked even longer hours than his usual fourteen, his whirlwind tours carrying him from one end of India to another, always in a rush. She had been living with him for the past ten years, ever since she had left school, dropped off every morning on his way to the courts at her sister, Shirin's house, to be picked up when he returned from work in the evening. But one day when he abruptly announced his resolve to get married, asking her to pack her bags and move to her sister's for good, she knew better than to argue with him. Once he had made up his mind to do something, nothing could ever shake his purpose, as she well knew. Neither tears nor coaxing worked at such moments; one devastating sentence, delivered in his cold, unruffled voice was enough to silence even her, his favourite sister. The 'onward rush of the mighty ocean of his will could sweep away all obstacles', as she put it in her memoir, *My Brother*.

But even with his inexhaustible willpower, the marriage seemed an impossibility. Viewed from any angle, the hurdles, whether personal, social or legal, were insurmountable. The easiest way out was what other young English-educated lovers from different communities had already started doing: go through a secret marriage, either civil or religious, and then bolt from their homes until the scandal died down. But Jinnah was far too fastidious for an elopement, even before Ruttie's father went to court as a precaution against it. Despite his arrogance and seeming indifference to public opinion, Jinnah had never once allowed a whiff of scandal to stain his reputation since he arrived in Bombay two decades ago. And he had no intention of doing so now, with his public eminence. Sir Dinshaw's pre-emptive move in going to court to stop the runaway marriage he feared was therefore more a boon than a handicap for Jinnah: while it tied his hands for nearly a year, until Ruttie turned eighteen and was automatically out of the court's jurisdiction as a minor, it also gave him plenty of time to consider all the options.

At first, Ruttie refused to accept that there was no way to dodge the court's order. And that there was nothing to be done but wait until she was eighteen. Convinced that there must be another way out instead of this interminable wait, she sought her own legal advice. This was done through Padmaja, her only confidante during this period of her prolonged secret engagement. Padmaja recommended a lawyer friend in Lucknow, Syed Nabiullah, an aristocrat barrister and member of the municipal board in Lucknow. He was both a 'progressive' from Aligarh and a friend of both Padmaja and her mother, and therefore could be trusted to keep the matter confidential, even from Jinnah if necessary. But for reasons unknown, Ruttie dropped the idea even before they could meet and discuss her situation—either she lost her nerve and was afraid that Jinnah would be angry with her for acting on her own or more probably, Jinnah finally prevailed on her that waiting was the best—and only—option before them. As Nabiullah wrote to Padmaja later, referring to her request for his professional advice on her friend's behalf: 'I am delighted to hear of my mysterious client. I had in fact a lurking idea of calling on her last September but I thought she may not like it,' adding on a more playful note: 'I would have enjoyed the very rare combination of beauty and great charm.'

But what Ruttie did not realize and what Jinnah knew full well was that the legal hurdles in the way of their marriage would hardly fall off by themselves once Ruttie turned eighteen, even after the court injunction against them automatically lapsed with her attaining her majority. There was the question of how to go about getting legal sanction for a marriage such as theirs, between a Muslim and a Parsi. So far, no one had dared attempt such a union. On the face of it, a civil marriage seemed the only possibility for such an unprecedented step. But far from being the liberal law it was meant to be, the Special Marriages Act brought its own peculiar set of difficulties. Under the law, while a girl could marry even at the age of fourteen, she needed her father's consent until she crossed twenty-one. Even then, the father was required to be present at the registrar's to witness the marriage, as his consent was mandatory to legitimize the marriage. Besides, if the bride and bridegroom belonged to non-Hindu communities, then they were both forced to file separate declarations swearing that they no longer owed any allegiance to the religion they were born into. It was tantamount to signing an oath denouncing one's own religion. For Jinnah, this was as good as being asked to commit political suicide. He had never really been a practising Muslim, having been brought up in a Khoja Ismaili household and educated in secular and missionary schools. The Khoja Ismailis followed an allegorical, symbolic interpretation of the Quran and therefore were not regarded as true Muslims by the majority Sunnis. Jinnah being aware of this handicap and knowing how vital his Muslim identity was to carve his own place in politics, shrewdly began to invent a Muslim identity of his own, ignoring the initial digs from the orthodox of his English manners and dress and clean-shaven face. Of course, now that he was the undisputed leader of the Muslim League and had won three times in a row as a Muslim representative in the legislative council, he was in a stronger position to face his orthodox rivals. Only five years ago, he had faced hecklers who wanted to know how he could call himself a Muslim if he was not dressed like one and spoke in English instead of Urdu. Jinnah had ignored the Muslim outcry against him and since then had become more confident of his identity as a 'political leader of Muslims and not their religious leader', as Jinnah put it. But defying Muslim orthodoxy in the matter of openly drinking whisky and smoking cigarettes was one thing, and signing a legal document forswearing his religion quite another. Even Jinnah didn't dare to go that far.

The only way out was for Ruttie to convert to Islam and marry under Muslim law. Luckily for him, Ruttie could not possibly have demanded that he convert to her religion instead of the other way around. As both were aware, under Parsi custom and law, it was prohibited for an outsider born of a non-Parsi father to convert to Zoroastrianism, let alone marry under Parsi rites. So far, no Parsi, man or woman, had ever dared to marry a Muslim, let alone undergone a conversion in order to do so. But, for Ruttie, that was hardly a reason to hesitate. In this again, her friend Sarup (Vijaya Lakshmi Pandit) did her a disservice by assuming that Ruttie's only motive in defying the community's diktat was her impish impulse to shock—'wake them up', as she was fond of saying. The truth was a little more complex. She could not have been unaware of the consequences she would face. Although Ruttie's attachment to her own religion left much to be desired, even she could not have been ignorant of the fuss within the Parsi community when her parents' friend Ratan B. Tata married a Frenchwoman in a Parsi ceremony. She had been only three years old then, but the incident had created too intense a controversy to have died down before she reached her girlhood. Countless meetings had been held, committees appointed and learned men from the community selected to report on the various religious questions that arose as a result of Tata's wife being invested with the sacred thread and vest and remarried by a Parsi high priest in a wedding ceremony that incensed the community's orthodox section. But Ruttie belonged to an exclusively English-educated generation who, as Justice Davar in his judgment on the controversy caustically put it, believed they 'were wiser than their grandfathers and were born with a mission to correct the errors of their elders'.

In an age of universal unbelief, most young Parsis of Ruttie's circle were unashamed atheists, refusing to go to the fire temples or even pray at home or sport the symbols of their faith. Nor did this worry their parents overmuch, with atheism having become fashionable worldwide. Of course, it did provide yet another reason for the orthodox within the Parsi community to attack this anglicized elite, carrying on a vigorous campaign against their irreligious and materialistic Western lifestyle, believing it would be the end of the Parsi community and traditions as they knew it. But the criticism from the 'riff-raff', with their 'jealous bigotry', as Sir Dinshaw's lawyers put it, had little impact on the Willingdon Club set. Having grown up watching this divide between Parsis like her and the other conservative Gujarati-speaking faction who left her with a need 'to shake them up', and having seen how easy it was for anyone in her father's circle to bribe the priests into bending the rules whenever it suited them, it was hardly surprising that Ruttie blithely assumed that rules were not something that applied to people like her. Of course, she had been through her *navjot* ceremony, a religious initiation rite performed by a priest in which a Parsi child, aged between seven and nine, is given a sacred thread and cotton vest which admits him or her into the Zoroastrian faith and Parsi fold. But with the navjot having been transformed by her new-age parents into nothing more than yet another occasion for lavish celebration, with a guest list of several thousand from both within the community and outside, it was unlikely that her navjot helped Ruttie deepen her appreciation for the religion she was born into. Like most of her circle, she was a Parsi only in name.

Certainly, Jinnah's own attitude to religion was not as casual and uncomplicated as his bride's. He was not a believer in the orthodox sense and had always remained above sectarian prejudices but he certainly did not belong to that class of the English educated who were raised like European children, taught by European governesses and tutors to disdain Indian culture and religion. As long as she was alive, he was devoted to his mother who was a deeply devout woman, if not in the purely Islamic way approved by the orthodox. And even his father, who was raised as an Ismaili to be half-Hindu in his customs and beliefs, had turned pronouncedly Muslim after his migration to Karachi. Jinnahbhai refused to give his children Hindu names or ceremonies, according to the Ismaili custom back home, and gave them daily lessons in the Quran while they were still young. While never overtly religious like his sisters, especially Fatima, Jinnah had a thorough knowledge of the Quran, having always allowed himself a rational, dispassionate interest in Islam, reading a biography in English of Prophet Muhammad while he was in England preparing for his Bar examinations. He also embarked on a study of Islamic jurisprudence while still a law student, supposedly because it would come in handy for his future law career whenever he returned to India. After his return too, Jinnah's religious sentiments could only be described as mixed.

Fastidious about being associated with Muslim backwardness and their many taboos and orthodoxy and superstitions, he refused to sport the outward identity of a Muslim, abjuring the round turban and spade beard and black gown that even educated and influential Muslim leaders clung on to. He not only defiantly dressed like a British gentleman but openly smoked, drank, ate pork and, more seriously, insisted on putting his sister into a convent boarding school in the teeth of stiff opposition from his own Khoja community. But he did not wish to turn his back entirely on his Muslim identity, carefully reinventing himself as a different kind of Muslim—one who did not go to a mosque to pray but still belonged to the community. It was as a part of this reinvention that Jinnah joined a reformist Muslim organization called the Khoja Shia Isnaashari Jamaat that was started in the beginning of the twentieth century by a few Khojas anxious to join the mainstream and to be seen as a more modern and progressive Islamic faith. Jinnah wasted no time joining this new organization with its own mosques, madrasas and *imamvadas* to distinguish them from the Ismailis, resulting, according to some biographers, in the rejection of a marriage proposal that his father sent on his behalf soon after Jinnah's return from England as a qualified barrister.

Overtly, his interest in Islam was purely legal and rational. When he joined the Imperial Legislative Council, for example, he took it upon himself to draft the first Muslim Wakf Bill, spending years reading and talking to Islamic experts to gain the thorough understanding of Islamic law he required in order to draft the bill.

And yet, whatever Ruttie may have concluded from his anglicized appearance and habits, her conversion to Islam was more important to him than merely a quick way of getting around the law. He was already fighting a stiff battle with Muslim rivals who insisted on labelling him a kafir, a non-believer, and now by marrying a *kafira*, the knives would be out again. He needed to find the right man to do the conversion, someone who would ensure that it would be so legally binding that it would stand up to his critics' scrutiny not only for now, but in the years to come.

He did not have to look too far. Maulana Nazir Ahmad Khujandi was not only a renowned religious scholar of the majority Sunni sect and a presiding imam of Bombay's Jama Masjid but also a member of the Muslim League. As his leader, Jinnah could expect the moulvi to accommodate him in any way possible as well as keep the conversion a secret at least until the wedding announcement was made. The date for the conversion, Thursday, 18 April, was carefully chosen, not because it was the anniversary of the Ajmeri Sufi saint Khwaja Moinuddin Chishti and was considered one of the holiest days on the Muslim calendar, as his Pakistani biographers conjecture, but because it was the most sensible way of holding his tightly plotted wedding plan together. It gave just enough time not to crowd up the wedding day but not enough time for the secret to leak out before they got away. All Ruttie had to do was walk into the Jama Masjid the previous day, accompanied by Jinnah's then trusted lieutenant, Umar Sobhani. No woman, veiled or unveiled, had probably stepped into the mosque before, but she was Jinnah's bride-to-be and therefore an exception. The ritual of conversion could not have taken very long, with her going through the prayers that she made no pretence of memorizing beforehand. She would have been back in Petit Hall well in time for dinner. The day of her conversion, incidentally, was also a Parsi festival day, Aban Jasan, dedicated to the angel who presides over the sea, when Parsis approach the sea to offer prayers with coconuts and flowers. It follows the day after the most sacred day on the Parsi calendar, Adar Jasan, the ninth day of the ninth month, when every devout Parsi visits a fire temple. It was an irony that was lost on both of them.

But what was not lost on Jinnah was the opportunity that the three public holidays in a row—Wednesday and Thursday for the two Parsi festivals, followed by the Hindu Ram Navami on Friday—provided him, especially as these were followed by the weekend. He was far too smart a strategist to miss such a rare advantage he suddenly held over Sir Dinshaw. The high court was already closed for the summer, but Sir Dinshaw had not relaxed his vigil, putting off his summer plans to keep guard over his daughter. But now, even were he to discover their plans and go after them, he would find his hands tied till the following Monday, when the police courts reopened. By then they would have safely escaped to an undisclosed destination that Jinnah arranged for them, but confided to no one. What is more, he could even think of sending out a press release announcing his wedding, giving the impression that it was conducted quietly but openly in the public eye and that there had been nothing clandestine about it whatsoever, knowing that by the time the newspapers came out with it, it would be too late to do anything about it.

The wedding ceremony itself couldn't have been more primly respectable. For Ruttie, accustomed to Parsi weddings with an open courtyard where white-robed priests performed a picturesque ceremony while guests feasted in the surrounding galleries, it must have seemed a poor show. Since neither the bride nor the bridegroom could recite the Arabic words of the nikah, others were deputed to do it for them. The moulvi gave a brief discourse praising Allah for his wisdom and recited three verses from the Quran that neither could follow. There was some discussion on her *mehr*, or dowry, and then a sign in a register, and it was over. It had lasted an hour, from seven to eight in the evening. The only memorable moment was when the bridegroom had to place a ring on his bride's finger and discovered that, with so much on his mind, he had forgotten to buy one. But the chief wedding guest, the Raja of Mahmudabad, an old friend and admirer of Jinnah's, came to the rescue, pulling off the diamond ring on his own finger. The marriage, according to Mahmudabad's son and heir, was performed according to Shiite rites, and a certain Maulana Mohammad Hasan Najafi was deputed as Ruttie's representative, signing the nikah document on her behalf, while Shariat Madar Aqai Haji Mohammad Abdul Hashim Najafi signed on behalf of the bridegroom. The attorneys and witnesses included Shareef Dewji Kanji, Umar Sobhani and the Raja of Mahmudabad. The wedding document was written in Persian, and the serial number in the nikah register was 118.37. According to the nikah document, the mehr was settled at Rs 1001. But quite apart from the mehr, Jinnah presented Ruttie with Rs 125,000 as a gift. This was almost as much as what His Highness the Raja of Rajpipli had just contributed to the War Fund, but the sheer magnificence of the sum was totally lost on Ruttie. Apart from her fuzzy head for figures, she had never handled cash before.

If refreshments were served after the ceremony, the newspapers, usually fond of dwelling on such details, did not mention it. The newly-weds, at any rate, would have been in a rush to get out of Bombay before the storm broke. Not that the prospect of it ruffled Jinnah's usual calm—he stopped long enough in his office at the bungalow to sign a letter requisitioning a public meeting three days later to be addressed by Gandhi. Jinnah, of course, would not be there to address the meeting according to the original programme, but he was too meticulous to leave without attending to this last detail. Apparently, even with Ruttie finally by his side, it was politics that continued to be topmost in his mind.

Chapter Seven

~

For those who saw them on their honeymoon, they seemed a perfect match: a dazzlingly handsome couple despite the twenty-four-year age difference; witty, intelligent and fashionable. And yet, no two people could be more unlike each other, even in their outward appearance. Jinnah was tall and thin with sharply chiselled features; he had fine eyebrows beneath which his rather narrow eyes shone with a calm intelligence. 'Aloof and imperious of manner,' he rarely smiled, spoke in a measured voice, each word perfectly pronounced and enunciated, tending to emphasize his points with a pointed index finger, especially when he mounted one of his polemical high horses, which was quite often. His expression of austere gravity was further heightened by the distinguished streak of grey hair right in the middle of his head. He was at all times immaculately clad, refusing even to step out of his bed without throwing on a silk dressing gown over his silk pyjamas. Such fastidious attention to his dress had prompted his more irreverent junior colleagues into dubbing him the 'Beau Brummell' of the Bombay High Court, after the regency buck who ruled over London's fashionable world in the early nineteenth century. The formal style in dress that he assiduously cultivated—well-tailored suits that sat so well on his graceful five-foot-eleven frame, correct to the last detail from the silk jackets and shirts to the stiff white collars, the matching tie and a kerchief in the vanity pocket and shining pump shoes—was more reminiscent of a generation that was already getting outdated, even before the conclusion of the War which overturned all the old notions of propriety and culture. In other words, Jinnah looked distinctly old school.

In contrast, Ruttie was dainty, warm, spontaneous, with a deep, mocking voice, and a look of sparkling mischief that made her irresistible. As on this first evening of her honeymoon, coming down to dinner with the Raja of Mahmudabad's family in his palatial residence in Lucknow. She was dressed unexceptionally—underdressed, in fact, for a newly-wed—in a plain white sari with a black and gold embroidered border, and with no trace of the shy, demure bride. Jinnah had accepted Mahmudabad's invitation to visit them in Lucknow before driving to Nainital where they would stay for a month in the Raja's house in the hill station. And as she stepped into the drawing room, frail and beautiful, besides her tall, composed husband, her charm was mesmerizing, as Mahmudabad's young son was to later recall. The four-year-old was so bewitched by Ruttie's first appearance that he could vividly recount the experience nearly seventy years later: 'She looked like a fairy . . . delicate as a doll made of glass . . . I never saw a lady so beautiful, elegant and graceful in my whole life.' The little boy gazed at her in wonder 'thinking it was a real fairy which has come down to our house'.

Seeing the little boy staring up at her with such astonishment, Ruttie swooped down in her quick, graceful way, picked him up and put him on her lap as she sat down on a sofa. As the eldest in an extended family of brothers and cousins, she had grown up with adoring little children hanging around her and it came naturally to her to reach out and pet the youngest, no matter how distracted. But at this moment, faced with the prospect of making small talk with relative strangers instead of being alone with her husband, the child's presence was very welcome. He broke the ice between the four adults groping for a way to get past that first, awkward pause, making them laugh by refusing to get off Ruttie's lap. 'I kept sitting in her lap for a long time, even when my father and mother ordered me to come down, until the supper started,' the boy who became Raja Amir Ahmad Khan of Mahmudabad later said, recalling her 'very charming and enchanting fragrance . . . which still lingers in my soul'.

For the host, whose hospitality was legendary, this was no ordinary occasion. He was one of Jinnah's closest friends, staying with the plain-spoken barrister when he visited Bombay and insisting that Jinnah stay with him whenever he came to Lucknow. They were the same age, although at first glance the Raja appeared at least twenty years older; and despite his superior lineage and rank, it was the Raja who treated Jinnah as his superior in both intelligence and character. They had met years ago, when Ruttie was still a child, and although very different in temperament, had soon become close friends. The friendship was based on their shared ideals of nationalism, and also on the Raja's genuine admiration for Jinnah, and his loyalty, which was always the way to Jinnah's heart. When they were together, they would talk until the early hours of the morning, but only about politics. Of a romantic temperament himself, the Raja was delighted when his 'calm and logical' friend—'no apostle of frenzy', as he once aptly put it—at last succumbed to passion like any other man. And since he regarded romantic passion as more his territory than his pragmatic friend's, he felt entitled not only to play chief adviser to the veteran bachelor in his matrimonial schemes but also to make the arrangements for their honeymoon which he was sure would not occur to Jinnah to plan.

The prince was well aware of Jinnah's aversion to holidays, unable to take even two or three days off from his work and politics without fretting. In fact, Jinnah had successfully aborted their first attempt at a honeymoon within the first five days of their marriage because he wanted to attend a conference of Indian leaders on the War called by the viceroy in Delhi. The announcement, splashed in the papers on the morning after they had fled Bombay following their wedding, was to demonstrate Indian support for the British government for the War, and apart from all the members of the viceroy's executive council, a number of Indian princes and leaders, including Gandhi, had been invited to present their views. There was no question, of course, of his skipping the meeting and although Delhi was hardly the place for a honeymoon, especially at that time of the year, when even the hotels were closed for the summer, Ruttie made no protest,

She wanted, with all her youthful ardour, to share in his enthusiasm for the conference. Jinnah was looking forward to voicing his views on constitutional reforms as the only price Indians were prepared to accept in exchange for fighting England's War, although he had spoken on this on innumerable occasions already. Only two days after their wedding, a delegation of Home Rule Leaguers had carried a memorandum he had drafted on the same theme to the viceroy in Delhi, with a copy of the letter also wired to the secretary of state in England. Of course, the government did not bother to respond, only making a note that Jinnah was to be carefully watched in future because he was an 'extremist' and an 'agitator'. But Jinnah's faith in his own persuasive abilities was unshakeable, and Ruttie preferred to swallow her disappointment and pack her bags for Delhi scarcely before she had unpacked them on their first holiday together.

Delhi was even duller than she feared. They were among the first to arrive because Jinnah wanted to attend the legislative council meeting before the main War conference. They stayed at the Maidens Hotel, reputed to be among the best in Delhi. Jinnah had always stayed there as a bachelor and now he booked one of the only two suites in the hotel. It was too nice and quiet, as she told the viceroy's ADC several years later at an official banquet, responding when he observed that the hotel she was living in was 'nice and quiet at night', that 'I don't like nice, quiet nights, I like a lot going on'. Not that the days were any less dull. The next two days when she was not stuck alone in this deadly dull hotel, cut off from the city, were spent in the visitors' gallery of the legislature. There were a hundred others, all of them old fogeys, listening to one long speech after the other, over thirty of them, beginning with the viceroy reading out the king's message, followed by the Gaekwad of Baroda proposing a royal reply in response to the message and then supported by other ruling princes and delegates in long-winded speeches. Jinnah was among the last to speak, which meant she could not even get away before the end. This was not the stirring political life that she had yearned to share with him, marching side by side, as she had fondly imagined. All in all, it was a 'sad fiasco', as the Bombay governor, Lord Willingdon, later described it, and for the first time Ruttie found herself in agreement with something the governor said.

She had also dreaded going to Delhi so soon after her marriage because of her recent notoriety, thanks to the newspapers. The Parsi and Urdu papers especially were at each other's throats over the marriage—as if it was anyone's business but hers and Jinnah's. Vicious things were being said, especially by the Parsi newspapers. They seemed even more incensed that she had converted to Islam than by the fact that she had dared to disobey her father. Even more offensive was their accusation that Jinnah and even the whole Muslim community had made her convert to Islam as part of a vile conspiracy against the Parsis, as if she was a puppet with no mind and will of her own.

The Muslims weren't thanking her either for her sacrifice. They were particularly outraged by some Parsi newspapers describing her wedding day, a Friday, as 'Black Friday'. An Urdu daily from Lahore, *Paisa Akhbar*, made threatening noises against those who 'dared to attack . . . the Muslim nation, a nation alive among the nations of the world, and the follower of a living religion'. And it more or less disowned J—she had decided to call him 'J' because Jinnah somehow sounded so unfamiliar and unlike the man she loved: 'Mr. Jinnah is not so illustrious and distinguished in the world of Islam that this one action on his part could prove to be a blot on Islam and its blessed horizon would be covered by dark clouds.' And although what the paper said was true—J was hardly Muslim at all except for his strange name—J himself seemed to be taking what they were saying more seriously than she had expected him to. It was all turning so strange and communal and had so little to do with them as two individuals in love.

As for her, the paper suggested in an editorial two days later that she had married Jinnah for his prestige and worldly fame, and had converted to Islam as a way to get this great catch. Under the headline 'A Parsi Baronet's daughter embraces Islam', the editorial said:

> Readers must have come across the news of the renowned Parsi Baronet Sir Dinshaw Petit's only daughter Ruttenbai embracing Islam and marrying the eminent nationalist Muslim Honourable Mohammed Ali Jinnah. Was it the truth and the divineness of Islam, or her love for him (that led to her conversion)? Whatever it was, the event nevertheless created a sensation in the Parsi community. If love has the power to change faith, then it has certainly produced much more magnificent results. In any case, to those liberal-minded people who have acquired materialistic views, religion and customs hardly mean anything. However, it is hoped that Sir Dinshaw and the Parsi community would see the incident in this perspective. Jinnah is a top-ranking advocate, lawyer and a leader of the nationalists and the darling of the Bar of Bombay Presidency, besides being a member of the viceroy's legislative council as the representative of the Muslims

of Bombay Presidency. In other words, there is no doubt in his being a celebrated lawyer. In terms of respect, renown and worldly grace, he could not but be the most deserving candidate for this marriage. The conversion of a renowned Parsi's daughter and her marriage to an eminent Muslim may not be the first incident in the present history of the Bombay Presidency but it is very interesting indeed.

In front of J she could laugh about it, but the tone, at once sneering and patronizing, got under her skin. Worse, she could see by the look in people's eyes that they had read these articles about her and J, and despite her mask of sophisticated indifference, she felt a creeping sense of shame, especially at the way her poor dear Papa's name was being dragged into the whole controversy.

But now, with the Delhi trip out of the way, she could look forward to a month's respite, spending the whole of May alone with J in Nainital. Mahmudabad had offered them his house in the hill station, Galloway House, for their honeymoon and they were going to drive there from Lucknow in a day or two. Mercifully, there was nothing further happening this summer on the political front to distract J's attention.

The month passed quickly, but not in that swell of passion and excitement she had dreamt about. Her life's only goal so far had been the pursuit of her grand passion, but having finally reached it, there had been so far only a sense, surprisingly, of disappointment which she hid even from herself. Having imagined that he was a non-conformist like her concealed behind his staid manner, his need to put his work above everything else, including food and rest, had been a big blow to her. She had yearned to break through the veils of his many self-repressions and discover for herself the real man with all his intense, impassioned longing for love, like herself. But the real J kept eluding her, hidden behind his cool and rational mind, never giving himself up to even a single display of deep emotion. Worse, sex with him was not thrilling, even before the initial novelty wore off.

In her inexperience, it had not occurred to her to make anything of J's long years of celibacy or even his lack of physical demonstrativeness while they were courting. If it had, she would have probably put it down to yet further evidence of his admirable willpower. It was not as if sex was something that could be discussed openly, not even in the girlish confidences she exchanged with Padmaja. The closest she ever got to raising the topic that was uppermost in her mind during her courtship was when she tentatively asked Padmaja if her current admirer was 'better in . . .' than a previous suitor. Even that had filled her with so much embarrassment that she had dropped the question midway.

But now that they were married and J's mask of self-assurance and worldly wisdom had begun to fall off, the man she discovered was not the fierce and passionate lover of her dreams who she thought would burn 'storming passions into the very fibre of her being', but someone altogether more timid and naïve, a child almost—spoilt but brilliant, and touching in his need for her admiration. And intuitively, she scooped him—metaphorically—up into her lap, as if he was really her child. As Kanji Dwarkadas later perceptively put it in his memoir of Ruttie, 'Though she was so much younger than he, she without his realizing it, looked after him.'

It was with this maternal indulgence she began to regard him—forgiving him his stiffness and egotism and his habit of being 'idiotically sensible', able to take his scoffing at her poetry and finer sensibilities sportingly, and keeping her own feelings apart. So what if he didn't really understand her, she could still keep intact the dream she had always nursed of 'pouring love on parched, unlighted souls and through sympathy and understanding' make them blossom, as she had once written to Leilamani. She could still build her 'whole character—(her) whole life' on love, making her personality 'the soul of love and sympathy', letting her 'passionate desire grow into a fair and fragrant flower—so beautiful that it shall draw and command love through its own loveliness'.

And so Jinnah found himself shaken suddenly out of his careful habits, teased and coaxed into abandoning his newspapers for riding and motoring in the countryside. Although he liked both horses and motor cars, the outdoors did not really interest him. He did not share her desire to feast his soul on nature, either for its 'exquisite and fierce grandeur' or to see if it was 'astir with song birds and little insects'. At nights, he had no wish to gaze at the stars and the fireflies; he wanted only to sit indoors with a drink, talking politics with an admirer or two, preferably male. And being a plain-spoken man, he was not afraid to tell her so, bluntly. But nonetheless, he did make an effort, even consenting to be drawn into the garden to plant a sapling as a memento of their love. But he drew the line at responding to the telegrams of congratulation pouring in from his friends on their nuptials. It was a waste of time writing polite nothings, according to him, but she, of course, was free to do as she pleased.

And it did please her to send off these little thank-you notes, just one line filling the whole page in her bold, graceful hand, so casual and un-copybook-like in the liquid ease of letters flowing informally into each other, the words coming easily. 'Dear Mr Syud Mahmud,' she wrote in one, 'This comes to thank you from us both for your wire of good wishes,' signing her new name for the first time: 'R. Jinnah'.

It gave her pride in her new marital status, as did her fussing over his food and appearance, ruling over him with such tender dignity that he became wholly dependent on her without knowing it, trusting in her taste and judgement, his eyes constantly seeking her approval in a way that made her feel both proud and powerful.

But all too soon it was June, and J was set on going back home to Bombay. Like it or not, it was time to face the music back home.

Chapter Eight

~

She knew that it could not be put off forever. Sooner or later, she would have to face her parents. And while she dreaded that first moment of their meeting, at least J would be there at her side, with his reassuring practicality, to smooth over the awkwardness. Although she had hidden away her doubts and misgivings from J, and indeed from her own self, she had faith that things would eventually work out between her father and themselves. Her father's conventionality behind his liberal exterior had enraged her when she lived with him, but now that she had had her own way and married J, she could afford to recollect the many ways he had indulged her throughout her life. She had always been his delight and joy, with him taking immense pride in her beauty and gift of repartee, especially in her love for reading, which he valued even more because he was not a bookish man himself. Her mother, she knew, would come around without difficulty—Lady Petit had always liked J, no matter how hard her husband tried to persuade her otherwise. And now that they were actually married, Ruttie could already see her Mama planning any number of grand saris for her trousseau and the receptions that would be held for them. But her father? Surely he loved her too much to hold on to his anger. Besides, what would be the point of him hanging on to his pride when they'd already been married for five weeks now? But still, as she watched their bags being packed at Galloway House, she simply could not share J's eagerness to return home even before the high court reopened after its summer vacation.

The reason for Jinnah's un-lover–like haste to get back from his honeymoon was the announcement of the Provincial War Conference.

Summoned by the Bombay governor as a follow-up to the Delhi War Conference in April end, it was a further attempt by the government to drum up support for the War, this time from the ruling princes, political leaders and leading citizens of the Bombay Presidency. And Jinnah, despite his failure at the previous conference to squeeze out any political concessions from the government, was just as keen to attend. He refused to believe in the futility of his memoranda and speeches, and in fact he and Ruttie had arrived in Bombay three days before the conference only in order to give him enough time to work out a fresh strategy for striking a bargain with the government on political reforms.

The four weeks in Nainital had been the longest break he had taken from all political activity, at least in the past decade, and having just got back, he had far too much on his mind to worry about his father-in-law's next move. In his usual thorough way, he had made sure that Sir Dinshaw's charge of abducting his daughter would not have a legal leg to stand on if he did decide to pursue them in court. And having plugged all possible loopholes, Jinnah now felt free to focus on the far more engrossing world of politics.

His young deputies in the Home Rule League had been keeping up the political momentum while he was away, with public lectures and even a large political meeting at Shantaram Chawl, where meetings were held when the crowd was larger than 2000. But now that he was back, he was eager to wrest the reins of leadership back into his own hands. On their very first evening back from Nainital, Jinnah decided to preside over a public lecture addressed by Annie Besant, and Ruttie went along with him, glad to put off for another day the dreaded meeting with her parents. And when Jinnah's faithful friend and lieutenant Horniman explained during his vote of thanks how Jinnah would lead a 'political agitation of an unparalleled kind in this country' if the government delayed political reforms any further, she could put her own fluttering fears about her parents aside and give herself over once again to her stirring dream of fighting by J's side for the country's freedom from the British yoke.

It was Jinnah who was the first to come face-to-face with her parents. This was three evenings later at the town hall where the Provincial War Conference was being held. Both Sir Dinshaw and Lady Petit had been invited for it—hand-picked by the governor for their unswerving loyalty to the British. And although both of them had been avoiding going out or meeting anyone since Ruttie's marriage, the War conference was far too important an occasion for Sir Dinshaw to turn down the governor's invitation. It might have occurred to them that they would bump into Jinnah there, but still it was hard to watch him walk in with his usual calm and self-assured demeanour, while they uneasily felt themselves the centre of all eyes in the town hall. But somehow, Sir Dinshaw managed to get through his short speech supporting the resolution on loyalty to the king, as was expected of him, and both the baronet and his lady got through their ordeal with whatever dignity they could muster.

It was much easier for Jinnah. Even if he had been the sort of man to be bruised by the cold looks directed at him, especially from the Parsi invitees, he had more practice ignoring what he did not want to see. Besides, there was far too much happening inside the town hall that evening for him to pay any attention to the personal drama of which he was the centre. There was a political drama unfolding there that held his attention so effectively that nothing else seemed to matter. The governor, Lord Willingdon, opened the proceedings in the hall by directly targeting the Home Rulers. In his speech, he not only questioned the sincerity of these leaders' support to the empire but even warned them that the government would not accept their 'half-hearted' assistance. The Home Rulers did not take this insult lying down. Tilak, who had been listed as one of the first speakers, began to protest against the governor's remark and was rudely interrupted by the governor for straying into what the latter considered 'a political discussion'. Tilak then stormed out of the hall, followed shortly by a fellow legislator, N.C. Kelkar, who was also silenced by the governor for putting forward his views on the resolution. Jinnah's other Home Rule associates, including Horniman, Jamnadas Dwarkadas and Bomanji, also walked out, but he decided to stay even though he was the only Home Rule Leaguer remaining in the hall. His stubborn pride would not allow him to walk out at the end of his speech like the others. Instead, he wanted to stick it out in the hall, facing the hostility directed at him from all sides, and register his protest by abstaining from voting.

The hostility that Jinnah faced inside the town hall from the Parsis spilled outside it as well. At first, it was difficult to tell how much of their sudden animosity towards him was because of his daring to snatch a Parsi girl of their top circle from under her father's nose and convert her to Islam; and how much of it had to do with his aggressive anti-government stance. All that was evident in the beginning was that the Parsis suddenly closed ranks and vociferously supported the governor's attack against Jinnah and his Home Rule League. Two days after the War conference, Bombay's leading Parsi, Sir Jamsetjee Jeejeebhoy organized a public meeting calling people to subscribe to the second Indian War loan, which Jinnah and other members of the Home Rule League boycotted as a protest against their treatment at the conference.

But the Parsis' ploy of banding together behind the governor and helping him bring down Jinnah didn't really work. The newspapers, especially the *Bombay Chronicle*, not only took his side against the governor, but he was projected on public platforms as the only leader who had the courage to stay back in the town hall after the other Home Rule Leaguers had walked out in order to 'throw into His Excellency's face the insult which he had thrown at them'. It ended up turning Jinnah into more of a public hero than he already was.

It was with this pleasant rush from his latest political triumph that the newly-weds finally met Sir Dinshaw. Contrary to Ruttie's expectations, they had not been invited to Petit Hall. Instead, they were summoned to court to answer a fresh charge her father had clapped on Jinnah. His daughter, he claimed in a fresh suit, had been abducted by Jinnah with a mercenary eye on her fortune.

Nothing could have offended Jinnah more deeply. He who had always prided himself on being a self-made millionaire, to be accused of being nothing but a common fortune hunter! Now certainly there could be no reconciliation with her family. He would be only too glad to cut himself away from them forever and they, and everyone else, would see how he could keep his wife in the style that she had been accustomed to.

Ruttie's feelings were more chaotic. Her father's appearance was a rude shock. She couldn't help but see that her Papa had aged visibly in the last five weeks. All his bonhomie had vanished, replaced with a bitter, defeated look that made him appear at least twenty years older than J. But she avoided his eye as she focused on what the judge was asking Jinnah: did he abduct Ruttie Petit from her father's home? And with a bold defiance that smote Sir Dinshaw even more than her elopement, she jumped impetuously to Jinnah's defence. 'Sir,' she said with that fierce protectiveness she had already developed for her J, 'Mr Jinnah has not abducted me; in fact I have abducted him.' Sir Dinshaw never forgot her words or her expression. His beloved daughter had just demolished the legal case he had taken such pains to put together for her rescue. But more heartbreakingly, she had chosen Jinnah over him. It was all over now, except for getting her to sign the legal papers renouncing her claims on her inheritance.

Ruttie was beyond noticing her Papa's hurt and disappointment. When she had rushed so recklessly to her husband's defence, Jinnah had been surprised like everyone else in the courtroom. But when he heard her words, he could not help smiling. Seeing that rare, sweet smile of his that she loved more than anything else in the world, nothing else seemed to matter. She had never before, not even when she walked out of Petit Hall with only her umbrella, felt so brave and noble and fearless. It was all worth it—yes, even cutting herself away from her Papa and Mama, who had never understood her.

But what neither she nor Jinnah seemed to realize—united now in their rage at Ruttie's Papa's unreasonableness and his stupid pride— was Sir Dinshaw's own compulsions. Their marriage, especially her conversion to Islam, had not just been a personal family problem but had put the entire Parsi community on the warpath. Sir Dinshaw was suddenly faced not just with the hostility of the orthodox and the less well-to-do, which he could, and had, ignored in the past. But this new belligerence of theirs was very different. Regardless of the fact that he had vehemently opposed his daughter's marriage and had even gone to court against Jinnah to prove it publicly, they were now screaming for his head in exchange for the couple's. Even his most anglicized friends and relatives, instead of rallying behind him, were quietly joining the witch-hunt. It left him with no real choice: it was either cutting off his daughter and Jinnah from his life and will or subjecting himself, his wife and sons to an excommunication from the community. This was the gun being held to his head, and the real cause of his anger and sorrow.

The protests had begun the previous month. On 26 May, before Ruttie and Jinnah returned from their honeymoon in Nainital, a few priests from the fire temples of Bombay gathered at the main Parsi cathedral, the Dadi Seth fire temple on Agiari Lane. It was a solemn occasion as befitted the gravity of the situation. The chief priest of Bombay, Shams-ul-Ulma Dastur Dorab Peshotan Sanjana, was voted chair of the meeting.

Although it was held on a Sunday and no outsiders were invited, the meeting of the Parsi priests—'to express its disapprobation of marriages of Parsi women with non-Parsis'—was widely reported, including for the first time by the British-run *Times of India*. And even though the names of Jinnah and Ruttie did not figure in the meeting, it was perfectly clear to all newspaper readers, especially the English-reading ones, who the priests were actually targeting: 'In opening the proceedings,' as the *Times of India*'s report said, 'the chairman stated that during the past few months the Parsi community had been greatly grieved by marriages of Parsi girls with non-Parsis . . . and this feeling of grief was particularly noticeable among the priestly class of the community.'

But the priests were not prepared to stop at merely condemning these marriages. Sensing that the moment was ripe for bringing the community back to the basics, they advocated a sweeping change in the lifestyle of their elite, especially in the way they were raising their daughters: 'Unions such as these were to be highly deprecated in the interests of the community,' the chief priest declared, 'and he exhorted Parsi parents not to allow their daughters to mix with non-Parsis until they had received sufficient instructions according to the tenets of the Zoroastrian religion.' Few could have missed the message behind the priestly injunction: Parsi girls, out of purdah for almost a century, were to be put back under the same restraints as girls from other communities. They were to be deprived of their English tutors and dancing teachers, their riding and shopping trips and garden parties, and even the Willingdon Club. It was nothing short of being told to lock up their daughters at home until they were safely married in the old, arranged way.

Other preventive measures were discussed with equal solemnity. One resolution that was passed unanimously by the priests addressed what they had long felt was the root of the whole problem: the neglect of religious indoctrination by the more anglicized Parsis. The resolution, moved by Dastur Dinsha J. Garda, after condemning marriages of Parsis with non-Parsis, 'and particularly marriages of Parsi girls with non-Parsis', called upon the Parsi community 'to give their children religious instructions and to teach them to follow in the footsteps of their great forebears who had left their mark on their ancient history'.

The second resolution laid down the punishment to be meted out to the guilty. And for the first time, the priests set down a severe penalty not just for the girl who had dared to marry outside the community, but her parents as well, holding them equally culpable in her crime. In the resolution the priests issued a warning to the parents of such girls, threatening to excommunicate them, along with their daughter if they tried to reconcile with their daughter or even continued to 'stay with or keep a close relationship with such a woman' after her marriage. In such a case, no Parsi priest would be allowed to perform any religious ceremony for them, including the death rites, according to the resolution.

That was only the beginning. The meeting of the priests in Bombay, although thinly attended, was so widely publicized that Parsi panchayats in other towns such as Deolali held similar meetings supporting the priests' resolutions. In fact, the press coverage of the meeting, especially by the Parsi-owned newspapers *Kaiser-e-Hind* and *Jam-e-Jamshed*, was so intensive that nearly every man in the community was soon persuaded to believe that it was his religious duty to stop 'these sort of marriages which do harm to the Parsi community'.

Encouraged by the popular response to their call, the priests held another meeting of their clan, much larger than the one held in the Dady Seth fire temple. The priests at the first meeting, although they had been severe in their condemnation, had carefully couched their injunctions as mere recommendations to the community. They could not forget that they were, after all, dependent on these fabulously rich Parsis, who had in the past bribed their way into being permitted to bring their foreign brides into the fire temples. But now, after the relentless press campaign, they felt more emboldened. This time they decided to crack the whip on those in their own profession who might be tempted to cooperate with their rich clients. Besides barring a priest from performing any religious ceremony for the erring girl or her near relatives who refused to disown her, even priests who unknowingly ended up at a Parsi home where the culprit was present would be severely punished, they declared in a new resolution. 'If you find in this gathering a Parsi who has married a non-Parsi or even her husband or both are present,' the resolution said, 'then the priest should not perform the ceremony and should get up and leave.' And the penalty for neglecting to do so? Excommunication, of course.

Nothing seemed to appease the priests or the community at large. Even Sir Dinshaw's unusually bold step of publicly disowning his daughter and son-in-law in a courtroom could not mollify them. Now the people began to press for a general public meeting of the whole community where the issue could be thrashed out. It was a rare thing, to hold a meeting of the Zoroastrian Anjuman, the entire adult male population of Parsis in Bombay. No one could remember when such a meeting had last been held, not even when a new member of the panchayat's board of trustees was elected to replace someone who had just died. But the situation now seemed to demand it—or at least that was what the head of the Parsi panchayat, Sir Jamsetjee Jeejeebhoy, thought.

A first cousin of Lady Petit's and inheritor of her father's baronetcy and estates, the fifth Sir Jamsetjee was no friend of the Petits. There was, in fact, an intense rivalry between the two baronets fighting for the coveted post of president of the Parsi panchayat's board of trustees. The rivalry had begun during the lifetime of the fourth Sir Jamsetjee, Lady Petit's uncle and successor to her father's baronetcy. Sir Dinshaw had filed a legal case against him as far back as 1906 (the same case in which he had championed the rights of R.D. Tata to marry an outsider according to Parsi rites and allow her to enter the fire temple as a convert to Zoroastrianism), challenging Sir Jamsetjee's right to head the Parsi panchayat's board of trustees as if it was an inherited right. By the time the case was settled, in 1908, the fourth Sir Jamsetjee was dead and his son had taken his place as president of the panchayat's board of trustees. And while it was Sir Dinshaw who won the case in principle, Sir Jamsetjee never vacated the chair because he was in any case acknowledged by all Parsis as their pre-eminent leader, with or without a proper election. After that their relations were anything but cordial.

And now this interloper cousin-in-law was taking the initiative in calling a public meeting to humiliate him further.

But Sir Jamsetjee was not wrong about the public anger against his niece's marriage. Around 8500 Parsis had signed up for calling a meeting of the community. For such a large gathering assembled at the venue, there were not enough chairs, leaving only standing room for many in the crowd. There was utter pandemonium, with many people wanting to speak at the same time. After trying to force order, Sir Jamsetjee finally adjourned the meeting. But the crowd left only after he promised that he would call a meeting of the general body of the panchayat, which would take measures to prevent such marriages in the future and to mete out fitting punishment to the culprits.

Sir Jamsetjee kept his promise. He accordingly sent out a requisition notice to be signed by all the members of the panchayat's board of trustees, summoning a meeting of the panchayat. Except Sir Dinshaw, all the trustees signed the notice, including the latter's cousin, Jehangir Petit.

It was even worse than what Sir Dinshaw had feared: to the last man, they agreed that it was their duty to stop marriages like Ruttie's. They declared her excommunicated and stripped her and her unborn children of all rights as Parsis, and warned that 'under no circumstances should she be allowed to enter the Parsi community again'. This included banning her from Parsi 'weddings, navjots and social occasions'. And as if that was not disgrace enough, the panchayat ordered that their resolutions be circulated to all Parsi communities across India to be held up as a warning to other Parsi parents and their daughters.

Never before in the history of the Parsis had there been such a savage witch-hunt. And yet, great care had been exercised both in the deliberations of the priests and the community to never once directly mention the names of either Ruttie or Jinnah. But stripped of its more civilized veneer, the impact was similar to medieval sanctions: the newly-weds may just as well have been paraded naked on the streets with their heads shaved for their crime of marrying for love.

Chapter Nine

~

Outwardly, Ruttie gave no sign of the humiliation she was undergoing. She resolutely ignored her extensive family of relatives and friends, avoiding the places where she was likely to meet them. The Willingdon Club, of course, being predominantly Parsi, was now enemy territory. Likewise, Jinnah resigned from the Orient Club, the only club he had ever belonged to, where he used to go occasionally to play billiards or meet his friends. While the Orient Club, a gentlemen's club, was not a Parsi ghetto like the Willingdon, it was still predominantly made up of Parsis, including her own uncle, and it became yet another place for the Parsis to show their hostility to him. In fact, the Parsis' hate campaign against them had become so widespread that for the first time in his life, Jinnah could find no one prepared to propose his name when he applied for membership of the Western India Turf Club. And Ruttie could not join even the Ladies Gymkhana, which was again run mostly by the Parsi women of her mother's circle.

The women, especially the younger girls, hated her even more than the men. They were now all coming under pressure, including the Willingdon Club set, just because of what she had done. With the orthodox Parsis attacking them on all sides, the anglicized Parsis had become defensive about their lifestyle, especially the way they were bringing up their daughters. There was even some talk of girls being forcibly pulled out of school and forbidden to step outside their homes. Whether or not any of these strictures would actually have been enforced, Ruttie and Jinnah found nearly all Parsi doors shutting on them. And those few loyal friends Jinnah still had among the Parsis did not let it be known abroad that they were still friends with him. As for Ruttie, she refused to go anywhere where she might bump into one of her parents' circle—which was nearly everyone who was anyone in Bombay.

She could have, of course, done what K.L. Gauba's wife, Husna, did two years after her, when she too found herself isolated by even the so-called cosmopolitan circles of Lahore, where they lived, on account of her Hindu–Muslim marriage. That is, set herself up aggressively and systematically as a popular society hostess whose invitations were so sought after that no one with social pretensions could afford to ignore her, no matter what they privately thought of her. But that was a survival strategy beyond Ruttie's capacity or even inclination, given her sheltered background and wrapped up as she was in Jinnah, wanting to belong in his world, uncaring, unaware even, of what it could do to her, to be banished thus from everything she had known so far.

For Jinnah, it did not matter that much, in fact, it even worked to his advantage. Far from upsetting his rather grandiose notion of himself, it only enhanced his image as a role model for progressive Indians, with the courage to take on a whole community's wrath to marry whom he desired. With a pride everyone considered more than justifiable, he declared publicly, on the floor of the legislative council, that Indians like him, modern and English educated, 'cannot simply sit quiet' while a community 'outcasts him or her for marrying outside their caste'. While he was indeed the epitome of the admirably progressive Indian, fighting for his right, and of others like him, to choose his own mate, it did not seem to occur to him that somehow it was Ruttie who was paying the price. After being worshipped as 'the Blue Flower' of Bombay, the admired and envied debutante of her generation, she had turned overnight into the city's most notorious outcaste.

It was true that Jinnah wasn't given to divining other people's emotions, and especially not his own bride's. But even the most perceptive of Ruttie's friends found it impossible to penetrate her lively, self-confident exterior and discover what she actually felt. She seemed to be as airily unperturbed by the Parsi panchayat's excommunication order as she was by her mother's total withdrawal. Perhaps following orders from her husband, Lady Petit had made no move so far to get in touch with Ruttie. Quite apart from his rage at his daughter's rebellion, Sir Dinshaw was afraid of making matters worse by inviting the community's wrath on his own head, or jeopardize his three sons' future by seeming to support Ruttie in secret. But whatever turmoil Ruttie might have been undergoing inwardly, she who had so far never left the protection of her powerful family circle even for a single day, faced the world now with a pride that matched Jinnah's, stubbornly refusing to play the victim.

In fact, even the one member of her family who did meet her went away without a clue to her inner distress. This was her brother Fali, the future baronet. Just a year apart in age, they shared the same high spirits that made them the life and soul of every party. They had been very close but now it was as if an invisible wall had suddenly sprung up between them. In later years their close resemblance, both in temperament and tastes, became more apparent—that same puckish sense of humour and impetuosity and generous instinct, the compulsive need to prick the bubble of the pompous and the vainglorious, and bring them down to earth, the love for dogs and books and all things exquisite, especially jade, and above all, an almost divine unconsciousness of money that only the very rich can have. But at seventeen, Fali was still unformed and more important, dependent on his father. For Ruttie, the leader of their childhood escapades and games of Three Musketeers, what could be more natural and gallant than to let him go on believing that all was well with her. At any rate, he was not going to remain at home for much longer, only waiting for the War to end so that he could go up to Cambridge, as his father had planned for him. Till then, they did keep in touch, however brief and covert these meetings might have been, and he must have surely come to bid her goodbye before leaving for Cambridge, for two years later, he makes a brief appearance in one of her letters. 'By the bye,' Ruttie wrote to Leilamani in a letter dated 18 April 1920, on a frivolous note, 'since you [intend] to marry him some day in the near future, it might interest you to know that Fali is leaving for England.'

It wasn't just Fali who was fooled by her response to her excommunication. She maintained such careless indifference in the face of the new indignities that she ended up shocking her acquaintances instead of winning their sympathy. And when she scoffed at the Parsi community and its absurd, childish prejudices, boasting gaily of wanting to 'wake it up', they mistook it for flightiness, hating her even more because it could have so easily been one of them in her place.

It would have been easier perhaps, especially in those first heady months of her freedom, if she had something to take her mind away from what she was going through. Perhaps then the insults would not have rankled so much. Why should she care so much that she and Jinnah were the only ones of their large circle of acquaintances not to be invited for a navjot dinner in the home of a family friend. Or mind that her aunt and cousins and grandmother, in spite of living right next door, had neither called nor invited them over. If only there had been more to do . . .

But there was so little happening at South Court. The house ran on well-oiled wheels, managed by the indispensable 'Visan', Jinnah's valet, accountant, bearer and housekeeper rolled into one, who had been with him since his earliest days in Bombay and knew exactly how to cater to his master's comforts. Jinnah 'had only to instruct Visan so many guests were to come for lunch or dinner on so and so date', according to one biographer, G. Allana, 'and he would make all the necessary arrangements'. Not the least of Visan's invaluable assets was, according to another biographer, Rizwan Ahmad, that 'he knew where every file and book was kept'. The cook, too, must have been around for years, considering how little his master required of him in terms of meals, and that too of the boiled and bland variety.

But he was a conscientious husband, punctiliously handing over the reins of the household to her, and determined not to question her on how she ran it and what changes she wanted to make, however perturbed he was inwardly by her extravagance. He had resolved to give her a free hand and he would not go back on it, no matter how shocked he was to see her throw away vast sums of money so casually on inessentials. Nor did he ever betray his feelings to her or anyone else, not by a word or gesture.

He gave up his old bachelor habits as well. When his sister Fatima had lived with him, as she had done for the last eight years since she passed out of her convent boarding school, he had come home as late as he pleased. Apart from having breakfast with Fatima and driving her to his other married sister Shirin's home on his way to the courts, Jinnah had not felt obliged to spend any time with her. He did not frequent the Bar Gymkhana like his other colleagues, wasting his time drinking and playing poker and bridge. But he loved to linger late in his chambers, talking to those of his young admirers who dropped in for a chat. He would willingly interrupt a legal conference with a client if one of them dropped in unexpectedly and seldom returned home from his chambers until late in the night, especially in the last two years when his political activity had outstripped his legal work.

And even when he did spend the evening at home, he was accustomed to retreat to his library with his newspapers. His sister was content to be left to her own resources, or at least rarely complained. And except for occasionally slamming a door or locking herself into her room in a sulk, she seldom demanded his attention.

But now he began to return home early, looking forward to spending the evening alone with Ruttie. But she missed going to the theatre and clubs, and it felt strange having no plans for the evening other than sitting down quietly with him over a drink while he pored over his newspapers. She had never before come across someone as devoted to the newspapers as Jinnah. In the first flush of home improvement, she had redone the room that Jinnah used as his library, stocking it with rare books and priceless first editions that made it a personal library any gentleman could be proud of. Jinnah had paid the bills without a murmur but he barely glanced at the new books she had added to his shelves. He had no time to spare from his newspaper reading.

If it was anyone else, she would have probably despised him for reading nothing else. It was like those diligent Indians who struggled to master the English language by poring over a newspaper, the sort of people who bought the *Aids to Newspaper Reading*, a popular dictionary of newspaper words—'choice words, phrases, idioms and proverbs as well as Latin and other foreign expressions'—that was forever being advertised in the *Bombay Chronicle*. Even her father, who never claimed to be a reading man, was acquainted with the major English poets and novelists, but Jinnah, in his blunt, honest way refused to pay even lip service to them. It both amused and exasperated her as she watched him come home every evening to sit down with his pile of newspapers, like a little boy poring over his stamp collection. He subscribed to everything, from the London *Times* to remote provincial newspapers and gazetteers, which he read from the first page to the last, not missing even the ads. And after that, instead of throwing the old newspapers out, he kept them aside to cut out items from them, which he then annotated and stuck into books. She did not have the heart to tell him how lonely she had begun to feel.

She had almost no one to talk to all day long. Sarojini was the only friend they shared in common but the poetess-orator was missing from Bombay all through those early months. Sarojini's second career as a popular political speaker was just taking off in that year and she had embarked on an extensive speaking tour across India, which took her from Madras to Sind, then to Baluchistan and Punjab. And when she did eventually return to her hotel suite in the Taj Mahal hotel, she was far too busy brokering peace between the leaders of the Congress to spend more than a hurried hour or two with Ruttie in her hotel suite and that too with dozens of other friends always dropping in.

Neither were Sarojini's two daughters available to her at this crucial time. Padmaja and Leilamani would have certainly helped her to cope with the current isolation from her own family and relatives, but they had been packed off from home once again, this time to a boarding school in Mussoorie, instead of Panchgani. At seventeen and a half, Padmaja's parents considered her as yet too young to be running a home for her father in Sarojini's absence and it was decided that she would go back to a boarding school at least until the War was over and a decision could be taken whether to send her abroad to college, or let her remain in Hyderabad as she wanted.

It was not as if the Parsi social boycott had isolated Ruttie completely. There were her friends from the princely set, for example. Or Kshama Row, a girl of her own age and from the same affluent background, but married several years before her and already the mother of a young daughter. They had many friends in common, including Padmaja and Leilamani, and shared the same tastes in travel and literature. Like Ruttie, Kshama too wanted to make something more of her life than merely run a fashionable home and raise children. She aspired, in fact, to be a writer of plays and novels, an ambition she was not afraid of telling her friends about, much to their amusement. The friendship had been sustained so far by Kshama's unalloyed admiration for Ruttie's beauty and style and wit, and on Ruttie's part by a good-humoured tolerance for her friend's conceits. But now with the balance of power suddenly shifting, Ruttie felt even less inclined to seek Kshama's company.

Instead, she decided to throw herself fully into Jinnah's life, determined to make it 'in all its aspects, pleasant, carefree and well worth living', as Kanji writes. It was a struggle. She took charge of planning his meals, but Jinnah found no joy in food, eating sparingly and sometimes not at all. Coming from Petit Hall, where every meal including breakfast was a multi-cuisine feast, this was difficult for her to take. When he was a baby, Jinnah's mother had agonized over his refusal to eat and although he had outgrown that phase and even cultivated a taste for roast beef and apple pie while he was in England, for the most part, he didn't care if he didn't eat at all. It was the least important thing in his life. Dinner or lunch would be announced but if he was busy in a discussion or dictating a letter, he took no notice. If he was reminded that the food was getting cold, he would politely reply: 'Just a few minutes more.' Or, 'Go and start and I shall join you in a little while.' But the little while often turned into a long while, and Ruttie had to coax and tease him into joining her at the table. And even when he did come to the table, it was impossible for Ruttie to tempt him into eating more than the quota he had fixed for himself. It was difficult even to make him try anything new.

It was even harder to change his reclusive habits. For Ruttie, who had rarely sat down for a meal in her previous life without at least a few guests at the table, it seemed unthinkable not to have people over at South Court. But Jinnah was at first adamant. He had long ago cut out all unnecessary socializing as a way of disciplining himself for his political destiny. There was no form of socializing that he did not consider unnecessary, including the garden parties and at-homes— the glittering outdoor and indoor receptions with live music and entertainment that fashionable Indians called by these misnomers. There were others, especially busy professionals like Sarojini's husband, Dr Naidu, who complained of whole days and even weeks being swallowed up by an endless round of breakfast, lunch, tea and dinner parties, music parties, theatre and picnic outings, at-homes and visits to each other's houses, not to speak of weddings and other festivities. It seemed as if nobody in the fashionable India of the new century ever went to bed at all, let alone do any work. But few dared go against the social trend except for Jinnah. He stoutly refused to either entertain or be entertained, not caring if he was called a miser by almost everyone he knew.

He even refused to call on anyone unless it was for work, even if the person was a close colleague who happened to be sick or dying. Because, as he explained to some of his youthful acolytes, 'if he took to visiting the sick and ailing once, he would have to devote most of his time to this duty and would not have enough hours in which to do his important work'. One of these admirers, M.A.H. Ispahani, was 'rudely shocked and tongue-tied' when he first heard Jinnah expounding such views, but was nevertheless awestruck by his idol's 'inexhaustible store of will power': 'Once he decided on a course of action, no persuasion would detract him from that course. If, for example, he decided to go somewhere, or not to take more than a quantity of food or other refreshment, no amount of persuasion and no temptation would wring a change in his resolve. He had so disciplined himself that he could, without stress and strain, resist all temptations and pleading.'

But Ruttie's coaxing and her subtle rearrangement of his life began to have some effect. Jinnah yielded but without actually giving up his principles. She wisely did not attempt to throw parties in the conventional sense of the term, certainly not the lavish extravaganzas of her mother's set, with music and dancing that he would have abhorred. Nor did she try to impose her own friends on him, knowing that apart from Sarojini and her daughters, none of them would be able to hold their own in a political discussion, which was the only dinner conversation that Jinnah could tolerate at his own table.

But she could, and did, collect a select list of guests that would be welcome in South Court. They were either his young associates or an occasional visitor from out of town like Motilal Nehru or the Raja of Mahmudabad. Jinnah's notion of entertaining so far had been to have a couple of his male friends over for an informal meal so that they could sit up until the early hours of the morning discussing politics over drinks and cigarettes, undistracted by the presence of ladies or the ceremonies of a splendid, multi-course dinner.

And now that she was there to arrange things for him, she began to not only invite his friends but also his young political associates in the Home Rule League, keeping it deliberately casual by renaming these gatherings as 'potluck'. She took care to invite only two or three of them at a time, issuing her invitations in her own handwriting, asking them to 'come and dine with us—quietly—perhaps another friend or two'.

Rarely were her invitations turned down. They looked forward to meeting Jinnah in his own home but it was she who dazzled them. Jinnah was adored no doubt, but they could always meet him in his chamber where they were welcome at any time. But an invitation to South Court meant spending a few hours in the company of Mrs Jinnah. For the young men especially, who came singly, even those few who were married, Ruttie was a source of the utmost fascination. They were mesmerized, not just by her beauty and style and charming informality but because they had never before come across a young and beautiful woman from the highest society who could stay awake all night discussing politics with them in a haze of cigarette smoke and alcohol. All of them went away a little in love with her, and at least one of them—Kanji Dwarkadas—was enthralled for life.

But she had eyes for no one other than Jinnah. To see him as he sat there—at his relaxed best, stretching out his long legs as he made a telling point; to catch him in one of those rare moods when he talked in a personal way, hearing him recount anecdotes from the past with his dry, sharp wit and dramatic flair, to listen with everyone else, with the same rapt attention, as he held forth on politics, demonstrating his quick grasp of political intricacies—was to fall in love again with the J she used to know before her marriage. And they both were at their best at these small gatherings—she, because she never felt so cherished by him than when he included her in his political plans, listening to her in all seriousness and good-humouredly taking the way she teased and pulled his leg in front of their guests. It gave her a secret sense of her own power over him, able to say aloud to him all the irreverent things that no one had dared to say to him before. The young men certainly were awestruck by the liberties she took with the great man famed for his haughtiness and reserve. And Jinnah too blossomed under her adoring attention, with his conversations at the dinner table becoming a virtuoso performance. She was seldom so happy as when there were one or two friends present and she could show how happily married they were.

Her other innovations in his life did not go down so well—not so much with him personally, but in the eyes of the censorious world outside South Court. She had taken to dropping in at his chambers every evening so that they could drive back home together. It was a harmless thing as far as she and even Jinnah were concerned. Everyone in England was doing it—in fact, after motor cars had taken over from carriages, the women drove themselves, 'returning triumphantly with their husbands by their sides', as the newspapers put it. Ruttie had not learnt to drive, but it was just as much fun to go to Jinnah's office in their chauffeur-driven car and come back with him, sitting side by side on the back seat with the top pulled down. It was the one thing Jinnah didn't baulk at, not letting his ever-present rationality get in the way. He didn't see the harm in it, and in fact prided himself on taking her everywhere with him.

But others didn't think the same way, especially Jinnah's colleagues in the court. They had never heard of any wife, let alone one as striking as Ruttie, walking in unannounced into her husband's office. And it shocked them even more that Jinnah of all men, with his reputation of being a 'lion of the court' should say nothing to put a stop to it, especially when she walked in while Jinnah was in the middle of a conference with a solicitor and other lawyers.

Even the most progressive youth of this legal circle, M.C. Chagla, who at this stage was very much under Jinnah's spell, considering him his 'beau ideal both in politics and law', disapproved of what he construed as Mrs Jinnah's very provocative conduct. 'I remember her walking into Jinnah's chambers while we were in the midst of a conference,' Chagla later wrote in his memoir, *Roses in December*, 'dressed in a manner which would be called fast even by modern standards, perch herself upon Jinnah's table, dangling her feet, and waiting for Jinnah to finish the conference so that they could leave together.'

Any husband ought to have been enraged at such 'uninhibited' behaviour, according to Chagla, but to his astonishment, Jinnah showed absolutely no reaction. 'He never uttered a word of protest, and carried on with his work as if she was not there at all,' Chagla recounted, adding: 'One can well imagine how the patience of a man of Jinnah's temper must have been taxed.'

But in truth it had not occurred to Jinnah to be ashamed of anything Ruttie did, and certainly not where her clothes were concerned. He trusted her judgement on aesthetic matters so implicitly that he had even surrendered himself into her hands for a thorough makeover.

She not only insisted on him getting a sleek new haircut, but also got rid of the woollen suits with the stiff collars and cravat that was still the trend, especially in the older generation. She picked out new jackets for him, made of light silk and worn open-necked without the constricting bow tie, which suited his slim, graceful form to perfection. It was a subtle change she worked on him, understanding his need to impress as well as escape the contempt of the British by outdoing them in sartorial elegance. It ended up lending him a new air of easy and graceful informality, much admired by British and Indians alike. 'Nobody knew how much Jinnah owed in this matter to Ruttie,' as Kanji was to write later.

Her own style, however, sprang from a different way of looking at the world. With her upbringing and self-assurance, she had none of his need to impress. She dressed as the new generation in England was learning to dress—'creating ever new and fantastic styles and imagery of their own with which to astonish the world and amuse themselves'. In her own circle, it was a style much admired, making her 'the daintiest, naughtiest, darlingest of the swish set, smarter than them all'. But it did not go down so well in the eyes of Jinnah's conservative circle of acquaintances, both British and Indian.

She had evolved by now her own unique style, combining Indian dress with the latest fashion from England, producing an effect so striking and aesthetic that nearly everyone in her previous circle of friends and female acquaintances had tried to copy her clothes. But it was a difficult style to imitate, needing a sense of immense self-assurance to carry it off. Her saris were no different from what every fashionable Indian girl of her age wore or at least coveted—gossamer-thin gauze in rainbow hues. The fabric was even more transparent than what women of Lady Petit's generation wore at the beginning of the new century—diaphanous chiffons and georgettes with intricately embroidered borders stitched on to it.

Although Ruttie would have hated to admit it, her style was, in fact, an extension of her mother's taste, rather than a departure from it. Both were discriminating in what they wore, shunning loud colours and anything elaborate or fussy. Rutty had an even more refined horror of anything flashy, especially gold zari work. And for this reason, she refused to buy anything off the shelves, believing that it was only possible to get the right sari by ordering it from the traders who came home with their tin trunks. She was prepared to wait for months for the sari to be specially woven for her in the plain, pastel colours she preferred, 'without vulgar tinsel marring it'. And among her friends, including Padmaja, her taste in clothes was considered so exquisite that they trusted her to buy their saris for them without even going along with her. 'Regarding your saris,' Ruttie wrote to Padmaja in a letter dated only 3 March (no year is mentioned), 'It is difficult to get the kind of thing that you would like. A friend of mine sent me a very beautiful purple shot a couple of days ago—it was on sale as having ordered it she didn't care for it when it came. It was ruined by some vulgar tinsel worked all over the surface, and as it was not a thing that I would have chosen for myself, I didn't select it for you. I suppose you know that most of my saris are made to order. Sometimes however it happens that the sariwallas have some really pretty things. But at present for some reason or other their trade is very slack and they have hardly any stock worth mentioning . . . Trust me however to do the best I can for you.'

Her blouses were also part of the new style much admired by the younger set. Parsi women of Lady Petit's generation imitated the English memsahibs' dress as closely as they could, adapting it creatively to suit Indian norms. Careful not to embarrass their English hostesses by baring too much flesh, fashionable Parsi women of Ruttie's mother's generation wore their chiffon saris with long-sleeved, waist-length European-style blouses. They thought nothing, for example, of paying 10 or 15 pounds for a trendy Parisian blouse which would anyway be hidden behind their sari folds. The style was universally regarded as 'Parsi'. But for most of the younger set of Indians among the top circles, there was nothing so 'hideous', as Vijaya Lakshmi Pandit described these Victorian blouses worn with saris. Instead, they dared to tailor their blouses in a new style that had become all the rage, close-fitting and cut low in the back and front, in imitation of the neckline which was the current fashion in wartime London but passed off as 'Indian' wear.

But the new style, while it had caught the fancy of the younger set, had not yet invaded the official set. The wives of British officials were especially shocked by the new trend. Of course, it was another matter altogether how much their disapproval had to do with their own racial prejudice, their 'silliness', as Bolitho puts it, undoing the good work of their husbands 'and responsible for our losing India'. After all, even twenty years before Ruttie made the Indian blouse a fashion statement, there was Lady Curzon writing home about one 'huge lady' at a purdah party in Hyderabad who 'amused us' in her 'green plush trousers, and above her waist was a broad expanse of nakedness, then a short transparent green lace coat, and over all a transparent gauze sari. So very little was left to the imagination . . .'

However, the English memsahibs were not the only ones to be shocked at Ruttie's daring dress. She created even more ripples among the conservative Muslims who considered her way of dressing as that of a 'fast woman'. Especially provoked were the 'bearded Moulvies and Maulanas' who formed an important part of Jinnah's political world. Chagla recounts an incident at Globe Cinema where a Muslim League conference was being held. When Ruttie walked in and took her seat on the platform meant for VIPs, Chagla writes: 'The hall was full of bearded Moulvies and Maulanas and they came to me in great indignation, and asked me who that woman was. They demanded that she should be asked to leave, as the clothes she flaunted constituted an offence to Islamic eyes.'

But instead of toning down her dress, Ruttie seemed to take a mischievous pleasure in provoking people further. Barely a month into her marriage, she made a dramatic entry into the Viceregal Lodge in Simla wearing her usual short, sleeveless choli under a transparent sari. Far from being intimidated by the disapproving stares, she took further liberties by refusing to curtsey to the viceroy, according to the protocol. Instead, she folded her hands in the Indian custom after shaking hands with him. Lord Chelmsford did not let the insult go unremarked. 'Immediately after dinner the A.D.C. asked Ruttie to come and talk to the Viceroy. Lord Chelmsford pompously told her: "Mrs Jinnah, your husband has a great political future, you must not spoil it . . . In Rome you must do as the Romans do." Mrs Jinnah's immediate retort was: "That is exactly what I did, Your Excellency. In India, I greeted you in the Indian way."' According to Aziz Beg, author of *Jinnah and His Times*, 'That was the first and the last time she met Lord Chelmsford.'

Several years later, another viceroy's wife, Lady Reading, left a sharp portrait of her first impression of Ruttie: 'In those days,' writes Lady Reading in a letter to a friend, 'Jinnah was . . . an object of

interest because of his startlingly beautiful wife . . . He came to lunch
with his wife. Very pretty, a complete minx . . . She is a Parsi and he
a Mohammedan (their marriage convulsed both communities). She
had less on in the day time than anyone I have ever seen. A tight dress
brocade cut to waist back and front, no sleeves, and over it and her
head flowered chiffon as a sari.' And in another letter: 'Her attire
was a liberty scarf, a jewelled bandeau and an emerald necklace. She
is extremely pretty, fascinating, terribly made up. All the men rave
about her, the women sniffed.'

Jinnah himself found nothing wrong with either her way of
dressing or what he regarded as her high spirits. It was, after all, her
vivacity and impish sense of fun that had so attracted him to her in
the first place. Nor did anyone dare to bring her conspicuity to his
notice. He was known to take offence easily and withdraw into a
cold silence that could last a lifetime. In the court, for example, his
cold war with Strangman, a barrister 'with a strong notion of his
own superiority both as a lawyer and an Englishman' was almost
legendary. As retaliation against an insult dealt by Strangman, Jinnah
not only refused to ever speak to him again but refused to enter his
chambers even for legal work. And when the two enemies appeared
in court, young lawyers went to see the 'fun'. As Chagla recounts,
'There would invariably be a scene in court with the poor judge trying
to pacify these two great lions of the court.'

It was eventually the governor's wife, Lady Willingdon, who
belled the cat, so to speak. 'The story,' as Jinnah's biographer Hector
Bolitho writes, 'is that Mrs Jinnah wore a low-cut dress that did not
please her hostess. While they were seated at the dining table, Lady
Willingdon asked an ADC to bring a wrap for Mrs Jinnah, in case
she felt cold.'

Jinnah's response was characteristic: 'He is said to have risen and
said, "When Mrs Jinnah feels cold, she will say so, and ask for a wrap
herself." Then he led his wife from the dining room, and from that
time, refused to go to Government House again.'

But the incident left Ruttie herself with more mixed emotions.
She was grateful for the way Jinnah leapt to her support and she
joined him too in his proud defiance. Henceforth, she refused to dress
in the subdued, modest style that seemed to be expected of her. But
the strain of dealing with so many people's disapproval on so many

different fronts was beginning to take its toll. Despite telling herself
how happy she now was, her health began to mysteriously fail on its
own. And by the time Sarojini finally managed to catch up with her,
more than three months after their marriage, she found Ruttie, to
her surprise, looking not half as glowing as she expected her to be.
Instead, she displayed that curious combination of feelings—'looking
very ill but quite happy', as Sarojini put it.

Chapter Ten

~

In December, the War having finally ended and with the winter session of the legislature closed, the Jinnahs returned to Bombay. The three months that they had spent in Delhi were among the dullest of Ruttie's life so far. There was nothing for her to do all day while Jinnah threw himself as usual into the business of the House. With the proposal for government reforms—the Montagu–Chelmsford proposals—just published, he found the legislative session even more engrossing than ever, and he was away most of the day and sometimes half the night as well, immersed in the debates in the House. The hotel they were living in, the Maidens, was just the kind to appeal to Jinnah, as it was cut off from the city and, as the viceroy's ADC famously said to Ruttie, 'nice and quiet at nights'; but quiet was the last thing she wanted, especially now—as if being cast into exile was not bad enough.

But now at last they were back in Bombay where there was more than enough going on. The season was in full swing, with the governor's imminent departure adding an even more feverish edge to the ceaseless round of garden parties and other glittering receptions held every winter. But instead of feeling the pangs of exclusion from all these festivities, Ruttie for the first time found herself drawn, heart and soul, into one of Jinnah's political campaigns. Usually these were dry and measured. They arrived at halls or public meeting grounds like Shantaram Chawl after things had been set up for them. She sat on the platform with him, subjecting herself to the crowd's gaze, not always friendly. Mercifully, Jinnah wasn't given to long-winded speeches, some of which could go on for more than four hours at a stretch. But there was really nothing for her to do except not to fidget and listen passively as he delivered his crisp, dispassionate talk. A beautiful prop, when her heart longed instead to fight 'side by side' with him, not just sit by listening to this endless talk but fight pitched battles for freedom 'with sword and dagger', as she had once fantasized, 'sacrificing all at the feet of the Motherland'.

But after seven months of enduring the tedium of those interminable public meetings and receptions, watching him fight what seemed to her shadow battles 'by pen or parchment' or 'through diplomatic parlance', here at last was some action. So what if J still kept his iron control, denying any personal passion behind the campaign he had started. 'In politics,' as he loved to say, 'you cannot be emotional.' But now at least she could bring her own ardour into the fight, sticking fierily to his side through every moment of it, fighting the good fight, just as she had dreamt it. She loved Jinnah as she had never done before as he allowed himself to respond to the crowd's emotion, not minding if other people thought of him as the kind of leader he had always detested: 'a tub-thumper'. And if it wasn't the swords-and-daggers stuff of her dreams, it came pretty close. It certainly was the first genuine mass agitation that she—and most of Bombay—had ever experienced. There were late-night meetings, rousing slogans, thousands of people coming out on the streets in his support, patriotic fervour and all the excitement of a hard-fought battle. It made her feel almost as if she had been transported into one of those militant suffragists' demonstrations in England that she used to love reading about—an Emmeline Pankhurst of India, almost. Except, there were hardly any women in the crowds besides herself.

The campaign had begun three weeks before. It started when a few of the Bombay governor's admirers decided to raise a memorial for him on his retirement later in the month. If they had decided to do it without petitioning the sheriff to call a public meeting on it, the memorial would probably have gone through without any contention. Ignoring the simmering conflict between Lord Willingdon and Jinnah, who in the past six months not only refused to go to the governor's house but boycotted along with his associates any meeting where the governor was present, they went ahead by calling a public meeting of citizens in order to raise the memorial. It was an opportunity that

Jinnah seized with both hands. He had always despised the cringing Indian attitude of 'automatic gratitude'—'automatic toadyism', as he and his friends called it, of men who had either accepted favours and titles from the British government or lived in the hope of gaining one someday. But so far he had not put his foot down on what other men in his position were doing in the name of the public, let alone going to the lengths he was now prepared to go.

If someone had told Jinnah even six months previously, when Ruttie was publicly snubbed by the Willingdons, that he would lead an agitation against the retiring governor where both he and his followers faced risk to their life and limb; when things would get so disorderly that chairs would be thrown and blows exchanged, he would have probably—not laughed, because he considered laughter too immoderate and therefore unbecoming in a gentleman—but smiled that slight smile of disbelief that he sometimes permitted himself. Unruly scenes had never been his style.

The governor and he had never got along. Quite apart from their political differences, their temperaments were inimical: Lord Willingdon, who hated his authority to be challenged, put his pleasures above his public duty, turning a blind eye to the faults of his administration, if not actually encouraging its abuse of power. Nor was he above petty machinations to get his own way. And there was Jinnah, with his austere sense of duty and the abrasive argumentativeness of a British parliamentarian (he could—and did— argue with even viceroys and secretaries of state, intimidating them into silence with his logic and reasoning); his stubborn insistence on British fair play and that impossible code of honour he had secretly devised for himself ever since he had been cast adrift at seventeen in London, with scarcely an idea of himself or his place in the world. Nor was his claim that he bore no malice to anyone despite political differences a mere idle boast. As he once recounted, 'I went to the chambers of Sir George Lowndes as a penniless man. He was to me like a father and treated me as a son. When he was in the Imperial Legislative Council as the Law Member to the Government of India, I bitterly opposed him. Withal, we have maintained our friendship unbroken to this day.'

These were values he had culled not from contemporaries but from ancient classics like the first-century Roman statesman Cicero's

The Offices—as though only letters and counsel from men long since dead would suffice to guide him in the destiny he had determined for himself. He would meticulously underline with a pencil words like 'pre-eminence', 'justice', 'prudence', 'magnanimity', 'fortitude' and 'moderation', taking them to heart with his passion and diligence, moulding himself carefully into that 'calm and undisturbed' personality with his 'whole life graceful and uniform', just as Cicero advised his son, emphasizing with two parallel lines running in the margin, thick with his own intensity of spirit that 'nothing is more brave than an evenness of temper in every condition' or 'not give overmuch ear to flatterers, nor suffer ourselves to be wheedled and imposed on by their deceitful words'. How could Lord Willingdon ever understand the sincerity of his aspiration? The governor was too bogged down in his own cynicism to be able to see the other man's disdain of 'baseness and treachery', qualities Jinnah regarded as not just immoral but 'unbecoming and effeminate'.

There had been clashes between them earlier. Three years ago, for example, Willingdon disappointed Jinnah by failing to live up to his expectations. Jinnah had complained to him of the police superintendent's conduct at a session of the Muslim League in Bombay. Instead of throwing out the intruders who were disrupting the meeting with their heckling, the police officer took the side of the intruders, hell-bent on breaking up the meeting. But when Jinnah complained to the governor, he merely brushed aside his complaint and, as a mark of how little he cared to please Jinnah, he invited both the superintendent and these opponents of Jinnah to an official reception he held soon after, treating them as honoured guests. Jinnah, of course, said nothing directly to Willingdon but exposed him ruthlessly in the press. It offended the governor but Jinnah was not acting out of personal rancour, as the governor presumed. He was only doing what he felt was his duty, as any friend of Jinnah's would have told Lord Willingdon had he cared to ask. And in fact, if anyone had asked Jinnah at any time if his relationship with the governor was strained, he would have denied it, asserting as he did later that there was 'no personal feeling, no personal ill will' between them. And it was the truth. His relationship with the governor had hardly changed since he took over the administration five and a half years ago: they had been cordial before and they continued to be cordial, as far as he was concerned. It was another matter that in Jinnah's dictionary the word 'cordial' did not extend beyond the frigidly formal civility with which the two men kept each other at a safe distance. For someone of Jinnah's temperament it was difficult to understand how unreasonably the governor behaved sometimes. It never failed to surprise him how personally Lord Willingdon took all criticism.

Six months ago the governor succumbed yet again to his personal pique, leaving Jinnah almost incredulous at his folly. He invited all the Home Rule League leaders, including Jinnah, for a provincial war conference, and having got them there proceeded to insult them in front of the whole gathering, accusing them of insincerity. And when they tried to speak in their own defence, he shut them up rudely which led to a walkout by all the Leaguers except Jinnah, who chose to stay on. Whether it was because it took him some time to digest the enormity of Lord Willingdon's stupidity or, as his friend Horniman put it later, 'to throw the insult back in the governor's face' is not clear. Either way, he lost all respect for the governor after that incident.

And what else could Jinnah do in such a situation but take full advantage of his enemy's weakness. It was the governor's 'greatest possible blunder', as he told the press with open contempt for Lord Willingdon's lack of good sense. Of course, he went at the governor hammer and tongs, in his best courtroom manner, denouncing his government from public platforms and in newspapers for its dishonesty and mistrust of Indians. He kept a strict control over his own feelings for the governor, keeping the fight as impersonal as only he knew how to do, attacking not the governor but his policies, or rather the lack of them. It caused serious damage to Lord Willingdon's image, both in Delhi and in London, possibly the worst thrashing a British governor had so far taken at the hands of Indians. It was only in September, after Jinnah left to attend the legislative session in Delhi, that Lord Willingdon got a respite.

But by mid-November when the governor's tenure was approaching its end, the hostilities resumed again. It started with a few of Lord Willingdon's admirers suggesting a memorial to him for the services he had rendered to the city. It was a harmless act of flattery with which the city's titled and privileged had indulged other governors with before Lord Willingdon, and certainly no governor was more badly in need of a balm to his bruised ego than the present governor. But Jinnah was in no mood for clemency.

It was the principle of the thing, he argued. Did the governor who was the head of the administration deserve a certificate from the public? His friend Benjamin Horniman, the editor of the *Bombay Chronicle*, carried a long indictment of the five and a half years of Lord Willingdon's administration in Bombay, outlining his many sins of omission and commission, including stifling democracy and harassing the Home Rule League leaders. Wisdom dictated that Lord Willingdon back off at this stage. Trying to take on yet again the combined might of the two friends was clearly an exercise in bad judgement. Between them, the two practically ruled Bombay—having at their disposal not only a very popular national newspaper but the entire organization and workers of the Home Rule League who were by now seasoned veterans of several successful political campaigns.

But Lord Willingdon's earlier battering at the hands of Jinnah's Home Rule League seemed to have taught him little. Besides, he had his future career in the Indian government to consider. His professional life as an Indian bureaucrat was only just beginning, even though his tenure in Bombay was coming to an end. It made him a little desperate to prove to the higher authorities in Delhi and London how well he was thought of by everyone in Bombay, excepting Jinnah. His strategy became to isolate Jinnah and his associates, making it appear as if Jinnah was agitating against him out of personal motives and vindictiveness. In fact, a former associate of Jinnah's in the Home Rule League who crossed over to the enemy's side actually went on record to say so. The 'renegade', S.R. Bomanji, gave an interview to a newspaper claiming that Jinnah was venting his personal disappointment on the governor because he had not been given a seat in the governor's legislative council. His interview appeared in *Jam-e-Jamshed*, a Parsi newspaper, and Bomanji's allegations went down well with its readers who were looking for another excuse to hate Jinnah apart from his daring to marry a Parsi girl. Bomanji provided another reason why people should support the memorial for the governor: now that Lord Willingdon was retiring and returning to London, Bomanji reasoned, he would be in a position to do some good to Indians from there. For the Parsis, this appeared like sound reasoning and they rose to the occasion, standing solidly behind the governor in pushing through the memorial proposal and dismissing the protests of Jinnah's group.

Instead of giving up in disgust, these underhand tactics from his opponents made Jinnah even more determined to stop the memorial at any cost. It brought out that side of him that his friends rarely glimpsed beneath his charm: that almost inhumanly obstinate streak which refused to submit under any circumstances. The issue itself was far too local and provincial to ordinarily hold his interest for very long, but now he threw himself into the agitation, turning it within a few days of his arrival in Bombay from a local protest that could be safely ignored by the authorities, into something on a more epic scale. For the first time, he was not content to merely turn up as chief speaker at meetings, leaving it to his juniors to make all the arrangements. He took charge of every aspect of the campaign, monitoring every move his opponents made. It challenged all his faculties. He had always been fond of the game of chess—that was one of the few pleasures he had indulged in during his club life—and now he set himself to checkmate his opponents, coolly and dispassionately. It, of course, meant sacrificing both his legal work and the few hours of sleep he allowed himself at night. But then he had never been in the habit of putting his personal comfort or legal career before his political activities.

Within his own head the conflict ran not as a clash of egos but a larger, more epic struggle it had become his sacred duty to wage. He argued persuasively that the time had arrived for self-rule and it was not just their right but their duty to fight against the government. The issue of the memorial, he decided, provided him with a timely opportunity to educate people on their political rights and duties. The War was finally over and it was time to put pressure on the government to deliver on its long-pending promise of reforms. In meeting after meeting, to ever-multiplying crowds, he began to drum the same point: allowing Lord Willingdon's admirers to go ahead and vote for a memorial for him in their name was to shirk their duty as citizens of Bombay. The governor's administration had flouted all principles of democracy and human decency, he said at every stop of his whirlwind campaign across Bombay. To passively accept this sycophancy towards British autocrats was to do themselves and the country a disservice. And then in that classic gesture that the crowds lapped up, he wagged his forefinger at the audience: Does the governor deserve a certificate from them? 'No!' they responded with an enthusiasm he had never seen before. That call to patriotism had touched a chord.

His passion was consuming. It infected everyone around him, including Ruttie. She went with him to every public rally he addressed across Bombay, no matter how late in the night it was held. And it was no longer from a sense of duty—she wanted to be there with him, part of the action and the crowds, even if she was usually the only woman at the venue. Seeing her so enthused, Jinnah was touched. He let her become involved in the campaign at every stage. She sat in on his meetings with his juniors, listening to the reports on how the enemy side was preparing to get the memorial passed despite the protest rallies of thousands that Jinnah was busy mobilizing. Aware that the popular tide was going against them, the pro-Willingdon camp began a last-ditch attempt to collect as many signatures as they could, regardless of who it was that was signing. Most of them had not a clue what they were signing for, as the *Bombay Chronicle* reported. They also roped in the indispensable Suleman Cassum Mitha, a prominent Khoja Muslim leader of Bombay extremely loyal to the British whose services in providing hired crowds of Pathans had come in handy for the government on previous occasions. According to the reports, Mitha had already brought 'battalions of foreign hirelings' into the city, putting them up in Muslim mohallas like Bhendi Bazaar, who were ready to fill up the town hall on the appointed day. The police force was also openly supporting the pro-governor camp, using intimidatory tactics to scare off the public.

But Jinnah wasn't having any of this. He got up on public platforms to declare that it was everyone's duty to come forward and vote against the memorial and if anyone told them it was against the law, he was telling them as a lawyer that it was their right to do so. Over twenty thousand people came forward at his call, ready to risk life and limb, even prepared to sleep overnight on the steps of the town hall if necessary, in order to force their entry into the hall on voting day.

The strategy was the same on both sides: since the town hall could accommodate no more than fifteen hundred people at best, the doors were closed as soon as the hall got filled up. This meant that whichever side managed to get in first would capture all the seats and control the meeting. Obviously the pro-governor camp had the advantage. They had both the police and the administration on their side. One of the first arrangements they undertook was to build a platform inside the hall large enough to seat over four hundred VIPs. These special guests on the platform would be issued passes that would permit them to enter from a side gate that was not open to all. They also issued special badges to volunteers and stewards picked from their side. In contrast, all that Jinnah's supporters could do was to queue up as early as they could so as to be the first to enter as soon as the doors were opened. Unsurprisingly, the authorities refused to disclose to Jinnah's side at what time the doors would be opened on voting day. When Jinnah demanded to know in his imperious way, the answer he got was the usual bureaucratic one: 'Don't know. Take your chance.'

All this raised the pitch of the battle to a level that Bombay had rarely witnessed before. On the night before the voting, the protesters gathered in the largest meeting place for public demonstrations: Shantaram Chawl. It was the biggest crowd Jinnah had drawn so far and the protesters could hardly contain their excitement. Cries of 'shame' and 'hear, hear' rent the air regularly as he spoke to them for the last time before the battle, and his appeal to them 'to get to the town hall today as early as they could' was greeted with loud and continuous cheers. Ruttie was there on the platform with him, listening with all her heart to the half a dozen speeches made on the occasion. She was so charged up that when Horniman put the question to the audience if they were going to the town hall, Jinnah heard her cry out with them: 'Aye!'

Although the town hall was no place for a woman, especially on a day when he and his supporters were going looking for trouble, Jinnah made no attempt to curb Ruttie's enthusiasm or persuade her to stay at home. Seeing how heartbreakingly determined she was to be part of the action, Jinnah held his silence. But he did leave for the venue without telling her. The voting was to take place at 5.30 p.m., but Jinnah, anxious to oversee his supporters, got there by 7 a.m. He did not want to wake her up.

The police had cordoned off the area around the town hall the previous night to prevent Jinnah's followers from sleeping overnight on the steps. Since seating in the town hall was on the first come, first served rule, they wanted to ensure that the pro-memorialists would not grab all the seats by reaching the town hall before them. The authorities usually made an announcement well in advance on what time the doors of the town hall would be thrown open to the public, but this time there was no announcement. Till late in the previous night, Jinnah's side was kept in the dark about the opening time. But that hadn't stopped Jinnah's supporters from gathering on the road as close to the venue as they could get. And by the time Jinnah and Horniman arrived the next morning, some two to three hundred of their supporters were already there, loudly cheering them as soon as they drove up.

The doors were not yet open, and the steps were being guarded by a posse of pro-memorialists—'European and Parsi gentlemen wearing badges as stewards of the meeting and various members of their committee'. Jinnah did not go up to join them as he might have otherwise done. Instead, he stood at the barrier on the foot of the steps, shouting up to the Parsi baronet Sir Cowasji Jehangir to ask: 'What time are the doors opening?' In better days, the Parsi knight had been a good friend of Jinnah's. Jinnah had dined on innumerable occasions at his fabulous mansion on Malabar Hill. But now, Sir Cowasji was not forthcoming, responding coldly: 'Don't know.'

Jinnah decided to wait with his supporters until the doors did open. Only he could ensure that the governor's camp would not intimidate his followers into a retreat. It took another hour and a half until additional men could be brought in by the pro-memorialists to match the enemy's side. It was an assorted crowd of 'millhands, Goanese clerks and Borahs and a number of Mohamedans of the Bhendi Bazaar mowali type' under the charge of Suleman Cassim Mitha, according to the *Bombay Chronicle*. Once they got there, the police gave the order to line up and despite trying to trick them into forming a separate queue, Jinnah's followers managed to rush to the front of the line. At about ten o'clock, the pro-governor camp had to concede defeat and open the doors for all. In a trice, Jinnah and his deputies took their place in the queue that their supporters were reserving for them, and perhaps for the first time in his long career in politics, Jinnah was the first to enter the hall at the head of the most enthusiastic following he had ever commanded. The meeting would not begin for at least another six and a half hours, and his opponents were waking up to a leisurely breakfast, unaware of Jinnah's strenuous efforts to subvert them.

The battle was only beginning. Forced to watch helplessly as Jinnah's supporters grabbed the best seats in the hall, the stewards took over now. They unseated them, sending them from the central row to the back of the hall. It was an unwise move, particularly when Jinnah was around. Unusually for a town hall meeting, several hundred volunteers, mostly Parsis, had been given special badges as stewards. There was little to do, with the volunteers merely walking around, 'more ornamental than useful', as a *Bombay Chronicle* reporter wrote with rare acidity. The Parsis had not forgiven Jinnah for marrying Ruttie and the steward's badge seemed to give them a chance to vent their feelings on him. The emotional undercurrents manifested in the form of what a *Bombay Chronicle* reporter described as 'officious bullying' by the Parsi gentlemen. It led to an argument, heated on their part, and handled with his usual composure by Jinnah. He wouldn't give an inch. As first-comers, he argued, his supporters had first choice of seats. The stewards then had no choice but to back off. But tempers were beginning to fray on both sides.

Within two hours of the doors opening, a scuffle broke out between the two camps. With six hours to go for the meeting and nothing to do but hang on to their seats, the rowdy gang brought in by the pro-memorialists was already beginning to get restless. They began some loud name-calling of their opponents who tried not to respond. But their restraint snapped when a Parsi volunteer lost his temper and manhandled one of the anti-memorialists. Jinnah, who had never once been tempted even in his youth to vent his anger through physical violence—it repelled him—would have preferred not to retaliate.

But it set them all off. Men on both sides lost their composure and lifted their chairs, hurling them at each other. The stewards, except the ones involved in the fighting, scuttled to the safety of the platform. In the melee that ensued, according to Aziz Beg's book, 'somebody even tried to push Jinnah down the stairs'. But he kept his cool and while he and his deputies repeatedly appealed to their side to sit down, it was a while before order was restored. The offending stewards were separated and taken to another part of the hall while

Jinnah's followers took back the chairs and sat down again. Two of their side were seriously injured and had to be taken out. Jinnah found himself shaken despite himself.

But it wasn't long before violence threatened to erupt again. This time it was over the seats reserved for ladies. The stewards who had fled to the platform when the two factions began hurling chairs at each other returned to find their seats taken by others. Instead of unseating them, they went and sat in the rows reserved for ladies. Jinnah's side objected vociferously to this. While the pro-memorialists were certain that no ladies would grace this meeting, Jinnah was expecting Ruttie and a few other ladies to join them at the scheduled time. Attempts were made to dislodge the men on the ladies' seats, but they wouldn't budge. As the *Bombay Chronicle* reporter put it: 'If ladies came, they said, they would be the first to get up for them, but in the meanwhile they had the right to occupy empty seats and they would wait and see, as they did not believe any ladies were coming. And none did come.'

But ladies did come, at least one of them—Ruttie. However, she was turned away at the door. Had she known what was going on inside, she would have been even more eager to get in—public brawls had always excited her fancy. But there was no way of getting past the Parsi stewards at the gate. Like the rest of her side who had not got in when the doors were first opened, she too was prevented from entering the hall by stewards who told her that the hall was already full. Meanwhile, Jinnah and the supporters who had managed to get into the hall were more or less trapped. If they left the hall even for a moment, the organizers were threatening not to let them in again. They had gone without food or drink since early morning. While this hardly mattered to Jinnah—he could go without eating for the entire day without any perceptible discomfort—his supporters were not so oblivious to hunger pangs. To add to their frustration, batches of their opponents were being taken to the verandah at regular intervals and returning to their seats with packets of biryani, 'and other refreshments'. All they could do was protest, until the organizers reluctantly agreed to keep the doors shut, both to the verandah and outside, from where the hired crowd was still trickling in.

But spirits still ran high even after six hours when finally Jinnah's side was permitted to bring in provisions for its starving horde. Two of Jinnah's team were allowed to step inside with baskets of food and water on the condition that they would leave the hall as soon as they delivered their supplies. Their entry was cheered vociferously.

In fact, except for the single incident of violence, the battle so far had been confined to an exercise of vocal chords: loud shouts of protest from Jinnah's side when the 'biryani door' was opened to admit a crowd of 'some two hundred men, mostly Mohammedans, some of them Pathans of the lowest class . . . escorted by one of Mr Suleman Casum Mitha's lieutenants and a European police officer bringing up the rear'; and even louder cries of 'Shame! Shame!' as the leaders of the pro-memorial side began to trickle in by five o'clock. The hall was by now uncomfortably packed. Wedged between the front row of seats where Jinnah sat with other leaders of his camp and the platform was 'a phalanx of about a hundred European, Parsi and Anglo-Indian stewards which made it extremely difficult—ultimately it became impossible—for the leaders of the anti-memorialists to see or be seen by those on the platform'. The sheriff was the first to arrive, greeted by loud cheers from the pro-governor's side, which were drowned immediately by prolonged shouts of 'Shame!' and 'Shame Sheriff!' The other leaders of the pro-memorial campaign—Sir Shapurji Broacha, Sir Dinshah Wacha, Sir Ibrahim Rahimtoolah, Mr Carmichael and others—were similarly hailed, with a special demonstration of vocal power reserved for Sir Narayan Chandavarkar who had been chosen to deliver the farewell speech for the governor. 'It seemed,' according to the eyewitness account of the *Bombay Chronicle*'s reporter, 'as though the solid body of opposition in the front and centre of the hall would never tire of expressing their indignation at the panegyrist-in-chief who had come to deliver the final and parting eulogy.'

But shouting apart, Jinnah was determined to lead this protest fully in accordance with his own principles—never digressing for a moment from the constitutional methods he believed in so implicitly. Exactly at five-thirty when the meeting was scheduled to begin, Jinnah hushed his crowd with an order to settle in quietly and listen to the proceedings. And had the pro-memorialists stuck to the rules of procedure, things would have probably never got out of hand as they did. Going by their plan, Horniman rose to his feet in protest immediately after the sheriff read out the notice convening the meeting. But instead of giving him a hearing, the pro-memorialists on the platform and near it began shouting him down. While he was still trying to be heard over the shouts of his opponents, the pro-memorialists took matters into their own hands. One of the leaders on the platform proposed Sir Jamsetjee Jeejeebhoy to the chair, and without putting the motion to vote and ignoring Horniman's shouted protest that they wished to propose someone of their own choice to the chair, Sir Jamsetjee hastily walked to the chair.

Such pre-emptory tactics were beyond what Jinnah and his supporters could bear. A noisy uproar broke out, with Jinnah's side shouting 'No! No!', while the stewards, volunteers and other supporters of the platform 'shrieked and yelled in derision, hurling insults and epithets at the opposition. What was happening on the platform, the rest could not see or hear. Then the resolution was declared passed. In the general clamour, it was unclear whether the vote was actually passed, with both sides claiming victory. As the *Bombay Chronicle* put it, 'It is said that Sir Jamsetjee put the resolution of appreciation of Lord Willingdon from the chair and declared it carried. It is possible. But the pretence that the resolution was carried by a meeting of the citizens of Bombay is farcical and an insult to Lord Willingdon, if he had the good sense to appreciate it.'

The clamour went on for nearly twenty minutes, making Jinnah more anxious by the minute. This was not his idea of how the meeting ought to have proceeded. He was wary, too, that somebody might get hurt again if he did not put a stop to it. He decided to call in the police.

But his faith in the system was to receive another severe blow. The police arrived in the hall, led by the commissioner himself, and ordered the audience to leave. But instead of waiting for Jinnah and his deputies to take their men out in an orderly way as Jinnah had expected, the police turned their batons on them, picking out the men on Jinnah's side and assaulting them as they tried to exit the hall. And to his lasting shock, the police dealt him a few blows as well.

The injuries, however, were minimal, at least to his person. What it did to his pride and dignity he had as yet no time to register. As he struggled out of the door, an extraordinary scene met his eyes and ears. From the top of the steps, he could see a sea of humanity stretching all the way down to Elphinstone Circle. Some twenty-five thousand people who had been denied entry into the hall were waiting for him to emerge from the hall. As soon as he and Horniman emerged together out of the door, a loud and continuous sound, like a roar, rent the evening sky. The cheering was coming not just from the road but from every balcony and verandah overlooking the street, crammed with people who were waving their handkerchiefs at him. So intense was the crowd's emotion that Horniman was seized as he came down the steps and carried shoulder-high through the street and around the circle. Had they dared, they would doubtless have done the same with Jinnah. But even strangers could sense that he was a leader who liked to keep his distance. He shrank from physical touch.

But they wouldn't let him go until he had addressed them, which he did briefly, appearing at the windows of a friend's office overlooking the road where the crowd had gathered and saying a few words in his crisp, dispassionate way.

While Jinnah and his men had been engaged inside the hall, Ruttie had not been idle. After she had been refused entry, she had found her way to the balcony above the town hall library. From there, she could see the immense crowd gathered on the other side of the police barricades at the Elphinstone Circle Garden. There was nothing much to keep them engaged, with their leaders locked away inside the hall. But they were expectant, standing around aimlessly waiting for the meeting to end and for Jinnah and the others to emerge from the door. On an impulse, she decided to go down to them. She had always liked the excitement and tumult of crowds, and there was nobody to stop her now. Reaching the crowd, she did something she had always longed to do but never dared: she climbed up on a soapbox and began to address them in English. It was her maiden speech but the words just seemed to flow from her without conscious effort. 'We are not slaves,' she shouted from her perch. The crowd went wild.

People were much moved by her lecture, according to a letter to the editor published the next day in the *Bombay Chronicle*. Almost every sentence she spoke drew 'loud cheering and constant ovation', the eyewitness wrote. But it was difficult to tell what exactly moved the crowd to such wild enthusiasm: whether it was her speech or the sight of a beautiful young woman standing up so daringly in the middle of so many strangers and addressing them with a total lack of any girlish inhibition. At any rate, her speech succeeded in bringing out the police commissioner from the town hall. The commissioner, a man called Mr Vincent, could do little about dispersing the crowd in a public garden but he could, and did, ask Ruttie 'to stop addressing the crowd for they were making a lot of noise'.

At the best of times Ruttie was hard to cow down, and here she was charged up and exhilarated by her first foray into political action. She stuck her ground stubbornly, refusing to move, finding the words she needed to confront the police commissioner: 'Mr Vincent, first of all you have no right to stop me from lecturing because I have a right to speak as a citizen of Bombay. Secondly, whatever you may do I am not going to move from here.' Clearly, she had learnt much by watching Jinnah at such close quarters, especially his art of throwing the law at the law-keepers. Short of using physical force, there was really nothing the commissioner could do to her. Mr Vincent withdrew quietly from the scene.

But the commissioner had not quite given up as yet. Instead of sending a police contingent with their batons to break up the impromptu meeting, he ordered that water hoses be turned on the gathering. Like Jinnah, Ruttie too was not spared. She was drenched from the dousing. But still she refused to budge from her makeshift platform, continuing to address the crowd with even more fervour. The crowd, all male, was spellbound, rooted to the spot despite the spray. It was their wildest dream come true. The image never quite faded away—half a century later, a Pakistani historian, Aziz Beg, rhapsodized: 'As she was completely wet, her curvaceous figure looked all the more attractive and prominent.' However, oblivious to the male gaze, Ruttie went on with her speech almost until the meeting within the hall broke up. According to Kanji Dwarkadas, she was sitting on the steps of the town hall smoking a cigarette by the time the men emerged from the meeting.

'With what feelings of pride her husband must have surveyed the situation,' wondered the *Bombay Chronicle*'s reporter in the next day's paper. But, of course, no one could tell what Jinnah actually felt. He did do a passable impression of being the proud but reticent husband. He had missed seeing Ruttie in action, but figured it out soon enough. He was mobbed by journalists as soon as he emerged from the hall, wanting to know, among other things, of his reaction to his wife's bravado. Jinnah did not snub them as they had half feared, making them bold enough to put a question to him: 'Could you not have persuaded Mrs Jinnah to stay at home?'

The innuendo that he should have somehow controlled his wife did not escape him but he did not duck the question, giving it the full weight of his gravity: 'Mr Jinnah gave us the history of her [Ruttie's] determination to be present at the meeting,' according to the *Bombay Chronicle*'s reporter. 'He told us that she was present at the meeting the evening before and when Mr Horniman put the question to the audience if they were going to the Town Hall, Mrs Jinnah was one of those who answered "aye". So there she was at the Town Hall.' It was the nearest Jinnah had ever approached to admitting that he did not have the heart to stop her, whatever his private doubts might have been.

In his head, of course, he was a staunch believer in women's rights. In fact, so strongly believing in women's equality that as a young student in England, he was a vocal supporter of the suffragists and attended their meetings. But somewhere in a secret corner of his mind that he was as yet unprepared to examine, it was beginning to strike him that it was not pure pride he felt in the situation, as the *Bombay Chronicle*'s reporter assumed. If there was pride stirring within him, and with it a generous instinct of solidarity with her, there was also something else he did not want to acknowledge: that he did not really want her to be making speeches; that was his territory. He could rationalize, of course, as he had done earlier with Kanji, when the latter joined the Home Rule League, asking the young man to choose the job of 'a worker and not a speaker', and liking Kanji all the better for agreeing to work backstage rather than giving speeches, praising him in front of others as 'my best worker. He works, the others make speeches.' But the fact is, quite apart from Jinnah's liberal values which he took seriously to heart, there was no denying that he and Ruttie came from two different worlds and not all his famous willpower or the smart clothes and Edmund Burke's speeches that he had soaked up as a young man could quite wipe away his disapproving father from inside him. It was easier, in short, to drop the 'funny long coat' of his boyhood than the boy who had once worn it. And yet, how could he ever voice this, let alone set it up with his usual assurance as a standard for her who was born to another way of life altogether. He, who had known no woman intimately except his sister or—remotely in his past—his first wife whom he had to coach not to drop the veil over her face each time she appeared before his parents, and his mother who had died in the service of his father.

But there were other doubts to do with his political career that he had no trouble at all voicing to himself, even in the midst of the celebration of his victory. Young and old, poor and rich (except for the Parsis) were hailing it as his finest hour. On the very night of the incident in the town hall at a public meeting to celebrate his triumph, Jinnah seemed bent on bringing the delirious celebrators back to heel. So drunk was the crowd on Jinnah's victory against the governor and his sycophants that they gathered in the thousands at Shantaram Chawl hours before he arrived, seeking standing space wherever they could find it, on balconies, housetops and windows and even trees overlooking the ground. And still the crowds kept gathering until the organizers were forced to hold an overflow meeting at the French Bridge on Chowpatty, where another fifteen thousand or so had gathered. But when Jinnah arrived, to 'a most touching and impressive demonstration of appreciation from the audience', he refused to either whip the crowd into further frenzy or pat himself or his deputies on the back, only pointing out that 'some of the men might have been killed if some little thing had happened'. And while he was ready, as he openly declared, to do his duty by them, he certainly had no intention of exposing Ruttie to 'the most disgraceful conduct of the police'.

Was she with him on the platform with the other ladies on that night of the celebration? The reports don't say, only mentioning a certain Mrs Kamdar, the wife of his barrister colleague, who made a speech expressing Bombay's gratitude 'to Mr Jinnah and others who had fought for the rights of the citizens and asserted these rights'. Their gratitude to her came a week later, at a reception held in Ghatkopar, where the residents presented Jinnah with a gold medal and paid a tribute to Mrs Jinnah's heroism. 'Just as Sita had stood by her husband and bravely faced the Police Commissioner making him quail before her,' an old resident said in his welcome speech. 'She deserved all praise and gratitude for vindicating the right of Indian womanhood to a high place of honour,' he added to loud cheers from the audience. But it wasn't she who thanked them for the honour done to her. It was Jinnah who rose to his feet to thank them 'for the honour they had done him and his wife', adding again 'that he would always do his duty'.

No word seems to have passed between them about the incident. But still, Ruttie, with her intuitive grasp, especially when it came to his feelings, had no trouble it seems reading his mind. It could, of course, just be that she was already five weeks into her pregnancy and he was too much of the old-world gentleman to be able to bear her exposing herself to danger. But after that she took care never to make herself conspicuous in the political sphere, not even if her ardour demanded expression. Her job, she decided, was to be a prop for him during his public appearances, sitting mutely by his side on the dais. And with a docility that would have shocked her father, she easily fell into her role, taking care to curb her natural instincts.

Chapter Eleven

~

The last thing either of them needed was a baby arriving on the scene. For Jinnah it was a time of intense anxiety, but it had nothing to do with either Ruttie or the unborn baby. Events were inexorably thrusting him into a crisis so acute that it was threatening to cast him into political limbo.

The year had begun promisingly enough. In fact, he had never had it this good before—his fame had spread after leading the anti-Willingdon protest, making him a household name not just in the Bombay Presidency but across India. Within days of the town hall meeting, his friends and admirers had spontaneously started a collection drive to build a public hall in his name, and money kept pouring in for the next two or three months, with the *Bombay Chronicle* publishing a list of contributors that grew longer by the day. It certainly kept the memory of his victory against the British governor alive and fresh in the public mind. However, neither he nor Ruttie stayed long enough in Bombay to really enjoy their triumph. In less than two weeks after the town hall protest, they were on their way to Delhi to attend the year-end Congress and Muslim League sessions. Then back home in Bombay for a couple of days for Jinnah to appear before the Government of India Reforms Committee before he set off for Calcutta to appear again before the same committee during its sitting in Calcutta. He was one of the principal Indian leaders to be interviewed by the committee in two consecutive sittings.

He was, of course, accustomed to shuttling back and forth across India as a bachelor, accompanied only by his valet. The valet, a Goanese, had been well trained to pack his master's bags at a moment's notice, not only packing the incredible number of suits and hats and shoes that a well-dressed gentleman seemed to need in those days even for an overnight trip, but also overseeing the vast amounts of his master's baggage and ensuring that they safely reached and left the various hotel suites that his master inhabited in the course of his busy twin careers. Jinnah was a hard taskmaster where his servants were concerned, refusing to listen to any excuses for lost or misplaced baggage. But on the whole, he left them alone to do their individual jobs, and his household had run so far with clockwork efficiency. But now that he was a married man, he found himself yielding on the domestic front. He insisted on taking Ruttie with him everywhere, even if it meant enduring the chaos that trailed her every arrival and departure. He was discovering a deep well of patience within him, willing to put up without a word of demur the mountains of luggage that accompanied Ruttie wherever she went, not to speak of the chaotic trail of maids and dog and its paraphernalia like special dog food and iceboxes for it for the summer months and even its own ayah. He took it all in his stride with his usual stoic composure, never showing a trace of impatience or questioning for a moment that perhaps they could have travelled lighter. So far it had occurred to neither of them to spare her this ceaseless travel up and down the country accompanying him everywhere; they were inseparable.

But now in her delicate condition, he thought it fit to leave her behind at home in Bombay while he did the strenuous shuttle back and forth from Bombay to Delhi, attending the legislative session and coming home over the weekends to look after the more urgent court cases that could not be put off till after the session closed. So for the first time since his marriage, he left for Delhi by himself, soon after returning from Calcutta for the Reforms Committee's hearing. It should have been a welcome change for her, considering how friendless and alone she had felt in Delhi, stuck in a hotel miles away from the city and with nothing to do but wait for Jinnah to return from the legislature, which was usually not until late in the evening, too late to go out in search of some entertainment or company. But although Bombay was her home, it felt just as friendless and lonely as Delhi had been. Worse, in fact, for at least in Delhi, she had Jinnah to await every evening no matter at what hour he returned. And then she could fuss over him and tease him as she liked to do in the few hours they spent together, until he had grown wholly dependent on her for all his comforts, expecting her to be there waiting for him whenever he returned, not pausing to wonder how she passed her time during the long hours he spent in the legislature.

But now, without her distracting presence, he lapsed as easily back into his old habit of becoming fully engrossed in politics all day and night, apparently not needing her at all. In February, a couple of weeks before her birthday—her first as Mrs Jinnah—he came to the first crisis in his political life which pushed everything else, including her, out of his mind as he became completely involved in the proceedings within the Imperial Legislative Council. The Rowlatt Bills had just been tabled. He was so taken up with the issue that he did not even return to Bombay for her birthday. It was the first time in her life that no one had made a fuss over her birthday. But he expected her to understand that politics came first for him, and she accepted it was so.

He was, of course, not the only Indian politician to be disturbed by the new legislation the government was bent on introducing in the council. With the Defence of India Act lapsing after the War, the British government tabled two bills in the House giving it the extrajudicial powers it needed to deal with Indian revolutionary activity that had begun during the War years. The two bills, based on the recommendations of the Sedition Committee headed by Justice S.A.T. Rowlatt, and therefore known as the Rowlatt Bills, gave the government extraordinary emergency powers on a permanent basis, including the power to arrest and sentence people without proper trials. Of the two bills—the Criminal Law (Emergency Powers) Bill and the Indian Criminal Law (Amendment) Bill—the latter was eventually discarded, but the first bill's introduction in the House was opposed by every non-official Indian member of the House. This was hardly surprising considering the many ways the proposed legislation could be abused by a government intolerant of any opposition. Jinnah, quite apart from his personal repugnance to such a draconian and arbitrary piece of legislation, was best suited to play the role of opposition leader. It meant that he had to be present in the House the entire time the bill was being debated, stepping in frequently to bolster the speeches of his colleagues who were less well versed than him in the intricacies of lawmaking, bringing the force of his legal acumen and incisive language to the aid of the entire opposition.

But the bill also stirred a depth of passion within him that he had not suspected he was capable of feeling. For the first time in his life, he felt shaken to his very foundations, questioning both his idea of himself and the world. The tabling of the bill dashed his high expectations of the political role he thought he would play now that the War was over, and forced him to re-examine his long-held faith in Great Britain, idolized so far as 'the home of his training and education', as he called it—and its tradition of fair play on which he had reared himself. It shook too his faith in his own strength as a leader, in his power to achieve whatever he set out to do, including unshackling his country from the British yoke, which he was determined to do in his orderly way, through the due processes of British law. It was his first political setback and left him with an unfamiliar feeling of failure.

He began by responding in the only way he knew: by reasoning with the government, pointing out the many ways in which the proposed legislation went against its interests and that of the people whose welfare it claimed to protect. But the more he tried to argue and reason, the more intransigent the government became, until it became apparent to even someone of his stubborn temperament that reasoning had its limits. So intent was the government on stonewalling its opponents that nothing he could do could prevent the law from being enacted, neither his well-argued and passionate speeches nor his exhaustive study of all its legal deficiencies; in desperation, he started pushing for a postponement of the legislation, suggesting that the government send it for further reconsideration to high court judges and local councils. It was sheer agony, as he admitted in the House with unusual feeling, 'to sit here [in the House] and see this mockery of debate', knowing all the time that nothing he could do or say would have the slightest impact. So pent up indeed were his feelings of anguish and frustration that he could barely trust himself to speak, and yet speak he did for one last time in the final debate that went on till late in the night, putting into that final speech all the passion and pain of his unutterable love for the country he felt he was born to serve as well as for that other country, Great Britain, which had given him his sense of purpose and destiny.

And then he walked out of the House in disgust, returning home to Bombay. But unlike Ruttie, he had plenty to occupy him even without his legislative work. There was his legal work and planning how to take the issue of the Rowlatt Act to the people. And the prospect, now that the War was finally over, that the British government would soon introduce the reforms it had been promising and he would once more take his place in the government, this time as the pre-eminent Indian leader. There was much he had to do before that in order to bolster his position.

But she, meanwhile, spent the months she was alone in Bombay fighting off her feelings of being closed in by the baby that was growing in her. She hid away her dismay, especially on the rare weekends when Jinnah was home, wanting to protect him from hurt. And her pride would not allow her to admit her feelings to anyone else, not even Sarojini.

Ruttie had barely seen Sarojini since her marriage, having met her only once in August the previous year when they both chanced to be in Bombay at the same time. Although Sarojini was by now a permanent resident at the Taj Mahal hotel, having taken a suite on monthly rent, she had hardly spent any time in it during the past year owing to her political tours. Her career as a political leader was beginning to take off, especially with the demand for oratorical skills calling her to unexpected corners of the country, leaving her with no time for either family or friends. In the past few months while Ruttie tagged along with Jinnah wherever his work took him, Sarojini had been touring the country far and wide, giving orations in places as far removed from each other as Benares and Coimbatore, or Madras and the Frontier Province. But finally, on 13 February 1919, their paths did cross again. It was Sarojini's fortieth birthday and by a happy chance, she happened to be in Bombay for a couple of days. Ruttie arrived at Sarojini's suite in the Taj, determined to see her after so long a gap. She carried a birthday gift—'an exquisite [sari] border embroidered in opal colourings'. Sarojini was ecstatic—among the passions she shared with Ruttie were poetry and clothes. The afternoon passed in making delightful plans for going shopping for the right sari to match such an unusual border. It would have to be, the two decided, 'a blue and silver sari which will look like a sunlit sea edged with seaweed and anemones', as Sarojini later rhapsodized in a letter to her daughter. The two parted in the best of moods, with Sarojini noticing nothing amiss. Nor did she seem to notice that Ruttie was pregnant. At least, she made no reference to it in the letter she wrote home that night. In fact, all she considered worth mentioning about her visit was the enchanting vision Ruttie presented 'in floating raiment, all blue and gold and orange'.

They met again two weeks later when Sarojini was next in Bombay. Ruttie dropped in at Sarojini's Taj suite for a casual lunch 'in a wonderful old embroidered Chinese sari and scarcely any blouse', as Sarojini took care to describe in her daily letter home. After lunch—fresh oysters, a treat that could only be had in the Taj or in grand households like Petit Hall—Ruttie lingered on. She stayed till almost seven in the evening, when she had to go in the car to pick up Jinnah who was on a short trip back home.

To Sarojini's increasing, but concealed, irritation, this became the pattern each time she visited Bombay. Ruttie would turn up at her hotel room around midday, always exquisitely dressed but apparently with nowhere else to go and with nothing else to do. She stayed the whole day in Sarojini's suite regardless of whether Sarojini had work or other visitors to talk to or simply wished to be alone, and would leave in the evening—if Jinnah happened to be in Bombay—to pick him up from his chambers. If Sarojini noticed that something was troubling Ruttie, she was far too tactful to pry. Outwardly, Ruttie appeared the same as ever, gay and stylish and full of fun. It was difficult for even someone as perceptive as Sarojini to imagine that a young woman of Ruttie's beauty and fashion could be grappling with feelings of acute loneliness. But here she was, walking in uninvited into Sarojini's suite every morning as soon as she had risen from bed and bathed, as if it was the most normal thing for a newly married woman to want to spend the entire day holed up inside a hotel room with an older woman instead of spending time in her own home or seeking the company of friends her own age. For the most part, Sarojini was all tact and affection with her uninvited guest, but she did complain now and then in her letters home of how Ruttie was monopolizing her, allowing her to do no work. But she was far too generous a host to be discourteous to Ruttie and order her off. Instead, she cheerfully ordered food for her from the restaurant downstairs, watching with maternal indulgence as Ruttie voraciously ate whatever the Taj kitchen provided. Sarojini herself held no high opinion of the Taj cuisine, considering it bland and tasteless compared to the rich, spicy Deccani fare she was used to. But Ruttie never seemed to tire of it, even playfully fighting with other guests in Sarojini's rooms for the last biscuit on the plate. Her old playfulness and the impish sense of fun were still intact, and how was Sarojini to guess that it only surfaced when Ruttie was in her hotel room, and that she dreaded the hour when it was time to leave and head back to her desolate home in South Court.

Cut off as she now was from her family, she yearned to be absorbed into Sarojini's family instead, embracing as her own not only Sarojini's four children but also Sarojini's various siblings, taking a lively interest in their doings. Discovering, for example, that one of Sarojini's colourful brothers, Harindranath Chattopadhya, had just written a book, *Fears of Youth*, she immediately demanded a signed copy for herself. But it was impossible really to ever find Sarojini by herself even in her hotel suite. A continuous stream of visitors poured into her room almost all day. The visitors, ranging from fashionable royalty to politicians and casual acquaintances, called either on work or for a chat, and invariably were all asked to stay for lunch or tea, depending on the hour. These impromptu parties in her suite were enlivening, with gossip and food adding to there charm. 'I had a funny little teaparty in my room yesterday,' Sarojini reported to her younger daughter, Leilamani, on 28 February, 'with Ruttie looking like a French Marquese in fancy dress arraigned in a wonderful, hand-painted crepe of mauve with scarlet lanterns and geishas and butterflies spiralling out in drunken delight'. Sarojini's other guests were equally fashionable, one of them being the socialite Leela Mukerji about whom she added with her characteristic bite: 'looking more fulsome than ever swathed in a yellow gauze spilled and sprawled with some cubic designs—bare feet tucked into gold slippers, a somewhat enamelled loveliness of face with a beauty spot (which by the way Liakat Ali—for a male—wondered how Mrs Mukerji's moles changed their places so often).'

These encounters with Bombay's society women were not always friendly, with some of them tempted to take sly digs at Ruttie in the safe environs of Sarojini's suite. But she did not take it lying down, fighting back as spiritedly as Jinnah was doing both inside and outside the legislative council. In one instance, as Sarojini remarked in the same letter to Leilamani, 'there was the mad Mehta with lantern face and bold eyes making malicious epigrams at them [Ruttie and Leela] both, which Leela couldn't follow but which Ruttie took up and answered with equally quick and clever malice'.

March was no different from February, although Jinnah was now back from Delhi for good, having walked out of the legislature. Ruttie's visits to Sarojini's suite were just as frequent and for as long. 'The day has been full of people more than things,' the exasperated poetess wrote home to say on 20 March, 'especially of Ruttie who turned up in an embroidered net sari and some new photographs of herself.' On other occasions, the two went shopping together. It was Ruttie who took Sarojini shopping to help her choose a wedding present for her friend Nellie Sengupta. They returned well satisfied with her purchase: 'a gold tissue sari and choli piece'.

Ruttie's eagerness to be part of Sarojini's family expressed itself in another way. She brought some fresh photographs of herself to be admired by Sarojini. She who had once been so impatient with her mother for wanting her to take fresh pictures of herself was now voluntarily putting herself to the trouble of going to a studio and getting her portrait done by a professional, even if it meant standing or sitting still for hours while the cameraman fiddled with his unwieldy equipment. She even volunteered to send a copy of it unasked to Leilamani. 'Ruttie is sending you a new portrait of herself,' Sarojini wrote to her younger daughter, adding, 'and I believe something for your birthday. I have suggested a box of watercolour paints. Or is there anything else you would like better?'

It is possible that the portrait was meant to be a gift for Jinnah on their wedding anniversary, which was the day before Leilamani's birthday. But clearly his lack of appreciation left her yearning for something more. The anniversary itself, their first, went almost as unmarked as her birthday. That week, the Jinnahs were in Hyderabad. He had to appear in a murder case for a client, and Ruttie, eager to meet her friend Padmaja, leapt at the chance to go with him. But the visit had to be aborted hastily because a public speech that Jinnah had earlier delivered in Hyderabad raised the ire of the Nizam's government and a ban order was slapped against his re-entry. The confrontation that followed between Jinnah and the Nizam's government wiped out any intention he may have had to hold a special celebration for their anniversary. But then, Ruttie was getting used to forgoing personal celebrations for political reasons.

It had been two months since Jinnah returned from Delhi, but Ruttie saw as little of him as before. Jinnah rose earlier than her and would have already breakfasted and left for the courts before Ruttie was up. In the evenings, after she picked him up from his chambers, they had a drink together and dinner, but after that he preferred solitude, retreating into his library supposedly to work on his legal briefs. For the first few weeks after he returned from Delhi, he was absorbed in his own dilemma. Should he resign from the legislature now that the government had passed the Rowlatt legislation ignoring the pleas and protests of members like him? He felt humiliated by the government's attitude, but there was also the fear that it might be the end of the road as far as his political career was concerned. To take the issue of the Rowlatt Act to the people as Gandhi was already doing involved a twofold loss that was hard to contemplate: it meant giving up his own faith in bringing freedom to India through constitutional methods; and worse, it meant giving up his hard-earned position as the undisputed future leader of India, and fall in line behind Gandhi, whom he neither respected nor trusted.

But in the end, reason won over his feelings, and on 28 March, he sent in his resignation to the viceroy, joining in the popular anti-Rowlatt agitation led by Gandhi.

However, having once decided to follow Gandhi, he was no passive supporter. He plunged into the popular movement with his usual zeal and focus. And in less than two weeks after his resignation from the House, it was Jinnah whom the government feared, considering him a far more dangerous power centre than Gandhi. Unlike Gandhi, who sent out mixed signals about his approach to the British government, even volunteering to recruit Indian soldiers for the War effort without placing any conditions, Jinnah took on the British frontally. As a result, Bombay's new governor, Sir George Lloyd, took an even more intense dislike to Jinnah than his predecessor, Lord Willingdon, had. In a letter to the secretary of state, Montagu, in London, he described Jinnah as 'one of the worse characters, attractive to meet, fair of speech but absolutely dishonest in every way'. And as Jinnah relentlessly built up the anti-Rowlatt campaign, the government was alarmed enough to consider deporting both him and Gandhi to Burma. It was only when Gandhi suddenly stopped the campaign midway that the deportation plan was dropped.

By April, Bombay wore a dismal, abandoned look. The hot season had set in and everyone on Malabar Hill had already deserted the metropolis for cooler climes. Ruttie's parents, along with her three brothers, had left for Matheran, the hill station where they owned their own mansion. Her friend Kshama had departed with husband and child to Mahabaleshwar. There seemed nobody of any consequence left in the city except for her and Jinnah. The only friend who was still around in Bombay was Sarojini. She was waiting for a passage to England which proved more elusive than before the War had ended. She needed to go to England to consult specialists for her heart, but with so many soldiers and officials returning home after the War, it was impossible to secure a berth on a ship, even for someone with her connections.

And because Sarojini was stuck in Bombay, her daughter Padmaja made a brief visit. It was a rare treat for Sarojini, who was ill and sorely missing her home. In honour of the visit from her favourite child, who, as her father's housekeeper, rarely got a chance to leave Hyderabad, Sarojini cancelled all but her most urgent political engagements. But her plans for spending time alone with her daughter were sabotaged by Ruttie, who was determined not to be away from her friend even for a moment. If she could not persuade her friend to spend time with her in the Jinnahs' home, at least nothing could dislodge her from Sarojini's suite.

But Padmaja's visit did not last long. Within four days of her arrival, her father was urging her to return home. The hours once again seemed to drag interminably, with nothing to look forward to except the arrival of a baby she did not want. And when something did happen, it was worse. A week after Padmaja's visit, Benjamin Horniman, the editor of the *Bombay Chronicle* and Jinnah's oldest friend and devoted follower, was picked up by the police and bundled into a ship bound for London. The unsuspecting Horniman was picked up in the middle of the night from a military hospital where he had been admitted for a routine treatment, brought to the docks and put into a steamship that was setting out at once for England without stopping anywhere on the way. His deportation, on the hastily cooked up charge of publishing a false report that British troops were using soft-nosed bullets to disperse crowds, caught his friends, especially Jinnah, unawares. But in retrospect, this was hardly surprising. As the editor of the *Bombay Chronicle*, Horniman had earned the government's ire by playing a leading role in exposing the establishment's high-handedness, especially after the Jallianwala Bagh firing and the subsequent martial law imposed in the Punjab.

Jinnah's friendship with Horniman dated back to his student days in London where they had both worked briefly at a theatrical company. While the two were very unlike each other—Horniman a bachelor several years older than Jinnah, of a sentimental and 'deeply unmethodical' nature, according to Sarojini, in contrast to Jinnah's unemotional and over-methodical persona—they were genuinely attached to each other. In fact, Horniman's interest in working in India appears to have begun with his friendship with Jinnah whom he followed to India, at first taking up a job in Calcutta as the editor of the *Statesman* before Jinnah provided him a chance to work in Bombay as the editor of the newly launched national paper started by his other good friend and patron, Sir Pherozeshah Mehta. The three men, all bachelors then, grew so close to each other that they spent all their leisure hours together, including holidays at Sir Pherozeshah's monsoon retreat in Poona. The friendship between Jinnah and Horniman survived even after Sir Pherozeshah's death and, in fact, led to Jinnah being appointed as chairman of the *Bombay Chronicle's* board of directors. In 1915, following a heated argument with the newspaper's board of directors, Horniman had walked out of the newspaper, taking his whole editorial team with him. His popularity was such that the board was forced to submit its resignation and a new board of directors was elected by the shareholders, with Jinnah as the chairman, whose first action was to reinstate Horniman and his team in their old jobs. After that there was no power that seemed capable of undermining their combined influence over the Bombay Presidency and beyond. While Jinnah took the lead on the political front, Horniman provided able support through the columns of his newspaper.

Horniman's deportation dealt a severe blow to Jinnah. The new Bombay governor, Sir George Lloyd, had engineered the deportation supposedly to calm the unrest in Bombay, but his real target was

Jinnah. Like his predecessor, Lloyd was convinced that Jinnah was the government's most dangerous enemy and that his political influence had to be undermined at any cost. But instead of taking him head on, Lloyd decided to order a closure of the *Bombay Chronicle* on a fabricated charge. By closing down the paper which he felt had become a virtual mouthpiece for Jinnah's views and political campaigns, the governor hoped to send his greatest enemy into political oblivion forever.

Of course, Jinnah fought back. But the new governor proved more adept than his predecessor in tiring Jinnah out. His strategy was to sidestep Jinnah, avoiding a direct confrontation with the ace lawyer who had in his time taken all his battles to the courtroom and won them. The government tied him up in bureaucratic knots, denying him direct access to the governor to plead his case and refusing to spell out its terms and conditions for lifting the ban. Horniman had already set sail for England, so there was little Jinnah could do to help his friend until he reached England. But he threw himself into the struggle to get the ban lifted on his newspaper. He began by negotiating with the government, asking for an appointment with the governor in order to present his case. But the governor refused to meet him, referring him instead to the secretary of the judicial department. For the next few weeks, Jinnah bombarded the secretary with letters that became increasingly desperate as the government refused to respond to his queries or explanations. It took him over a month of daily correspondence for the government to finally relent and allow the newspaper to resume publication. But there were stiff conditions imposed, including a pre-censorship order on its editorial content. The shadow-boxing with the government consumed Jinnah to the exclusion of everything else. He became even more disassociated than before from his home front.

But this time, Ruttie hardly minded the distraction because she too had grown extremely attached to the kind English editor who had become more Indian than most Indians. She too immersed herself in the campaign to get Horniman back, made more confident by having Jinnah's full approval. While he was mostly busy sorting out the affairs of the *Bombay Chronicle*, Ruttie even attended a trade union congress held for the first time where she moved a resolution protesting against Horniman's deportation. The congress was a big gathering of important men, but sitting quietly by herself in a side-box, Ruttie not only moved the resolution but spoke from her heart, 'fluently and faultlessly', according to eyewitnesses, for five minutes—so important was the issue for her personally. But after that, for reasons that she could never explain even to herself, she never found the drive or the conviction to ever speak in public, considering that as exclusively Jinnah's sphere.

In all this renewed political activity the baby was quite forgotten, although it was due to arrive in less than three months. Instead of making plans for her confinement in Bombay, they now set off on a sea voyage to England for an indeterminate period. The Home Rule League leader Annie Besant had made an offer Jinnah could not refuse. She asked Jinnah to join her delegation to England to discuss the Montagu–Chelmsford proposals before Parliament in return for making all the arrangements to get him there. Since the War had ended, a passage to England was hard to arrange, even with all the money in the world, because the soldiers were going home. For Jinnah, it was an opportunity he could not miss. Having fallen foul of the local government, he wanted to appeal to his friends in higher authority in England who he was convinced would help Horniman to get back his passport and return to Bombay. The journey by sea would last at least twenty days and since Parliament would not start its hearings for at least another two months, it meant that he could not return in time to be there for the childbirth. There was no way he could leave her behind, cut off as she was from her own parents and family. Loath to lose this opportunity and yet a dutiful husband and would-be father, he took a risk that few would have dared in his place: dragged her along to England with him. Not that Ruttie needed any dragging—she was overjoyed at the prospect of this trip abroad, their first since they had married. Once they were in England, perhaps they would be as she had imagined their life together to be. As for the baby, she did not want to think about it as yet.

Chapter Twelve

~

It had been almost six years since Ruttie had been on a ship. The last time she had been a mere schoolgirl of thirteen, accustomed to going on summer vacations abroad with her parents and brothers and the large retinue of servants that accompanied them everywhere. It was the custom for rich families to go abroad for their summer holidays, and the Petits, with their own estates in the south of France and a summer residence in England, were more privileged than most. Coincidentally, Jinnah had been travelling on the same steamer, on his way to England, like them, for his summer vacation. But then she had been nothing more to him than the young daughter of his friend, with whom he might have occasionally stopped to converse if they ever met on deck. At thirteen, she was still something of a tomboy, more interested in playing pranks with her brothers; and when she tired of their games, retreating into her own world of books. And in the excitement of travelling abroad she had lost her taste for the long political talks that she occasionally had with Jinnah when they met in Bombay. He too had other things on his mind, primarily to use the journey to hold political talks with Gokhale who was also travelling on the same ship. In fact, Jinnah had made sure his travel plans coincided with Gokhale's trip to England so that they both would have the leisure for uninterrupted political discussion during the journey, as Sarojini told Gokhale in a letter she wrote to him on board. And apart from paying his usual courtesies in his old-world manner to the Petit ladies, he wasted no time on them or anyone else. It turned out to be her last trip abroad as Miss Petit, with the War starting the following year.

If the War had not lasted so long, they would have surely gone abroad for their honeymoon. Ruttie had been longing to escape from the country, not just to get away from all the unpleasantness and scandal, but so that she could get Jinnah away from the politics that was consuming him. In England they could at last be themselves, as she felt they were meant to be—a loving, smart, social couple, with their passion for politics leavened with visits to the opera, art shows and the Broadway. Life wouldn't be just about staying home and eating alone by themselves, but full of dinner parties, travel, fun. Once they got away from Bombay, Jinnah would surely be that old self that she had once briefly glimpsed while they were courting. Her spirits rose at the prospect, making it easier to ignore the fact that they had barely two months' time to themselves before the baby arrived.

To add to her eager expectation of the joys ahead, Sarojini had also decided to join them on the same ship, *S.S. Merkera*. Having waited futilely for weeks to find a passage to England to consult doctors on her heart condition, she had finally managed to find a berth by becoming, like Jinnah, part of Annie Besant's delegation going to England to appear before the parliamentary committee on the reforms bill. For Ruttie, this was even better than going to England with Jinnah, who, in any case, would get caught up in talking politics non-stop with other members of the delegation while they were on their voyage. She, who had tried and failed to get Sarojini's undivided attention while they were in Bombay, had a whole stretch of twenty days now to look forward to, with no one intruding on her time alone with her favourite person—just lying down on a deckchair next to her doing nothing more strenuous than reading and talking and snoozing between meals.

But that turned out to be yet another vain hope. Ruttie was in no condition to enjoy the voyage or Sarojini's company. During the first half of the journey, until Aden, she lay prostrate in her cabin, overcome by the extreme heat and rough seas. They did not go ashore at Aden, on their midway stop, but as Sarojini remarked in a letter home from the ship on 15 June 1919, there was plenty to see and enjoy, including 'the funny little roaming boats coming alongside full of curly-headed negro boys selling all sorts of wares—desert wares—of ostrich eggs, coloured baskets woven of date leaves, bundles of dates,

cigarettes, buckskins, beads and shells'. But always oversensitive to
heat and the rocking of boats on rough waters, made worse by her
present condition, Ruttie was in no state to enjoy the floating market
or anything else for that matter.

Jinnah, too, may as well have not been there with her. Although
he was physically in the same cabin with her, his mind was far away
in Bombay, where his real concerns were. The government had not
yet lifted its pre-censorship orders on the *Bombay Chronicle*. He had
tried everything, seeking appointments with the governor and his
officials and meeting every term and condition that the government
laid down, but they kept changing their terms and conditions, making
it impossible for him to escape the suspicion that the government was
determined to send him into political oblivion by whatever means
they could. And finally tiring of their dilatory tactics, he gave up and
resumed publication of the newspaper without the editorial pages.
This was only a week before his departure and it made him anxious
about leaving Bombay at such a time. He had little faith in the ability
of those he had left in charge of the newspaper's affairs to handle
the government, especially the assistant editor, S.A. Brelvi, who had
taken Horniman's place. He was nagged by worry throughout the
journey and by the time they reached Port Said, he could no longer
contain his anxiety. He sent off a letter from the port, which would
have amused Ruttie who knew only too well how much Jinnah
loathed writing letters. But she was feeling far too ill to appreciate
the irony. The letter was brief and displayed all his hidden anxiety to
know what was going on in Bombay during his absence: 'Dear Mr
Brelvi,' it began stiffly, 'This is just a line to inform you that we have
now reached Port Said.' And then without wasting time on further
civilities, Jinnah asked for news of what was going on in Bombay: 'I
shall feel greatly obliged if you will send me [the] *Bombay Chronicle*
to my address.'

Then, without willing it, he revealed himself, exposing his real
motive for writing the letter: 'How are things getting on? I am anxious
to know. Please keep in touch with what is going on in Bombay. I
wonder whether the order of pre-censorship continues.' And having
said what he wanted, he probably felt that some small talk was
in order: 'We have had a nice voyage on the whole,' he wrote, an
observation that Ruttie could hardly agree with. 'We almost escaped

the monsoon and it has been quite pleasant all along,' signing off abruptly with 'Hoping you are well, Yours sincerely, M.A. Jinnah.'

The other letter he wrote on board was equally forced out of him by his need for news from home. This letter was to Gandhi, requesting him to send him news of political developments, including Gandhi's own views on the reforms bill. Gandhi replied promptly, but instead of discussing the reforms or giving him the political news that Jinnah craved, he sent some gratuitous advice to him, suggesting he learn Gujarati and Hindi before he returned to India, and asked Ruttie to join the spinning classes that had now started in Bombay under his supervision.

Sarojini, on the other hand, with none of Jinnah's anxiety to know what was going on in India during their absence, and with a sturdier stomach than Ruttie's, could afford to sit back and enjoy herself during the voyage. 'How the sharks follow the ship for the garbage and how the porpoises play all round taking leaps into the air and then diving into the sea. Such a pretty sight,' she wrote from the ship to her daughters back home. She had plenty of time to look around her and enjoy the various human dramas on board the ship: 'The humour on board . . . are many and varied—and as I sit in my corner all day—quite aloof and quiet, I can watch all the fun. People have by now divided themselves into natural groups and rather sniff at one another—the bridge players, the snobs, the flirtatious, frivolous—the dowdy and domestic and the rag-tag and bobtails generally are herded together! But, of course, there are some very nice and interesting people . . . I do nothing all day long but lie in my chair and dream, read or sleep. I hardly talk to anyone except for a few minutes and I get to bed by 8.30 or latest by 9 o'clock.'

'Every now and then we pass a ship and that marks an event in the day,' she wrote in another letter. 'We reach Suez tomorrow and Port Said, which is like a city of the Arabian Nights, on Friday and then we get into the Poets' Mediterranean, the sea of song.'

After crossing Aden, according to yet another letter home from the sea, there was a respite from the oppressive heat. 'We expected blazing heat after Aden and everyone turned out in their thinnest summer clothes, prepared to be uncomplaining and cheerful martyrs to the Red Sea of tradition. But such a strong head wind started directly we set going again that everyone was glad of wraps and rugs and sheltered caverns.' And here Sarojini gives her only news of the silently suffering Ruttie, valiantly struggling against the heat, and her seasickness: 'Even Ruttie has begun to respond to the beautiful cool weather and comes up in the evening all glimmering like a mayflower and all the women gape at her because she looks so fragile and lovely—and fantastic.'

Nor did it get any better for Ruttie after they landed. Jinnah had, of course, the practical sense to rent a house for the duration of their stay in London. He would have preferred undoubtedly to have lived in a hotel, taking his usual suite in his favourite hotel in London, the Ritz, but had decided that it wouldn't do, especially with Ruttie's confinement approaching. But having installed her in their temporary home, he took off almost instantly, feeling his husbandly duties were done.

There was much to keep him busy and away from home. He had arrived in London not prepared to take it easy like the other delegates arriving in various deputations waiting their turn to give their evidence before the committee. His sense of duty drove him to meet as many people of influence as he could because he felt he had 'arduous work to do for the cause of India', as the Bombay Chronicle put it. They had reached London well ahead of some of the other Indian deputations. The committee was to begin its sittings nearly a month later, in the first week of August 1919. But first, he had to go meet Montagu in the hope of getting him to use his influence to release Horniman's passport and lift the deportation order against him. There was also the matter of the Rowlatt Act that he wished to discuss with the secretary of state, confident that he would side with him on the issue.

But his confidence in Montagu proved misplaced on both counts. For one thing, Jinnah's refusal to heed personal gossip had left him clueless about the changing power equations in London. Montagu's star was now waning. This was partly due to his fading health which reduced his previously formidable style of debating; but it was mainly because the government's attitude to India had lost its liberal hue after the Jallianwala Bagh incident. Montagu himself was no longer as sympathetic to Jinnah as he had been two years ago when he was in Bombay interviewing national leaders on the contents of the reforms bill. The good impression he had then formed of Jinnah had been entirely dissipated by both the present governor of Bombay, Sir George Lloyd, and his predecessor, Lord Willingdon, who turned him against Jinnah, with Lloyd even writing to Montagu warning the secretary of state about Jinnah's unreliable character. It was Lloyd who had engineered the deportation of Horniman and the temporary closure of the *Bombay Chronicle* in order, he claimed, to calm the unrest in Bombay and undermine the position of Bombay's extremists, of whom he considered Jinnah to be the prime leader. And now, with Horniman's removal, Lloyd was able to convince Montagu that he had achieved calm in Bombay by removing the 'daily ration of sedition' that Horniman was providing his readers through the newspaper.

Clueless about what was really going on under the surface, Jinnah busied himself setting up meetings with both Montagu and other people of note in London. What little time he spent at home went into reading newspapers. He had been starved of news from back home on the long voyage to London and was now eager to catch up with all that he had missed. He went through not just the day's newspapers, both from India and in London, but carefully read old issues as well, making copious markings and issuing clarifications and press statements whenever he felt they were necessary. The news famine had also made him uncharacteristically social, inviting any young Indian student he met to his Pall Mall home so that they could talk politics with him.

By the end of July, his attention shifted to the reforms bill. All the Indian deputations had arrived by now and receptions were being held in their honour by unofficial organizations friendly to India's political aspirations. Being the best known among the Indian representatives, Jinnah, naturally, was invited to address the gathering. Now he took on yet another self-imposed mission that kept him busy at all hours of the day and night. Believing that it was important to show the British government that Indians were united in their demand for self-government and wanting to dispel the general impression in England that only a 'few educated agitators and lawyers' were demanding the reforms, he held long discussions with all the Indian deputations to persuade them to speak in one voice. But this was yet another wasted effort on his part. Despite his strenuous efforts, neither the Congress nor the Liberals were willing to give up their extreme positions on whether the reforms were workable or just rubbish. While he succeeded in getting Mrs Besant's Home Rule League team to sign a joint memorandum on the bill, the Congress and the Liberals stuck to their position at both extremes of the middle path he was suggesting.

There was no time in all this to pay much attention to what was going on in his own home. Even less to wonder what Ruttie felt about having a baby abroad with no support except what his money could buy. Ruttie herself felt as if she had exchanged one place of solitary confinement for another. England, especially after the War, was 'no place for anyone without a definite purpose', as Sarojini put it. The London of Ruttie's girlhood memories no longer existed. The house that they had settled into was in Pall Mall, which was a convenient address for both their interests, within calling distance of Jinnah's various work appointments and close to the shops in case Ruttie wanted to go shopping by herself. But there was so little to see or shop for, with all the post-War shortages, including even of coal and food. Nor did she know anyone she could go and call on. The few acquaintances from her maiden days were all associated with her parents' circle, and therefore to be avoided. Once again, there was only Sarojini to turn to, but she had decided to use the one month before the committee began its sitting, to go on an extensive tour of the Lake District and Ireland.

Jinnah, on the other hand, was focused on his upcoming interview with the joint select committee, and sent out summons to several young Indian students he knew to visit him at his flat so that he could discuss with them the questions likely to be asked by the select committee's members. Diwan Chaman Lal recalls being 'summoned' by Jinnah to his flat near Regent's Park and 'hardly had got down to my cup of tea with a [half-] bitten sandwich in my hand' when Jinnah got down to discussing what was on his mind—how to answer a question he was anticipating from the committee on India's low literacy, which Chaman Lal was delighted to be able to provide an answer to, with all the confidence of a fresh Oxford graduate. Chagla, an Oxford undergraduate then, similarly recalls Jinnah receiving him warmly when he went to call on him and 'talked to me about politics and what was happening in India and what was likely to come out of the labours of the Joint Select Committee'.

A month later, the committee began its sittings and Ruttie saw even less of Jinnah than before. The sittings, held three days a week, lasted several hours each time, but Jinnah in his thorough way was determined to attend every sitting, following word for word as each delegation came up before the committee of twelve British parliamentarians. And with so many deputations to appear before it, the committee was expected to go on with its examination of the Indian deputations for at least a month, putting paid to any hopes that Ruttie may have had of spending some time alone with Jinnah.

His own turn to appear before the committee came earlier than most, on 13 August, just a week after it had begun its sittings. He had prepared meticulously for the occasion and put forward his views with his usual brutal frankness. It surprised him, of course, when Montagu, as the author of the proposals, took his forthrightness to heart. The secretary of state, walking into the hearing after Jinnah had already begun his speech, was no doubt put out to hear Jinnah describing the proposed reforms as 'timid and prejudiced'. Jinnah, unconscious as ever of the effect he sometimes had on others when all he felt he was doing was arguing his case forcefully, further put off Montagu by expressing his deep admiration for his predecessor, Lord Morley. Jinnah declared roundly that in his opinion, Morley had been the best secretary of state that India had ever had and that none of his successors had matched him so far or could hope to do so in the future. Had Ruttie been there at the hearing, she would have probably been amused at the effect her husband was having on Montagu and the other members of the committee. She was familiar by now with his brutal frankness, never stopping to consider how his remarks would be construed by those to whom he addressed them. A disconcerted Montagu, who had formerly liked and even admired Jinnah, receiving him in his home, hit back by accusing Jinnah of continually accentuating and increasing his demands.

Jinnah ruffled other feathers in the committee by his hard-hitting arguments on why the reforms in the bill were too little, too late. With the exception of one question that was put to the other member of his deputation, the committee members focused their entire attention on trying to trip Jinnah up on the statements he had made or at least attempted to get him to admit that he had not done enough homework on the suggestions he was trying to include in the bill. But he was more than a match for the British parliamentarians, as one eyewitness, B.G. Telang, observed, describing Jinnah at the sitting as 'the equal of everybody where question and answer and repartee were concerned'. Telang was not as impressed with Jinnah's grasp of the nitty-gritty of the bill though, claiming that he had been caught on weak ground where practical details were concerned, 'without any mastery or study of the subject' and tending towards 'controversial frippery'.

But Jinnah did not share in this view of himself. In fact, his good opinion of himself and the sense of satisfaction at a job well done were strong enough to allow him to take an evening off from his political work and go with Ruttie to the theatre. During their courtship, he had impressed her with his fondness for theatre, and now that they were in London, she had been coaxing and teasing him into taking her to see a play. They set out the very next evening after he appeared before the committee, a carefree, smartly dressed couple that turned heads when they entered. But Ruttie's pleasure in this rare evening out with Jinnah was destined to be short-lived. Halfway through the play, the baby decided it was time for its arrival. They had to leave the theatre hurriedly.

The baby arrived around the midnight of 14 August. It was a girl, with Ruttie's exquisite mouth and her large, dark eyes. There were no visitors, neither family nor friends, to admire the baby or fuss over the mother. Lady Petit was back in Bombay after their holiday in the hills, taking lessons in spinning under Gandhi's tutelage (causing Sarojini to write home in amusement: 'think of Lady Petit in her chiffons and Lady Tata with her pearls, solemnly spinning thread like the Fates!'). Sarojini might have still been in London—her letter to her son, Ranadheera, is datelined 'London, August 13th', just the day before Ruttie's delivery. But having given her evidence before the select committee a little before Jinnah, she might have been about to take off for a well-deserved vacation in Ireland, after having spent the last few weeks giving lectures all across England to spread the Congress's point of view on the reforms bill. In fact, her next letter home is not until the following fortnight, 27 August 1919, datelined Dublin, and makes no mention of Ruttie or her baby. But even if she had indeed been in London around then, it is doubtful if Jinnah, with his stubborn pride and independence, would have thought it necessary to ask her to be there to at least provide some moral support to his young wife, so far away from home. Sarojini makes no mention of it in any of her many letters home from London. Left to himself, Jinnah, no doubt, rose to his duty, as ever—appointing the best professional caretakers that his money could buy, and then, after consigning both mother and newborn daughter into their hands, returning calmly to his own concerns.

Nor did Ruttie seem to consider the baby her particular concern. She, who had always lavished her tenderness on weak and helpless creatures, was curiously detached from her own infant girl. Jinnah would have spared no expense in hiring nannies and nursery maids and whatever staff he might have been told a well-born baby required, and with a bevy of so many professionals at the baby's beck and call, Ruttie could have easily persuaded herself that the baby was in better hands than her own. She was ready, at any rate, to accompany Jinnah wherever he was invited, whether it was public meetings or receptions in his honour, leaving the newborn to her nannies and nursemaids.

Within weeks of the baby's arrival, she had apparently bounced back. But there was something indefinably tragic about her, as Sarojini was quick to notice when she finally returned to London and called on the Jinnahs. 'Ruttie is looking for all the world like a fragile moth with black gold-spotted wings,' she wrote to Padmaja on 8 October 1919. 'She does not look excessively happy but beautiful with a courageous pathetic beauty.'

Less than two weeks after Sarojini's visit to meet the mother and her newborn, the Jinnahs boarded a steamer back to India. The baby had just turned two months old, and Jinnah could wait no more. It was more than four months since he had left India and he needed to get back. Confident though he continued to be of his unassailable position in Indian politics, recent events had made him nervous of being cast into political obscurity. It was a question of his political survival.

Chapter Thirteen

~

Three weeks later, the Jinnahs were back in Bombay. The baby presumably took the sea voyage better than her mother, with Ruttie's 'intestine ever on the defensive against the surging surface', as she once put it in a letter to Kanji. At any rate, there was no mention of the new addition to the Jinnah family in the notice that appeared the next day in the *Bombay Chronicle*'s popular 'Official and Personal' column, which merely said: 'Mr and Mrs Jinnah arrived in Bombay per S.S. Malwa on Friday morning.'

They had arrived over the weekend but Jinnah allowed himself no rest. Almost the first thing he did on landing was to summon a reporter from the *Bombay Chronicle* to give his views on what he had managed to accomplish during his London visit—the 'arduous work for the cause of India' and the 'many people of note' he'd met and his cautious optimism on the government reforms that were soon to come. For Ruttie, who had always loathed any premeditated and 'calculative' action, whether in politics or personal life, his long interview splashed in the newspaper the following Monday might have appeared embarrassingly like self-promotion, but Jinnah was a practical man. He was not going to shy away from building himself up in the media when it was his only way of keeping his hold in a fast-changing political scenario.

Quite a lot had changed since he'd gone to England, making him fear that he would lose his grip on the political scene unless he got down to work at once. For one thing, he discovered that while he had been pouring all his energies in England on pushing for more drastic reforms in the new Government of India Act, Muslims had moved away even further from issues of self-government. In fact, the only political issue they were concerned with was the Khilafat question. The fact that the Caliph, who was also the Turkish sultan and had been on the wrong side of the War, was now being stripped by the Allies of his control over the holy places of Arabia overshadowed everything else in the eyes of Indian Muslims.

For someone like Jinnah, who had striven throughout his political career to keep religion out of politics, it was difficult to take the Khilafat issue seriously. He had been facing pressure from the pro-Khilafat elements within the Muslim League even before he left for England, forcing him to put in a perfunctory note of protest with the British government while he was there. But by the time he returned to India, the Khilafatists had entrenched themselves in power, forming committees in every province and making themselves heard. In November, soon after he returned from England, they even called an All-India Muslim Conference which was to be held in Simla. He had been invited, of course, but declined the invitation on a flimsy pretext, sending them a telegram of support instead. On the other hand, when the government appointed him to its peace celebrations committee, he promptly distanced himself from it by identifying himself as a sympathizer of the Khilafat cause. But this fooled neither the government nor the Muslims, who thought his gesture of solidarity too perfunctory to be sincere.

It was the same in the Congress—a hard struggle to keep his position from being undermined. There were no takers for his moderate views on the reforms and his conviction that the Congress should cooperate with the government on, even if what they had to offer was disappointingly little. His only way of getting heard now within the Congress seemed to be through joining forces with Gandhi, which was both humiliating and unavoidable.

Of course, he spoke of none of these concerns to Ruttie, even though she had not quite given up as yet in trying to involve herself in his political life. But in this he did not encourage her, not because he wanted to deliberately keep her out, but because it was simply not in his nature to share his political dilemmas with anyone until he had sorted them out in his own mind. Nor did she try to wheedle or coax them out of him as she would have done in the past. The issues that were agitating him seemed to her, in any case, too dry and legalistic to hold her attention. It could have been the arrival of the baby, but she was in a strangely restless mood, as if her youth and freedom were deserting her, although she was only nineteen. On the surface, their life settled into a routine. No longer needing to go to Delhi for the legislative sessions now that he had resigned, Jinnah still followed his strict regime of leaving for work in the morning and then immersing himself in more work when he returned home in the evening, with no break for rest or entertainment, while she was left to her own resources. But there was little she could find to occupy her. Unlike some mothers, she preferred to leave the baby entirely to the ayahs and nursemaid, as her mother had once done. But whereas Lady Petit's pride and joy was inextricably tied up with her children, wanting to dress them up in beautiful lace longcoats and have their portraits taken and fuss about their common cold and flu, Ruttie felt no interest in the baby at all, apart from making sure that it had a nursery and staff of its own. She had already overhauled their household, bringing it up to fashionable standards in the number of footmen and butlers and cooks and valets and maids required to wait on them. And with that running in order, there was little to do other than ordering their meals, which in Jinnah's case was merely ensuring that his breakfast was served on time. As for the other meals, he hardly ate at all, and that too the most spartan of fares, posing no challenge at all to her who had been raised on Petit Hall's legendary table. But still, perhaps to keep her boredom at bay, she did try to invest her daily task of choosing the day's menu with a touch of individuality, and sometimes it was, to say the least, eccentric—ordering, for instance, a vegetarian meal when they had guests for dinner because, as she explained to Chagla when he asked why, 'her cat was sick'. There was shopping, of course, something she had always loved, but even in this her enthusiasm was waning. On the day after they arrived from London, she had summoned a sari vendor to come home with his trunks to show her his wares. But she was not tempted to buy anything he showed her from his trunks and although she ordered a few saris for herself out of old habit, she had grown so indifferent that she did not even bother to follow up on the order for months afterwards.

At the end of December 1919, Jinnah and Ruttie took their first trip out of Bombay since arriving with the baby. Leaving it behind with the nurse and nanny, they left to attend the year-end sessions of the Congress and the Muslim League in Amritsar. It had been only three years ago when a sixteen-year-old Ruttie had set out on a train with her aunt to attend her first Congress session, filled with excitement at the prospect of listening to three days of long speeches. But that wide-eyed excitement had long since died and now it was all as dull as she had feared it would be. Amritsar was rainy and cold and depressing, and there was thin attendance at the sessions of the Muslim League, with the opening day going only into reading aloud the presidential address which stretched for several unbearable hours. Then midway through the session, the Ali brothers entered and took over the stage and the hearts of the audience and the air was rent with cries of 'Allahu Akbar' and loud weeping. It was a scene that appealed to neither of them.

The Congress sessions which took place simultaneously were equally tedious, with leaders spending hours debating over a single amendment to a resolution. Like her youthful self, the days of stirring political speeches that had so fired her up with patriotic zeal seemed to have suddenly ended. She felt burnt out.

The only thing she could think of that might help lift her sinking spirits was to plan a trip alone to visit Padmaja in Hyderabad, leaving both Jinnah and the baby at home. It was a city that she had never visited before, except for the aborted trip she made with Jinnah the previous April when they were forced to take the next train back because the Nizam's government objected to a speech he made there and banned his entry into the state henceforth. She had always longed to go there, especially after she got to know Sarojini and her daughters. As a girl, Padmaja's description of the life they led there, the impromptu parties and picnics and fetes and the warm friendships, with people visiting each other for breakfast and midnight music sessions, had made a deep impression on her, and now, being the social outcast she was in Bombay, she yearned to become part of this charmed social circle where no one ever seemed lonely or depressed. 'Hyderabad, it seems, could quite well give Bombay a lesson on "How to make things hum a bit,"' she had written wistfully to Padmaja at fifteen, when she was convalescing in the Petits' monsoon retreat in Poona. And to Leilamani a year later, imagining a city of romantic charm: 'of beautiful Begums and warrior Nawabs, of fragrant white jasmine and passionate burning incense sticks, of luxurious diwans and rainbow coloured sticks, of mosques and fortresses and muezzin cries, of throned elephants and oriental pomp'.

Except for the short trip she had made to Mussoorie to visit them in their boarding school shortly after her marriage and an equally short visit Padmaja made to Bombay just before her mother's departure for England, Ruttie had not spent any time with either of the Naidu girls for the past two years. Caught up as she was in her new life, even the correspondence between them had stopped, with not a single letter exchanged between them since her marriage. She longed to get close to them again and spend at least a fortnight with them in their home when they could once again tell each other their secrets, and she would no longer feel so lonesome.

Not the least of its attractions was, of course, that it would give her the break that she badly needed, both from Jinnah and the baby. With the ban order against him, Hyderabad was the one place he could not possibly propose joining her. It was to be her bachelor trip, without him or the baby to hamper her, free to bond with her girlfriends. Sarojini was still in England, convalescing from the surgery she had undergone, but both her girls were in Hyderabad with their father, with the younger one, Leilamani, having just finished school. They greeted her plans to visit with a warmth and enthusiasm that made her even more determined to go, although it left Jinnah less than enthusiastic.

Jinnah, of course, would have felt it beneath his dignity to argue with her, and it was only after she had actually left that he sunk his pride and began 'writing and begging her to return', as Padmaja wrote to her brother, Ranadheera, during Ruttie's visit. Hurt he must have surely been, given his 'over tuned senses', as Ruttie termed that hypersensitivity he hid behind his impassive exterior. For her to abandon him like that, when she knew very well that he could not enter Hyderabad because of the Nizam's order, probably cut him to the core. But more important, it would have triggered that conflict between his old and new selves that he had begun feeling ever since his marriage—the urbane gentleman of liberal ideas at war with his father's son. It was not the first time—and certainly not the last— when he would have realized the abyss between them—he, born of a mother who had never once gone anywhere without her husband;

in fact, her devotion to his father was so total that she even refused to stay a while longer in the village during Jinnah's first wedding because her husband was going back to the city and she could not bear him going without her. While here was Ruttie, from such a different world, setting out on a pleasure trip without him, as if it was the most natural thing to do—as indeed, it was, having seen her mother and her set living in a world quite apart from their husbands. But still, whatever his feelings might have been, he kept them stoically to himself, saying nothing while she made her own plans.

Funnily enough, neither of them seemed overly concerned about her leaving the baby behind, although it was only five months old. Having installed her from the day they returned from London in her own nursery, they seemed to have almost forgotten her existence. It would take at least another year before Ruttie's unnatural lack of attachment to her baby would attract comment, but even in these early months there was less than the usual weak connection that seemed to exist between infants in well-born modern households and their otherwise busy parents. So little did either of them involve themselves in the baby that it had not even occurred to either of them that she would soon require at least a name of her own.

It was a puzzle why Ruttie, of all women, who even as a child could not bear to see a suffering creature without rushing to its aid, turned her face away so resolutely from her own infant daughter. Could it be perhaps her resentment, hidden so far under her guise of careless insouciance, but chafing nevertheless at this 'slavery', as she later put it—this double bondage of wife and mother that she had not bargained for in her passionate eagerness for life, not yet daring to spill out into open rebellion, but still unable to resist her heart's stifled cry of 'Let me be free. Let me be free'? Panicked suddenly that 'her youth is going and she must live', that 'life is passing her by', she was determined to try and recover her old self, 'longing to be free of all her shackles'. She needed some time alone with her friends, to immerse herself once again in the old life that she had so foolhardily turned her back on. Of her family, Lady Petit, at least, was eager to make up with her daughter, yearning to see her little granddaughter but Ruttie, with a pride as stubborn as Jinnah's, wanted to have nothing to do with her, turning instead to her friends in Hyderabad as if they were her one and only family.

But while it was easy, even imperative, to leave behind both Jinnah and the baby, Arlette, her precious dog, had to go with her because she could not bear to part from her, even for a fortnight. And although the Naidus' home was already overcrowded with a menagerie of pets, including several dogs, cats, a squirrel, deer and a mongoose, she insisted on not just taking Arlette along but its attendant as well and the boxes of its special food, watched mutely by Jinnah, his face giving away nothing as she set out on her first holiday without him.

Chapter Fourteen

~

The quarrels started as soon as she returned. Of course, there could be no quarrels between them in the ordinary sense, no raised voices or scenes, or slamming of doors, or such venting of tempers. At least that would have been a relief, because then one could hope for it all to end soon, the making up compensating for the sulking, with a clearing of air that she longed for as one way of getting closer to him. But with Jinnah, there could be no slanging matches. Losing his temper would have been beneath him; he did not even raise his voice against a servant. With her, he just withdrew, retreating into a cold silence which not all her teasing and coaxing could penetrate, leaving her wondering whether he was really angry with her and, at the same time, what she could have done to offend him. That he was displeased with her from the moment she returned from Hyderabad was apparent enough to her, but what she had done to deserve his cold treatment she could not quite figure out. It certainly made it even harder to reconcile herself to getting back to her own home, especially after the warmth and hospitality of the Naidu household.

Padmaja had not exaggerated the charms of her native city, and the Naidus' wide circle of friends had taken her to their heart at once. She was not just included in all their schemes of fun and entertainment but sought after in a way that made her oddly grateful after months of being ostracized. Most Hyderabadis who met her were immediately bewitched by her beauty and glamour, making no secret of it, and she blossomed under the adulation, becoming her old, friendly, open self all over again. The persona she had recently adopted—the mocking, chain-smoking sophisticate who was beyond being hurt and existed only to shock others—dropped away effortlessly, revealing that sympathy of soul that was her most attractive quality.

She went riding with Padmaja and her friends, drawing them out in intimate conversations that they would not have dared to initiate with her. She showed such tact and discretion that they warmed to her, overcoming their awe of her. Many of them were unused to the sophisticated world she came from, but they were so warm and affectionate that she could not help being touched, taking great pains to hide her amusement at some of their gaffes, and all along putting them at ease. After being starved all these months of the company of young people and having felt a pariah in her own city, it felt good to be sought after again. Her defences crumbled under their simple adoration and she felt eager to please and be pleased, as she used to be as a young girl. They insisted she visit them in their homes, and they treated her with such old-world hospitality and affection that she was in a mood to be charmed by all that she saw—recklessly ordering replicas of everything that caught her eye, from furniture to brass urns and clay palm stands and even a horse, to take back home with her. In short, she made more friends and dined at more homes in the eighteen days she was in Hyderabad than she had in the eighteen months of her life in South Court. She revelled in the freedom to be entirely herself and to be loved and admired for it—instead of the sidelong looks and notoriety that was her lot in Bombay. And though she always put up a spirited defence against such tactics, the way she was treated in Hyderabad made her feel more at home than she had felt since her marriage.

And what perhaps did her more good than meeting Padmaja's friends was the chance at last to unburden herself, at least a little, with Padmaja. There had been few secrets between them, especially on Padmaja's part, who trustingly confided her private concerns, mostly about her romantic attachments and the proposals she had received, to all her girlfriends, including Ruttie. But now it was Ruttie's turn to open up, trying to convey her very mixed feelings about marriage and Jinnah, and the half-exasperated pride of having him so dependent on her that he could not bear even this short separation from her.

The house itself, 'The Golden Threshold', named after Sarojini's first book of poems, was, as a visitor described it, 'a quiet bungalow set in the midst of a walled-in compound and nestling in the shade of noble trees . . . in the verandah a huge swing common in South Indian homes . . . [it] combined eastern tastes with western comforts'. There was something magical about Ruttie in its ambience. It was not just its 'delightful unconventionalism', as she put it, but the sense of freedom and warm spontaneity that was all-pervasive. The girls, now that they were out of school, were free to do what they liked with their day, waking up when they liked and following their own pursuits. There were no set times for meals, the servants were free and easy in their manners, the garden was charmingly disordered, books lay carelessly about, pets ran around with no leash, and visitors dropped in at any hour, sitting down informally to eat with the family, making plans on the spur of the moment and carrying them out instantaneously. The contrast to the rigidity and formality of her own home must have struck her, making her wistful for the life she had so carelessly walked out of, unmindful of the consequences.

Even the garden with its delightful unkemptness—'well filled with the most beautiful flowers and shrubs and then allowed to run into wildness', as the Naidus liked their garden to be—was such a pleasing contrast to South Court, with Jinnah's passion for tidy flower beds and everything in straight rows, unable to bear what he called 'a jungle'.

She felt drawn to each member of the family, especially Dr Naidu whom she was meeting for the first time. He was a quiet man, almost silent, but she had always prided herself on being able to read people's souls through their eyes and now she felt she had divined his true spirit, telling the two sisters that he had the most remarkable pair of eyes she'd ever seen on a man's face. Although he was rarely at home, his devotion to his children, especially his two daughters, was apparent to even a stranger like her. They, in turn, worshipped him for assuming the role of a single parent, setting free Sarojini from her domestic responsibilities to enable her to pursue her rising career as a poet and politician. It made Ruttie wistful and she spun stories in her head of the sacrifices he had made for the family; when back in Bombay, she fed her gullible friend Kshama with fanciful tales of how he was, in fact, the real genius in the family, composing all of Sarojini's poems for her and generously letting her take the credit for them.

Her interest in him would have surprised Dr Naidu had he been aware of it. He had barely been home while she stayed with them.

As a military doctor, he usually worked long hours but in those weeks while she was there, he had to keep even longer hours because of a flu and plague epidemic that erupted simultaneously. Whatever might have been his opinion of his house guest, he kept it strictly to himself. He had always been a little wary of Sarojini's smart friends, and the fact that Ruttie had chosen to make a pleasure trip on her own, leaving behind her husband and infant daughter, made him even more aloof than usual. He said little, only observing carefully in a postscript to a letter to his son in Bangalore that 'Mrs Jinna [*sic*] arrived today and is a guest in our house.' Nor did he say much more in the letter he wrote the following week; the only sign that he was better acquainted with his house guest being a correction in the spelling of her name: 'Mrs Jinnah is still here.'

The burning topic in the Naidus' home that fortnight was the question of sending the two girls to England for further education. It was something that both Dr Naidu and Sarojini had set their hearts on since they were little girls. True liberals, they had long decided that their two daughters would be provided the same opportunities for further education as their two sons. And now that Padmaja had passed her Senior Cambridge examination, they had begun preparations to send her abroad. An English acquaintance, a missionary in Hyderabad called Mrs Wigel, was approached to make the necessary arrangements for Padmaja's admission into Oxford. But while the arrangements were being made, the usually gentle and biddable Padmaja inexplicably refused to leave home. One reason possibly was the financial strain she knew this would put on her father. Dr Naidu's salary as a military doctor under the Nizam was certainly handsome by Hyderabadi standards, but would certainly not stretch to cover the costs of putting four children through university abroad. Either that, or a secret romance with a young officer in Hyderabad may have made Padmaja decide to turn down her father's plans for her, and nothing or nobody could change her mind, forcing Dr Naidu to give up the arrangements being made for her admission to Oxford.

But Leilamani had no such qualms and readily seized the chance to go in her sister's place. A self-willed, boisterous girl of fifteen and a half, Leilamani certainly did not dwell on the financial burden she might be imposing on her father, especially as she would have to spend an extra year in an English boarding school preparing for her university entrance examination. With Sarojini still in England recovering from her surgery, she was easily able to persuade her father to send her in Padmaja's place. And with his progressive ideas of women's emancipation, far ahead of his times, and no Sarojini around to veto the scheme, he made no objections, allowing Leilamani to have her way. It was at this poignant point in the Naidus' lives that Ruttie descended on them, plunging herself at once into the family discussion as if she was indeed a member of the family she had always longed to belong to.

Ruttie had always been a vocal and impassioned believer in women's equal rights, particularly on their right to equal education, inspired by suffragist Emmeline Pankhurst's autobiography, *My Own Story*. Having bought a copy of it soon after it was published in 1914, and signing her name in her fourteen-year-old hand, 'Rutty Petit', in ink on the front page that has leaked and stained on to the next page, she embarked on an enthusiastic reading of the autobiography, heavily underscoring entire passages of it with pencil, particularly on the discrimination daughters faced in education compared to sons, including a sentence on page six—'I didn't want to be a boy'—and writing next to it on the margin an enthusiastic 'bravo!' It's not hard to understand why a young and ardent Ruttie at fourteen would have set Emmeline Pankhurst up as her role model. Emmeline, like herself, had married a barrister twenty-four years her senior in age and a believer in women's equal rights. (Richard Pankhurst believed so deeply in a life of public service that he had decided to remain a bachelor until he met and fell in love with Emmeline.) And she, after flouting her mother's injunction 'to stop throwing herself at him', toyed with the idea of living with him outside marriage, had eventually married him, and despite five children, had embarked on a life of public service along with her husband. But now, when Leilamani had got the chance that Ruttie had wilfully denied herself by choosing to get married rather than wait for the War to end and go abroad to study further, Ruttie surprisingly found herself on Padmaja's side of the family tussle, trying to dissuade Leilamani from making something of her own life. Could it perhaps be a twinge of envy—not wanting the younger girl to have what she herself had opted out of? A little envy would only be natural considering her current chafing at her own 'fetters', while there was the young and brash Leilamani with her freedom stretching before her, unobstructed, and with her father's full support behind her. Without stopping to examine her own feelings too closely, Ruttie seems to have used her considerable influence on the younger girl to give up her plans, and was, in fact, quite confident of having succeeded by the end of it. As she wrote later to Padmaja, 'By the bye, was I right in my surmise or *is* she still talking about going to England quite seriously?' But Leilamani, far from being scared off by the prospect of spending four years in a cold, distant country with no home comforts or family support and depriving herself of the privileges that girls of fifteen or sixteen enjoyed in India—allowed to freely enter the adult world of drawing rooms and parties and even secretly indulge in romantic pursuits that their purdah-free environment enabled—proved Ruttie wrong.

The fortnight passed all too soon, even though Jinnah did not think so. Abandoning his usual stance of resolute detachment, and letting her decide when she wanted to return home, he gave in to an irrational impulse and wrote to her at least two or three times during the fortnight, urging her to come back home soon. She, however, was in no mood to oblige, stretching her fortnight's holiday by yet another three days before she reluctantly decided it was time to go back to her 'fun-forsaken' home. 'Ruttie has been staying here for over a fortnight,' as Padmaja wrote to her younger brother, Ranadheera, from their home in an undated letter, 'and how the poor kid has been enjoying herself.' And since she was now part privy to Ruttie's marriage, was able to add: 'Jinnah has been writing and begging her to return and she is leaving on Saturday, only because she is afraid that otherwise she might not be allowed to come again here.' Meanwhile, Ruttie was bent on squeezing every last drop of fun out of these remaining few days of her holiday without him. 'Just now,' Padmaja wrote in the same letter, 'she and Papi [Leilamani's pet name] and Toufik [one of their many friends in Hyderabad] are out for their morning ride.' Ruttie managed to pack in so much partying that even Padmaja was quite sick of it by the end. 'We have been very busy with parties and lunches and dinners etc. and I am so tired of it all.'

The highlight of Ruttie's trip, however, was a dog that she found and adopted, planning to take it home with her. As Padmaja recounts, 'The other morning a crowd of them rode to Golconda and Ruttie bagged a lovely Banjara dog that she saw. Since it came she has spent

I don't know how much over soaps and brilliantine for the dog—but he is very beautiful and Arlette hates him.'

Jinnah, too, seems to have taken an instant dislike to it. Or perhaps it was a vent for his pent-up resentment against her for abandoning her responsibilities, always a touchy subject with him. But at any rate, he now put up a brief show of husbandly assertion, so unusual for him that it left her unnerved. It had to do with the dogs. He had so far suffered in silence the two dogs that Ruttie had already introduced into the household—besides Arlette, a replacement for Fido, the lapdog who used to accompany the sixteen-year-old Ruttie to parties dressed in a bow matching his mistress's sari, there was another dog, Bolsh or Bolshie, short for Bolshevik, who also had the run of the house like Arlette, petted and indulged and not allowed by their mistress ever to be leashed, let alone disciplined in any way. Till now, he had shown exemplary forbearance towards her overindulged pets, but Loafer-ul-Mulk—that was the name the new dog had been given by Ruttie as a tongue-in-cheek acknowledgement, presumably, of his gypsy Banjara antecedents—seems to have triggered his extraordinary bout of aggression. It was possible that the scene was the result of the natural mayhem that must have ensued with Loafer's admission into the household where Bolsh already reigned as the alpha male. But Ruttie does not refer to any doggie battle for turf, only writing to Padmaja the next day to complain of the severe shock to her nerves as a result of Jinnah deciding to teach her dogs a lesson. 'Although I had fully intended writing to you yesterday, I couldn't find the nerve to settle to it,' she wrote in a letter, datelined Bombay, 9 February 1920, 'as J insisted on keeping Loafer-ul-Mulk and Bolsh on either side of him with a cane between his knees.'

To most people, the incident which she scathingly called 'J's super training' would hardly have seemed worth getting so upset about, but clearly it perturbed Ruttie deeply, bending helplessly, and worse, silently, to his will. As a child, Ruttie had flown into a rage, on separate occasions, at both her governess and her mother for even lifting a cane threateningly at one of her dogs, so passionately did she believe in her dogs' rights to have the run of the house and not be restrained in any way. And it was a measure of how much she had changed in the last eighteen months that she could sit by and watch without intervening while J had his way with the dogs. In her frustrated fury, she wished the dogs would attack him but that was impossible—they instinctively bent to his will. As she wrote: 'Of course I was hoping that they would make him the common foe—but in vain!' And with a submissiveness that would have surprised her family in Petit Hall, she closed the painful subject with: 'The result of all this super-training is that Bolshie is limping and Loafer evincing his strong dislike to the chain by howling.'

It is easy to read between the lines and sense the depth of her wistfulness to be back again among her dear friends instead of this place she had to call home. 'I have had such a ripping time with you all in Hyderabad,' she writes in the same letter, 'that I am quite spoilt for this fun-forsaken place.' She tries to adopt a light-hearted tone which she gives up midway through her sentence: 'It is impossible to offer you "formal thanks in formal words" (De Profundus!!!) when I think of the delightful unconventionalism of "The Golden Threshold" but you will understand how very much I appreciated *everything* when I tell you that it will remain among the happiest of my' . . . 'memories', she was about to write but changed it to 'recollections'.

Even the memory of two old-worldly acquaintances of the family who paid her a customary courtesy gets a fond mention: 'Haider was a perfect brick and old Ansari turned up at some station or another with a bottle of scent (which I have no doubt Papi would have loved) and gave it to me with all due ceremony.'

To add to her sense of alienation at being back home, Fatima, whom she was beginning to dislike intensely, came to spend the day with them because it was Sunday and her appointed day to meet her brother. Unmindful of her manners, she began to tease her serious-minded sister-in-law, pretending to make a joke of it. As she recounted in her letter: 'By the bye, I told Fatima that I went to Hyderabad to look up some eligible man for her and I showed her Taufik's photo as being one of them.' Oblivious to both Jinnah's and Fatima's reaction, she kept up her merciless ragging, taking pleasure in putting Fatima down as a confirmed old maid still unmarried at the advanced age of twenty-six. But something in Jinnah's expression must have shamed her into stopping—those eyes, 'twin lamps of truth', as someone later called them—and she was still smarting the next day at the look she received from him. As she wrote: 'She quite believed it at first, but

J didn't quite play up to his part and I observed fast a shadow of a doubt in those deep grave eyes of hers.'

But while she was left with some uneasiness at this 'joke' of hers that had misfired, Ruttie was as yet unaware of the other subject on which they were soon going to disagree sharply, and that was her careless extravagance. She had done some shopping while in Hyderabad—casually ordering whatever caught her eye—bric-a-brac and wooden furniture and brass and clay palm-stands—in her effort to try and refurbish the rather dingy South Court into a house that was more to her taste. She had, of course, not yet told him how much she had spent—nor did she need to—but knowing what a stickler he was for accounts, and sensing how much her vague indifference to money must irritate him, and even anxious perhaps to regain his approval after seeing the recent condemnation in his eyes over the Fatima incident, she was suddenly interested in finding out from Padmaja how much money she might have actually spent while in Hyderabad. She got down to it with a would-be air of businesslike efficiency: 'And now I am going to worry you—regarding my bills for which I have enclosed cheques. If the furniture man from Secunderabad has sent all the articles will you please forward this cheque in his name.' But it was difficult for her to focus on settling the bills even as her mind ran to other things she still wanted to get from Hyderabad: 'If you can manage to get hold of somebody who you think understands the type of work of the [clay] palm stand and urn at Mahomed Ali's please show it to him and let me know.' And then flitted back again to purchases that were about to arrive: 'Burton hasn't yet sent in his bill. I am writing to him directly and I really don't think that there is a likelihood of his ignoring my instructions.'

And having got the tiresome business of bills out of the way, she could get back to being herself, ending with a breezy: 'Please give my love to your father and Baba [Padmaja's brother, Jaisoorya],' going on to add a personal message to one of Padmaja's friends, a keen rider like herself: 'and tell Naik that I have not forgotten the talk we had on our last ride'.

But by her next letter, she is seething again. Written a fortnight later, on 25 February 1920, it begins cheerfully enough, recounting to Padmaja the contents of an amusing letter she had just received from one of her new acquaintances in Hyderabad, a young woman who presumably ran a small business in home-made cosmetics, and was seeking Ruttie's sponsorship: 'What do you think old Rehana has done? Written to me advising me not to use the lotions she sent me. And (at the same time) begging for my "patronage and photograph". I personally think that her frankness deserves some return, don't you? However I really don't intend sending her my photograph. For heaven's sake don't tell Papi this, as she is sure to go and ask *her* [Rehana] all about it. I sat convulsed for quite half an hour after reading her letter, it was so funny. And the idea of her advising me not to use her lotions tickled my sense of humour.'

But her simmering resentment against Jinnah had to be vented: 'It is rather a shame about the horse,' she wrote, referring to a horse she bought on impulse during her visit to Hyderabad which Jinnah vetoed on the ground that it had not been properly vetted. 'I wish the owner had succeeded in his ruse of bribing the vets. At any rate I do hope J won't be idiotically sensible about it. After all, I never had him vetted before I married him! But horses I suppose are far more valuable!'

In her desire to be independent of Jinnah and his criticism, implicit or otherwise, of her spending decisions, she tried once again to get a grip over the accounts of her shopping spree in Hyderabad. But it was no use; she continued to be befuddled, with one of the cheques she issued being returned to her. 'The cheque along with your letter arrived just as J and I were going out, so I am afraid I cannot enclose a fresh cheque in this. I shall however send it to you tomorrow.' But on the morrow when she tried to clear her debts without Jinnah's assistance, her pride coming in the way, she got mired in difficulties, her confusion increasing manifold because of the conversion she had to do from British Indian rupees to Hyderabadi rupees, or the 'Moghlai' currency, as she called it. 'I owe the stand man 335/- in British money, that is equivalent to 245/- in Moghlai roughly. The brass fellow has to be paid 463/- British, or 485/- Moghlai—463/- + 235/- = 698/-. I am not a bit sure of all these mathematics so please correct it if there is a mistake. Of course I shall be owing you more, as I have asked for a professional packer and the deal cases etc. I shall send you the sum on hearing from you,' she wrote in yet another letter, undated, to Padmaja.

By the following week, the friction between them had come to a head, with Jinnah, who had thus far suffered in silence her penchant for thoughtless expenditure, no longer mincing his words about her extravagance. She was wounded, of course, but not so mortally that she could not give it back to him in her spirited fashion. The letter to Padmaja, written on 3 March 1920, begins on a note of attempted lightness too feeble to pass off as humour and was evidently to oblige Padmaja who specifically begged for an amusing letter from Ruttie to raise her flagging spirits. She picks on the subject of their mutual friend Kshama Row's writing ambitions, an unfailing source of amusement apparently. 'It is always rather fatal to ask for an amusing letter,' Ruttie writes. 'I am however going to rely on the green of my paper to dispel the clouds from your chaotic mind. Kshama hasn't been particularly amusing of late. She tried very hard to pump me about you people in the interests of literature, specially about Dr Naidu, so I told her that among his more prominent characteristics is his passion for devouring little boys. I am afraid she did not believe me! Her object is to write a play centred round the lives of your father and mother—And as she doesn't know the one and cannot understand the other, she looks to me for enlightenment. I have half a mind to tell her that . . . Dr Naidu writes the poems and in his magnificent generosity lets your mother take the credit. It might appeal to her sense of sacrifice!'

'J for his part hasn't been so alarming of late,' Ruttie writes, referring to the incident with the dogs that had caused her such trauma. 'Every now and again he seriously shakes his head at Loafer-ul-Mulk and calls him a treacherous animal.' But her resentment against him now spills out despite herself: 'In consequence of my extravagance—and here she interjects two words as an afterthought—'I suppose'—'he has been trying to convince me that *he* is not the calf that lays the golden eggs.' While Jinnah uncharacteristically mixed up two metaphors to make his point—referring at the same time to the biblical sacrificial lamb and the Aesop's fable of the goose that laid golden eggs, the barb was not lost on Ruttie, who was left smarting at his unfairness, considering that it was she and not Jinnah who had made the sacrificial offering of herself at the marital altar, having flung away her fabulous inheritance in order to marry him. But if she was silent about his unjust barb, she was in a mood to subvert him.

'But alas!' she writes in kindling defiance, 'This is all futile!' In the same spirit, refusing to feel compunction just because he expected it, she is delighted at more packages arriving at South Court: 'The brass arrived last night. It was beautifully packed; whoever did it deserves to be congratulated!'

But these were minor squabbles, insignificant compared to the other source of friction that was threatening to split them wide apart, and that was their differences over Fatima. Ruttie had never liked the older woman but she had been accommodating of her till now, not stopping Fatima from spending every Sunday with them, monopolizing the one day of leisure that Jinnah allowed himself in his busy week. But now that the gloves were off between her and him, she didn't see why she had to put up in silence with this 'deadly serious' sister of his.

Chapter Fifteen

~

They had ample reason to hate each other. Ever since she left school nine years ago, Fatima had been encouraged by her entire family, including Jinnah, to groom herself into being her brother's sole companion. And now, after having earned their esteem—not to speak of envy—by the close bond she managed to build with him, and after being accepted by everyone around her as the only woman in her beloved 'Jin's' life, to be ejected so summarily from his home, asked to come and see him once a week like a poor relation—it was a state of affairs unlikely to endear her to the usurper of her brother's heart. But Fatima was not the sort who would make a fuss openly in front of her brother—or anyone else, for that matter. Instead, she turned those weekly visits into a torture for herself and Jinnah, her grave, silent presence a constant reproach to him for his betrayal.

It wasn't easy for Ruttie either, to be stuck with her dour sister-in-law for the whole of Sunday. Nearly seven years older than her, Fatima had little charm or sympathy, nor was she by any means anxious to please despite her friendless state. She was never really 'herself', as Sarojini once put it, having 'always been so repressed'. Had she been younger perhaps, and not so disapproving of Ruttie, she might have tried harder to get along with her. There was a time, even at twenty, when she had been eager to reach out and make friends, and Sarojini, ever generous and warm, especially with the young and lonely, had suggested to her thirteen-year-old daughter that she befriend the lonely Fatima. 'I am asking Fatima Jinnah to write to you,' Sarojini had written to Padmaja from London in 1914. 'She is twenty but very fond of you from all I told her about you in Bombay and as she is constantly writing about you to me, she may as well write to you and I hope you will write to her nice letters.' But that penfriendship, if it ever began, seems to have died a natural death, given the difference in their age and temperament.

Ruttie, too, must have felt the difference, but she had put up with her sister-in-law as long as she believed that J was on her side and felt—like her—that Fatima's presence was an intrusion and imposition on both of them. But lately, she had begun to doubt it— far from sharing her opinion of his sister, he regarded her with an affection that surpassed his love for any of his other four siblings, all of whom he kept at arm's length, unwilling to share either his time or himself with any of them unless it was to give a handout now and then, when one of them was in obvious distress. And this too was done dispassionately, especially with his brother who was never allowed to drop in at the house, only visit him in his chamber. But with Fatima, it was entirely different and Ruttie was far too quick and perceptive not to see that, even though neither brother nor sister ever betrayed by sign or word the strong bond between them.

They seemed strangely unlike any brother and sister she had ever known. She herself had been close to all her three brothers, especially Fali, closest to her in age and temperament. As the eldest and the only girl, she mothered them all. They, in turn, had adored her, looking up to her to lead them in their games and pranks which she did with boyish zest; but they also left her alone when she wanted to be by herself. As the only bookworm in the family, they knew and respected her tastes, even little Manik knowing at the age of eight or nine exactly which novel of Charlotte Bronte to get his sister for her twelfth birthday. There had certainly never been a dull moment when the four of them had been together, with laughter and jokes, and playing Three Musketeers or going riding together. Whereas these two, Jinnah and Fatima, barely exchanged a word with each other even though Fatima came religiously every Sunday, spending the whole day with her brother, who mostly ignored her, not even bothering to glance up from the book or newspaper he was reading. And while it was true that Fatima's eyes often rested on her brother, either in reproach or devotion, she hardly ever spoke to him unless spoken to, just sitting there silently every single Sunday, with her book open in front of her in a way that filled Ruttie with extreme irritation.

There seemed to be no resemblance between them, either in features or temperament, with Fatima's thin lips pressed in perpetual disapproval and her deep-set eyes in such contrast to J's chiselled charm and dry humour and his openness towards the young, unlike his sister's severe disapproval of the young generation's free and modern ways. What intrigued and fascinated Ruttie—apart from arousing her envy—was the silent connection between two such apparently dissimilar individuals. She could not resist trying to get a reaction out of Jinnah when Fatima was around; while he, in his stubborn way, refused to be provoked into shedding his wooden mask and revealing his true feelings.

The first time Jinnah really upset her was the day she returned from her holiday in Hyderabad and when she thought she was just having some innocent fun at Fatima's expense, pretending that she had gone to Hyderabad only to hunt for a suitable husband for Fatima. Jinnah simply refused to play along, making her feel like an outsider in her own home. Even worse than watching the silent solidarity between brother and sister, was to see the silent condemnation in his eyes and know in her heart that it was richly deserved. It was true that she had always loved playing pranks, especially when she was still living in Petit Hall, but her jokes had never been this malicious; this taunting of a confirmed spinster, even if it was a sister-in-law who was so provokingly judgemental.

But the next time there was friction between her and Fatima, she didn't think she deserved to have Jinnah punish her with his cold look. It upset her that J did not support her even though Fatima was talking down to her. At the best of times, Ruttie found Fatima irritatingly self-righteous and solemn; but on a day when she was already jarred by Jinnah's unfair accusations of spending too much money, she could not suffer her sanctimonious sister-in-law in silence. As she wrote to Padmaja in her letter on 3 March 1920: 'Fatima's deadly reason quite upset the last Sunday. She was reading the Quran, so I told her that it was "meant to be talked about and not to be read". So in all seriousness she asked me "how one could talk about a book one hadn't read".' Jinnah's unspoken solidarity with his sister in this instance must have made Ruttie feel suddenly that he too was a stranger that she hardly knew, and she felt an alien in her own home.

She was pushing his buttons as well without knowing it. For all his outward appearance of being a born and bred Englishman, somewhere inside him was the Mohammed Ali raised to put family duty and honour above all else. Even as a young student in England, while at a safe enough distance from home to start shedding his old baggage, his father could recall Jinnah back to who he was with a mere few words. 'Do not bring shame on the family name,' Jinnah Senior wrote to his son when Jinnah joined a drama company in London and wrote to his father afterwards outlining his plans for a stage career. But his father's words were enough to make Jinnah quit the stage and return home to take up his duties as the head of the house. Although Jinnah was only twenty-one then and had yet to establish himself, his father had already begun to lean heavily on him, expecting him to handle all his tangled business and personal affairs.

Chief among these problems was to arrange suitable marriages for the two elder daughters. This was by no means easy. Rahmat, the sister who was born two years after Jinnah, was already nineteen. At that age most girls in their community were already mothers of several children. But Jinnah's father, broken by his wife's untimely death and his bankruptcy, had left her marriage hanging until Jinnah got back and took care of it. Against all odds, even though he was just twenty-one himself and without a job or connections, Jinnah did manage to settle her marriage soon after he returned from London with a well-to-do businessman from Calcutta.

But it came at a price. Since the only match they could find for the overaged Rahmat was a widower from outside their own Ismaili sect of Khojas, it meant risking excommunication for the whole family and also reduced Jinnah's chances of finding a second bride among the Ismailis. Jinnah's maternal uncle, a close aide of the Aga Khan, who had been of much help to the family during Jinnah's absence, had, in fact, intended giving his daughter in marriage to Jinnah, now that he was single again, but he warned Jinnah's father that he would go ahead with the marriage only if they did not insist on marrying Rahmat outside their own community.

Not that Jinnah paid much attention to his uncle's threat. In fact, he may have even rejoiced secretly. Jinnah had married the first time against his own inclinations because of his mother's insistence. But now that both his mother and bride had passed away—his first wife,

Emibai, died in a cholera epidemic a year before his mother—he was certainly not disposed to shackle himself with a wife again.

There were other ways in which his decision to get Rahmat married to a Sunni Khoja set him free. He could now afford to discard his past and reinvent himself, just as he had done in London, discarding his old clothes and beliefs, and assuming the mind and manners of a pucca Englishman. But this turning of himself into a modern, rational Muslim above all sects and castes was an even more daring transformation because it had to be done in spite of the stink it raised. But with Jinnah, as he was fond of saying, once he decided to do something, he simply did it. And it was not long before everyone, even the most orthodox Muslims, accepted him for what he was. His success as a barrister and his wealth certainly silenced any reservations that his community might have had. Besides, as if to hammer home the point that he wanted nothing more to do with the Ismaili community, he soon enrolled himself and his father in a new reformist Islamic organization called the Isnaasharis who set themselves apart from all sectarian divisions.

The change came in handy for his other sisters' marriages as well. He could now look for suitable matches based on his own criteria of affluence and background, casting the matrimonial net further than any Muslim had done before him. And such was his standing within the community that when he arranged a marriage for his second sister, Maryam, with the well-known merchant family of Bombay, the Peerbhoys, not a single eyebrow was raised, even though the Peerbhoys were Khoja Sunnis like Rahmat's in-laws.

But besides arranging his sisters' marriages and paying his father's rent and living expenses, Jinnah kept his life apart from them all. He lived away from them, visiting them occasionally. When he returned from London, his father had already shifted from Karachi to Bombay and they were living in a small rented apartment in the crowded by-lanes of the city's Khoja neighbourhood. Instead of moving in with them or moving them out of there to live with him, Jinnah decided it would be better for him to live separately. And despite being desperately short of money, he moved into an English-run hotel, the Apollo, in Fort Bombay, which was across the city from them.

But he did pay them regular visits, dazzling the neighbours and his own siblings whenever he dropped in with his immaculately tailored

Sir Dinshaw Petit, Ruttie's father

Lady Petit, Ruttie's mother

Jinnahbhai Poonja, Jinnah's father

Sir Jamsetjee Jeejeebhoy, Ruttie's uncle
and head of Parsi panchayat

Lady Petit in a studio portrait

Fatima Jinnah as a young woman

Ruttie (centre) at six with her
brothers, Fali (left) and Manek

Leilamani Naidu as an
Oxford undergraduate

Padmaja Naidu, Ruttie's dearest friend
and correspondent

Dr M.G. Naidu, head of the eccentric
Naidu family

Sarojini Naidu was in her thirties when Ruttie first met her

Jinnah as a young barrister

Jinnah before his marriage

Jinnah in his forties

Syud Hossain as a young journalist

Ruttie as a teenage wife

Ruttie in her black drapery

Jinnah with his sister, Fatima (left), and his daughter, Dina (right)

Jinnah with his daughter and dogs

Dina Jinnah outside her father's home

suits and tie and stiff collar, and shoes and socks which he refused to take off even within the house. Even when he eventually shifted out of the Apollo to his own apartment, the family was not invited to live with him. He was able to somehow juggle this double existence—the dashing, single barrister in his bachelor apartment, cutting a figure in Bombay's high society with an ageing parent and siblings tucked away in a hidden corner of the city. This double life of sorts continued for the next six years until his father died.

His father died in April 1902, saddling the debonair Jinnah with three minor siblings—Ahmed Ali, who was sixteen, and two sisters, Shirin and Fatima, fourteen and nine respectively. His first instinct must have been to get them all off his hands as quickly and efficiently as he could manage. Ahmed Ali was packed off to the Anjuman Islamia School as a boarder. Having attended the school himself as a young boy, Jinnah probably felt it was the best place to lay the foundations for a future professional career he had in mind for his brother.

But there was little he could do about Shirin. At fourteen, she was at the lawful age to be married but he was yet to begin the matrimonial hunt for her. Meanwhile, he was forced to keep her at home with him, however much it inconvenienced him—conveying her in his carriage to his sister Maryam's house every morning on his way to work and picking her up in the evenings on his way back. But mercifully, he soon found a suitable match for her. When Shirin married into the eminent merchant family of Bombay, the Currimbhoys, he was finally relieved of all responsibility for her.

That left little Fatima. With Jinnah's English training and habits, it seemed the most logical solution was to put his orphaned little sister into a good boarding school. Keen to give her the best English education his money could buy, he picked a convent school in Bandra, St Joseph's. It was a rational decision based on his understanding of what kind of education was required for a modern girl. But little did he anticipate its personal repercussions on himself.

Till then, no Muslim girl had ever been admitted to a Christian missionary school, and that too as a boarder. It set tongues wagging both within his extended family and among other Muslims. They were scandalized—even for someone as rich and indifferent to orthodox opinion as him, this was carrying things too far. He would, of course, have been aware of the risks. And if he was not, there would have been plenty of people to point them out—that a convent-educated Muslim girl was likely to become a huge liability when the time came to arrange her marriage within the community. Bandra being nine miles away from Bombay, and at least a couple of hours' journey by horse carriage, the child would be virtually isolated from all her relatives for the next seven or eight years except during her holidays, brought up by strangers and unable to speak or relate to anyone in her own community—who would marry her then? Until two decades ago, Muslims were so suspicious of Christian missionaries that they refused to send even their boys to English-medium schools. And here was Jinnah daring to propose sending his sister to a convent school as if it was the most ordinary thing in the world. But by now, he had become immune to all criticism, especially when it came from orthodox Muslims. It only made him more determined to do what he thought was best for her.

He couldn't, of course, be so peremptory with Fatima herself. The little girl was terrified of being sent away so far from home. Having been raised by a succession of her older sisters ever since their mother died, Fatima was a shy, repressed child who shrank from strangers. She was born a few months after Jinnah went to London and even when he returned, she had been too small and insignificant for him to take more than a perfunctory interest in her. But now Jinnah needed to calm her fears. And he did it with a patience and tenderness that would have surely surprised his other siblings and relatives—he usually had so little time to spare for the personal touch.

But here he was now, taking time off from his own schedule, driving his little sister in his carriage to Bandra, and showing the timid girl around the school. Then taking her aside to reason with her, just as their father had done with him at her age—he asked her to choose for herself between school and the life of liberation it offered or that of a conventional woman's life behind purdah. But Fatima was no strong-willed Jinnah capable of thinking for herself; she chose him, or rather his approval, agreeing to join the boarding school only because her brother wanted her to.

By wilfully changing his sister's destiny, he had bound her to him forever. He took to giving up his precious Sundays to go and visit her in school. He rode the nine miles back and forth to Bandra on horseback, carrying gifts of chocolates for her. He started taking a keen interest in her schoolwork. And insensibly, although they were nearly sixteen years apart, he was drawn closer to her than to any of his other siblings—or any other person in his life.

Fatima, in turn, was lonely and isolated. She had no friends, she played no sports and hardly anyone else in the family visited her. By the time she left boarding school eight years later—four years in the Bandra convent before she shifted to St Patrick's School in Khandala from where she passed her matriculation exam—she needed no one else. Her handsome and clever brother had become everything for her.

It was taken for granted that once she was done with school, she would move in with him. He now lived in a larger house, on the first floor of a building in Colaba, having shifted there from an apartment on Bandstand, and she fitted in unresistingly into his rigid daily routine. He had suggested to her to study for the Senior Cambridge examination under his tutelage and she did some desultory reading for it, starting with a book of essays, painstakingly underlining difficult words with a pencil, just as he had done as a student in London. The arrangement was the same as he had with Shirin—after breakfast together (always at the same hour), he dropped her off in his carriage on his way to court at their sister Maryam's, to be picked up by him on his way back. But the difference was that he made no attempt to find her a suitable husband. Nor did she ever hint to him or anyone else in the family that she would have preferred to leave him for a home of her own. It was, in fact, a family myth, well established in the years after Fatima finished her matriculation and came to live with her brother, that she meant to devote the rest of her life to him, and she did nothing to dispel it. Her choice of a life as her brother's keeper satisfied her, not only because of her devotion to Jinnah but also because of the enhanced prestige this undoubtedly earned her from the rest of the family.

There would have been the usual pressure, of course, especially from her sisters, to marry. At seventeen, despite a matriculation degree and her fluency in English weighing her down, there was still a chance of finding someone suitable. But living with her handsome and famous brother, any suitor would have paled in comparison.

They were good companions. They went for walks, had dinner together, and occasionally she accompanied him when he went riding.

It was the only sport she ever took to. And since she was such a willing listener, almost adoring, he could hold forth at the table whenever he felt like it. They quarrelled only occasionally, usually when his cavalier treatment became too much for her to take. There was the instance when she opened a window in the house without his permission and he ticked her off for it, telling her shortly to go to the other room if she needed some fresh air. Fatima flounced out of the room and banged the door shut in the other room, locking herself in and refusing to come out even at dinner time.

Opening the windows while he was around was always something of an issue between them—Jinnah was bothered by the noise from the street below and in one rare burst of temper had even thrown down a bucket of water to stop the ruckus. But her tantrum made him anxious. He went up to the locked door, pleading with her, 'Fati, open the door.' Fati was his name for her and she called him 'Jin'. She emerged out of the room eventually but he was not quite forgiven. They ate their dinner in silence and were not on talking terms until he finally bought peace with a piece of jewellery. She loved baubles and he knew exactly how to placate her.

It was this hidden and unspoken bond that Ruttie had stumbled upon, making her strangely uneasy. And instead of backing off, something drove her to keep prodding the silent Fatima. Everything about her—her 'deadly reason', her 'deep grave eyes', her self-sacrifice, and now her show of piety—annoyed Ruttie. The last was something of a recent development. Despite her expensive convent education—or perhaps because of it—Fatima had turned by now into a devout Muslim. Her staple reading was the Quran. And she had taken to arriving at South Court with her own copy of the Quran, sitting down to read it at all times instead of picking a book out of Jinnah's vast library as she once used to do. Having endured it all these weeks, Ruttie had suddenly snapped, making that remark about the Quran—that it was a book 'meant to be talked about and not to be read'.

It was a remark that Jinnah ordinarily wouldn't have even blinked at. Apart from whatever religion he had imbibed as a child (mostly his mother's blind faith in the miracles of saints), he seemed to have a purely intellectual interest in the Quran, having studied closely the orientalist D.S. Margoliuth's *Mohammed and the Rise of Islam.*

He openly flouted Islamic tenets against drinking and smoking even in the presence of moulvis, and the first time he ever entered a mosque to pray was nearly two decades later.

But his sister was quite different—she and his other siblings had been reared by their father when he had changed considerably, having taken in his later years to gathering his children around and reading aloud to them from the Quran.

So, with Fatima taking umbrage, daring for once to speak up in front of her brother and taking on Ruttie frontally, Jinnah found matters getting out of hand.

In the next few days, friction within South Court had risen to such a pitch that Ruttie was even threatening to leave him. She made plans to go to London with Padmaja's sister Leilamani, who was preparing to sail the following month. That she was in earnest became clear from the agitated letter Sarojini wrote back to her daughter from London, complaining of the 'shock' she had received when she heard that Ruttie was planning to come to London 'minus Jinnah and Baby' and taking only her beloved Arlette with her.

By now, Jinnah was learning the hard way, as he once feelingly put it, 'never to argue with a woman'. Instead, he directed his energy into persuading Fatima, who at least was more susceptible to his reasoning. It was at his prodding that Fatima agreed, however reluctantly, to enrol herself in a dental college in Calcutta. It was the sensible thing to do, considering how few professional courses were available to women at that time—it would take another two years for the legal profession to open its doors to women, and a medical degree meant at least five years of study abroad. Her brother was ready to fund her studies as well as her stay in Calcutta (even though her eldest sister lived there, Fatima had no intention of staying with her), and by July, Fatima was out of the scene—at least for the next two years.

Ruttie celebrated her victory by taking Jinnah on a holiday to Ooty. She was in excellent spirits. 'I have insured myself quite an "exciting" time having sent up two horses and a car,' she wrote triumphantly to Leilamani from Bangalore, on her way up to the hill station.

Chapter Sixteen

~

But getting Fatima out of their lives seemed to bring them no closer to each other. Instead, Jinnah spent their holiday in Ooty obsessing about a thin, half-naked man with a weak voice and the habits of a crank who was keeping him awake at night with his unpredictable moves. The man who was threatening his political survival was a fellow Gujarati whom everyone called Mahatma Gandhi.

Gandhi had not impressed Jinnah to begin with. In this, Jinnah had been no different from most of Bombay's high society. He had arrived in India five years earlier in 1915 with a huge reputation made in South Africa, and people had been eager to meet this world-acclaimed leader. But he had cut a poor figure at the receptions hosted for him in Bombay, arriving barefoot, dressed in a short dhoti, an *angarka* and *sapha* in Kathiawari style and speaking in Gujarati. They had not taken to each other right from the start. At the very first reception given to Gandhi in Bombay, a garden party thrown by the 'Gurjar Sabha', or the Gujarati Society of Bombay, Jinnah, who was presiding over the function, voiced his doubts about Gandhi's intention to devote himself to the Indian cause, saying, 'what a pity it was that there was nobody in South Africa to take his place and fight their battle'. In his turn, Gandhi offended Jinnah by labelling him a Muslim, saying, he was 'glad to find a Mahomedan a member of the Gurjar Sabha and the chairman of the function'. After that first flurry of receptions held in his honour, Gandhi then disappeared off the political radar for almost a year, making a brief appearance at the Congress session held that year-end in Bombay where he disappointed his admirers once more by dressing in the same peculiar fashion and delivering a speech that was almost inaudible.

While the War lasted, Gandhi scrupulously kept himself out of politics. He refused to take part in any demonstration against the government and offered the British his full support, even volunteering to recruit soldiers for them. He dismayed young people who came to him for advice by coming up with the most hare-brained of solutions. For example, when the British government clapped Annie Besant into jail, he suggested to her supporters that the best way to secure her release would be to march peacefully all the way from Bombay to Coimbatore, a distance of over a thousand miles. And to others interested in political work, he suggested they work in rural Bihar as carriers of night soil. As a result, he was dismissed as a political maverick, although he soon began to be worshipped as a saint by ordinary people. To Jinnah, he remained something of an enigma. He could not tell if this former barrister was an astute Hindu politician or a genuine social reformer with no interest or talent for politics. On the one hand, Gandhi made a show of being disinclined to join politics, and on the other, he deftly turned any social reform programme he led into a high-voltage political drama that got him maximum publicity. As an experienced lawyer, Jinnah could hardly take Gandhi at face value.

As for his personal habits, there was no dearth of stories floating about him. He heard from his young associates how Gandhi received his visitors sitting on a mattress on the floor; his strange austerities, including shaving 'with a broken blade and without using soap, only water'. But his habits were not half as shocking as his political views—his 'vague philosophical absurdities', as Jinnah put it. Jinnah first became acquainted with Gandhi's peculiar views the day he urged Jinnah, in all earnestness, to turn his Home Rule League into a recruitment centre for soldiers for the War, assuring him that the British would reward Indians with self-government for this unconditional support.

It was difficult for Jinnah to take Gandhi seriously after that. Especially during the next two years when Jinnah was re-elected to the legislative council and had reached the height of his glory as a national leader, what with the Lucknow Congress session in 1916 and his talks with the visiting secretary of state for India,

Edwin S. Montagu, the following year. Gandhi took no part in the Lucknow Congress proceedings or made much of an impression during Montagu's interactions with various Indian leaders, whereas Jinnah held centre stage on both occasions. And as for the anti-Lord Willingdon campaign that Jinnah led to such popular acclaim, Gandhi had nothing to do with it, wriggling out of participating in it by making the feeble excuse that he was not a citizen of Bombay.

Having turned into one of the two political power centres in the Bombay Presidency, the other being Bal Gangadhar Tilak, Jinnah could afford to be generous with Gandhi as with other nationalists, including Tilak who ran a rival Home Rule League. In fact, Jinnah went out of his way to help Tilak, appearing in court for him without charging a fee and springing to his defence when he was snubbed by Lord Willingdon. And with Gandhi, he felt even more kindly disposed as he did with anyone who liked to remain in the background and let others take the political stage. As long as Gandhi stuck to his work as a social reformer and did not meddle in political issues, Jinnah was more than happy to provide him with a platform or cadre whenever he needed it or even his own services as a speaker.

But what came as a shock to Jinnah was to discover that under the meek and humble demeanour, Gandhi was just as determined to lead. It was true that Gandhi was seven years older and many times more famous, especially in the international sphere, but on home turf no one had doubted so far that it was Jinnah who was the superior both in experience and natural talent. Still worse was Gandhi's habit of proselytizing. In his gentle but persistent way, Gandhi was resolved to play mentor to Jinnah, not understanding how averse Jinnah was to being led by anyone. The more Jinnah resisted, the more persistent he became, as if the social reformer in him could not resist the challenge that Jinnah presented.

He worked especially hard to get Jinnah to give up speaking in English and switch to Gujarati as he had done. Jinnah resented the presumption but more than that it seemed insane to him to give up, of all things, English—the language that he had worked so hard to cultivate, knowing it was the only way for the British to take him seriously. But Gandhi kept at it, refusing to be snubbed by him.

At first, Jinnah tried ignoring him. At the Gujarat Congress session in Godhra, for example, when Gandhi who was chairing the session wanted Jinnah to speak in Gujarati, Jinnah simply humoured him. He rose to his feet and said, 'Gentlemen, I am speaking today in Gujarati as ordered by Gandhiji.' Then, having got his mandatory Gujarati sentence out of the way, he continued, 'Having now made this part of my speech in Gujarati, gentlemen, I shall complete my speech in English.' The audience went into 'roars of laughter', allowing him to continue uninterrupted in English for forty-five minutes. It was the beginning of their lifelong misunderstanding, with Gandhi going so far as to persuade himself that Jinnah felt so humiliated by the audience's laughter—as Gandhi undoubtedly would have felt in Jinnah's place—and surmised that Jinnah 'took it as a personal insult' and never forgave Gandhi for it. Whereas, according to Kanji, the first round in this clash of wills had definitely gone to Jinnah, and not Gandhi, with the audience lapping up Jinnah's speech regardless—or because—of it being in English. Most leaders, including Sarojini, were uneasy speaking on a public platform in any language other than English but no one dared to defy Gandhi's idiosyncrasy except Jinnah.

But it became increasingly difficult after that to stand up to Gandhi. In less than a year, from the Gujarat Congress session in October 1916 to the Champaran and Kheda satyagraha of 1917, his work as a social reformer had turned him into a national hero and something of a national tyrant as well. Politically, Gandhi's rise to supreme power started with his civil disobedience movement against the infamous Rowlatt Act in 1919. Almost overnight, he was transformed from a half-naked fakir into a full-fledged politician with hundreds of thousands of ordinary people responding to his call to join his anti-government agitation. After that he became so hugely popular that no Congress leader dared to openly oppose him, pretending to go along with his oddball ideas and programmes rather than risk public ire.

Pretending was, of course, out of the question for someone of Jinnah's temperament, but political compulsion had forced him to fall in line behind Gandhi after he quit the legislative council because Gandhi was already leading a full-blown public agitation against the legislation. He would have preferred an agitation less coloured by the pseudo-religious tone that Gandhi always brought to his demonstrations, with prayers and fasts and marches to temples and mosques, and holy dips in the sea. But he had no choice. It was either joining Gandhi's side or the government's, which was why he had put aside his personal reservations and supported Gandhi's movement.

It had its downside, of course. Although he had little choice then, his decision to join Gandhi's anti-Rowlatt Act agitation in 1919 had proved costly, with the government labelling him as a terrorist, along with Gandhi, and even planning to deport him to Burma, along with Gandhi and six others. Nothing came of it ultimately because Gandhi called off the agitation but Jinnah had ended up suffering the most because he lost both his editor and political aide when the government bundled Horniman off to England after that.

But despite his reservations, Jinnah was far too pragmatic not to be able to see the importance of working with Gandhi rather than cutting off from him altogether, especially now that he had clearly emerged as a mass leader who could not be ignored. Jinnah had, in fact, made an attempt to reach out to Gandhi soon after the latter called off his civil disobedience movement against the Rowlatt Act. This was while he was in England in the summer of 1919 waiting for the joint parliamentary committee to start its hearings. He wanted to both keep in touch with what was going on at home as well as find out Gandhi's views on the reforms bill.

But it seemed that Gandhi had learnt nothing from the failure of his experimental anti-Rowlatt agitation. The only reforms Gandhi seemed to be interested in were personal ones, including Jinnah's. 'I have your promise,' Gandhi wrote in his letter, presumably in reply to Jinnah's letter which is lost, 'that you would take up Gujarati and Hindi as quickly as possible. May I then suggest that like Macaulay you learn at least one of these languages on your return voyage? You will not have Macaulay's time during the voyage, i.e., six months, but then you have not the same difficulty that Macaulay had.'

In the same letter, dated 28 June 1919, Gandhi was equally bent on proselytizing Ruttie: 'Pray tell Mrs Jinnah that I shall expect her on her return to join the hand-spinning class that Mrs Banker Senior and Mrs Ramabai, a Punjabi lady, are conducting.' Unlike his unusual stiffness with Jinnah, Gandhi was more himself with Ruttie, able to be warm and close with her in a way he failed somehow to be with Jinnah, unable to get past his defences. He had probably met Ruttie several times through Sarojini and they seem to have hit it off quite well, judging by the one letter from Gandhi to Ruttie that remains of their correspondence, and the jokes they shared at each other's expense through Sarojini's witticisms. Jinnah, of course, was not part of this good-humoured ragging, possibly with his sense of dignity coming in the way.

After that one letter from Gandhi while they were in England, Jinnah seems to have not bothered to get in touch with him again. In fact, it was Gandhi who next sought him out, addressing his plea to Jinnah through Ruttie. It was the same old thing again. Dated 30 April 1920, the letter said: 'Please remember me to Mr Jinnah and do coax him to learn Hindustani or Gujarati. If I were you, I should begin to talk to him in Gujarati or Hindustani. There is not much danger of you forgetting your English or your misunderstanding each other, is there?'

'Will you do it?' he went on in his insistent way. 'Yes, I would ask this even for the love you bear me.'

But by now—Jinnah was holidaying in Ooty with Ruttie from 19 April to 3 June 1920—Gandhi was giving him much more to worry about than merely proselytizing. While Jinnah had been away in England for five months the previous year, Gandhi had once again changed tack and bounced back into the political mainstream by changing the rules entirely. He used a gambit that no politician before him had ever tried: uniting Hindus and Muslims by espousing a religious cause that concerned only Muslims. This was the 'Khilafat' issue. After the War, Indian Muslims were concerned over the fate of defeated Turkey facing dismemberment of its Ottoman empire and with it, the threat of their holy places in Arabia slipping from the custody of the Turkish Caliph into non-Muslim hands. The matter was serious enough to make Muslims want to protest against the peace treaty that the Allies were drawing up, especially because the British government was going back on its word given before the War that the Caliphate would not be disturbed.

In Jinnah's view, the Khilafat question was unfortunate, but not really a political issue at all. Of course, he took an interest in it, representing to the government both in India and Britain, but it was more to appease his Muslim constituency than because his heart was in it. Gandhi, on the other hand, took it up with his usual missionary zeal. While Jinnah had been away, Gandhi had befriended the more radical Muslim leaders who wanted to fight for the Khilafat cause and had been spurring them on into forming their own organization so that he could have their backing for his non-cooperation programme. He had become such a champion of the Khilafat cause that he started writing and speaking on it wherever he went. With his help and guidance, Khilafat committees sprang up in every province of the subcontinent. And by the time Jinnah returned, with his head full of the reforms bill and what could be done with it, Gandhi had effectively shifted public attention away from the reforms to the Khilafat issue. Even worse, the movement had acquired enough momentum for them to hold a political convention in Simla that was so big that it cast the Muslim League into shade. Representatives of every sect of Muslims from across the subcontinent were expected to attend, giving the convention a pan-Indian character that undermined the Muslim League's importance.

On the surface, Jinnah showed no alarm at the developments. He was even able to put up a show of great liberality by expressing his 'happiness' at the growing signs of Hindu–Muslim unity, which he called the 'most important thing necessary for success' in an interview to the *Bombay Chronicle* the day after he landed. But his pride would not let him attend the conference in Simla, although he did receive an invitation. The prospect of being overshadowed by Gandhi at a Muslim conference was hardly an incentive.

It was a mistake, though, to allow Gandhi to take the field by himself and emerge as a leader of both Hindus and Muslims. Gandhi had attended the Simla convention with prominent Hindu leaders and after that had stepped up his involvement with the Khilafat issue by writing newspaper articles and giving speeches. His call for a 'Khilafat Day' got a huge response from both Muslims and Hindus, enabling him to re-emerge as the tallest national leader. And by the following month in Amritsar, where the Congress and Muslim League were holding their annual sessions simultaneously, Jinnah was literally forced to take a back seat, sitting directly behind Gandhi at the Congress sessions and helping him steer a difficult resolution past his opponents in the Congress.

At the Muslim League's convention also it was Gandhi's protégés, the Ali brothers, who stole the limelight. They had just been freed from imprisonment and arrived midway through the session and the proceedings were interrupted as members stood up to welcome them with loud cheers of 'Allahu Akbar!' The older of the two brothers, Shaukat Ali, took over the stage, delivering a thundering speech that called on 'forty lakhs of Mussalmans to come forward and die for their religion' while the audience fell to weeping at his words. His brother, Mohammed Ali, followed with another tearful speech and on that high note of emotion, regular proceedings had to be suspended for the day.

At the Khilafat conference, which was the highlight of this Congress session, Jinnah was again sidelined. He sat on the platform squeezed between dozens of Gandhi's supporters, both Hindu and Muslim, facing a record 16,000 Muslims who had turned up at Gandhi's call. He listened impassively as Gandhi demonstrated the power of speaking in Urdu rather than English, outshining even the Ali brothers, who were meant to be the star attraction. Gandhi's speech delivered in his diligently acquired Urdu was of such 'incredible power and lucidity', as the *Bombay Chronicle* reported the next day, that 'he captured the Muslim heart and mind'.

After Amritsar, Gandhi stepped up his Khilafat campaign even further and went on an extensive tour with the Ali brothers in order to rally support for the cause among Hindus across the country. Gandhi had once again cast Jinnah into a major dilemma: he could not afford to detach himself from the Khilafat cause because of its significance to Muslims; yet he did not want to yield to pressure from Gandhi or Gandhi's Muslim friends. His reason pulled one way while his pride pulled in the opposite direction. But he kept his troubles close to himself as was his habit.

If there was something troubling him, Ruttie would have no way of divining it, so impenetrable was his silence when he wanted to be alone with his thoughts. She was clueless even about the undercurrents between him and Gandhi. She was not the sort to seek her husband's permission for her friendships, and it had not occurred to her to take his prior permission before corresponding with Gandhi. Nor did she tell him of the cheque she had sent to Gandhi sometime before they left for their holiday. It was a generous impulse on her part, wanting to contribute to the fund that Gandhi had started for a memorial at Jallianwala Bagh to commemorate the killings. 'The memorial would at least give us an excuse for living,' as she must have said in her accompanying note, for Gandhi quoted her in his next newspaper column, taking care to mention how 'Mrs Jinnah truly remarked when she gave her mite to the fund, the memorial would at least give us an excuse for living.' The article, 'Neither a Saint Nor a Politician', which appeared in Gandhi's weekly newspaper, *Young India*, on 12 May 1920, would have probably escaped Jinnah's notice—at least till he got home from his holiday in Ooty—but even had he read it, it was not in his nature to raise the subject with Ruttie, considering it strictly her business whom she chose to write to or send his money to.

So, while Ruttie had been looking forward to their time alone in Ooty and thought she had 'insured myself quite an exciting time' by leaving the baby back at home and sending up two horses and a car ahead of them, it did not turn out as she had hoped. Instead of spending their days outdoors in the hills and going riding all day— Ooty was famous for its hunting season—Jinnah was preoccupied throughout the over forty days they spent at the Savoy Hotel with his political anxieties, for which he blamed Gandhi. He not only found himself out of his depth in this religion-tinted new politics that Gandhi had started but was also dismayed that Muslims were deserting the Muslim League and moving towards the Khilafat committees run by Gandhi's friends—or at least those Muslim leaders who were inspired by his methods of mass mobilization. He felt that unless he took some pre-emptive steps, the Muslim League would start losing out to the Khilafat conference committees. And brooding over the problem that the Khilafatists posed to his Muslim League, he wrote to the secretary of the League less than ten days after their arrival in Ooty, asking him to call a meeting of the League's council in Bombay in mid-June 'to carefully consider', as Jinnah put it, 'the whole question of securing a Khilafat', and suggesting as a counter-step to the falling attendance at their meetings that 'You should give long notice to the members so as to get a proper and full attendance.'

Apart from being oblivious to the fact that every good Muslim was aware of—that mid-June would be in the middle of the Ramazan month when most Muslim delegates would prefer not to travel, as the secretary had to gently point out to him—Jinnah's letter came too late. The Khilafatists had already beaten them to it and were holding a meeting in Allahabad to back Gandhi's non-cooperation programme.

The reply from the secretary of the Muslim League only arrived at the end of their trip—or perhaps even after the Jinnahs returned to Bombay—but for Jinnah, brooding on his political problems, there was no time to spare for Ruttie, even though that must have been fully his intention when they set out together. He had time, though, to answer all his official mail by hand, including a letter from the acting editor of the *Bombay Chronicle*, S.A. Brelvi, who had sent him a cutting from a newspaper called *New India* commenting on the *Bombay Chronicle*'s policy being still 'inspired' by its deported former editor, Horniman, and 'that the directors of the *Chronicle* should appoint a responsible Editor'. Replying almost as soon as he received Brelvi's letter, Jinnah was quick to rise to Brelvi's defence, calling *New India*'s comment 'malicious and impertinent besides being an unjust attack on you', and asking Brelvi to publish Jinnah's letter in the *Chronicle* as validation of how highly the board regarded Brelvi's services.

And before she knew it, their holiday was over, leaving her unfulfilled—always so, 'a tragedy of unfulfillment', as Padmaja was to put it several years later in a letter to Chagla, 'so young and so lovely' and loving 'life with such passionate eagerness and always life passed her by leaving her with empty hands and heart'. But Jinnah did not see it in his hurry to get back home in order to come to grips with the political situation that Gandhi was forcing on them all.

Much to his alarm, Gandhi was using his new-found popularity among Muslims to push through his non-cooperation programme on a national scale. If Gandhi succeeded in getting the Congress to accept it, Jinnah felt it would be nothing short of disaster for the country, calling as it did for the boycott of all government institutions, including schools, courts, legislatures and councils. The only way to stop Gandhi now was to somehow separate him from the Muslims. And for that the Muslim League would have to snatch back the initiative on the Khilafat cause. With these urgent thoughts preoccupying him, Jinnah retreated within himself, paying no attention to Ruttie, but nevertheless expecting her to understand and be a supportive wife, albeit a silent one.

It took another three months before Jinnah could get his Muslim League office-bearers to organize a special session in order to assess the situation. However, by that time, it became pointless because Gandhi was poised to take over the Congress, with his Khilafat allies supporting him solidly.

But Jinnah was not yet ready to give up. The battle shifted to Calcutta, where a special session of the Congress had been called to discuss whether it should adopt Gandhi's programme of non-cooperation. Although Gandhi had won Muslims to his side, there were still enough Congress leaders as determined as Jinnah to oppose Gandhi's programme. They were particularly resistant to the boycott of courts which meant giving up flourishing legal practices and also staying away from elections to the legislatures and consequently giving up their seats to the Liberals who were determined to contest in the coming elections. They were Jinnah's last hope.

As he boarded the train to Calcutta with Ruttie and his Home Rule League colleagues, there seemed little to worry him. There were nearly 250 delegates from Bombay travelling on a train specially hired for the Calcutta session and the majority seemed opposed to Gandhi's non-cooperation movement. Throughout the journey there were lively discussions, much to Ruttie's delight. It was a pleasant change from being cooped up in a first-class coach with only a brooding Jinnah for company.

Gandhi himself had left on an earlier train with his entourage and principal ally, Shaukat Ali. They were greeted wherever the train stopped by huge crowds that had gathered from miles around and kept shouting 'Gandhi-Shaukat Ali ki Jai'. But the crowds were hardly going to help him win votes in the Congress.

Frantic lobbying to consolidate the opposition to Gandhi started as soon as they stepped out of the train. Motilal Nehru, who had come specially to meet Jinnah at the Howrah station, greeted him with the glad tidings of a combine being formed against Gandhi. Prominent leaders willing to join were Pandit Madan Mohan Malaviya, C.R. Das, Lajpat Rai and Annie Besant. Das, the lawyer-politician who was the tallest leader from Bengal, took the lead by organizing a series of breakfasts, lunches and suppers for Congress delegates so that they would vote against Gandhi.

It made Gandhi's supporters insecure enough to redouble their efforts to keep their flocks from straying. It was unclear till the last minute which way the voting would go. But it looked as if the opposition had the edge over Gandhi's side. But at the last minute, Gandhi's supporters resorted to going out on the streets and picking up random strangers to swell their numbers. Nearly a hundred outsiders were brought into the Congress pandal on the morning of the voting to ensure Gandhi's victory. But that was not the only trick that Gandhi's supporters resorted to. Motilal Nehru, who had throughout been lobbying for the opposition, ended up voting for the resolution. He had been persuaded to cross over to Gandhi's side by his son, Jawaharlal. Jinnah took the betrayal calmly—as he did that of his two young associates in the Home Rule League, Umar Sobhani and Shankerlal. The two had not only crossed over to the enemy's side but were directly involved in the vote rigging. Not everyone took it with his stoic composure. Shaukat Ali, who had been increasingly incensed by Jinnah's stubborn refusal to yield to popular pressure and back down on his fierce opposition to Gandhi's resolution, almost beat him up as they dispersed after the meeting. A large man, he lunged at Jinnah as if to strike him but was held back by other delegates. Jinnah walked away, seemingly unperturbed.

For Ruttie, who had not left her seat in the Congress pandal while the session was on, the proceedings seemed to be disappointingly dull. The implications of what Gandhi's triumph meant for Jinnah's political career had not yet sunk in. But the sounds of a scuffle outside the pandal prompted her into action. Instead of making her way out of the pandal through the crowds, she ran to her friend, Kanji Dwarkadas, who was still lingering in the tent. He, too, had heard the sounds of fighting going on outside and was waiting for it to subside so that he could escort his leader, Annie Besant, out of the venue. She tugged at his sleeve, saying, 'Come on, take me out!' Kanji, who could refuse her nothing, tried to reason with her: 'We cannot go, there is some fighting going on outside.' But she was not to be put off. 'That is exactly what I want to see, let us go quickly,' she said imperatively and Kanji obediently led her outside. 'Fortunately,' as he recalled years later, 'the fighting had come to an end.'

But the fight didn't really end—at least in Jinnah's head. It took another month before his rage and frustration against Gandhi finally boiled over. The issue was the way Gandhi broke all the rules and completely changed the Home Rule League which Jinnah had built up from scratch. It enraged Jinnah that Gandhi had once again outmanoeuvred him and gone several jumps ahead, leaving him feeling cheated.

Six months ago, when he was still deluding himself that he could control Gandhi, Jinnah had invited Gandhi to take over as head of the Home Rule League. 'He thought he would be able to keep some check on Gandhi if he would agree to work with him,' as Kanji recounts in his book, *India's Fight for Freedom*. But far from wanting to work together, Gandhi went over Jinnah's head and changed the constitution of the Home Rule League, and also renamed it Swaraj Sabha. Unable to stop him, Jinnah and nineteen other colleagues were forced to resign. Jinnah's patience was by now exhausted and instead of trying to sort out the issue with Gandhi in person, he took the extreme step of publishing the letter of resignation in the *Bombay Chronicle* the next day.

Gandhi's reply, arriving twenty days later, infuriated Jinnah even further. Apart from the less than lukewarm appeal to reconsider his decision, Gandhi stoked Jinnah's already sore temper by his patronizing tone and refusal to admit that he had broken the rules. It was enough to make Jinnah forget himself and pour all his derision for Gandhi in an open letter to him. The letter, several pages long, published the next day in the *Bombay Chronicle*, attacked Gandhi for his 'methods [that] have already caused split and division in almost every institution that you have approached hitherto, and in the public life of the country not only amongst Hindus and Mohamedans, but between Hindus and Hindus and Mohamedans and Mohamedans and even between fathers and sons'.

And as if he had not gone far enough with his personal attack on a leader worshipped by all as a Mahatma, Jinnah proceeded to commit political hara-kiri by his forthright opinion of Gandhi's followers: 'People generally are desperate all over the country and your extreme programme has for the moment struck the imagination mostly of the inexperienced youth and the ignorant and the illiterate.'

This was the very first time in twenty-three years of his public life that Jinnah lost his temper, and, of course, he had to pay for his indulgence. Almost overnight his popularity crashed, plunging him from the heights of 'Bombay's uncrowned king' to its lowest point, hated by the very Muslims who had admired him and followed his lead for at least two decades.

But the full effects of what he had done became apparent only seven weeks later at Nagpur, where the annual Congress session was being held that year to vote on adopting Gandhi's non-cooperation programme as a national plan. In the three months since Calcutta, Gandhi had turned into a living god, with people gathering for a mere glimpse of him wherever he passed on his tour of the country. To oppose him now was to be branded a national traitor. But there was a covert rebellion brewing among the major Congress leaders against his drastic non-cooperation move, although none of them dared to be as openly critical of Gandhi as Jinnah was. And it was towards them that Gandhi made an effort to reach out and build a consensus, using Shaukat Ali as an envoy. But leaving his peace talks to Shaukat Ali had at least one unexpected consequence. Shaukat wooed each and every opposition leader within the Congress except Jinnah, whom he had begun to regard as a personal enemy. Jinnah—and Ruttie because she was with him—became the untouchables of the Congress session of December 1920.

The leader in the opposition camp that Shaukat Ali courted most assiduously was the barrister Congressman from Calcutta, C.R. Das. Das had arrived in Nagpur with a contingent of 1800 delegates whom he had brought along with him from Bengal at his own expense. It cost him a whopping Rs 50,000 to transport these delegates and to lodge them at the Congress camp, but Das was determined that Gandhi's supporters would not again push through their agenda by questionable means. By its very size, the 'Bengali Camp' became the scene of all action before and in between the sessions, with Shaukat Ali holding 'continuous negotiations' with Das, while their men came to blows outside. Several heads were broken in the Bengali camp, according to Gandhi's own admission but he chose to turn a blind eye, dismissing the violence as a mere 'family dispute'.

Shaukat Ali's combined tactics of intimidation and coaxing yielded rich results. One by one, the leaders of the opposition camp keeled over, leaving Jinnah standing alone in the field to fight against Gandhi before a crowd baying for his blood. Annie Besant, who had already got a taste of the crowd's hostility in Calcutta when she put up a fight against Gandhi's resolution, wisely decided to stay out of the Nagpur session. Motilal Nehru was, of course, emotionally blackmailed by his son into falling in line with Gandhi. And the crowds led by the Ali brothers gave Pandit Madan Mohan Malaviya such a rough time during the earlier session that he stayed away on the last day, pleading an attack of malaria. G.S. Khaparde, a co-worker of Tilak's and an opponent of Gandhi's resolution, was booed so relentlessly with cries of 'Shame! Shame!' that he had to give up halfway through his speech. But the most sensational crossover was that of Das, who turned overnight from fierce 'anti-non-cooperator' into the meek mover of Gandhi's resolution. The battle had been lost but Jinnah refused to retreat.

If Jinnah had listened to his reason rather than follow his stubborn refusal to yield under pressure, he would have packed his bags and left straightaway. There was no doubt left that Gandhi single-handedly ruled the Congress and that his word was law. But that only made Jinnah more determined to stick it out until the end. It was by no means easy with the crowd out to jeer at him and not letting him speak. He faced the crowd's hostility with his usual impassivity, refusing to be bullied by them which only infuriated them further. He was treated so badly that one of the British Labour Party invitees finally protested, saying from the dais that 'it pained him to remember the bad treatment accorded to Mr Jinnah in the Congress' and appealed to the delegates to 'behave like gentlemen even towards the opponents'.

But the appeal fell on deaf ears. On the final day, when he got up to oppose Gandhi's resolution, the crowd would just not allow him to speak. The pandal was packed with anywhere from 16,000 to 50,000 delegates crammed into a space meant to accommodate 3000, but they had been surprisingly disciplined and courteous while listening to the two earlier speakers, Gandhi and Lajpat Rai. But as Jinnah rose to address the gathering with the words, 'I rise to oppose the motion,' there was an explosion. A cacophony of hooting, shouting and catcalls rose up from the audience, drowning his voice. But he would not yield. 'He stood there, without twitching a muscle, and when the shouting died down, he again said, "I rise to oppose the motion."' Again he was drowned out by the crowd. Three times he tried to speak, pitting his indomitable will against 'that vast ocean of humanity' ranged against him, refusing to retreat, until they had to let him speak. But now they began heckling him, shouting each time he said 'Mr Gandhi': 'Call him Mahatma Gandhi!' Thinking to buy himself a few minutes' time to reason with them, he agreed readily. But it was not enough: they next demanded that he address Mohammed Ali as 'Maulana'. This was beyond his forbearance. 'No, I will not be dictated [to] by you,' he shot back. 'If you will not allow me the liberty to speak of a man in the language which I think is right, I say you are denying me the liberty which you are asking for.' This only enraged them further, especially Shaukat Ali, who came forward to the platform ready to hit him. He was stopped by other delegates, but Jinnah still refused to step off the dais. Whether anyone listened to him or not, he would not stop until he made one last, desperate attempt to reason with the crowd. This time his appeal was to Gandhi himself, urging him to use his 'vast influence' to stop a programme that was sure to end in disaster. Then he walked out, impassive as ever while the crowd raised frenzied cries of 'Shame!' and 'Political impostor!'

Ruttie had missed this scene of his final humiliation. Nothing could have torn her away from him just then, but she had been forced to withdraw. As soon as they arrived in the pandal that morning, some delegates had sent up a chit to the president, objecting to Ruttie's dress. Clearly, it was part of the hate campaign the Jinnahs had been facing ever since they got to Nagpur for the session. According to an unprejudiced eyewitness, there was really nothing about Ruttie's dress that day to offend the most strait-laced of moralists. She was dressed, according to him, in the current fashion 'in a beautiful sari and an armless blouse'. But instead of tearing up the note as a frivolous interruption, the Congress chief took the extraordinary step of passing on the note to Jinnah. This meant, according to the convention of the party meetings, that Jinnah would either have to rise to his wife's defence, opening themselves up for a further mauling by the crowd, or else she would have to accept that she was in the wrong and withdraw from the Congress. For Jinnah, there seemed only one way to deal with the note. He glanced at it and passed it on silently to Ruttie. She got up and left.

There was another parting kick. Jinnah decided to leave Nagpur without attending the Muslim League session, but Gandhi's non-violent non-cooperators were determined to strip him of even this last shred of his dignity. They hounded the Jinnahs on their way back to Bombay by shouting invectives at him at the stations. At Akola railway station in particular, Shaukat Ali, who was travelling by the same train, incited an emotional crowd to hoot at Jinnah, who was seated in the first-class compartment, with cries of 'Shame!' It upset Ruttie but seemed not to bother Jinnah at all. Or so he would have the world believe.

Chapter Seventeen

~

Almost the first thing that Ruttie did when she got back home was to dash off an angry letter to the *Times of India*. The letter, protesting against the way Jinnah had been bullied on the train, was her way of telling him—and the world—that she was unflinchingly by his side.

To see him hurting behind his impassive exterior brought out all her fierce tenderness, and she was ready in her brave, impetuous way to rush to his protection, not caring for the consequences. But he was the careful kind, and the letter would have taken some unusual pondering on her part. It was a delicate task, beginning with the question of where to send it for publication. It could not be to the paper that was her natural choice, the one that everyone she knew read, the *Bombay Chronicle*. That would be embarrassing, with Jinnah there as chairman of its managing board—not for her, but him. So it had to be the rival paper, and even so, she had to be careful not to use her own name, again for his sake rather than her own. The letter, written with the fluid ease with which she wrote anything, never at a loss for the right word, and yet with uncharacteristic restraint, appeared the next day in the *Times of India*'s letters to the editor column. Signed 'R', under the headline 'Non-cooperation in Practice', it was terse, attacking the one man she felt safe to attack because she could at least discern how Jinnah felt about the Ali brothers. But Gandhi she left out altogether—her feelings towards him, coloured by Jinnah's own ambivalence towards his great rival, were altogether mixed. 'At Akola,' the letter said, 'Mr Shaukat Ali delivered a short lecture to those who had assembled on the platform; and at the end of the lecture, he incited them to hoot Mr Jinnah, who was seated in the first-class compartment, with cries of "Shame". Sir, this sort of thing is the negation of non-cooperation of which non-violence is the essence.'

It must have pleased him, this little show of loyalty from her. He liked nothing better in a woman than her loyalty. But now he was all the more anxious to prove to her and himself that he was not upset at all. A politician had to grow a thick skin, as he loved to tell his young associates. They had all left him, incidentally, the young men, some lawyers, others in business, well educated and wanting something more out of life than merely making money. They used to love dropping in at his chambers, loved hearing him hold forth, and counted themselves honoured if they received one of Mrs Jinnah's casual notes asking them to drop in for 'potluck'. But the potlucks were now a thing of the past. After Nagpur, the young men had all disappeared one by one—Umar Sobhani, Shankerlal Banker, Syud Hossain . . . all rebuffed by his rude and brusque manner brought on by his growing political frustrations. He could not forgive them for going over to Gandhi's side. But there was his legal work to take their place and he plunged himself into work with a vengeance. People assumed it was his greed for money, but money had never interested him much, especially now that he had made his 'packet', as he called it, and invested it wisely, leaving him free to pursue the only career he had ever wanted—as a political leader. But at least court work was something to keep him engaged, taking up his time until late into the night. He still came home punctually at six in the evening but shut himself up in his library, refusing to emerge even for dinner. Ruttie had a hard time even getting him to eat his meals, let alone open up and talk to her. He had a habit, as she later complained to their friend Kanji Dwarkadas, but fondly, 'of habitually over-working himself'. Others knew how hard it was to get him to not work so hard or even eat if he didn't want to, but in her tender, solicitous way she kept at him, knowing as she told Kanji, that if she didn't 'bother and tease him he will be worse than ever'. His silent withdrawal must have dismayed her sometimes, struggling as she was with her own feelings of loneliness and disappointment. She dared not as yet acknowledge it even to herself but the shadow of a doubt was beginning to grow in her that Jinnah could never 'satisfy her mind and soul', as she eventually confessed to Sarojini. But her love and solicitude for him kept her bound to him—a tender, hovering love such as she had not felt for anyone, wanting fiercely to protect him from all hurt.

What would have touched her the most was that somewhere inside that icy hauteur, there was his boyish determination to prove that he wasn't beaten yet. The fight had by no means been squashed out of him. In less than three weeks after his Nagpur mauling, he was back for more, literally walking into the lion's den. He descended on a public meeting addressed by Mohammed Ali and took his seat among the audience, as if he was a nobody. Seeing him, Mohammed Ali took a few potshots at him, making suggestive remarks about people who refused to join Gandhi's movement because they were afraid to 'leave law and suffer for the country'. But his courage was never on better display than when he had to stand up to a hostile crowd. It was impossible, of course, to try and cow him down—his very presence, with its natural sense of power and authority, made him impervious to intimidation. In fact, it was he who assumed a tone of condescension, even though he was addressing Mohammed Ali up on the stage while he sat in the audience, calling him 'young man' and asking him searching questions on how exactly they proposed to bring in Swaraj within eight months as they were promising to do. Of course, it did not make him any more popular with the crowd but he affected not to care.

Four weeks later, he was once again inviting the crowd's wrath upon his head, trying to reason them out of their blind faith in Gandhi. This time he was on the platform, one of the main speakers at a public meeting to commemorate national leader Gopal Krishna Gokhale on his death anniversary. As a well-known friend and admirer of Gokhale's, the audience was ready to overlook his differences with Gandhi and even gave him a generous round of applause when he took the stage. But it was Jinnah who would not let matters rest. He was bent on bringing up Gandhi's non-cooperation resolution, trying to explain yet again how disastrous it would be for everyone. He felt it to be his duty to enlighten them, to explain how Gandhi was 'taking the country to a wrong channel', and he ignored them when they got restive and broke into cries of 'No! No!' Something seemed to drive him on. Nothing mattered more than the public's love and acclaim, and yet he had to shake them out of their 'hysteria'.

At least no one tried to beat him up this time. Other leaders who took on Gandhi, even though they were much more circumspect than Jinnah, were facing a rough time from the public. Annie Besant, whose Home Rule League had started bringing out pamphlets and leaflets against Gandhi's programme, was not allowed to speak at a public meeting in Bombay. She stood mute on the platform for one whole hour while the crowds shouted, booed and hissed at her and she had to eventually withdraw without being able to say a word. At another anti-non-cooperation meeting held at Bombay's popular venue, the Excelsior Theatre, the pro-Gandhi crowd got so violent that the main speaker, the Liberal leader Srinivas Sastri, had to escape by the back door. Kanji Dwarkadas, who was then secretary of both Annie Besant's League and the 'Anti-Non-Cooperation Committee' set up by some anti-Gandhi leaders, had the clothes torn off his back in an assault by Gandhi's supporters.

Even Jinnah was forced to curb his usual forthrightness when it came to denouncing Gandhi. Public sentiment would simply not allow him to speak out openly against their idol, their 'Prophet of Ahimsa', but in his heart, he was seething. In less than twelve months, the political career that he had built up so assiduously over twenty-three years had unravelled in a way he had never thought possible, reducing him to virtually a nonentity. He had been forced to resign his seat in the legislature, walk away from the Home Rule League he had helped build up and quit the Congress as well. He didn't entirely blame Gandhi for all of it—that would be giving him too much importance. But he did blame the British government, convinced that it was their blunders that were making people desperate enough to fall into Gandhi's hands. What frustrated him was that between Gandhi and the government, he was stuck in a bind. He could now neither contest for the newly reformed councils—because that would make him look as if he was more pro-British than the other Congress leaders—nor could he take his rightful place in the struggle because he would have to submit to Gandhi's crazy ideas. There was no way out for him now except to wait until Gandhi's movement collapsed under the weight of its own absurdities and people lost faith in him. But that was the hardest thing—to merely sit around and do nothing. He had never had a hobby and hated wasting time on holidays.

It wasn't easy for Ruttie either. All around her, friends and acquaintances were getting swept away by Gandhi's movement, galvanized by his call to boycott schools and colleges and government jobs, and join up for national work. It left her feeling more isolated than ever. Within weeks of Gandhi's call, students were leaving Bombay's colleges by the hundreds to join up for national service. Her friend Padmaja's brother Jaisoorya was one of them. 'Baba [Jaisoorya's name within the family] has written a pathetic letter of his mental struggle with the wave of non-cooperation that is sweeping over the students of Bombay,' Padmaja's father Dr Naidu wrote to his younger daughter in England. 'He feels that he must give up his college and I agree with him.' Padmaja herself was so fired up by Gandhi's programme that she was determined to take up 'some national work in Delhi or anywhere else', despite her father's misgivings about her fragile health. And even though he was afraid for his children, Dr Naidu was equally carried away by the patriotic fervour that had reached everywhere—except South Court, it seemed to Ruttie.

It made her restless—this sense of a new national spirit stirring up everywhere and the deadness within their own home. She longed to get away from it all, go away somewhere far away where politics would no longer matter, this cruel reminder of what they'd been through already—so resonant of that first expulsion, this sudden inexplicable plunge from Bombay's most popular political couple to its most reviled. At least then, when both the Parsis and Muslims were up in arms against them, they had their friends; now there was no one, just the two of them it seemed against the whole world which had gone over to Gandhi's side. And unlike Jinnah, Ruttie had no stomach for more fight; she preferred, indeed dreamt, of starting afresh somewhere far from here, a new life among people who did not know them and wouldn't judge. But, of course, Jinnah would not hear of it—had he not spent twenty years diligently creating this space for himself in public life, and now to give it up for one man. Others were ready to give up, either falling in line behind Gandhi's strange new agitational politics, whatever their reservations, or dropping out and returning to their private practice. But not him; he was even more obsessed with the political scene now that he had no part in it, trying to figure out some way of fighting his own insignificance. There was really nothing to keep him in Bombay, with even the high court closed for its two months' summer break. But he wouldn't budge; the last thing he wanted was to leave the field wide open to his detractors, unchallenged, while he spent the next four months doing nothing more stimulating than accompanying her on an extended tour of Europe that she had been dreaming about ever since the War ended. Eventually, realizing perhaps that even her coaxing and teasing was not working, she decided to go away by herself, leaving him and the baby.

Of course, tongues began to wag almost at once. Except for her closest friends, everyone she once used to know in Bombay had been expectantly awaiting news of their inevitable split. Perversely, she wanted to keep them guessing. Her plan, as she airily informed anyone who asked her, was to make her leisurely way via the French Riviera and Monte Carlo to England. 'Ruttie will be in England soon,' Padmaja wrote to her sister, Leilamani, in a letter dated only April 1921, by which time Ruttie was already living it up in Monte Carlo, as Padmaja goes on to add: 'That is, if she does not become penniless at Monte Carlo.' Nobody knew when Ruttie would return, if at all, and her plans for herself seemed grandiose. As Padmaja wrote: 'I hear she has great ambitions of acting for the cinema and has some plutantophoric scheme of supporting Jinnah by her earnings as a "vampire".' 'Plutantophoric', incidentally, is Padmaja's invented word, a spontaneous creation she came up with by ingeniously welding 'plutocrat' to 'philanthropic'—a combination word that oddly enough best describes Ruttie's whole attitude to wealth, or rather, her sudden lack of it, that is, if only she could somehow become rich enough to support Jinnah rather than be dependent on him and suffer his disapproval, voiced or unvoiced, on her excessive spending. But apart from that, Padmaja's rather elliptical statement is interesting for another reason: why, of all roles in the world, is Ruttie drawn to that of a vampire which is not, as one would assume nowadays, a monster who sucks human blood but the liberated woman of the early 1900s reviled for a similar sin—a man-eating home-wrecker and painted flirt, the irresistible 'vamp' of later years, the prototype of the bad girl in the silent film era? Did the role fascinate her, or was there inside her still, the good little girl of Petit Hall fame struggling against this new image of herself as the 'flapper' of her time?

Nor would she say how long her trip was going to last, giving the impression that she was a free woman, unfettered by her marriage.

In June, when Ruttie had finally reached England after her long trip to the Riviera and Monte Carlo, Padmaja asked Leilamani: 'How long is Ruttie going to be in England?' Presumably for another two months at least, as Padmaja pointed out in her letter: 'Leila told me that she was going to write and ask her to stick on until she went in August so that they could have a rare old time together—they have become violent chums evidently.' And adding, because being around Ruttie was always fun, as the two Naidu girls well knew, 'It will be great luck for you. Give my love to her.'

But behind her mischievous playacting of a would-be screen vamp, inspired perhaps by the American star Theda Bara, who had already made by then more than three dozen films that made her the world's most famous 'vampire', Ruttie was still very much the devoted wife. She made sure she left Monte Carlo and arrived in London on time to join Jinnah there for his much shorter visit of a few weeks. He had, of course, followed her, as they both knew he would, giving himself a brief respite before resuming his struggle to regain his political clout. Things had only got worse after she had left, forcing him to resign his last public position, as chairman of the board of directors of the *Bombay Chronicle*. He had to sever all connections with it following a conflict with the *Bombay Chronicle*'s editor, a certain Picthall, who had been picked personally by Horniman to succeed him, but with whom Jinnah now had sharp differences over his coverage of Gandhi's non-cooperation movement, compromising, according to Jinnah, the *Bombay Chronicle*'s policy of 'neutrality'. Having sent in his resignation letter, it seemed a good time for Jinnah to take a break. Besides, the trip would give him a chance to reconnect with his political contacts in London. But more to the point, although he could not bring himself to admit it, he missed Ruttie. He had not spent this much time apart from her since their marriage, having, as Kanji later put it in his memoir of Ruttie, 'no separate existence away from his wife'.

So effortlessly was she able to slip into her accustomed role as his supportive wife that he had no clue of her growing discontent. Nor did he want to know, happy in his belief that they were, as an old Parsi acquaintance later said of them to Bolitho, 'two sweethearts', devoted to each other in their own peculiar way. He could refuse her nothing, no matter how extravagant and unreasonable he thought her demands, although he did grumble about it; and good-humouredly put up with all her teasing, especially about his parsimony. He could be cold and stand-offish with everyone else, but around her he suddenly blossomed into something else, warm and expansive— 'almost human', as Sarojini put it. She bossed him around and put him down in front of others, teased and cajoled him and indulged her vanity by showing everyone how she could twist him around her little finger, but she too was more attached to him than she let on, attentive in every detail to his comforts in a way that was quite contrary to the emancipated times, especially for someone from her high-society upbringing. She would get up and leave, for example, from wherever she was at exactly five in the evening so that she could get home in time to receive him when he got back from court. And they always had a drink and dinner together, no matter what social engagement she had to skip in order to fall in with his rigid routine. In innumerable ways, she looked after him and made his life comfortable, including choosing his clothes and perfume because she was the only one apart from himself that he could trust to meet his fastidious tastes. He leaned on her, took her everywhere with him and cast little looks at her whenever he made a winning point, as if it was an offering to her. Sometimes her adoration shone out of her eyes, especially on the rare occasions when he relaxed, stretched out his long legs and launched into one of his anecdotes, full of dry humour.

It was different with the baby, though. With this infant, she felt no need for putting up any show. She simply ignored its existence, as if she was done with playing roles and couldn't be bothered keeping up appearances. She did her duty by it, as Jinnah expected of her, setting up a nursery for it in a separate wing of the house and assigning its care to a retinue of servants. After that, she never went anywhere near it, leaving the infant entirely to the servants' care. And although the child was now twenty months old, she refused to even give her a name. In her letters to Padmaja, which were quite frequent at least for the first year of the baby's birth, there was not even a passing reference to the child although she took care to send Padmaja greetings from all her three dogs in each letter she wrote to her. This was all so incomprehensible, so unlike the Ruttie before her marriage that no one, not even a friend as loyal and sympathetic as Padmaja, knew what to make of it. Padmaja dropped in at South Court after

Ruttie had left on her grand tour, and her heart went out to the lonely child for whom neither of its two parents seemed to have any time. 'Her little baby is one of the most pathetic, heart-breaking things I have ever seen,' Padmaja wrote to Leilamani in her letter of April 1921. 'I simply cannot understand Ruttie's attitude—I do not blame her as most people here seem to do, but whenever I remember the little dazed, scared child, like some mortally hurt animal, I come very near hating Ruttie in spite of my great affection for her.'

Jinnah was still around in Bombay then, not yet having left to join Ruttie in London. But his presence could have made little difference to his infant daughter even when he was home, considering his own preoccupations. Nor did he spare his time for her dogs that she had left behind, including Arlette who she usually took with her no matter where she went. The thought of caring for a dog in a hotel in Monte Carlo, and that too without an attendant, had probably deterred her from carrying Arlette along. But they were missing her even more than her baby, as Padmaja wrote: 'Loafer and Arlette and Bolshie were delirious with joy and excitement at seeing a friendly face and nearly overwhelmed me with greetings when I went there,' adding: 'Poor little Arlette has grown quite matronly and has quite lost her slim figure.'

But this daring attempt to unshackle herself from her domestic fetters hardly seems to have helped. After having got her own way and apparently living out her life's dream of the free and modern woman—travelling around Europe without husband or baby—Ruttie seemed no more at peace than before. 'I had a brief and wistful letter from Ruttie,' as Sarojini wrote to Leilamani on 11 June 1921. 'She seems so hungry and restless and I think she needs me as much as Bebe does, only in a different way.' But with Gandhi keeping Sarojini so busy that she had no time to visit her dear 'Bebe', as Padmaja was called by her family and friends, or even call her to Bombay, where was she to find the time for Ruttie's angst, inexplicable as it seemed to her impatient soul. Having grown more pragmatic with age, Sarojini was almost in a fever of irritation with Ruttie's 'clamouring for freedom', as she later put it, especially the way she had abandoned her baby for it.

Sarojini had hardly seen Ruttie since the baby's arrival. When the Jinnahs returned from England with their two-month-old, Sarojini had remained stationed there for another year and a half, taking on the role of a political and cultural ambassador for the Congress. She had returned to India only around the time Ruttie was setting off for Europe again, shockingly 'minus Jinnah and Baby', as she put it. But with both Ruttie and Jinnah now away in Europe, Sarojini dropped in at South Court to see how it was doing in their absence. The baby had just returned from Ooty where Jinnah had packed her off for the summer with the servants. And had returned to Bombay that very day with her retinue, as Sarojini wrote to Padmaja to say. 'I went to see the Jinnah baby this morning,' she wrote in her undated letter. 'It returned from Ooty in its pathetic servant-fostered loneliness. It looked so sweet, fresh from its bath. I stayed and played a little with it, poor little pet.' Then she added: 'I could beat Ruttie whenever I think of her child.' But in another letter, dated 5 July 1921, to Leilamani, evidently written on the same day as her previous one to Padmaja, she was a little more reconciled to what Ruttie had done: 'I went to see Ruttie['s] baby today. She has just returned from Ooty. She was looking sweet and happy. The dogs too are well.' And in a curt message to the errant mother, she added: 'Tell Ruttie I'd love to beat her but that I love her in spite of all her wickedness.'

But with Jinnah, there was no abandoning the role Ruttie had so lovingly and conscientiously donned since her wedding day, the ever-dutiful wife, accompanying him wherever he spoke. There she was, by his side, silent and approving and beautiful, just as he liked her to be—first on 20 June, at the Connaught Rooms in London where Jinnah was the chief speaker at a public meeting organized by the 'India and Near East Bureau'. Their friend Horniman, still waiting patiently for the government to return his confiscated passport, was there too, in a show of solidarity that must have pleased Jinnah. And she went with Jinnah to Oxford too where he addressed the Indian students' debating society, the Majlis. And also to the reception held in his honour by the Indian community. Evidently his unpopularity at home had not affected his image abroad.

But except on these public occasions when he wished her to be by his side, he did his own thing, almost ignoring her as was his habit. He had come to London with plenty of plans of his own, although this was supposed to be a holiday with her. But then, she knew how much he hated to 'waste' his time, even during holidays. He had, in fact, come to England fully prepared with a scheme that he was sure would topple Gandhi from power by splitting the Khilafatists away from his side. And since this involved getting the British government to grant a few sops to Turkey so that he could lure the Khilafatists away from Gandhi, he was bent on cultivating parliamentarians and newspaper reporters who could put the necessary pressure on their government. Then there was, of course, his old friend, the secretary of state for India, Montagu, to pursue as well; and if there was any time left from all this running around, there were all his newspapers to read.

It certainly gave her plenty of time alone to brood on their differences, which now seemed to her unbridgeable. It was not really the age gap that bothered her, as others thought, as his old-fogey habits, all the more glaring in this new post-War culture sweeping across Europe, with young people making a swift, clean break from the past and its inhibitions. She, of course, took at once to the new age, recognizing bits of herself in its new culture and embracing the new licence to freedom with all her usual ardour. But Jinnah was by no means ready to give up all that he had worked so hard to cultivate within himself. Having groomed himself with such diligence and persistence during the puritanical Victorian times, he would not give in to the free and easy new age. He refused in his stubborn way to change anything, not even his high, stiff collars or his now quaint habit of an elaborate change of attire for different hours of the day. He was especially horrified by the new craze for dancing and would have forbidden Ruttie from ever taking to the floor if his liberal principles would have permitted. At one gala they attended, for instance, at the residence of a rich Muslim admirer of Jinnah's, he had to be led away to the billiards room downstairs as soon as the band began to play and couples took to the dance floor, because he could not hear himself talk, and sat in the basement the entire time with a young man for company, talking politics, while Ruttie, who loved to dance, was left in the lurch.

Going shopping with him was equally exasperating. He had a fussy habit of turning everything over without picking up anything even after spending hours in a shop. He either complained about the poor quality of the cloth or demanded to be shown clothes made before the War. And if he did find a shirt or a collar from pre-War times, he snapped it up, gloating over the bargain price that he had got it for, not caring how hopelessly dated it was. It took enormous effort on her part to make him switch over from his bargain-conscious dressing mode to the fabulously expensive tailor in Paris, at Charves, although she did have her way in the end. She had a hard time even persuading him to keep his hair the way she had insisted he wear it, long and backswept. He grumbled about wanting to cut it short until she had to remind him that it was the condition on which she had accepted him. She, on the other hand, maybe partly because he insisted on being so tiresomely staid and middle-aged, wanted to go to the other extreme, and began to dress in a style that was over-emphatically modish—bare back, a bob cut, paint on her face, long cigarette holder and all—as if to prove that she at least was still young and with-it.

They were both, in their own ways, lovers of drama, and if he liked to play the ageing Victorian gentleman with his old-world quaintness and his paternal 'my boy' and 'young man', she too relished her new persona as chic, young, eccentric, gay and frivolous as the fashion demanded. It took her no time at all to convince everyone around her that she was indeed 'Mad Little Ruttie', someone who, as Leilamani admiringly put it, was 'always so unique'. No mean accomplishment, incidentally, in an age when everyone was vying with each other with competing eccentricities in order to be noticed.

She had met Leilamani when she went to Oxford with Jinnah for his talk at the Majlis. Sarojini's younger daughter, now studying in a women's college at Oxford, was overjoyed to see her former idol. Leilamani, of course, could see no trace of that sadness within Ruttie that had disturbed her mother a few weeks earlier. Instead she wrote to Padmaja, saying, 'Ruttie has arrived looking so childish, naughty and beautiful!'

Ruttie too was glad to have found a friend to lessen the chill of 'this marriage ice', as she later put it. Not content with spending all their holiday in Oxford hanging out with Leilamani and trying not to mind Jinnah's preoccupation, Ruttie then carried Leilamani along with them to London. The Jinnahs had taken a suite at the Ritz for their two months' holiday and Leilamani was only too glad to leave her student digs for a while and enjoy a holiday in London at their expense. Jinnah did not seem to mind the new arrangement at all.

He went about pursuing his own interests, hardly noticing Ruttie and her friend as they went to town spending his money. As was expected of a surrogate older sister, Ruttie indulged the homesick college girl. 'She gives me delicious food and stuffs me with lovely things,' Leilamani exulted. They went shopping together and Leilamani could once more enjoy the thrill of walking on the street with her strikingly beautiful friend. As she wrote to Padmaja on 15 July 1921: 'Yes, Ruttie is Naughty still but even more charming and lovely than before. It is one of the most amusing and charming occupations to walk down Piccadilly and Bond Street with her and all the dowdy Duchesses and all the young Dukes, all the Nouveaux riches flashing in brilliants and diamonds gaze in delight at this lovely thing and turn and crane their royal necks to see and see her again!'

The threesome continued even when the Jinnahs moved to Paris on the last leg of their holiday. Ruttie had once again urged Leilamani to join them and all three stayed together in the same hotel, the Claridge's, with Leilamani only returning to her college when it was time for the Jinnahs to board a steamer back to Bombay. And far from feeling left out, Jinnah found a better way to occupy himself than going around Paris with Ruttie: he sat in their hotel room to write to Montagu, reminding him to set up an appointment for him with the new viceroy, Lord Reading.

Nor did the journey home bring them any closer. Ruttie, as usual, was confined to her cabin by her violent seasickness, while Jinnah, who had never had any patience with any form of illness in himself or others, promptly left her to her own devices, and stayed absorbed in his future plans. He could see himself playing the mediator's role in the political crisis he saw looming ahead of them all and the prospect of meeting the viceroy to discuss his scheme made him so eager to reach home that they landed in Bombay a whole week earlier than Ruttie had expected.

Absence had not made her any fonder of their child. It had been five months since she had left home and child, but on the very day they landed in Bombay, she felt the need to get away again. She fled to the Taj Mahal hotel, planning to spend the day with Sarojini in her suite. But Sarojini was not in. Undeterred, Ruttie decided to come back the following day, expecting to find Sarojini in her suite as usual and taking her welcome very much for granted. She left Sarojini a note, which the latter described dryly as 'characteristic'. It said: 'I have come. Tomorrow with just me here at 11 am. Woe to any intruder, man or Mahatma.'

She didn't know it as yet but everything had changed while she had been away, including Sarojini herself. Gandhi's mass movement of non-cooperation had its ups and downs politically, but he had performed a miracle on high society, transforming them both spiritually and culturally. Friends and acquaintances whom Ruttie had known from her garden party days had given up their homes and cars and gold to be auctioned for national funds, and were now filling up jails, considering it an honour to be arrested by the government. Women who used to spend their days partying or shopping had given up their silks and chiffons, making bonfires of their foreign clothes and going from door to door 'begging' for funds to run Gandhi's campaign. Even old Mrs Dadabhoy made the rounds with Mrs Mohammed Ali for collecting funds, as Sarojini proudly reported in one of her letters. There were other elegant ladies and gentlemen who now prided themselves on running khadi shops or attending spinning classes. Even Lady Petit had succumbed, 'torn between her accustomed pearls and embroidered georgette and a white khadi sari to attend the national meeting', as Sarojini put it. So had Ruttie's friend, Kshama Row, whom she had never rated very highly either in intelligence or commitment. It was as if, unbeknownst to her, everyone she knew had embraced a new faith while she had been away. Sarojini, of course, was among the first to take Gandhi's 'Swadeshi vow' to abjure mill cloth and had switched over to unbleached homespun cotton. Usually the first to poke fun at her beloved idol, the 'little tyrant' as she fondly referred to Gandhi, refusing firmly to follow any of his fads and become like the rest of his devotees, she had given up her colourful silk saris and went about looking, in her own words, either like a 'dhobi's bundle' or 'a wind-blown balloon of white khadi'.

But the outer change was nothing compared to Sarojini's inner transformation. Inspired by Gandhi and filled with a new sense of purpose and meaning, she was no longer the easy, laid-back hostess who had turned her hotel rooms into a salon and sanctuary for lost and vagrant souls, welcoming with open arms anyone who turned up at her door, with meals and gossip sessions. For the last five months, Sarojini had been thrust into the centre of Gandhi's political struggle and her responsibilities now ranged from mediating between the Khilafat and Congress leaders, presiding over public meetings across the country, raising funds to the tune of several million rupees for the Congress, organizing a women's wing of non-cooperators and holding khadi exhibitions, besides leading marches and boycotts of foreign cloth. She was kept so busy working 'night and day without food, without sleep', that, as she wrote to her daughter, the only thing she could be certain about in her day was her morning bath. But she was loving every moment of it, 'proud and grateful', as she said, for the 'privilege to share in the great work'. It hardly made for a frame of mind to receive Ruttie back into her life. Sarojini had, in fact, been dreading Ruttie's return, as she told Leilamani in a letter dated 10 August 1921: 'I am glad that Ruttie has been so good [to you]. She is returning here on the 7th September and I am wondering if I shall ever get any work done when she returns!' As it turned out, much to her dismay, Ruttie landed up even earlier than she was expected, as Sarojini wrote to Padmaja: 'Ruttie returned last week [28 August 1921]—a whole week earlier than she was expected. And of course she came the very day . . .'

Another week went by before they could meet. And while both found each other much altered, it was Sarojini who put her feelings down in a letter to Padmaja (undated but obviously written in the first week of September 1921), saying that Ruttie 'is looking lovely but not in the same radiant and touching fashion. There is something hard and cold about it all—paint, powder, bare back and the rest of it.' But under the paint, she could still discern the loving Ruttie of Petit Hall days, making her add: 'And yet at the core of her, she is a wonderful flame of purity and nobility. She loves you, my little girl—and she understands you.'

It was that core which Ruttie had not quite rid herself of that made her so uneasy with herself. Unable to bear her isolation from the others now absorbed in the national struggle, and tied to Jinnah inextricably by her love and loyalty, she fled every morning to the Taj for some relief from her rising anxiety. To Sarojini's increasing dismay, Ruttie arrived at her suite every morning at eleven, soon after Jinnah left home for the courts. She hung around there for the rest of the day, refusing to leave until it was time for Jinnah to return home from his chamber. 'Ruttie takes up her abode here between 11 and 5 regularly and prevents me from doing any work,' Sarojini complained to Padmaja in a postscript of a letter dated 3 September 1921.

What made her even more annoyed with the way Ruttie casually dropped in and spent her whole day in her room was that she now had so little time for herself, serving not only as the chief of the Bombay Provincial Congress, which was the hub of all Gandhi's activities at this stage, but also heading the Swadeshi Sabha that had started dozens of new activities, including as she said in the same letter, 'Today the Dadabhoy Jayanti . . . [which] for my sins of course I am deeply implicated in the celebrations. Next week I have endless Ganapati puja festivities; and I have been receiving simultaneous "urgent" calls from UP, Punjab, Bihar, Bengal, Central Provinces, Berar, Surat, Gujarat, Kandahar, Maharashtra and Andhra! I leave out Assam and Madras because I have regretted them both!!'

With that much happening in her own political life, it was easy for even someone as friendly and sympathetic as Sarojini to become somewhat sententious about Ruttie's idleness, enforced though it was because of being married to Jinnah and sharing the political exile he had brought upon both of them. 'The Jinnahs are back,' Sarojini wrote on 9 September 1921 to Syud Hossain, their common friend now living in London, 'and very out of place in the India of today where there is no room for any kind of slacker. Ruttie spends most of her time here as usual.' As for Sarojini herself, as she makes a point of mentioning in her letter: 'I am desperately busy and rather ill—or should I say very ill, but I cannot afford to be a slacker even for an hour. Things are very grave . . .'

In this new work environment that Gandhi had created even in Bombay's high society, suddenly giving their lives a new meaning and purpose, even to fall sick was to be guilty of being a 'slacker', as Sarojini sternly pointed out to Padmaja when she heard of her illness. 'No man, no woman today can dare to be a coward, a backslider, a self-centred self-pitying weakling when the very soul of India is at stake,' she wrote, adding, 'I know you will do your best to get quite strong and take your share of the work as other girls of your age and your own friends are doing.'

Given that punishing environment, Sarojini's suite proved to be the worst place for Ruttie, making her feel resentful and excluded. 'Ruttie comes nearly everyday,' Sarojini complained again in her letter to Padmaja the following week, on 19 September 1921, 'and laments all the people who come to see me. She is in a very restless, hysterical frame of mind and her manners are becoming intolerable.' And then the unkindest cut of all—'Poor child,' Sarojini added condescendingly, 'she has nothing but her beauty to interest her and how to clothe, or rather, unclothe it artistically!' It was a measure of how desolate her life had become that she still landed up at Sarojini's suite every mid-morning, putting herself through the daily torment of watching others bustle about with purpose and importance in Sarojini's suite which had become the hub of party activities, while she whose passion had been political work from the age of fourteen was forced to stand by, out of it all.

Understandably, it made her a little insecure, wanting to establish her proprietorial rights over Sarojini, the one friend remaining from her once full life. But Sarojini, instead of understanding, seemed to be running out of patience, and was almost peremptory with her. One day, for instance, Ruttie brought her a gift of an exquisite statue. As a solace perhaps or a cure for her boredom, Ruttie had been tapping her Petit gift for beauty and had become a discriminating collector of antique statues, with an impressive collection of jades, and wanting to give Sarojini something truly exquisite but knowing her habit of carelessly passing on any gift she received either to one of her daughters or a friend, Ruttie made her promise that she would keep this gift for herself. It was a simple thing after all, a young friend yearning in her loneliness for some special connection with her mother figure, and yet, Sarojini, with an insensitivity that was so unlike her, promptly brushed it away, forwarding the gift to Padmaja, with a casual line in her letter saying: 'You will be wondering at my sudden affluence in statuary. Ruttie gave it to me with the express injunction—which I promptly ignored—that I am not to give to you, Papi, Umar [or] Syud because it would be an insult to her gift and herself.'

Yet, Ruttie clung to her, despite Sarojini's severity, needing her desperately in this time of her utter isolation. Sometimes, especially when one of her children came to her on a visit, they unwound enough and Sarojini once more caught a fleeting glimpse of the Ruttie she had once adored. 'Ruttie is getting more and more self-centred and self-worshipful,' she began in her by now usual tone of disapproval, but suddenly changed tack, recalling Ruttie's other aspect, which she was apt to forget. 'And yet she is full of childish charm.' Her letter to Padmaja, dated 4 October 1921, went on to say: 'She and Mina play together like two babies and she is altogether natural and simple when she is here . . .' And Ruttie, as if to establish her claim to somehow become part of the Naidu family and lose her orphaned state, could then make simple demands on her, as one makes at home with one's own family, without it being misconstrued: 'By the way Ruttie wants,' as Sarojini added, 'one dozen bottles of the tomato sauce to be sent VP to her address.'

To other people, she could come across as bold and daring and different, 'a complete minx', as Lady Reading sniffed, playing the 'vamp' in real life. And she could be cutting when she wanted, able to put even a viceroy in his place with her quick-tongued retorts that she had no doubt learnt from that idol of her youth, Oscar Wilde, whose witty epigrams she had been so fond of throwing about, just as Jinnah had sedulously cultivated the speeches of his role model, Edmund Burke. Grown fearless now in the art of inspiring disapproval, and with her impish need to unsettle the sanctimony of the devoutly khadi-clad women around her, she had taken to dressing even more daringly than before, arriving in Sarojini's suite in transparent gauze saris and backless and sleeveless blouses that she had specially tailored at Emile Windgrove's, the exclusive European-owned tailor's shop on Hornby Road. But with Sarojini and her children, she could be her real self, dropping all her armour of paint and camouflage.

It helped, of course, that Sarojini knew her so well and refused to be shocked, even willing, to Ruttie's great delight, to join her in making fun of the great Mahatma who had taken over both their lives, in such different ways, casting one as his loyal but still healthily sceptical lieutenant and the other into the lifelong perdition of exile, bringing out all her spirit of defiance.

By October 1921, both Ruttie and Gandhi seemed to have perfected their sartorial style, meant equally to shock and to set standards. As Sarojini put it with her unique mixture of reverence and irreverence where the Mahatma was concerned: 'Bombay has another epidemic on at present—an epidemic of leaders. They are pouring in today from all parts of India because Manucci [Sarojini's nickname for Gandhi] the Greater than Buddha is here and has summoned or summonsed us to an informal gathering of the Clan to plan our future work and play. He is a heroic and pathetic figure,' she wrote in her letter to Padmaja on 4 October 1921. 'He arrived minus cap, coat and half his dhoti. He has only a big piece of loincloth around his waist tied on with a string,' and added dryly: 'I told him that the only fit companion from the point of view of quantity not quality of clothes was Ruttie!!'

But there was no denying Ruttie's sense of style, no matter how much they might sniff at her, covertly measuring her up, fascinated by her originality and unerring good taste. They envied her, especially in an era when Gandhi was conspiring, as Sarojini once complained, to impose ugliness and drabness on the whole world, with only Ruttie standing out, defiantly stunning, amidst the dowdily khadi-clad or frumpily over-clad ladies of her time. So admired was her style and beauty, especially among the royalty, that one admirer among them— the Spanish-born rani of Kapurthala—openly sought Ruttie out to ask for tips on what to wear, even giving Ruttie a free hand to give her a complete makeover, including sharing tips on how to wear jewellery to create her unique style—using elaborate nose ornaments, for example, as earrings or a diamond necklace as a tiara, adding an exotic 'oriental' touch that was especially appreciated by the artists and photographers roaming Bombay in search of the picturesque and aesthetic. In fact, Ruttie even lent her own sari and jewellery for a photo shoot the rani had for the English magazine, the *Tatler*, even though the rani's own collection of jewellery, specially ordered from Cartier's by her doting husband, the maharaja of Kapurthala, was said to be fabulous, even by royal standards. 'By the way,' as Sarojini wrote to Padmaja on 19 September 1921, 'I am sending you a copy of the *Tatler* with the Spanish Rani's picture in it, dressed in Ruttie's black and gold embroidered sari and jewels.'

It was an odd friendship for Ruttie to strike up with this 'Spanish Rani', a low-born, almost illiterate flamenco dancer called Anita Delgado who at the age of sixteen bewitched the maharaja, Jagatjit Singh, of Kapurthala. The prince then pursued her for another two years, had her groomed in Paris at his expense, and at the age of eighteen, brought her home as his fifth wife. But she, after bearing him a son, felt increasingly stifled in the marriage and cast adrift in an alien world, eventually managed to make her escape sixteen years later. If there was any call of a kindred spirit, it did not seem to have struck a deep chord, and apart from lending her sari and jewels, and occasionally playing her stylist, Ruttie did not feel she shared anything in common with the rani and they never became close friends. Except, they were once again thrown together three years later at the Savoy Hotel in London, when according to at least one biographer of Delgado, Jinnah was obliged to be the mediator between the enraged prince and the rani because of an adventure she had the previous night, leading to their separation.

Playacting as a vamp or not, as the mood took her, and regardless of her disenchantment with Jinnah's staid habits of mind and temperament, Ruttie's sense of loyalty and duty to him never wavered. In November, when Jinnah finally got his appointment with Lord Reading as Montagu had promised him, and he was invited to Delhi to explain his scheme to the viceroy, Ruttie went along with him regardless of what she might have privately felt about such formalities, and calmly endured Lady Reading's disapproval, however unexpressed—'she had less on in the day time', as the vicereine later observed in a letter, 'than anyone I have ever seen'. Nor was she overly deferential to the viceroy, in fact, a little too irreverent. But in this their temperaments—Jinnah's and hers—were in perfect consonance. He, too, was temperamentally disinclined to try too hard to please. At lunch where she was seated next to the viceroy, she proceeded to snub him in her insidious way. According to their friend Kanji, who wrote about it later in his memoir of Ruttie, Lord Reading raised the subject of how much he wished to go to Germany but couldn't go there. Then she asked him, 'Your Excellency, why can't you go there?' Reading replied, 'The Germans do not like us, the British, so I can't go.' Ruttie then quietly asked him, 'How then did you come to India?' Reading is said to have immediately changed the subject. It would have been the kind of thing Jinnah would have said—or at least wished he had.

It turned out to be a waste of time for all concerned. While the viceroy was just as keen as Jinnah to end Gandhi's non-cooperation, he was neither willing to trust Jinnah to be the go-between nor willing to make substantial sacrifice to achieve what Jinnah proposed.

Mercifully, it was a short trip and when she reached home, there was some good news that seemed to make up for all the wifely duties and constrictions of the past few months. Padmaja was coming to

Bombay for a few days, on her mother's suggestion, taking a break from her duties in Hyderabad as a birthday treat to herself. It was a chance, at least for a few days, to forget all the political divisions and bitterness and be herself at last. What excitement, what planning! 'Ruttie is planning all sorts of things for you when you come,' as Sarojini wrote to Padmaja on 8 November 1921, reminding her again to 'bring Ruttie's tomato sauce also!'

But it was not to be. Duty called again. Padmaja arrived in Bombay in the same week that the Prince of Wales landed for his month-long visit. And with his arrival, politics seized them by the throat again. The prince was greeted by a big bonfire of foreign cloth as the Congress held a demonstration as planned. But the plans went awry, with riots erupting on the streets, and some of the protesters targeting Parsis and anyone else dressed in foreign clothes. The rioting and violence embarrassed the government but it affected Gandhi even more, devastating him with the failure of his call for non-violence. To his political rivals, including Jinnah, this was the moment they had been waiting for all these months, when Gandhi would be forced to admit defeat and retreat from the political scene. Sarojini tried to stop some of the protesters and got hit on the head with a stick, and Padmaja was hastily recalled to Hyderabad by her concerned father, while Ruttie took her place next to Jinnah at the round of official receptions held for the prince, putting paid to their innocent holiday plans.

Jinnah, bending over backwards to prove that the Congress boycott of the prince's visit served no useful purpose, made a point of attending every official function connected with the visit, of course, taking Ruttie along with him. It was the sort of thing that her mother would have enjoyed, to not only meet the prince on so many occasions but to actually sit next to him and even exchange a few words with him. But to Ruttie, that irreverent soul who liked 'to offend genteel proprieties', as Bolitho put it, it meant nothing more than enduring the tedium of long evenings spent in exchanging meaningless words and courtesies, but so strong was her sense of duty that she did not cry off from any of those many functions, even earning herself a favourable mention from the historian of the royal tour. '. . . I was interested to see how quickly Mr Jinnah and the Prince came to understand one another,' the historian, Rushbrook Williams, later recalled. 'Mr Jinnah and his beautiful wife, Ruttie, met the Prince on many occasions; I am sure that the Prince learned much from them, while on their part they were impressed by his unfeigned interest in India and her people.'

But that too mercifully was eventually over and the following month there was another fleeting moment when she could forget that she was Mrs Jinnah and be herself. Once more it was when one of Sarojini's children was visiting her, this time not Padmaja, but her younger brother, Ranadheera. Mina had always been a favourite with Ruttie and on this visit she was in particularly high spirits, perhaps feeling unconstrained for the first time in months. Sarojini, who was in the middle of writing her fortnightly letter to Leilamani at college in Oxford, left a graphic description of the scene of Ruttie cavorting around the room in an old sari, mimicking the Mahatma in a loincloth. 'The little wretch Ruttie half-clad in one of my cast-off garments, eating cake, is using abusive language and preventing me from writing to you,' Sarojini says in the letter dated 14 December 1921. In her general exuberance, brought on by the rare joy of spending time alone in Sarojini's rooms with no others except Mina and Sarojini's younger brother, Rana, Ruttie snatched the letter away from Sarojini before she could complete it and added her own postscript: 'Your mother is begging me to return the sari which she gave me two years ago—but since it is sufficient to cover but half of my sacred being—it would hardly be worthwhile to make the sacrifice, since it wouldn't do for an All India Khaddar to gag around with nothing to cover her co-operation.'

But there was no more horsing around after this. Political events took over their lives entirely, leaving no room for any personal indulgence—or that is what Jinnah would have liked her to believe. He himself had ignored the humiliation he had faced in the last Congress session at Nagpur and decided to attend this year-end's session in Ahmedabad. He felt he had to intervene in the political impasse between the non-cooperators and the government. The government, in its anxiety to avoid any embarrassment during the prince's visit, had sent a feeler through the former Congress president Madan Mohan Malaviya, offering to hold a round table conference to discuss all political demands if Gandhi called off his agitation. And Jinnah, unable to sit still and watch as Gandhi squandered a golden opportunity, took himself to Ahmedabad for the party conclave, regardless of how he felt personally about Gandhi or the rest of the Congress leaders. And, of course, she went along, eager to be of some use to him.

Once they got there, there was not much for her to do except stand by and watch Jinnah get down to the business of persuading the Congress to deal with the government. What this, in fact, meant was trying to get Gandhi to the negotiating table, since after his non-cooperation movement, there was no more Congress, only Gandhi. In his eagerness not to lose this opportunity, Jinnah even went along with Malaviya to Gandhi's ashram, something he had never done before, only to try and persuade Gandhi to see sense. But Gandhi, beneath his gentle demeanour, could be just as obdurate as Jinnah when it came to giving up his dearly held principles, and having failed to bring him around to their ways of thinking, Malaviya and Jinnah then focused their energy on the other Congress leaders, getting them together for an informal meeting to discuss the developments. It was a hectic time, with the Muslim League Council meetings to steer as well, and it seemed on all those four or five days they spent in Ahmedabad that any moment they were about to make a significant breakthrough.

This breathless sense of anticipation that something crucial was just about to happen pursued them to Bombay. Jinnah had come up with a plan he thought would help resolve the political impasse that Gandhi had thrust them all into with his impractical programme. There was suddenly a new energy around, not just in Jinnah but in their home as well, buzzing with the plans that Jinnah was making to call an all-party meeting in Ambalal Sarabhai's home in Bombay. His plan, as he told Ruttie and their friend Kanji, was to rope in leaders of various fractured groups of nationalists to bring pressure to bear on Gandhi so that he would agree to make peace with the government.

All through this period of renewed hope and activity, Ruttie was there, by his side, effortlessly filling in as sounding board, organizer of potluck dinners to facilitate his plan, enthusiastic participant of all-night political sessions, his cheerleader and acolyte rolled into one. And then suddenly, as if in reprisal for not heeding that restlessness and wistfulness within her that Sarojini had noticed six months ago, she collapsed.

Chapter Eighteen

~

For two nights in a row, she was the young Ruttie Petit again, eager to merge into him, share his passion, sitting up all night smoking and drinking and talking politics.

He was excited now that he had something concrete to do; she was carried away, seeing freedom at last from the British yoke, not in some dim future but around the corner, in the next few months. At last he could see his way out of the mess that Gandhi had made for all of them. He must gather all the nationalists together and they would force the viceroy to call a round table conference, putting an end to this political impasse once and for all. Gone were the irritations of the last three years, his cold withdrawals and refusal to engage and her chafing at his fixed, old-fogey ways. He was the old J once more, eager to talk, and she listened with all her heart. They were at last one, on the same plane, not two widely disparate temperaments that she had despaired of ever bringing together.

And best of all, there had been an outsider, someone young and charming and male, to bring out all that was best in J, keeping him talking all night. It was Kanji, who dined with them two nights in a row. The first evening he had dropped in uninvited, wanting to be the first to give them the stunning news: that the government had offered Gandhi what any politician in India would have killed for—a round table conference to arrive at a political settlement. But incredibly, Gandhi had turned down the offer without consulting anyone. Jinnah was astounded at this new instance of Gandhi's idiocy and the discussion on why and what this meant went on till three in the morning. And the next day Kanji came back again, this time on both their invitation, and the three of them talked once more till four in the morning.

But on the third day, Ruttie collapsed. Her stomach caved in without warning. As a child she had been prone to bilious attacks, occasionally gripped by stomach cramps and nausea, unable to stir out of bed. But in Petit Hall there had been nurses and nannies and governesses to keep an eye on her, along with her overanxious mother, restraining her from eating too many sweets or fried and spicy food and even from getting too highly strung. But she had always been impatient of their restrictions and for the last four years had thrown all the old restraints away, living exactly how she pleased, making do, like J, with three or four hours of sleep a day. But lacking his iron control over himself, her body collapsed, unable to take the abuse any more, retaliating against the chain-smoking, drinking and serial late nights and eating the spicy food that she craved, sometimes even making Jinnah climb out of the car to fetch her a plate of chaat from a roadside eatery or going by herself to dubious shops selling kababs.

It was bad timing. Jinnah's conference, which was going to bring together nationalists from all over the country, was less than two weeks away. Worse, it was going to be held in their own house and she was not well enough to take part in it. Her body simply refused to move, overcome by sudden fatigue. All through the two weeks leading up to the conference and during the conference itself, while Jinnah was caught up drafting the agenda and sending letters to the viceroy's secretary and trying to keep the conference going, Ruttie was lying upstairs in her bed, too ill to stir. It was the beginning of an illness that puzzled everyone, including the doctors, having no known cause but devastating in its effects.

At first, neither she nor Jinnah took it seriously, thinking it would pass. It was Sarojini who was the first to grow alarmed at Ruttie's state. Accustomed to seeing her every day, spending the hours while Jinnah was at work in her suite at the Taj, Sarojini began to miss her constant presence that she had so often chafed at. 'Ruttie is ill,' she wrote to Padmaja on 9 January 1922. And four days later, on 13 January, a day before Jinnah's conference was about to start: 'Ruttie has been very ill, poor child! I have not seen her for a week.'

The conference ended in a fiasco, with Gandhi playing hot and cold, raising his demands so unreasonably high that the viceroy withdrew his tempting offer. But even after that, Jinnah stubbornly refused to acknowledge that all his efforts had come to nothing even after weeks of the conference ending: it had collapsed on the last day under the weight of its own contradictions. He continued to bombard the viceroy with official letters, sending him the minutes of the conference, chasing Gandhi at his ashram, anything to get the government to renew its round table offer. Her illness was the last thing on his mind; he, who hardly remembered to eat or sleep and was impatient of all weakness, even in himself, how could he even pretend concern for what seemed to him mere self-indulgence? Outwardly at least, there seemed little wrong with her other than what he took to be her lack of willpower in not overcoming that restlessness and fatigue and lack of appetite or whatever it was that was keeping her from resuming her duties by his side as she would have surely done. It took a whole month before it even occurred to him to call a doctor.

Not that the doctor really knew what was ailing her. The symptoms—sleeplessness, restlessness and a deep, utter fatigue when she could hardly lift herself up—were common enough, afflicting thousands of well-to-do women like her, judging by the advertisements for 'liver tonics' splashed in leading English dailies of the time. In addition to these mysterious 'women's disorders' to which doctors could not quite fix a name and yet were unwilling to admit ignorance of, there was Ruttie's acute abdominal pain and bouts of high fever to confound the doctors further. Depression, though common enough, especially among the young and idle, was not something that doctors in India had as yet learnt to take seriously or knew how to handle. A few years ago, for instance, when Sarojini's older son, Jaisoorya, finding himself unable to cope with the pressures of his parents' high expectations of him and his own sense of worthlessness, had suffered from mysterious attacks of fever and blindness. He consulted a doctor for depression; the doctor's response had been one of bewilderment and helplessness: 'Why are you depressed?' It took another decade and a half and several months' stay in a sanatorium in Europe before Jaisoorya could even begin to answer the doctor's question.

But in Ruttie's case, the doctor could fall back on her 'biliousness', the medical term then for excessive secretion of bile leading to nausea and vomiting. Bilious and other liver complaints had become part of the medical lexicon by the mid-nineteenth century, encompassing any illness doctors could not specifically diagnose; it would be attributed, among other things, to 'intemperate habits of drinking and gluttony'. And the cure seemed just as vague, requiring, as the doctor prescribed for Ruttie, an immediate change of air from the presumably 'unhealthy tropical clime' of India. In short, a lengthy sojourn in Europe.

That was news to gladden her heart. Or so Sarojini imagined. 'Ruttie will be going to England in March,' she wrote to Leilamani on 2 February 1922, literally the instant after hearing from Ruttie. 'How she must rejoice that she has been ill enough lately to make the change necessary for her. She is coming here now. She has got out of bed for the first time after a month or so.'

But Ruttie's hidden conflict between desire and duty continued. Still bent on ignoring her instinct to flee, she struggled instead to get out of bed in order to stand by Jinnah's side. Politically, it was going to be an exciting time. Just three days after the doctor's visit, Gandhi had called off his non-cooperation movement and retreated from politics, leaving his colleagues in the Congress and the Khilafat Committee seething. His abrupt withdrawal was because of a stray incident of violence involving a few supporters who attacked a police station in Chauri Chaura, burning to death twenty-one constables and a sub-inspector of police. With such a stirring political situation before them, it was easy for Ruttie to convince herself that things would be better now. And summoning all her depleted energy, she got down at once to her old business of pleasing him, organizing one of her little potlucks. It was just Kanji, and the two of them—discussing what lay ahead for the country. And in the excitement and plans for the future where Jinnah seemed once again poised to rise to the helm of affairs, she stayed up talking again all night with the two of them. It almost seemed like old times.

But this proved costly, and the very next day, she collapsed again. This time there was no bouncing back any time soon. While lying ill in bed, the thought of fleeing the marriage that was making her sick— at least for a short break—seemed the sensible thing to do, even if it hurt Jinnah deeply, as she knew it would. In England, Leilamani was looking forward to her arrival by spring. 'O! Cheers!' she exclaimed in her letter from Oxford to Padmaja on 22 February 1922. 'How Ripping it will be to have little Mad Ruttie here again in spring—she is always so—*unique*, if nothing else, and a most welcome diversion after college work!' But Ruttie's body seemed unable to rise to the ordeal of breaking free.

A whole month went by with her lying prone in bed, too weak to even go calling on Sarojini at the Taj. 'Ruttie is still ill,' Sarojini wrote to Padmaja on 20 March 1922, and in her concern for Ruttie, so cut off from all family and friends, she added: 'Do write to her.'

Usually, Padmaja did not need pushing from her mother in these matters. At nearly twenty-two, she was as empathetic as her mother when it came to meeting the needs of her large circle of friends and relatives, including her own parents. But it was a busy time for Padmaja, now that she was also managing a spinning and weaving centre in Hyderabad besides her father's home. Her handloom 'factory' had been keeping her so busy supplying Bombay's fashion-conscious with khadi saris that even her occasional visits to Bombay to see her mother had stopped for the present.

Sarojini, too, had been swamped with political work. She had been ordered by her 'slave driver', Gandhi, to undertake an extensive tour of riot-hit provinces, leaving her with scarcely a moment to herself. Alone and unable to escape her feelings any longer through her usual frenzied activity, Ruttie's condition became worse, as Sarojini discovered when she saw her a fortnight later. She was, by now, on the verge of madness. 'I am so desperately anxious about Ruttie,' Sarojini wrote in her next letter to Padmaja, on 26 March 1922. 'She is very ill—and I fear not quite normal. She has taken to getting out of bed and coming to see me about midnight every night, hardly able to stand.'

It lasted over a month. And throughout those weeks when she wandered about at midnight in her mental anguish, Jinnah apparently took no notice of her, going about his own work. It was the time when he was trying to persuade the viceroy to renew his offer of a round table conference that Gandhi had rejected, and it kept him occupied to the exclusion of everything else. Sarojini, though made of less stern stuff, was also forced to put politics over personal concerns and it was almost another month before she met Ruttie again. Even then, there was little she could do for her except to feel some concern. As she wrote to Leilamani on 20 April 1922, the day after the Jinnahs' fourth wedding anniversary: 'Ruttie is very, very ill, but she gets out of bed at midnight to come and see me in black draperies and a mad look, poor, suffering, pitiful child!' But there seemed no way for Sarojini to help her, as she wrote six days later: 'Ruttie is very, very ill and yet no one can do anything for her, poor child!'

In April, Sarojini's younger son, Ranadheera, came on a brief visit to Bombay. He was attached to Ruttie, like most of his family, and called on her. He was in for a shock. He got 'a fright' when he saw her so 'pale and drawn in the face', as he wrote to Leilamani on April 25 1922, telling his sister that 'Ruttie is still in bed and much worse than before'. Then, as if her illness reminded him of something unrelated, he suddenly brought up news of an acquaintance of theirs in Hyderabad: 'I wonder if you know that Hadi (Khan's brother) created quite a sensation in Hyderabad by suddenly marrying "Chinu Begum".'

Only Padmaja, who had not seen Ruttie since the end of last year, still believed that Ruttie was soon going to leave for Europe. 'Perhaps Ruttie will get to England before your holidays are over and then you are sure of a great time,' she wrote to Leilamani on 20 April 1922, completely unaware of Ruttie's state of mental and physical distress.

A month later, Ruttie was still no closer to resolving her issues. In May, she was lying prone in bed, while the world around her became even more absorbed in politics. Communal riots were erupting everywhere and Sarojini had been sent by Gandhi on a peace mission that kept her away from Bombay for over a fortnight. Jinnah was in town but may as well not have been. Still refusing to acknowledge that she was really ill, or perhaps he felt she was not trying hard enough to get well, he ignored her. Many years later, incidentally, when he himself was very sick, Jinnah told the story of a woman who could not be persuaded to get out of her bed even though there was nothing wrong with her, until her doctor put a flaming stove under it to drive her out! Apart from his impatience with any illness, his or hers, and his well-known aversion to doctors, Jinnah was busy now with the new party he wanted to start with his high court colleague, the politician M.R. Jayakar, and it was left to Sarojini, who had just returned from one of her political tours, to find out how Ruttie was doing. Not good, as she wrote to Padmaja on 16 May 1922: 'Ruttie continues [to be] desperately and defiantly ill, poor child.'

All through June it was the same. 'Ruttie is still mysteriously ill and in bed,' Sarojini wrote in a letter to Leilamani on 2 June 1922. And twenty days later, returning from an official trip to Lucknow, she wrote again, this time to Padmaja, on 22 June 1922, saying: 'Ruttie is still ill in bed—I am very anxious about her.'

She was not the only one, as it turned out. Kanji, who until then had hovered on the periphery of Ruttie's circle of friends, felt an urgent need to go and see her after a disturbing dream he had of her. As he later recounted in his memoir of Ruttie, he had not seen the Jinnahs for a few months, being too tied up with his legislative work in the Bombay Council. But three months after his last visit to South Court, Ruttie suddenly appeared in his dream, calling urgently to him: 'Kanji, help me!' The dream recurred the following night, and her evident distress affected him so deeply that overcoming his inhibitions and the fear of appearing overfamiliar, he called on her the very next day while Jinnah was at work. Told she was ill, he almost turned back and was about to drive away when the servant asked him to wait until he took his card to her. Starved as she was for company, he was invited in and found her lying down exactly as she had appeared in his dream, reclining on a 'peculiarly shaped' sofa in a verandah she had converted into her day room. Kanji could tell, of course, that she was sick but either did not see, or deliberately omits to mention, the acute emotional distress that had called to him so urgently in his dream. Even though she was so unwell, she was apparently still her usual charming and hospitable self, and they talked non-stop for two and a half hours, with Kanji only leaving after Jinnah returned from work, at 7.30 p.m. Jinnah was as glad as Ruttie to see Kanji and pressed him to stay on for a drink. And although Kanji did not stay that evening, it set the trend for the future. After this visit, he felt free to come and go as he pleased, marking the beginning of an extraordinarily close and triangular friendship, with Kanji becoming a close friend to both Jinnah and Ruttie.

It was, of course, Ruttie who drew Kanji to South Court, although Kanji does not say it in so many words. It was her he wanted to serve in any way he could, bringing her books to read and writing reviews of books that might interest her when she was too ill and tired even to read, and talking of mutual friends—anything to keep her spirits from sinking too low. In return, she took an interest in his work as a labour leader and drew him out and gave of herself. Jinnah was eager to share in the friendship, unwilling to be left out. They hit it off well together and it is not hard to see why. Kanji was a well-turned-out, amiable young man, married with a baby son, but he socialized—in the custom of those purdah-ridden times—as a bachelor. He was an acolyte of Jinnah's, very loyal, and an excellent listener; what is more, he had a fund of good stories about all the important leaders in the country, including Gandhi, which made him a popular dinner guest with Jinnah, who loved a 'good gup', as he called it.

Adoring her as he did, and putting her on a pedestal, Kanji was certainly not the friend with whom Ruttie could lay down her defences and share what was troubling her. Instead, in his lively presence, it was easy to go with the flow and love Jinnah for what he was and repress that sinking feeling that she had made a terrible mistake in marrying him, as she later confessed to Sarojini. When Kanji was around, they both joined in teasing Jinnah either about his arrogance or his quaint touches of miserliness, and he good-humouredly put up with it. Those moments were a joy to share and it's not surprising that Kanji's was such a rosy picture of their marriage, seeing only her tender, teasing solicitude for Jinnah and how he leaned on her for everything. He did not see the Jinnah who lacked understanding and 'the spirit of the joy of life', as she later put it to Sarojini, which was unknowingly stifling her soul and making her yearn to break out of this 'marriage ice'.

But if she could not open her heart to Kanji about Jinnah—and this was surely as much because of her own natural rectitude and loyalty to J as her reluctance to end Kanji's illusions about her— Kanji's adoration and friendship nevertheless helped to pull her out of her depression. It even seemed to melt the hardness in her heart towards the child. For the first time, she made an attempt to reach out to her little girl, now almost four but still nameless, offering her the ultimate token of her love—a newborn kitten from her beloved cat's recent litter. But it was not a success. The child took the kitten away and promptly 'drowned' it, according to Sarojini, with a bottle of expensive cologne that she stole from her father's dresser.

For Sarojini, who heard the story either from Kanji or Ruttie herself on the phone, the episode was only an entertaining titbit to pass on to her children—and to take a sly dig at Jinnah. 'Here is an amusing story for you,' Sarojini wrote in the postscript of her letter to Padmaja on 1 July 1922. 'Ruttie (she's very ill) gave Jinnah a very expensive bottle of eau de cologne and a kitten to her baby. The baby got hold of the scent and drowned the kitten in it. Jinnah was so upset at losing his scent that he sent for the baby—of three!—and *reasoned* with it. How characteristic of Jinnah!' But, for Ruttie, this was no joking matter. It gave her another reason not to reach out to her child. And to sink a little more into her spiral of despair and sadness.

But hope, or at least some validation for her feelings which gave her the courage to hope, arrived unexpectedly. It came in the form of Sarojini's younger son, Ranadheera, who arrived on a longish visit to Bombay. Ranadheera, who was a couple of years younger than Ruttie and the black sheep in the Naidu family because of his drinking problem, knew better than most young people of his time what it felt like to cope with the high expectations of others. With him, Ruttie could be herself, as childish as she wished, with no need to put up a show. She turned to him now for all kinds of advice. And to Sarojini's amusement, Ruttie began to lean on Mina for everything, from consolation for the kitten's death to making its funeral arrangements, and even advice on living abroad with her cats on a shoestring budget—something that she was notoriously poor at. 'Mina's functions are very varied,' Sarojini wrote to Padmaja on 28 July 1922, six days after 'a very untidy and travel-stained Mina' arrived at her hotel. He had been sent to Bombay expressly to look after Sarojini who had just had a heart attack and had been advised to rest for some weeks. 'He is *supposed* to be looking after me but Osman (Umar Sobhani's younger brother) needs him for business advice and Ruttie for consolation because her kitten died. He is also her counselor apparently on *economy* and has been counseling her about taking an electric cooker with her to Paris and the Riviera so as to cook her cats' food because meat is so expensive at hotels!! How I laughed when I heard that.'

Sarojini might laugh, but Mina's visit did Ruttie untold good, and was more beneficial than the doctors and medication. Ruttie now turned to him for everything, instead of leaning on his mother as she used to do. Sarojini, with her tact and sympathy, could be the ideal confidante and often was—all sorts of people took their personal problems to her for advice and kind words. But with Ruttie, as with her own children, she could be a harsh disciplinarian sometimes, unable to stop herself from trying to shield them from what she considered their headstrong and foolhardy ways. Anyhow,

Ranadheera's regular visits to South Court for lunch and pep talks made such a difference that within days of his arrival, Ruttie was able to shake off her apathy and actually book her passage to Europe. As Sarojini wrote in the next mail to Leilamani in England on 29 July 1922: 'Ruttie is better but very weak and cannot go out as yet. She is going with Fatsy (Umar Sobhani's sister Fatima) on the Kaiser-e-Hind on the 23rd September and will stay in Paris and the Riviera and get to England next year.'

It was not that the voice within her head urging her to stick to her self-assigned duties as Jinnah's wife and caretaker had been silenced for good. Having set out across the sea to Europe, she was still worrying about Jinnah and feeling guilty about leaving him to the servants' care. Writing to Kanji the very day after her ship left Bombay, with at least another week before it docked at Aden where she could post her letter, she begged him to 'go and see Jinnah and tell me how he is'. Adding, 'He has a habit of habitually over-working himself, and now that I am not there to bother and tease him he will be worse than ever.'

The forwarding address she sent Kanji was in London—'C/o Messrs. Henry S. King, London W'. But she was in such a hurry to get to Paris that she did not stay in England long enough even to visit Leilamani in Oxford. It was Paris that had been calling to her so insistently, with its promise of unfettered freedom and gaiety and excitement, and the hope of starting a new life without her 'shackles', as she called this feeling of being closed in by her marriage, in a disclosure she made to Sarojini only several years later.

At first, the freedom was heady. After the War, Paris had become the meeting ground of the disenchanted everywhere, fleeing the fetters of their own societies in search of artistic freedom, and was a refuge from the old values. While the city had its little circle of Parsis, all well connected and with business interests there, including members of her extended Dinshaw Petit family, she turned her back on all of them and sought out the Paris of her dreams. There was nothing to stop her now from plunging headlong into its pleasures—the fashionable world of art and jazz and soirees and nightclubs. And it was not long before the beautiful 'Madame Zhinna', living in dashing style with the funds Jinnah uncomplainingly provided, found her feet among the idle rich set, including several exiled royalty and French aristocrats, throwing herself into the social whirl with as much zeal as Jinnah back at home was trying to rebuild a political platform for himself.

But there was still something holding her back. It was apparently not possible to wipe away the last four years, or even her love for him. And when she met someone connected to her past, it again touched off those mingled feelings of guilt and shame. In her inchoate longing for home, she had sought out the exiled Parsi revolutionary Madame Bhikaiji Cama. Bhikaiji's home in Paris had become a sort of pilgrimage for both Indian revolutionaries as well as curious visitors from India. She was also a friend of Ruttie's aunt Hamabai Petit. And even knew or at least had heard of Jinnah and evidently admired him. Ruttie went to see Bhikaiji but the visit was not a success. Ruttie's flippant way of talking did not go down well with the old firebrand, in her sixties then. According to Cama's biographer, Khorshed Adi Sethna, she took instant umbrage to a story that Ruttie recounted, thinking it would amuse her. The story, of a marquis who had taken Ruttie out to a nightclub but crashed his car on the way back because he had too much to drink, brought out the puritan in Bhikaiji. Despite being a fiery rebel who had separated from her husband in Bombay and was now settled abroad on her own, Bhikaiji had not lost her Parsi roots. She became so enraged by the deracinated Ruttie that she apparently burst out in a tirade: 'When such a remarkable man has married you, how could you go to a nightclub with a tipsy man?' Nor did she ever forget the incident, as Sethna recounts in her book, erupting into rage when Leilamani, who visited her much later, brought up the beautiful Ruttie in her conversation with Bhikaiji. As Sethna writes: 'Only Bhickoo could have ticked off Mrs Jinnah with such spirit—no one else would have dared. And it is doubtful if the aristocratic Mrs Jinnah would have accepted such a stricture and scolding from anyone else.'

This odium, whether expressed so openly or not, no doubt worked its insidious effect on Ruttie, especially now when she was at her most vulnerable, struggling with the conflicting pulls of modernity and duty without anyone to turn to. It was true that other English-educated young Indians of her generation were finding themselves similarly adrift in a confusing new post-War world, severed with a brutal suddenness from their own past and unsure of how much of it to retrieve from the debris. But most of them, if they were either sensitive or lucky enough to be drawn into his movement, had found Gandhi. His movement, as Jawaharlal Nehru was to say later, was as much about rescuing the spirit as about politics. But Ruttie, without sharing Jinnah's animus against Gandhi, turned away from the one man who might have saved her.

Paris was exactly the wrong place for her, especially now. Although she did not lack either funds or friends, it simply did not have the environment to nurture someone like her. Coming from her privileged hothouse existence in India, Ruttie was plunged, without training or temperament, into the ferment that was the Paris of her time, with its drugs and bohemianism, in a Europe gone mad in the aftershocks of its collapse.

She herself could feel it, and like someone drowning, reached for the only support she could think of—Sarojini, the friend whose judgement she had once totally trusted. Somewhere in her lost, confused wandering around the Riviera or Paris, seeking solace in new friends and excitement, and finding none, she at last reached out to Sarojini for help. But, of course, none was forthcoming. As Sarojini later admitted to Leilamani, Ruttie's letter left her feeling both anxious and helpless. 'I wonder if you ever come across Ruttie at all,' says the letter from Sarojini to Leilamani, dated 5 June 1923, from the Taj in Bombay, nine months after Ruttie's departure. 'I am dreadfully sad and anxious about her. Because, poor child, she is passing through a very tragic time and is desperately lonely and restless and tries to find relief in mad excitement and sensation.' But Sarojini's deep anxiety for Ruttie only made her angry, wanting to knock some sense into her stubborn head, and roundly blaming her for her own unhappiness: 'She has everything—beauty, youth, wealth, love, intellect but not the power to live a natural life true to herself, poor little Ruttie. Unless one lives true to one's ideas—and out of *oneself*—happiness and content[ment] are mere words of ironic mockery and emptiness. I love Ruttie but I am powerless to help her. She will not accept reality but crave for illusion in rainbow colours all the time.'

Someone of her own generation, undergoing the same torment of desire and guilt and yearning for liberty and its attendant anxieties, might have understood Ruttie better perhaps—or at least enabled her not to take Sarojini's words to heart. Sarojini's letter to Ruttie is lost but one can guess its contents from the tone of the former's letter to

Leilamani. As the more headstrong of Sarojini's two daughters and at more risk, so to speak, because she had chosen to go abroad to study, Leilamani had often been at the receiving end of such advice from her mother. Almost every mail from Sarojini brought a maternal assault of injunctions and cautions, so unlike the laid-back mother of liberal values that she usually was, growing increasingly insistent that Leilamani never forget her 'Indian Womanhood' and bear that load wherever she went, and to think and behave accordingly and to never 'misuse' her freedom.

But Leilamani was also blessed with older siblings, especially Jaisoorya, who could confidently advise his sister to do exactly the opposite of what their mother was preaching. 'If you do a thing,' he wrote to Leilamani from Berlin while undergoing therapy at a 'nerve clinic', 'it is not what others say is right or is wrong but because you want to and it is your right to do so. It is just as much your right to make of your life what you desire; it is yours to do what you like with it. Therefore if you choose your own path you did not only right, but if you did otherwise, it was a wrong to yourself. Youth must go its own way, seek its own path and salvation, suffer and learn and find its freedom. Not to have accepted the challenge and asserted your own individuality at that psychological moment as a woman would have been fatal. The tragedy of womanhood is not that her freedom is too much, but too little and her experiences too few. The road to progress is filled with one more duty repudiated and one more religious law defied.'

But Ruttie, it seems, had had enough freedom. She was already losing faith in herself and in her difficult journey of making it on her own. Her dream of finding herself someday as a published poet perhaps or a writer had remained just that—a dream. Plagued by her inner turmoil and unable to figure out, as Jaisoorya was slowly learning to do through his psychoanalysis, 'that a person with too many emotional conflicts is incapacitated from action', she saw it instead as how Jinnah perhaps would have seen it—as a failure of her willpower and lack of discipline. Filled with self-doubt, she let opinions like Sarojini's, that she should try to 'accept reality' and stop craving for 'illusion in rainbow colours all the time', chip away at her morale. And whether it was Sarojini who urged her to return to Jinnah, or her own craving for him—for she had not got over him as yet—she decided to end her adventure in single life and join Jinnah when he arrived in England in the middle of June 1923. She was ready to start on a fresh note, or more accurately, persuaded herself that this time it would be different. Time and distance had blurred her memory of what it had been like before.

Jinnah did not seem in any hurry to see her, although it was now almost nine months since she had left him and the child. With his hypersensitivity, it is not difficult to imagine how deeply he must have been hurt by her desertion, even though it was not in his nature to ever talk about it. He retreated into his usual vice of overwork. Fortunately for him, there was much to do, thanks to Gandhi having cast him into political limbo, with some help, of course, from himself. Now he threw himself into rebuilding his political career almost from scratch. At first, he put all his heart into exploring whether he should join the rebel group of Congressmen who were forming the Swaraj Party in order to fight the elections. But he fell out with them when they refused to break away from Gandhi's brand of politics.

Next he became preoccupied with trying to revive the Muslim League. He needed the League, which had become almost defunct since the rise of the Khilafatists, to provide him with a political platform, especially now that he had given up hope of ever rejoining the Congress. But here too he faced stiff resistance, this time from the Khilafatists who were determined to edge him out of the leadership. It was only when all his efforts came to nothing that he finally decided to give himself a break and take a trip to Europe. In his pragmatic way, he thought of it as accomplishing two tasks at one go. He could finally go and meet Ruttie without compromising his pride or showing any eagerness on his part, having survived more than nine months without her. And he could also turn the trip into a useful working holiday by using his presence in England to try and influence politicians there, having failed to make a dent with the government at home.

But it was no joyous reunion. They must have quarrelled almost as soon as they met because within days of Ruttie joining him in London, she had left him at the Ritz where they were booked for the summer and taken off by herself to visit Leilamani in her college in Oxford. Her trip was obviously a last-minute decision, judging by Leilamani's dismay when she heard of Ruttie arriving with hardly a day's notice. 'Ye gods!' Leilamani wrote to Padmaja on 14 June 1923, 'Ruttie is coming up to visit me on Saturday . . . I shall not have much time to see [her] as I wish to reserve my energies for these last few days [before her exams].'

It was a short visit. She arrived, trailing cigarette smoke, a Persian cat and a French maid, determined to prove both to herself and Leilamani that she was by no means too old and jaded like Jinnah for simple, collegiate pleasures. She put up such a convincing show of enjoying it all that Leilamani was taken in. 'I've just seen Ruttie off,' Leilamani wrote to her father on 19 June 1923. 'She came down for the weekend (plus her French maid and a Persian Pussycat!!) to see me—I think she loved the welcome Oxford gave her and was very happy to be in the midst of "youth", even though for a fleeting hour'—the quotation marks around the word 'youth' were, of course, meant to be ironic—but not about Ruttie, who at twenty-three was by common consensus among them on the borderline, if not having already crossed the border of middle age. It was Leilamani's way of being ironical about her own age; she had turned twenty that year, a cause of some dismay because she too was getting old. 'We took her on the river and gave her the best time we could—incidentally having a little relaxation ourselves, to be refreshed before the ordeal that starts on Thursday,' Leilamani wrote.

But the trip did not resolve whatever problem Ruttie had tried to flee from. Within three days of her return from Oxford, she was off again by herself, this time back to Paris, leaving a rather depressed farewell note for Leilamani. 'I am afraid that it will be a long, long while before we meet again as tomorrow I' (and here she had almost written 'we' but scratched it out, replacing it with 'I')"leave England and not again till the next season should I be back if at all,' she wrote in a letter dated 22 June 1923, unusually full of gaps and scratches, indicative of her troubled mind. 'I'll say goodbye therefore and wish you the best of luck.' On the same funereal note, as if this was indeed the end for her, and time to clear all her debts, with this one presumably incurred by her self-assumed role as Leilamani's proxy older sister, she wrote: 'Simultaneously with this is being sent a box of Desti's Amber according to my promise,' referring either to the perfume or scented cigarettes of the same brand that had become all the rage in Paris. There was one more debt to settle before leaving, of a trifling nature but nevertheless revelatory of Ruttie's attitude towards money—blissfully unaware of what things cost, how much money she had on her or even when she had actually run out of it. She was not at all embarrassed to be broke but happy to borrow from the nearest person, and that too only in order to pay for some treat for the very person she had just borrowed from. This spontaneity and generosity may have once endeared her to Jinnah, but no doubt was now grating on his nerves, considering the bills she would have run up in these last eight months of holiday without him. And now, before leaving London perhaps never to return, she conscientiously squared her accounts, returning the quid she had borrowed, not from Leilamani, who evidently had none to lend her, but from one of her student friends, probably as impoverished as her. 'Am enclosing the one pound for Ghose which *you* [underlined twice] lent me—thanks. Have had it enclosed in the envelope since Monday! However!' She wrote in a postscript, failing, even with her usual liberal use of exclamation marks, to disguise the bleakness with which she was looking towards the future.

Jinnah's mood was no lighter. Meeting the new secretary of state for India, Lord Peel, soon after Ruttie left, Jinnah was presumably at his dourest and most abrasive, prompting Peel to remark that Jinnah was 'the only Indian I have yet met who really was disagreeable'. But two months spent alone in the Ritz with almost nothing except his newspapers to keep him from brooding over his marital issues, appear to have made up his mind for him. He had suffered, of course, as no one would ever know—so severely did he impose a seal of silence on his personal life, confiding in no one, as Sarojini remarked about him several years later. But failing at his marriage would be worse—failure was a word, as he liked to say, unknown to him. And having stuck rigidly to his pre-planned schedule of spending his entire summer holiday in London, he made an unexpected detour to Paris on his way back home to see Ruttie. A few days later, Mr and Mrs Jinnah headed home together.

On the surface, it seemed as if nothing had changed between them, with Jinnah getting immediately busy with his court work and interviews to the press, while she slipped into her old role of making herself indispensable to him—'looking after him without him realizing it', as Kanji put it. But under the apparent preoccupation with his work, he had, in fact, withdrawn from her into his stony fortress, as was his habit when he was hurt. Apparently she had not yet been forgiven for those eight months of desertion. He showed nothing, of course, of his real feelings, only erected this wall she could not pass through. The elections to the legislature were almost round the corner and Gandhi was in prison, with his movement called off, but the old excitement of political plans being discussed all night and the camaraderie had gone. In fact, he was still in two minds whether he should contest or not. He wanted to get back into the legislature, of course, but not if the Congress boycotted the elections, leaving him in the same dilemma as when he resigned from the legislature three years ago: not wanting to be seen as pro-British but not agreeing with the Congress policy of non-cooperation either. And while the Congress and the Khilafatists fought it out among themselves, threatening to split the party on whether or not to stand for elections, Jinnah issued his own version of an election manifesto, asking people through an appeal published by the *Bombay Chronicle* to tell him whether he should contest or not. And while he waited to see what he should do next, he kept his own counsel, making himself even more unapproachable.

There was an occasional thaw when she could tease him like the old times, usually when Kanji was around, such as when Jinnah eventually decided to contest the elections but would do no campaigning for himself. Knowing he would win his reserved seat without difficulty, Jinnah was focusing his energy on campaigning for weaker candidates, with an eye on forming a loose party of like-minded legislators after the elections. But his 'over-confidence', as Kanji recounts in his *India's Fight for Freedom*, both amused and worried Ruttie, with Jinnah saying, 'The electorate is on trial', and leaving it at that. He won, of course, with the other two contestants beating a retreat before the election. But other than those rare moments when both Kanji and his other friend, Sir Purshottamdas, were there to join her in her teasing, she felt shut out by him.

It only got worse after that. Even before he could be sworn into the new legislature, he had already given notice for moving two resolutions, one of them calling for the immediate release of Gandhi from prison. And within days of his swearing in, he was holding meetings with like-minded members of the central assembly to form a party of independents. Although he managed to get only seventeen legislators to join him, he became the power centre within the House. But even that was not good enough for him. Now he aspired to seize control of the legislature. And within a month of his joining the legislature, he had achieved the impossible—forming an alliance with the forty-eight-member Swaraj Party until it was his tiny party of independents that was really calling the shots in the House, not the larger Swaraj Party or the government. Now he had a hand in all the laws that came up before the House and he was on all the committees and a star speaker. All this, of course, involved energy of manic proportions, and she was ignored even though she had moved to Delhi with him into the confines of the hated Maidens' suite.

Her energy, meanwhile, went into somehow trying to stop this rising tide of uneasiness within her. There was a price to be paid for having repudiated her freedom and come back to her duty, as Jaisoorya so rightly pointed out to Leilamani. She was stuck alone in their hotel room with nothing to do and no one to meet. Now that Jinnah was a legislator again, she was condemned to spend the better part of the next three years alone in a hotel suite, either at Maidens while the session was on in Delhi or at the Cecil when the assembly moved to Simla. The child, of course, had been left behind at home, out of both their ways, looked after by the best staff that money could buy. And other than walking her dogs and being stared at by people in the bazaar, there was nothing to occupy her. She had no friends and no interest in going to either women's clubs or cultivating the company of the wives of other legislators. With Jinnah gone for most of the day and even night—except when he sat up late working on some papers to do with his work in the legislature the next day—her life stretched out in an unending tedium.

Occasionally, they attended a dinner together, but this was no fun either, being either one of those stiff, formal receptions where she was expected to be seated by her host's side at the table, making polite conversation, or make do with the company of women she had nothing in common. The only company she actually welcomed was Motilal Nehru's, Jinnah's good friend and ally in the House, who sometimes took pity on the neglected Mrs Jinnah and dined with her at Maidens. It was true that he was more than twice her age but she cheered up when he dropped in to dine, this old man so unlike the other legislators in the assembly, not only a connoisseur of good food and lover of hearty meals, like her father and other Petits, but someone who knew how to laugh and make others laugh, unheard of in this Delhi environment where jokes seemed almost anti-national. But his visits did nothing to stir Jinnah's husbandly conscience. Someone with his impeccable manners, who could put everything aside and be a charming host if there was a guest for dinner, preferred now to ignore them both. He noticed, of course, but remarked on it only to make a political point—that even if 'Pandit Motilal and I used to fight like a pair of wild-cats on the floor of the Legislative Assembly yet on the same evening of our altercation he used to dine sumptuously with my wife,' unable to resist adding (he was his father's son, after all) 'at my expense'.

Several times, as Ruttie told Sarojini many years later, 'it came to almost breaking point and she never meant to return'. But perhaps because she did not have the heart to leave him again, when his political career was once more rising to its former heights; or because, despite ignoring her and focusing only on his politics, he still seemed to need her around, or so she hoped; or maybe simply because she had lost her nerve, with that one failed attempt to break free—she stayed put.

But some vital chord that had kept him bound to her despite his undemonstrativeness seemed to have mysteriously snapped. Under the chill, he, too, was unhappy in his own way, revealing himself in sudden and inexplicable bouts of irritation. The first time it happened was when she, with all good intentions, intervened in an acrimonious war of words between him and his arch-rival, Mohammed Ali. The bitterness between Jinnah and the two Ali brothers dated back to when the former walked out of the Congress four years ago, heckled by their supporters. And with the collapse of the Khilafat movement, their rivalry had only sharpened, with both fighting for the same space: to retain their hold over the Muslim community. They went for each other in public, with Jinnah scoffing at Mohammed Ali by calling him 'the little Maulana', and his Khilafat Committee as 'not worth respect'; Mohammed Ali called Jinnah 'parasitical'. And when Jinnah published an article in the *Bombay Chronicle* attacking the Congress's 'unconstitutional' policies, Mohammed Ali took him on, writing a series of letters attacking Jinnah which the newspaper readily published in full. But after two or three of these articles had appeared, while Jinnah stonily refused to react to his rival's personal taunts, Ruttie felt compelled to respond on his behalf. She called at the newspaper's office and through the editor, appealed to Mohammed Ali to stop his articles 'as this would create bitterness' rather than resolve issues. A year back, Jinnah would have probably smiled indulgently at her concern and let the matter drop, but now he was enraged at her interference. 'Ruttie had no business to intervene,' he snapped at the editor when he was told of what had transpired. After that, Ruttie kept out of his affairs.

But some devil seems to have got into her as well. Knowing how deep was his sense of correctness and propriety, she began to needle him, knowing that he would not retaliate either by word or gesture. Bolitho describes how she went out of her way to 'offend his genteel proprieties in public'. One evening in Simla when they were driving to dine with the governor, as Bolitho recounts in a passage later expunged from the biography of Jinnah he had been officially commissioned to write, 'she stopped the carriage and bought a roasted corn-cob from a man beside the road. She began to eat it as they came near Government House.' Of course, he said nothing to her—it would be beneath his dignity to either protest or plead with her. 'He accepted the foolish hurt in silence,' as Bolitho adds. How hurtful the episode would have been to a man of his acute sensitivity to proprieties, who would literally rise from his deathbed only in order to do the proper civilities, can only be imagined. The wound stayed in his mind, recalling the story years later, as Bolitho wrote, 'to a woman he trusted, and said, "It was not level-headed: would you do a thing like that?"'

Even she never knew how deeply she could hurt him, so wooden was his exterior, infuriating her into making more attempts to breach his fortress wall of impregnability. It brought out that mischievous streak in her, but now no longer innocent of malice. She went for him whenever she could, not when they were alone, for that would be pointless, but in public, wanting to get under his skin and draw blood. It would take the form, as Chagla wrote in his memoir, of walking into his chambers while he was in the midst of a conference, perching herself on his table, dangling her feet, unmindful of how uncomfortable the other men in the room were by her presence. He had always welcomed her dropping in at his chambers, even allowing her to do it up for him in a style that raised it to a level of smartness unknown in the dingy lifestyle of the high court. Nor did he mind what she wore, far from it—he was enormously proud of her beauty and style; yet he was far too smart not to know when she was deliberately trying to provoke him by her behaviour or dress, verging as it was now on insolence. His response, as Chagla witnessed, was to never utter a word of protest, and carry on with the conference 'as if she were not there at all'. But she did drive him crazy, as he admitted years later, in the only self-revelatory admission he ever made about his marriage, confessing to another friend whose marriage had just broken how Ruttie 'got on my nerves—she drove me mad'.

And he drove her mad with his inhuman lack of all emotion, or so it seemed, and his punctilious sense of duty, as if she was no more to him than a duty he must discharge. In the past, she would have been able to laugh at him—at that rather sanctimonious way he had of pronouncing 'I have my duty to do.' But now she couldn't—at least, not unless Kanji was there to lend her some moral support. But this sinking feeling that she was being erased as an individual; that the only part of her that still existed was the role he expected of her, doing her duty by him as he did for her, bothered her. Eventually, she had channelled it into a poem—the only one she wrote after her marriage—a 'song', as she called it, lacking in lilt but not sense. It was the sort of scribble that she would have probably hidden or thrown away—for, that was part of her problem, especially after her marriage to Jinnah, letting her self-doubts chip away at her confidence and her cherished dream of becoming a published poet like Sarojini, only because he did not admire poetry. But the ever-sympathetic Padmaja, to whom she must have recited her poem in private and who too, like Ruttie, wrote poems in secret but rather overcome by her mother's great repute as a poet lacked the courage and faith in herself to find a publisher, drew it out of her against her will. The poem went:

> Not for the sake of the husband is the husband dear, but for the sake of the self is the husband dear.
> Not for the sake of the wife is the wife dear, but for the sake of the self is the wife dear.

Not for the sake of the son is the son dear, but for the sake of the self is the son dear.

Not for the sake of the Gods are the Gods dear but for the sake of the self are the Gods dear.

The ink had hardly dried on the paper, when the doubts began assailing her again, making her write in self-deprecation in the accompanying note to Padmaja, 'I warned you, did not I, that its only appeal rested in its thought and so far from being a "song" it hadn't sufficient lilt . . .' But still, it had a resonance for her that she could not explain to Padmaja or herself—'wonderful to the understanding if not the ear!', as she put it. It marked her disenchantment with love, but that craving for 'illusion in rainbow colours all the time', as Sarojini dismissively put it, refused to go away. There was no getting rid of that yearning and finding the will to 'accept reality', as Sarojini so badly wanted her to do.

From the outside, it certainly looked as if she was finally settling down, falling unresistingly into her role as dutiful wife and homemaker, as thousands of modern young women like her were doing all around her, unable to resolve their dilemma of what to do with this new freedom that an English education had given them. So flawlessly did she play the part that even Sarojini, with whom she was closest and most candid, was taken aback four years later, in 1928, when she confessed how trapped and unbearably stifled she had, in fact, felt during those latter years of her marriage. As part of her effort to settle down and stop dreaming, she had poured all her creativity and gift for beauty and, of course, a small portion of Jinnah's money—he was worth millions by now—into transforming South Court into one of the most enchanting homes on Malabar Hill, unique in its style, like her. It took away one's breath, as one caller, Sayyada Badrunissa Begum, who was just married to a well-known lawyer of Delhi, wrote later. The newly-wed had sought out Ruttie through their mutual friends, the Sobhanis, and had called on her one evening, accompanied by Umar Sobhani's younger brother, Osman. Sayyada Badrunissa's account of that visit, published years later, in 1929, in a Urdu monthly, *Humayun*, gives a graphic portrait not only of the Jinnahs' home but also their differing temperament and the distance between them. She recalled being asked to wait in the hall—an intimidatingly splendid room of antiques and Persian carpets and tapestries besides bronze and copper casts of ancient animals. Unused to such a startlingly exotic departure from the current fashion of very 'English' furnishing and décor, and the distinctive fragrance floating in the air, the Begum thought 'the place looked like a house of magic'—an impression that was only heightened by the entry of a 'vicious looking' dog, followed soon after by a black Angora cat that fixed its unblinking gaze on her. The Begum was transfixed in her antique chair, trembling with fright, before Ruttie finally walked in, fresh from a bath.

She was like a beam of light in the dark room, according to the Begum, her beauty stunning, like 'a fairy come down to earth'. Speaking in 'exquisite English', Ruttie soon put her guests at ease, even leading her into her bedroom to show her collection of saris because the Begum was so impressed by her taste, and then later into the library ('filled with books in leather matching the colour scheme of the furnishings') because Ruttie had, in her impetuous way, offered to write a letter of introduction to a friend in Delhi so that the Begum would have some company when she got there. And while she was at it, Jinnah returned from work, tall and lean and very correct, knocking on the door of the library and asking permission to enter before stepping in and after a formal introduction, leaving the room to Ruttie and her guests. But Ruttie, presumably to give him his space, took them to 'her' part of the house—the verandah facing the sea—and gave them sherbet to drink and made polite conversation until it was time for her guests to leave.

Beside the verandah, she had by now created a sitting room for herself which Jinnah rarely entered unless she had a visitor he wanted to talk to, like Kanji. It was, like the rest of the house, exquisitely done up in an eclectic mix of the occidental and the oriental, with a Buddhist touch, as Leilamani vividly described it when she visited South Court in late November 1924. 'Yes, Ruttie's drawing room is almost as enchanting as her clothes, her three Persian pussies and her latest fads. It seemed to me, on first tremulously entering, as if I were treading on the mind shadow of some once martyred Buddhist Priest—martyred because he loved and dared to beckon the wild gypsies and watched them dance at dawn upon the carpet of his dreams,' Leilamani wrote to Padmaja on 26 November 1924.

Leilamani, who had come home on what was supposed to be a short holiday from college but turned out instead into a six-month forced break, was even more impressed by Ruttie's cooking skills. This was a hitherto-unexpressed facet of Ruttie, with her having little need to cook while she lived with her parents, and was possibly inspired by her constant craving for Petit Hall's rich, spicy cuisine. It was yet another of those little differences between them, endearing while in love but by no means an insignificant factor in their growing apart. Jinnah's taste buds, such as they were for a man of his abstemious habits, ran mostly to bland English fare. She could never hope to tempt him with her home-cooked meals, so this was evidently a hobby she reserved for the rare occasion when one of her friends dropped in for lunch. As Leilamani added in her letter: '*Need* I add that Ruttie is as delicious as ever . . . especially since her "cuisine" has creditably and considerably improved of late—The prawn curry was scrumptious.'

And in a mirror image of what Jinnah seemed to be doing to her, raising a wall between them, she, in turn, did to the child, enclosing her in a sealed compartment, both literally and figuratively. The child was still apparently confined to her nursery, well out of her parents' sight, even though she was now over six years old. As Leilamani wrote in the same letter to Padmaja, 'The one dark shadow (an exquisite little shadow, really) i.e. the unnamed and unloved little baby, clung to me and begged me "not to go" when I was leaving her nursery after an hour's play with the little one's toys.' Having already heard from both her mother and sister about Ruttie's strange indifference to her child, and now seen it for herself, Leilamani still could not bear to fault her adored friend for the child's unloved condition, preferring instead to shift the blame to the supposed faults in Ruttie's super-rich upbringing. 'Ruttie, however, can't be blamed for her innate lack of motherly affection,' she added, providing a feeble but nevertheless plausible explanation for her idol's unmaternal aspect—'she got so little parent love herself, poor kid.' For Leilamani, brought up by two exceptionally warm and demonstrative parents, it would have been easy to have misinterpreted Ruttie's privileged background, raised practically by servants and governesses, as a sign of an unnatural emotional reserve within the Petit household. It was a sign too of how much Leilamani had changed since she left home four years ago, having given up her envy of Ruttie's super-rich background for a better appreciation of her own upbringing, raised in a household of modest means but with parents who gave them, among other inalienable rights during those more formal times, the licence to climb into their bed every morning for a cuddle, bringing their dogs and cats with them.

Leilamani had returned from Oxford in September 1924, 'plus luggage and new ideas and quite minus good manners in the main', as Sarojini caustically put it. The change in her daughter alarmed Sarojini enough to decide that what Leilamani needed now more than a college degree was 'a prolonged stay in India to get back the true Indian perspective and to correct all those mental and moral traits in her which distress me beyond measure', as she told Padmaja in a letter on 12 September 1924. And the last person Sarojini wanted on the scene at such a time was Ruttie whose 'unbalanced company and conversation', as she wrote in another letter to Padmaja, would hardly promote Sarojini's project of force-feeding her youngest on a diet of 'Indian' culture. But there was little Sarojini could do to prevent the two friends from meeting every day. While Leilamani stayed with her mother in Bombay, most of her day—and night—was spent with Ruttie, either going to South Court for lunch where 'Ruttie fed me on absolutely wonderful things' or Ruttie coming to spend the day in Sarojini's Taj suite, 'fighting with me like a baby over "tea cakes".' Or, 'Just off to the cinema with Ruttie and the cats', as she wrote to her siblings over the next few weeks. The cinema outing, incidentally, was an evening show—a time of day that Ruttie had until recently dutifully kept aside to spend at home with Jinnah because he liked to have her at home when he returned from work.

There were other ways in which she began to court his displeasure. Much to his distaste, she had taken up dancing. It was all the rage in Bombay then—not the sedate ballroom dancing of the old, pre-War days but the new, uninhibited forms that had sprung up along with the growing popularity of jazz. In Willingdon Club, members were enthusiastically learning the new steps. Kshama Row took Leilamani there to dance (the latter wrote to Padmaja). And while Leilamani did not think much of their friend's dancing—'Kshama's dancing made me roar so much that I quite recovered from the "tired feeling",' she wrote. But she soon caught the current craze, telling Padmaja in her next letter four days later, on 16 September 1924, that 'I'm liking dancing nowadays—I suppose because I'm tired of languishing with "ennui"!'

Ruttie herself preferred to dance elsewhere. While the Taj moved into the Edwardian trend 'at a steady but none too confident pace', it was at the hotel next door, the Greens, where the city's smart set 'leapt and pranced with few signs of inhibition', as the *Times of India* put it, with its little dance floor becoming so crowded that 'they will soon have to have somebody to direct the traffic or perhaps the jazzers will have to wear buffers'. And since the Greens had a not-undeserved notoriety 'for its racy, honky-tonk atmosphere', Jinnah was understandably disapproving. It reached a stage, according to an interview which Kanji gave late in his life to Pakistani writer Shahabuddin Desnavi, where Jinnah became so unreasonable that he tried to forbid Ruttie from dancing with any man, even in the respectable Willingdon Club. Kanji was made the sole exception, according to the interview—and that was only because, as Kanji pointed out, Jinnah was well aware that he did not know how to dance.

If the 'cold logician' was indeed seized by such an irrational impulse to control her, it seemed to have only made her more defiant. She started going out on 'dance nights' a day of the week when hotels invited live jazz bands to play and all were welcome on the dance floor. She was escorted by idle, rich young dandies for whom Jinnah had nothing but contempt. In a few months, even the staid Taj Mahal had succumbed to popular demand and started its own dance night with performances by live jazz bands and a Mlle Singy—'Professoress of Dance'—arriving in the city to introduce the even more shocking tango at a series of 'Tea Tangoes' in the Taj. For Ruttie, this was a double bonus—she could not only dance all night but save herself the inconvenience of going home afterwards by sleeping over in Sarojini's rooms until the next day. In this—as in most things—Sarojini's sympathy was entirely with Jinnah, and her opinion of Ruttie's new fad and her choice of dancing partners was no less scorching. It crept out in the occasional remark in one of her letters to her children, as for instance to Ranadheera: '[Ruttie's] new craze is for dancing and her chief partner, a bumptious youth who knows you, Ali Kurrimbhoy . . .' Or to Padmaja: 'Today Ruttie having danced all night is lying asleep on my bed.'

And it was not just this one act of childish rebellion. The frigid silence between them seems to have grown with the months. Her tenderness for him, the cajoling and teasing and almost maternal indulgence had disappeared; and on his part, the loyalty and trust in her had gone. Neither ever spoke of it. But one hint of what might have possibly been going on behind Jinnah's mask of iron composure is suggested in a few lines of a book that he underlined several times, as if they had struck some personal chord within him. It was one of those biographies he occasionally found the time to read, titled *Napoleon: Lover and Husband*, by Frederick Masson. Marked on one of the pages in pencil are these lines about Napoleon's struggle to come to terms with his wife's infidelity: 'It was no half pardon which was extended . . . (Bonaparte had the wonderful faculty of forgetfulness). He argued that those men were not to blame, but that the fault was his, for he had not taken good care of his wife, that she had not been properly guarded, but left too long alone and unprotected, and so another had been able to penetrate into his harem. It was natural, the necessity of sex ordered that man should be insistent, that woman should succumb; it was the law of nature. Bonaparte reasoned that if the erring wife was no longer beloved, she should be repudiated; if she was still dear the only thing to do was to take her back; reproaches were senseless.' And enclosed in a box, as if to highlight their significance further, underlined over and over again in curly and straight lines, are these three words—'reproaches were senseless'. Was this the problem then—Jinnah's struggle to reassert his reason over his feelings of injury and betrayal?

There was certainly nothing to stop her had she ever wished to even experiment on that score. She had always scorned conventional morality and now, after the War, there had been a great awakening of women's sexual freedom, especially in Paris where she had spent a lot of her time. It was reflected in almost all the books she read—scores of novels and collections of short stories that she gobbled up without bothering to put her name on the front page, as she used to do before her marriage, when she took her reading seriously. These books— 'bestsellers' before the word was even coined—seemed to take an almost malicious pleasure in bringing down the edifices of Victorian marriage and morals, using parody as their weapon. But with her, if there had indeed been 'another', it would have been a passing thing, perhaps even a desperate call for Jinnah's attention. Philandering was not a part of her temperament. Hidden under all that extravagance and frivolity was an almost ascetic streak. She now entered a phase of what can only be construed as self-loathing. From being someone who had relished 'dressing up' in a playful way, in sharp contrast to Jinnah's deadly seriousness when it came to clothes, she suddenly lost all interest in her appearance. With her sense of drama, even this was theatrical: the sudden and inexplicable transformation of Bombay's most dazzling beauty into 'the miserable remnant of Mrs Jinnah', as Motilal Nehru lamented to Sarojini. The gulf between them had led not just to separate sitting rooms but presumably to separate bedrooms as well, judging from their contrasting sleeping habits. (It is very curious that among the household effects of Jinnah, who hoarded everything that once belonged to Ruttie, there is no sign of a double bed!) Jinnah slept very little, but as Fatima Jinnah says in her book, he had a 'life-long habit of sleeping when he willed'. Sleep, however, had deserted her of late, along with her peace of mind, leaving her tossing all night, making it impossible to share a bed with anyone, least of all Jinnah, with his extreme aversion to any sign of restlessness around him. It was doubtless far more convenient for both to sleep separately, enabling him to get his few allotted hours of sleep, while she could toss restlessly about or get up, as she chose, leaving her bed at least on two instances to write a letter to Kanji well past midnight, without disturbing Jinnah. He was, moreover, a stickler for routine, unable to bear even the slightest departure from his clockwork timetable—the day beginning on the dot at 7 a.m., no matter how late he slept; with his personal valet entering the room with his tea on a tray and the newspapers; exactly an hour later, his bath, while the valet laid out his clothes; and then sharp at quarter past nine, breakfast, and out of the house by ten. All this while Ruttie was still asleep, having finally snatched her few hours of slumber with the help of a medication that had become all the rage among a restless new generation chasing sleep by means of a new invention called the 'sleeping pill'.

How much of Ruttie's sleeplessness had to do with the emotional toll of his frigid withdrawal and the retribution, as Jaisoorya called it, for repudiating her duty to herself, and what portion of it was due to her growing addiction to the barbiturate called Veronal, is hard to determine. Veronal was by now indiscriminately prescribed by most doctors for any patient of nervous disposition who complained of sleeplessness. Except for a cautious few, like Dr Naidu, who advised Padmaja not to use medication to treat her insomnia but to try instead a hot spinal bath—even sending her a cutting from a newspaper on the method to be followed—doctors throughout the world saw no danger in the new barbiturate. And it would take at least another half-century before they found out its lethal side effects, including the risks of addiction and requiring ever higher dosages to counteract its wearing effect, with overdose leading to death in many cases. How long Ruttie had been on Veronal is uncertain but by mid-1925 she evidently was accustomed to taking sleeping pills, judging by her complaint to Kanji in a letter dated 7 April 1925, of her dreamless 'heavy druglike sleep' which had no redeeming feature except 'the five, or at the most six hours rest it ensures a restive mind'.

Even when they were thrown close together, as in their hotel suite while the assembly session was on, she found ways of avoiding being alone with him. Jinnah, in any case, had ensured that the suite he booked for them at the Maidens had two sitting rooms so that they could each have a living room to themselves, but that did not seem to suffice for her need to get away from him. Instead, she hit upon a plan to invite Padmaja to go along with them. Dreading the reopening of the assembly, when she knew there was no way out of going with him to Delhi, and in a fever of apprehension in case Padmaja rejected her proposal, she nevertheless plucked up the courage to write to Padmaja, inviting her to come to Delhi with them. Ruttie's letter, dated 2 January 1925, says very little about her unhappiness in her marriage—in fact, portraying Jinnah as a fond and forbearing husband, happy to give his wife and her friend their space when they wanted it, which, of course, was true, even if she had brushed the rest of the truth aside. But the letter says a great deal more of the changes within her since their marriage. Sarojini, of course, was the first to notice it, observing in a letter to Ranadheera (wrongly dated April 1921, when Ruttie was in Monte Carlo): 'How she [Ruttie] has altered physically and mentally . . . She has lost much of her beauty and yet continues to be better looking than most people anywhere.' But even Sarojini seems to have missed the utter decimation of Ruttie's self-confidence since her marriage and the social ostracism that had followed, turning her from the bright, confident young woman of sixteen who could almost peremptorily summon Padmaja, as if she was a princess, to come and visit her in Mahabaleshwar, into this craven, almost abject supplicant nine years later, afraid of being spurned by the very same friend. So devastating apparently had been the effect of her isolation that every line in her letter to Padmaja seems to reflect this desolation within her, beginning with her choosing to write to Padmaja, rather than ask her directly. At the time Ruttie was writing the letter, flinching in anticipation at a possible rejection, its recipient, Padmaja, was not only in Bombay, but had, in fact, visited Ruttie the previous day, giving Ruttie ample time and opportunity to make her request in person, as friends normally do when they plan a trip together.

But instead, here was Ruttie beginning her letter with the utmost trepidation, as if their roles had reversed, she now the nervous schoolgirl while Padmaja who had once been too embarrassed to confess that she had no car at her disposal now had the power to reject her proposal. 'I hadn't the courage to ask you when you were here yesterday as I was afraid that you might give me some hasty reply in the negative,' Ruttie wrote, 'and I hadn't the heart to face that as it would mean the wrecking of very many dreams and illusions I have been nurturing since the last few weeks or more.' And having begun, she still needs to brace herself again not to stall and come to the point: 'You see, I feel quite nervous to come to the point, as your answer is going to mean so much to me. Anyhow you must be getting rather fed up with this endless preamble so I will come to the point.'

Then at last it is out: 'I want you to come and stay with us for a couple of weeks or more at Delhi. We shall be putting up at the Maidens Hotel and directly I hear from you I shall arrange for rooms for you. We have already booked for ourselves one of the only two suites in the hotel and as it has two sitting rooms we can always lock J up in one of them when we want to be by ourselves. Besides I shall do my best to get you as nice a room as possible and in the same passage as us if not exactly next door.'

'J will have to be there about the 17th instant,' she wrote, hastening to reassure her friend that it was not J's programme that was as important for her as having Padmaja come along with them, 'and I am not sure that I shall go with him as I would much rather follow in about a fortnight later. Anyway it all depends on you. About the first week of February is by far the best time to come up and we can travel together.' And having at last come out with her invitation, the almost pathetic eagerness with which she waited for her answer: 'Do, do say yes as I have dared to build on your answer and my disappointment will be great. However, your own inclination will be your only guide. Please let me know as early as you can, firstly as I shall be hopping about for the reply and secondly as I must write for rooms at once. Love, Ruttie.'

But to Ruttie's ill-luck, before Padmaja could make up her mind, she was suddenly recalled home to Hyderabad on a summons of an urgent and mysterious nature, a 'cry of despair' apparently so compelling that she had to abruptly cut short her holiday with her mother and sister, and return to Hyderabad by the next train. The only hint of this summons—or possibly her errand of mercy—is in Leilamani's letter to Padmaja from the Taj on 16 January 1925, saying that their mother has asked Leilamani 'not to worry you with questions so I sadly pocketed my desire to console you and of course my curiosity'.

It would take another couple of weeks before Padmaja turned down Ruttie's invitation, in all likelihood because she was still caught up in whatever errand had taken her back to Hyderabad so suddenly. The disappointment must indeed have been great, as Sarojini wrote to Padmaja as soon as she learnt of her decision, 'Ruttie will be heartbroken at you not being able to join her.' But there was also some relief commingled with the commiseration. 'On the whole,' Sarojini wrote to Padmaja on 30 January 1925, 'when I think of it, having been to Delhi, for now you would not have stood the crowds and bustle at Maidens Hotel.' Leilamani concurred—except it was not the bustle she thought was the problem so much as the boredom. 'I cannot tell you how sorry I am you could not join Ruttie,' she wrote from the Taj to Padmaja in Hyderabad. 'Although the little woman apart, you would (I feel from our last visit to the Imperial City) have surely died of *cold* there had you succeeded miraculously in surviving the *Boredom*. But then, you'll add, I've survived worse things than either . . .'

But even before Padmaja's rejection could do its work in demoralizing her further, something else occurred to shatter what remained of Ruttie's self-confidence about her social life. Very soon after Padmaja's abrupt departure from Bombay, Ruttie had an unpleasant scene of some sort with Leilamani which led to a severing of their friendship that was to last all her life. It had to do with Ruttie's friendship with Umar Sobhani's younger sister, Khannum, who was also a friend of Leilamani's. 'Khannu', much to her brother's dismay, had become so close to Ruttie in the past couple of years as to be virtually inseparable. In his desperation to put an end to a friendship he considered unsuitable for his sister, Umar resorted to underhand means, paying a visit to Ruttie at South Court without telling his sister and carrying a message purportedly from Khannum that destroyed Ruttie's faith in her friend. He played the same trick on his sister, lying to her that 'a most insulting letter' had arrived from Ruttie 'but that as she was too ill to see it he had destroyed it'. Somehow Leilamani's name also seems to have been dragged into the story that Umar had concocted, and given her 'terrible tempers and her even more disgusting manners', as her unindulgent mother believed, it lent credibility to Umar's story. In happier times, Ruttie would have perhaps laughed it off and moved on, unaffected, or even perhaps confronted her two friends with what Umar had said, and sorted it out with them. But the past few years of her largely undeserved notoriety and the constant odium directed at her from all sides, and the disapproval, either open or covert, of parents and guardians of the young women she tried to befriend, finally insinuated itself deep within her. It made her touchy, quick to withdraw in hurt pride at insults, imaginary or real. Ruttie cut herself off from both Leilamani and Khannum without giving or demanding an explanation from either, just as Umar had hoped. 'Ruttie and Khannum have ceased their wonderful friendship and no longer talk to each other, much to Omar's relief and joy,' Sarojini wrote a year later to Padmaja, on 16 January 1926, still unaware of what had transpired.

To Leilamani, it seemed to be a minor misunderstanding that would soon clear up. 'I've not seen Ruttie since you left,' she wrote to Padmaja in her letter of 16 January 1925, 'only heard the tail-end of the quarrel from "Khannu" who came to inquire why I had called her a "D- -n liar"!' I've made my peace with her [Khannum] but Ruttie I shall leave alone as I am weary of strife and a patched up peace will help neither of us—I shall continue to be her friend whether she likes me or no—I cannot help that—misunderstandings when they cannot be unravelled, should be left alone for time and loyalty to diminish.' But time never healed the wound, cutting deeper into Ruttie's fragile sense of her own worth than either of her friends suspected.

It was Khannum who eventually made the first move, desperate to patch up with Ruttie, arriving at her doorstep the day before Ruttie sailed, possibly on her trip abroad with Jinnah for the Skeen committee almost fifteen months later. As Ruttie wrote to Kanji in an undated letter, on board a steamer, also unnamed: 'By the bye, Khannum came to see me the day before I sailed and she asserts that Umar told her that a most insulting letter had arrived from me but that as she was too ill to see it he had destroyed it. She also denies all knowledge of her brother's visit to me and his message from me was the first that she had heard about it!!'

But she was still in denial about her own vulnerability, feeling instead pity for Khannum. 'Poor little kid,' Ruttie wrote, 'I didn't like to say anything but I told her that I would ask Umar about it on my return. Life has been very hard for her and the world a fearsome relentless monster but unless she pulls up and takes herself in hand she will fall all to pieces, both physically and mentally. The strain of circumstances is too much for her, as it would be for me were I in her place.' The 'strain of circumstances' that Ruttie was talking about was probably a reference to the crash of the Sobhani fortune after the government withdrew contracts to them because of the Sobhanis' anti-government politics during Gandhi's non-cooperation agitation. But it did not once occur to Ruttie that her life had been even harder, and the world an equally, if not more, 'fearsome relentless monster', and that unless she too 'pulled up' and took herself in hand, she was even more likely than Khannum, with her large family to buffer her from hard knocks, to 'fall all to pieces, both physically and mentally'.

The first sign that she was not as impervious as she had assumed was another bout of her old illness. Whether it was the strain of cutting out Khannum and Leilamani from her already depleted social life or the disappointment of Padmaja declining her invitation, she was seized again by the illness that doctors had no name for. Within days of Padmaja's decision to turn down Ruttie's invitation, she had collapsed. But in her unhappy, restless state of mind, she refused to stay in bed. Instead, she dragged herself out to visit Sarojini at the Taj.

As Sarojini wrote to Padmaja on 5 February 1925: 'Ruttie is really very ill, I think. She was here yesterday, about half her usual size and hardly able to sit up, poor child.' One good thing about it though was that she could now put off the dreaded shift to Delhi, perhaps for the whole session. A fortnight later, she had still not joined Jinnah in Delhi but, instead, was taking around one of Leilamani's friends from Oxford who had turned up in Bombay while both Leilamani and her mother were away. The friend, 'a graceful little person of beautiful manners who I am told is a brilliant student and an allround sportsman as well', as Sarojini wrote to Padmaja on 21 February 1925, arrived the day Sarojini was leaving for Patna on official work, taking Leilamani with her. And it was only natural for Sarojini, who knew nothing as yet of the quarrel between her and Leilamani, to ask Ruttie to step in and do the needful. 'Ruttie took him in charge for the day,' as she wrote in her letter to Padmaja.

Ruttie's delicate manoeuvre of cold-shouldering Leilamani, who was still living in the Taj with her mother and going with her wherever Sarojini's official duties took her, while at the same time continuing to drop in on Sarojini as if nothing was wrong, apparently had fooled Sarojini for a while and she did not notice their strained relationship for at least another month. When she did, her sympathies were with Ruttie, as she was fed up with Leilamani by then. 'Papi [Leilamani's name in the family] needs a first class whipping, poor beast,' Sarojini wrote to Ranadheera on 23 March 1925. 'She'll get it soon enough from life. I cannot help being very sad for her deliberate mockery of her best self, alienating every single friend by her terrible tempers and her even more disgusting manners. But she will find her level very soon. Meanwhile till she goes the strain on my nerves is *awful*.'

Throughout that year, Ruttie continued to fall ill off and on, enabling her to skip both the winter session in Delhi and the summer session in Simla. After seeing the pattern—short bursts of restless high spirits before she collapsed, unable to climb out of bed for days on end—it occurred to Sarojini that Ruttie's illness might be at least partly self-induced. 'She is usually ill and when she gets better she starts overeating to get ill again,' she observed much later, but this was possibly Sarojini's busiest year in politics, and her subsequent election as president of the forthcoming session of Congress, left her no time to spare for Ruttie's seemingly capricious self-destructive behaviour.

But Ruttie's mother, although similarly helpless to intervene, was seriously alarmed—not about her headstrong daughter as much as her unloved granddaughter, as Sarojini wrote to tell Padmaja on 25 March 1925. On a visit to Petit Hall to deliver a lecture at one of Lady Petit's garden parties, Sarojini wrote: 'Petit Hall was en fete today and the beautiful French lawn was a mass of red and violet flowers for my lecture to a huge crowd of fashionable women . . . But before the lecture I spent the day with Lady Petit who is full of sorrow because she thinks Ruttie is going to die and full of anger against her because of the little girl who is worse than an orphan.'

Others, including casual acquaintances, had also begun to notice that shadow behind Ruttie's vivacious exterior. According to one acquaintance, Jahanara Shahnawaz, who met Ruttie more frequently than most because of the parties hosted by her father, Sir Muhammad Shafi, at his home in Simla, Ruttie was 'a very vivacious person and full of life . . . Whenever Ruttie attended a function at our house, she would take part in the games wholeheartedly and would make the party come to life with her charming personality.' But being the life and soul of the party was not the only thing Jahanara noticed about her. 'She insisted on eating things like green chillies that were forbidden by the doctors, and I remonstrated [with] her for doing so, she would not listen,' Jahanara writes in her memoir. 'She was a person who felt lost and was deliberately trying to shock people around her.'

This need to shock took various forms. 'Whenever she went to the Viceregal Lodge [in Simla, when the assembly was in session in the summer capital] she would never stand up to pay her respect to the Viceroy,' according to Sir Yameen Khan. 'She argued that being a woman she was not required to pay him respect in this way. After all he was a man.'

And then, Khan writes, she would walk into the Lower Bazaar—where ladies from the upper class never ventured out alone—to eat chaat by the roadside. 'Mrs Jinnah with her dog would visit the Mall Road in a rickshaw every evening,' Khan writes in his memoir. 'First she would buy chocolate for her dog from the shop of Hussain Baksh General Merchants, and then from Lower Bazaar she would buy herself some *chat* served on a large leaf. Once, when a friend asked her about it, she said, "I do it to tease people like you." ' Jinnah, by all accounts, instead of trying to discourage her from calling attention to herself, sometimes got out of his carriage to fetch her a plate of *chat*, ignoring the doctor's warning to Ruttie to avoid spicy and unhygienic food. Nor did it seem to matter to her that the chocolate was as bad for her dog as the roadside snack was for her.

'She often used to be in the mood for shocking people,' as Jahanara put it, 'which some people did not approve of, but those who knew her well would laugh over it.'

Jinnah, however, was no longer as amused as he once used to be by her now almost desperate need to shock, although he never betrayed what he felt either by word or gesture. But under the almost inhuman composure, there must have been at least a trace of relief at the fact that she remained in Bombay for the next two sessions. As a legislator he had never been this busy, focusing on his work in the legislature as if 'we need not bother ourselves outside the assembly', as one of his own partymen remarked. He stood up on the floor of the House to speak on almost every issue which meant, of course, hours and weeks of diligent reading in preparation for the interventions. And even after his acrimonious split with the Swaraj Party, he kept up his punishing pace, having been elected to two important legislative committees that would keep him busy for the remaining year of this assembly. Living in the hotel without Ruttie and 'her zoological department', as Sarojini once called it, was by no means a deprivation. Nor were his brief visits to Bombay as frequent as they once used to be when he would commute between Delhi and Bombay to keep up with his court work. Having made ample money for a lifetime of ease, he was not interested in making more, and would rather not lose a single day of the session, even if it meant sacrificing his legal practice.

His icy withdrawal from her, however, was now past. Having once made up his mind to take her back, reproaches were indeed senseless, as his pencilled lines in Napoleon's biography reminded him. Moreover, it was not in his nature to mull over grievances, imaginary or real, and while he was home between the two sessions he was ready to fall in with whatever plans she made for them—that is, of course, only if they did not clash with his other work, political or legal.

But in April when he returned from Delhi after the session closed, she was already deep into an obsession of her own. This was her passion for what she called 'spiritual phenomenon' and the clairvoyants and mediums who claimed to be able to get in touch with spirits outside the physical world. As she wrote to Kanji: 'Lately I have been very much drawn towards the subject of Spirit Communication and I am *most* anxious to know more and to get at the Truth. It is such an elusive Subject and the more I hear of it the more puzzled do I become, though still more passionately interested.' Her intense craving to find out for herself rather than depend on what other people told her led her, according to Kanji, to conduct 'difficult and dangerous experiments on herself. As Kanji was a member of Annie Besant's Theosophical Society of India, Ruttie assumed he would be able to put her in touch with the right circles in Bombay where she could join their séances. As she says in her letter to him: 'I don't profess any creed nor do I subscribe to a belief, but of late willy-nilly I have been propelled towards the study of so called spiritual phenomenon and I am too deeply immersed in the matter now to give it up without some personal satisfaction for I cannot content myself with other people's experiences, though I fully realize that in a matter of this nature one doesn't always get the evidence one seeks.'

Her friends were dismayed. There was no dearth of clairvoyants and mediums in Bombay, mostly from Ireland or England, making a lucrative living by foretelling the future. Nearly everyone in Ruttie's circle had been to an astrologer or face reader or some other form of fortune teller, but with Ruttie's tendency to go overboard with her fads, they were afraid for her. As Sarojini wrote to Ranadheera: 'She [Ruttie] lives in a vague, half-dreaming condition steeped in spiritualism which I think [is] a source of danger to one of her excitable and unbalanced mind.' Even Kanji had his reservations. To his mind, 'Séances were not only unsafe guides for getting such knowledge and experience, but they were dangerous to all those who participated in them . . . séances weakened the mind and the spirits of those who indulged in them and further they made people credulous.'

This interest in the otherworldly had, in fact, begun towards the end of the previous year, 1924. Jinnah was then at home for nearly two months. But while Ruttie was increasingly becoming deeply immersed in her 'Spirit Communication', asking Kanji to find her a clairvoyant or a medium she could consult without giving away her identity, Jinnah was preoccupied with first the Hindu–Muslim Unity

Conference, with Gandhi in the chair, and also with his efforts to put some life back into the Muslim League and bring Muslims together under one political platform. He hardly cared what Ruttie was up to. They each followed their predilections, with Ruttie attending a meeting of the Theosophical Society which was holding its annual convention in Bombay in December 1924, while he was busy refusing to move a Muslim League session in Bombay to Belgaum, where the Congress was holding its year-end session. When he did notice, on the occasions when he found her conferring seriously with Kanji about 'this business of magnetizing and thought transference', as Kanji put it, he 'used to laugh at Ruttie and me'.

It was left to Kanji, as he writes in his memoir of Ruttie, to deflect her from what he thought was her dangerous pursuit of the occult, nudging her towards the study of theosophy instead. But as with politics, she was more interested in people than their ideas and philosophy. She went readily to the annual theosophical convention that was being held in Bombay that year and listened to the speeches, including 'a most inspired address by Mr Jinarajadas' (C. Jinarajadasa, an official at Annie Besant's ashram in Adyar, Madras), as she later wrote to Kanji on 28 December 1924. But she was more entranced by his wife, Dorothy. It was love at first sight, as Ruttie said in her letter, thanking Kanji profusely for introducing her to 'a very charming and rare type of womanhood'. Her enthusiasm was so great that for a while she seemed like the old bubbly Ruttie, with her passionate attachments and fine appreciation of beauty in others. 'Looking into her face (it is one of those faces one looks into and not at),' Ruttie wrote, 'I understand for the first time what is meant by a "radiant face". I must confess I fell for her absolutely and I hope that you will try and arrange so that I may meet her some time when she happens to be in Bombay.'

While it lasted, Ruttie was so swept away by her enthusiasm for the theosophists that she even contemplated sending their child (now six) to a school for girls the society ran at their ashram in Adyar in Madras. She made inquiries through Kanji about the school, and Dorothy, a little overcome by the honour being done to their school by admitting the child of such an important personage, sent him the details. But by then, Ruttie had either been overruled by Jinnah or had lost interest in the project; there was no more talk of it from her end. Dorothy sent several reminders, writing to Kanji on 29 August 1925: 'I do hope Mrs Jinnah will send her daughter to the School, for I am sure she must be a very intelligent girl, and it will be worthwhile her having a good education.' And again two months later, on 29 October 1925: 'I hope you have received satisfactory answer regarding the School and it would be good for Mrs Jinnah's child to go there.' But Ruttie was no longer interested.

She was even more fascinated with a painting that caught her eye at the convention. Of the painting she says nothing except that it is 'of Chandrasekhara', who might have been a revered figure among the theosophists but whose name has not survived in their annals. But it appears to have struck such a deep chord in Ruttie that she immediately placed an order with Dorothy Cousins for three reproductions of it in varying sizes. One would have expected her enthusiasm to have waned in the three months that the package took to arrive, but when she received only one copy instead of the three she had ordered, and discovered that Dorothy had already sailed for England along with her husband and could not be reached, she became unaccountably desperate, as she wrote to tell Kanji. Unable to locate another person in the society's headquarters in Adyar who could help her get the remaining two copies of the painting, she turned to the unfailing Kanji. 'I *must* get those other copies or I shall be quite frantic and I am sure you don't want me to lose my equilibrium!!!" she wrote in her letter to him dated 31 March 1926, a few months after she thought she was done with the Theosophical Society forever.

In her eagerness, she tried to carry Jinnah along as well, despite his avowal of scepticism and wanting nothing to do with this 'business', as he put it. He was home for the summer, and because there was nothing much happening politically to occupy him, she was able to renew her efforts to draw him into her current enthusiasm. Both she and Kanji were convinced that Jinnah had an intuitive side to him, a 'sixth sense' which he refused to acknowledge in himself, even though, as Kanji pointed out in his memoir of Ruttie, he used it to such good effect in his political career. Having picked a book which she thought would be a good bait for him, Ruttie was able to make him read it by using her old methods—'alternate bullying and coaxing', as she put it. *The Spirit of Irene,* as Ruttie describes it in

her letter, was an account of a murder trial in England of a case that
became famous as the Boscombs Murders, where the baffled police
apparently resorted to a séance to find the clues that helped them
solve the murder mystery. Either to humour her or because he sensed
she was drawing away from him and wanted her close to him again,
Jinnah, as Ruttie writes, 'had to admit that it was remarkable and
irrefutable'. If not exactly convinced, as Ruttie adds, 'J was not at all
events able to find any flaw in the case.' But her eagerness to convert
Jinnah was palpable in how frequently she refers to him in just this
one letter to Kanji, beginning with: 'I am slowly, but surely drawing
J's interest into the matter . . .'

That eagerness to win his approval for this new interest, or at least
not have him scoff at her for it, seemed related in some curious way to
her growing sense of alienation from his politics. It was as if because
of her disillusionment with politics in general and Jinnah's politics
in particular, she needed some other link, however tenuous, to hold
them together for fear of growing more apart. It was a time when
Jinnah, having just split up with the Swaraj Party, was being roundly
condemned by them as a rank communalist, a charge the newspapers
had taken up, while he did very little to correct the impression. She
knew there was no truth in it, yet his increasing focus on building
a base for himself among Muslims was making her increasingly
uncomfortable.

The week when Ruttie dropped in at the theosophical convention
in Bombay, for example, and got so carried away by everything to
do with theosophy, was also the week when Jinnah had been busy
planning his Muslim League session. But she kept her distance from
both him and the session, leaving him to turn instead to his assistant in
court, M.C. Chagla. It was Chagla who was now the sounding board
for his ideas. Chagla buoyed him up with his admiration and youthful
enthusiasm, as Kanji and Ruttie had done on earlier occasions when
his politics had nothing to do with Muslims. And while she went with
him for the session in Bombay's Globe Cinema, sitting beside him
on the platform—for it meant a lot to him to have her attend these
sessions, as a political gesture he wanted to send out to these all-male
gatherings—she would rather have not been there. As it turned out,
it would perhaps have been better for everyone if she had listened to
her own feelings and kept away.

Her mute presence, instead of adding to his image as a progressive Muslim leader, only detracted from it, as Chagla points out in his memoir, *Roses in December*. The overwhelmingly male audience resented her presence in the hall and some of them were shocked at the way she was dressed. It was her usual fashionably transparent sari with a sleeveless blouse—a dress in which she could step into the theosophical convention the previous day without raising an eyebrow—but it outraged conservative Muslim sensibilities. As Chagla recounts: 'The hall was full of bearded Moulvies and Maulanas and they came to me in great indignation, and asked me who that woman was. They demanded that she should be asked to leave, as the clothes she flaunted constituted an offence to Islamic eyes. I told them that they should shut their eyes as the lady in question was the President's wife and I could not possibly ask her to leave the hall.'

She did, in fact, avoid going for the next session of the Muslim League held in Aligarh the following year, in December 1926. Finding her sense of duty to him competing with her own desire to go with Kanji and his wife and their four-year-old son to the headquarters of the Theosophical Society in Adyar, where a jubilee convention was being held in the same week as the Muslim League session, Ruttie informed Jinnah that she would not go to Aligarh with him.

But it turned out that Ruttie could not go either with Jinnah or Kanji. Her beloved cat, Shapurjee, fell ill and she had to stay behind in Bombay to nurse it. Ruttie's emotional bond with her pets had always been deep, but in her isolation and the loneliness within her marriage, they had come to mean even more to her, the only objects of her love and a means of maintaining her fragile mental equilibrium. Despite the brittle mask she put up for the world to see, the emotional toll had already begun its devastating effect, erupting in those frequent bouts of illness that were becoming by now an almost permanent state of invalidism, and sudden fits of despair that resulted at least on one occasion, as she later confessed to Sarojini, in an attempt to kill herself. Jinnah, of course, was as oblivious as ever to the real state of her mind, but even Kanji, who had become so close to her as to count as her only real friend, was equally taken in by her light-hearted manner of normality. But Shapurjee's illness, coming on top of all the emotional strain that she kept locked up so tightly within her, appears to have shaken her badly.

She became so distraught by the cat's illness that the frail composure that she had found for herself in recent months, thanks to Kanji and theosophy, threatened to fall to pieces again. She badly needed someone to talk to but there was simply no one she could turn to, with even Kanji having left for Adyar. Sarojini, who had so far been her one refuge, had become increasingly unavailable of late, with either her overcrowded schedule keeping her out of Bombay or her impatience getting in the way of her sympathy. She was again out of town, caught up in her own programme for the year-end Congress session in Kanpur over which she was to preside in a few days. Jinnah was as usual unavailable, particularly during her emotional meltdowns. In her desperation, Ruttie clung to Kanji even from a distance. Kanji was, by now, in the thick of the jubilee convention he had gone to attend. But she insisted on sending him a daily wire updating him on Shapurjee's condition, more to relieve her own feelings than to inform Kanji who, as she well knew, was not interested in her cat or its health.

A week later, when Shapurjee recovered, Ruttie followed Kanji to Adyar for the convention, not fully recovered but intent on her search for some light to ward off the gathering darkness. She was so hopeful that this at last was the path she had been looking for, that she came all ready to join as a full-fledged member of the society and take her initiation from Annie Besant in person.

But again, what she found was disappointment; and that lost feeling of not belonging anywhere. She felt an outsider among the theosophists, and much as she wished to blend in, could not. Jinarajadasa, sensing she would be uncomfortable in the temporary huts set up at the ashram for the delegates, suggested she stay in a hotel in Madras instead. But she turned up every afternoon at Adyar, diligently attending the meetings and lectures. One evening while at the ashram, she became unaccountably upset and Mrs Besant had to take her to her rooms to talk with her in private. They spent half an hour alone together. Ruttie told her that she had come to Adyar to join the Theosophical Society but was upset because of the society's practice of having recitations from scriptures of different religions during the morning meetings. And according to Kanji's memoir of Ruttie, she informed Mrs Besant that she no longer wanted to be a member of a society that was bringing back these forms of religion.

Mrs Besant calmed her down by reassuring her 'that it was not essential for a serious minded and genuine person like her formally to join the Theosophical Society as a member'.

It could be that the prayer meeting reminded Ruttie too sharply of other betrayals on account of religion, particularly the way J was moving irrevocably closer to his Muslim identity and therefore away from her. At any rate, Mrs Besant sensed at once that there was something more than theosophy that was troubling her. After their meeting, Mrs Besant told Kanji: 'Look after your great friend, she is unhappy.' And when Kanji was surprised at that, she exclaimed: 'Don't you see unhappiness in her eyes? Look at her.'

There was another Irishwoman with psychic powers, a friend of Sarojini's called Mrs Harker, who too had been able to see beyond the light-hearted, almost frivolous exterior to the despair lurking in the shadow of Ruttie's beauty. 'My dear,' she is supposed to have remarked to Sarojini when she met Ruttie in her room as far back as 1919, 'I see a dreadful sight. I see this beautiful child dead before my eyes, dead ten years hence on her birthday.' But Sarojini had merely brushed it aside, disbelieving, so convincing was the front that Ruttie put up.

Just as now when Kanji looked, all he found was the very social and confident Ruttie attending a glittering dinner party hosted by Lady Emily Lutyens at the Adyar headquarters, a party that impressed Kanji because it was an international gathering with guests speaking in English and French. It did not seem to him that anything was troubling her at all, even when she asked Jinarajadasa during a dinner he hosted for them to 'magnetize' something for her in order to protect her from some imminent danger she felt from either outside or within her. 'Magnetizing', the process of transferring thoughts of positive energy into an object, usually a precious stone, which the owner believed would keep her safe from harm was one of those 'spiritual' practices that the theosophists frowned upon and Jinarajadasa fobbed Ruttie off by saying: 'Why ask me? Your friend Kanji can do it very well for you.'

Chapter Nineteen

~

The visit to Adyar marked the end of Ruttie's short affair with theosophy. She came back from Madras thoroughly disillusioned with theosophy, much to Sarojini's relief, and wanted to engage in something quite different, something like youth issues. 'Ruttie is fed up with theosophists after attending their great jubilee at Adyar,' Sarojini wrote to Leilamani on 16 January 1926, after Ruttie's return to Bombay. 'She is going to preside at a students' debate on inter-communal marriage but is frightened now because she has to make a speech.'

This was odd, because stage fright had never been Ruttie's problem. As a young bride of eighteen, she was able to stand up before a crowd and deliver an impromptu speech that kept her audience entranced outside the town hall during the anti-Willingdon protest. Even in the following year, 1919, she rose to the occasion, effortlessly delivering an impromptu speech from the side-box where she sat at a large trade union convention in Bombay while moving a resolution against their friend Horniman's deportation.

But her interest in the occult survived a while longer, flickering on for a few months more, before that hope died out as well, leaving her defenceless against the encroaching sense of despair and emptiness from within. From the beginning, her interest had been in what she called 'Spirit Communication' rather than theosophy, and obsessed with finding out how to contact these spirits, as if that would save her somehow from this anguish of the real world and its bonds that she longed to escape. Even when Kanji was able to interest her in theosophy as a way of taking her mind off séances and other occult subjects, he was still not quite able to cure her of her craving for supernatural experiences and séances. 'What I am after,' Ruttie wrote to Kanji on 28 December 1924, the very day, or day after, attending her first theosophical meeting in Bombay at his urging and being apparently so swept away by its charms, 'is a Séance controlled by some experienced medium, professional or otherwise; as I am most anxious to get a personal experience of this matter in which I so passionately believe.' Equally futile was his attempt to deflect her search away from séances towards telepathy and 'dream travel'—the belief he shared with other theosophists that people with karmic connections could send messages to each other through dreams. This she resisted because, as she pointed out, she not only had trouble sleeping but when she did, her sleep was disappointingly dreamless. 'Yes, I know of the dream travels of which you speak,' Ruttie wrote to Kanji on 7 April 1925. 'But I do all my dreaming in my waking hours. I am not being waggish. There is nothing I would welcome with greater rejoicing than an experience of the sort to which you refer in your letter but in my heavy druglike sleep there is no redeeming feature and besides the five or at most six hours' rest it ensures a restive mind, and a correspondingly restless physical state it has *no* value. I don't dream excepting very rarely and then I wake up only to the consciousness of having dreamt, and no more.'

By now, this search had become so urgent and vital for her, that nothing else seemed to matter, and yet, she could not get rid of that restlessness that was troubling her, as she confides to Kanji in her letter: 'My soul is too clogged! And though I aspire and crave, God knows how earnestly! how intensely, my researches remain uncrowned—even by thorns! I am feeling peculiarly restless and wish one with psychic powers would come to my assistance.'

Her pursuit seemed at least partly to do with her struggle to reconnect with herself,; she had the feeling of being lost since her marriage and she hoped perhaps spirituality would provide the meaning she was unable to find and the lack of which made her life so unbearable. 'My proud soul humbles before the magnitude of this subject,' she wrote, 'and in my estimation those of us with Second Sight and other such psychic powers should rank with the world's poets and songsters for their gift if more intelligible is also more divine. The seers and saints should stand among the world's prophets. After all we are at present too blind and unseeing to comprehend what the psychics would reveal to our half demented senses. But what the mind often revolts at, and refuses to accept, the intrinsic self within us admits with certain ease which makes the more thoughtful ponder, as though it had some ancient and original knowledge of its own.'

And the more it eluded her, the more determined she was not to give up, as she writes: 'There is much to clear away, and almost as much to mend, before I can dare to feel disappointment, because certain signs and manifestations for which I long and contrive do not occur. But I am weak and spoilt by indulgence, and to drive myself is a task to which I don't impose a time limit for obvious reasons.' Till now, Ruttie had been on somewhat formal terms with Kanji, ruled by the convention that you could not pay a personal call on a member of the opposite sex unless you were related to them, and she still needed to reassure him in her letter that all he had to do was 'let me know by phone or a written word when you are free to come, and you will be more than welcome'. But for the time, she felt close enough to him to say what was on her mind, and trusted in his sympathy and understanding. 'I have written much,' she wrote, 'but I feel confident that it is in sympathetic hands and they will be understanding eyes that read what I have said.' What she does not say, however, is why with Jinnah at home right then—probably sleeping in the next room, considering that her letter, which began at midnight, had by now stretched well into the next day, as her postscript clearly says—she needs to lean on a relative stranger like Kanji for closeness and understanding rather than on the man she had married at such cost to herself.

At its height, this chasing after the unreal served another useful purpose: she was able, quite unintentionally, of course, to keep her feelings from overwhelming her—no trifling thing in her fragile state. For example, there had been another pet tragedy in South Court six months before Shapurjee got ill. As Sarojini pithily put it in her letter to Padmaja on 10 April 1925: 'Ruttie has been bitten by Arlette who has gone mad.' Something like this would have ordinarily shattered Ruttie for weeks on end, as it almost did when Shapurjee fell ill at a time when her intoxication with the other world was beginning to wear off. But at this point she was so thoroughly oblivious to everything but her pursuit of the otherworldly that the tragedy seemed to pass her by without rousing any feeling, even though it involved, among other things, putting down Arlette who had been her life's companion, going everywhere with her from her Petit Hall days. In the letter she wrote to Kanji only two days later, on 12 April 1925, she talks of everything, from the books on theosophy he has sent, Blavatsky's *The Secret Doctrine* and its challenges, Jinnah and the challenge of making him read *The Spirit of Irene*, and even a word of thanks to Kanji for forwarding her the address of the artist who did the portrait of Chandrasekhara, but not a word, even in passing, about either Arlette or her grief at her passing. In fact, Arlette seems so completely forgotten in the excitement of having at last seen a 'manifestation' that she declares herself to be even happy that day. 'I am very excited,' she wrote, 'and equally happy as at last I have two manifestations, one was a most extraordinary luminance—a sort of perpetual flash suspended midway at the corner of Hughes Road and Sandhurst Bridge.'

Her excitement over the manifestations also blunted her disappointment at J yet again cancelling the holiday in Kashmir they had been planning for so long. She was now able to brush it aside in two casual lines: 'It doesn't look as if we are going to Kashmere after all, as J is engaged in the Bawla case. So it is more than likely that we shall remain in Bombay.'

The Bawla case itself obsessed her for a while. It was a sensational murder case revolving around a young and beautiful singer called Mumtaz Begum, who escaped to freedom from the court of the prince of Indore and was ambushed while she was driving near the Hanging Garden on Malabar Hill by the jealous prince's goons, killing her lover, a wealthy merchant called Abdul Kader Bawla. Mumtaz struggled with her assailants and called for help from a group of British army officers who were passing by. They rescued her, and her assailants were handed over to the police. The case was splashed in all the newspapers and attracted so much public attention that when the trial started, there was no room for the crowds that pushed to get into the courtroom.

But Ruttie's interest in the case was not so much with the drama of sex, mystery and violence that were drawing the crowds, but with the plight of the young singer. It was as if she identified with her—this young woman who had been taken possession of by a powerful prince at the tender age of fourteen, isolated from her mother and shut away for his occasional enjoyment, but pursued and hunted down when she tried to escape from his court. Ruttie became so fascinated with Mumtaz Begum that she not only read every word of what the newspapers said about her, but sat through the trial, missing nothing. Access to the courtroom was easier for her than for most people because Jinnah was the lawyer for one of the nine accused, for whom he managed to get an acquittal. She did not stir out of the courtroom for as long as the trial lasted, and was seized by a desire to help Mumtaz Begum after that to try and rescue her from her circumstances. 'Don't you think that this would be the critical moment to approach Mumtaz Begum to wean her away from the life to which she seems predestined?' she wrote on 1 May 1925 to Kanji, who, as a legislator and social worker, had the power to help her in this matter. 'When I saw the witnesses one by one who gained connection with her I was frankly disgusted. Her associations are horrible—but I can't help thinking that she is above them as she is above her associates . . . If she is allowed to remain in her natural surroundings a reversion to type is inevitable. Can't anything be done?'

Apart from serving as her sounding board, Kanji had become important to her by now as an emotional support and for boosting her morale. All through 1925, as Kanji writes in his memoir of her, they met regularly three or four times a week. Besides their shared interest in psychic and spiritual matters, Ruttie threw herself into his work as she had once done with Jinnah's politics. Here again it was his work in the brothels of Bombay that fascinated her, although she did not as yet push him into taking her along for his investigations into their living conditions.

And yet, despite how far they had grown apart, she was nowhere close to getting over J. Some part of her still clung to him, even as the rest of her struggled to break free. In July, when he left for the new session in Simla, she kept intending to join him there but fell ill each time. As Sarojini wrote to Padmaja on 1 September 1925, 'I told you, didn't I, that Ruttie couldn't be with Jinnah in Simla at all. She has been ill all the time, poor child!' Having all the time to herself, she felt restless and unhappy, turning up every night at Sarojini's to escape her solitude. As an exasperated Sarojini wrote to Ranadheera on 14 September 1925: 'What was left over [of my time] especially between

10 pm and 4 am was cornered by Ruttie who simply *won't* go home. She is ill and lonely and restless. She looks haggard and weary and is always in pain. I am glad that Jinnah will be back in a day or two to take charge of her.'

It was a part of Ruttie that Kanji never saw. To him, she was all in all: a source of inspiration, one of the two most helpful and healthy influences on him and his work (the other being his mentor and spiritual guide, Annie Besant). According to him, Ruttie was 'extraordinarily clever, full of understanding, full of affection and [with] a noble heart'. Her health, if it ever cropped up at all, was lightly dismissed—'I have been ill again,' she mentioned casually in her letter to him on 5 June 1925, 'so almost any evening will find me at home.' Nor did Kanji seem to notice her anxiety attacks and sleeplessness. She had fled from home in her usual fit of restlessness and then recalling an appointment she had made with Kanji, she had raced back only to find that he had left a few minutes before. And that troubled her so much that she could not sleep, and at 2 a.m. she wrote a letter of apology. And yet when she wrote in the same letter 'It is nearing 2 am. I am frightfully tired and sleepy but the thought of you having come to me I simply had to crawl out of bed to write to you—to ease my conscience if nothing else,' Kanji took it as a sign of their growing friendship rather than a symptom of the nameless anxiety that was taking over her life.

When Jinnah returned, it was back to the usual routine: they were friendly and even fond of each other, but starved of all intimacy. He, too, saw no sign of anything troubling her, and was happy to accompany her to a birthday dinner party that Sarojini was hosting in her suite for Jaisoorya. Jinnah even wore the clothes that Ruttie had obviously picked out for him because Sarojini had organized a 'Hyderabadi' dinner, made by her sister's cook and brought to the Taj for the occasion. To Sarojini's surprise, as she wrote to Padmaja on 27 September 1925, 'Jinnah invited himself and appeared in real Lucknow costume and fed daintily as befits a dandy.' It was a small gathering of friends, including Jai Joshi, another young friend of Sarojini's who frequented her Taj suite. Jai, around Ruttie's age and equally fashionable, was a qualified doctor but also adrift, not knowing what to do with her life, but strangely enough, with so much in common and meeting often in Sarojini's rooms, had never become a good friend of Ruttie's. 'Jai failed us at the last moment owing to and [an] appointment in the "sooburbs",' Sarojini wrote, making fun of Jai's accent. 'But Ruttie more than made amends in the matter of appetite.'

Meanwhile, Gandhi had withdrawn again from politics and retreated into his ashram life, and everyone was feeling a bit like Ruttie—aimless and drifting after the excitement of being part of his mass agitation. As Sarojini wrote a week later to Leilamani, on 3 October 1925: 'Everyone is as usual, only more so than usual! Ruttie with her dogs and cats. Jai [Joshi] with her alternate cynical smile and womanly tears, Osman brave and horribly in need of work and money [the Sobhanis went bankrupt after taking part in Gandhi's non-cooperation movement]; Omar with his proud air that defies the poverty of seven worlds; Shuab [Qureshi, another young Muslim nationalist like the Sobhani brothers who had been active during the non-cooperation movement] with his hair wilder than ever with a flat of his own now and a growing circle of lady-friends. And so on and so forth.'

Jinnah, too, was his usual self, showing no signs of being discouraged. He had put in extraordinary effort into the last couple of legislative sessions, but politics had ground almost to a halt, particularly for him, now that he was out of the Congress, at odds with the Swaraj Party, and with almost no Muslim League to speak of. Anyone else in his position would have probably thrown up his hands and sunk into his legal work, which at least made him money, or have taken his wife on that long-promised holiday. But Jinnah was Jinnah; refusing to give up, he now poured all his energy into rebuilding his Muslim base. He had plenty of work to keep him busy, starting with his plans to hold the next session of the Muslim League in Aligarh, including doing all his own correspondence related to it, true to his reputation as 'a one-man secretariat'. In between, there were his public engagements, and to make up for the time he had been away on legislative work, he now accepted whatever invitations he received to address Muslim gatherings as part of his work of rebuilding the Muslim League. In mid-January, he left for the winter session in Delhi, leaving Ruttie to follow. But after returning from her trip to Adyar with her great hope of finding her mission among the theosophists evaporating, her precarious health once again broke down. For Sarojini, sending her weekly bulletin of news about their friends to Leilamani was all part of the usual: 'Sarup, bobbed and beautiful, is sailing on March 1st with Ranjit,' her letter to Leilamani on 21 January 1926 says. 'Jawahar is taking Kamala by the same boat to Geneva for treatment. Poor Betty [Sarup's younger sister, Krishna]—also bobbed and beautiful—is already looking and feeling forlorn and Bebe [Padmaja] went and bobbed her hair again today. She looks about fifteen. Ruttie has been ill again. Jai Joshi is still full of complaints against life and the living.'

But a week later, Ruttie's illness seemed to have left her as mysteriously as it had erupted. Her recovery, or at least her willingness to be up and about, coincided with one of Padmaja's visits to Bombay. As Sarojini wrote in her next letter to Leilamani on 29 January 1926: 'It is 2 am. Ruttie has just gone and Bebe is tumbling into bed. We all went to see the dancer Ruth St. Dent and her company—beautiful dancing and yet after Pavlova—very tame.' The famous Pavlova had come with her troupe to India four years earlier, leaving Sarojini so deeply moved by her dancing that she had gone for all her performances in Bombay, despite her tight schedule.

The week after, everyone, including Sarojini, was in Delhi for the Hindu–Muslim Unity Conference. Everyone except Ruttie, who had found another reason to postpone joining Jinnah in Delhi. 'Ruttie is not coming here,' Sarojini wrote to Padmaja from Delhi on 7 February 1926, 'to apparently knock off the extra pounds.' Adding: 'She is ailing quite often.'

It was either the fastest weight loss ever or Ruttie changed her mind driven by her loneliness, because she arrived the following week to join Jinnah at their suite at the Maidens. 'Ruttie arrived this week with the dogs and cats, an enormous amount of luggage and a new ayah who is already driven to distraction,' Sarojini wrote in her next letter to Padmaja on 13 February 1926.

But once in Delhi, instead of fleeing her solitude as she did at home, restlessly in search of distraction, Ruttie stuck to their hotel rooms, refusing to stir out even to walk her dogs. Jinnah, of course, was busier than ever in the legislature, not missing even a day while the assembly was in session. And with the unity conference going on, he had even less time for her, although he did not get too involved with the conference, considering it a Congress, or rather a Gandhi show. But there was no dearth of company if Ruttie had the will to seek it. Delhi was, as Sarojini wrote to Leilamani on 23 February 1926, 'full of people you know. Goswami has brought his shy, just-coming-out-of-purdah wife, Mrs Chaman Lal is here, the Maharani of Baroda . . . [and] Mrs Sultan Singh [who] is becoming a public person nowadays founding clubs and schools and what not.' The city was at its best too, at the close of winter, its gardens bursting 'with sweetpeas as large as your eyes and every kind of glowing purple and blue and crimson flower in full bloom', Sarojini wrote to Padmaja, and 'so peaceful too, so far away from the dead on one side and the living on the other'. But instead of going out and enjoying herself as the others were doing, Ruttie hung about in her own rooms, getting 'very ill and restless and so on', as Sarojini put it, impatient and annoyed with Ruttie's inertia.

It was foreign to Sarojini to understand Ruttie's shrinking from people, fearing hurt and rejection. To someone of Sarojini's self-assured temperament, it seemed almost as if Ruttie was deliberately wallowing in her loneliness. As she wrote to Padmaja on 27 February: 'Ruttie is not well. She looks like a lovely ghost and spends her time buying more and yet more clothes, not particularly pretty. And she seems to have no friends except (me) or the hangers on of [illegible] kind and of course the animals which never get *any* exercise and are overfed . . .'

But still, Sarojini made an effort to pull Ruttie out of her hotel room. She herself loved shopping, especially in the local bazaars where she spent hours looking for pretty, affordable gifts for her daughters, mostly handwoven saris and ethnic knick-knacks for their rooms. And one day when she was not sitting in the assembly and listening to 'endless drivel and wonder[ing] why some men should waste good time in such footling ways', she took Ruttie shopping with her. It was not a success. She wrote to Leilamani on 3 March 1926: 'I took Ruttie out to Chandni Chowk to buy Delhi shoes today. Never again! I marveled at the patience of the shop man!'

It was another month before they met again. After Delhi, Sarojini had gone on a village tour of north India, returning to Bombay in early April. The Jinnahs, too, were back in Bombay by then, and on their way to England. Jinnah had been appointed a member of the Sandhurst, or Skeen Committee, which was going on a four-month study tour of Europe, Canada and America for setting up a military training school in India, and he was taking Ruttie along with him. While Jinnah could not—or did not want to—see the signs, to Sarojini it seemed clear that something was seriously wrong with Ruttie. 'She is the wreck of herself in body and mind!' Sarojini wrote to Padmaja on 8 April 1926, and again, two days later, to Leilamani: 'Ruttie and Jinnah are sailing today by the Kaiser-i-Hind. She is looking just the very shadow of herself—a wreck of what was once a beautiful and brilliant vision.'

Dimly, she too could sense that she was going down somewhere deep beyond recall, and tried feebly to fight it off. Unable as yet to identify what it was that was crushing her, she clung desperately to her faith in charms to save her. Turning to the only person she could trust in these matters, she spoke to Kanji a few days before they sailed. 'You will not be with me to protect me and help me,' she told him. 'Do please, therefore, magnetise something for me to keep me in touch with you.' Kanji hesitated but she was insistent. Her need for some magic to help her cope had become urgent by now. So he asked her to give him a precious stone and promised to do his best. She gave him one of the jades from her beautiful collection and he 'magnetized' it 'with thoughts of love and protection with particular reference to protecting her from any adverse effects of séances'.

If Jinnah thought he would make up to her now for the past years of overwork, she did not give him a chance. She had decided even before they sailed that she was not going to stay with him in England. As Sarojini wrote in her letter to Leilamani on 10 April 1926, the day they sailed for England, 'I don't think she will be more than a very few days in England but spend her time in Paris and go to Canada and America with Jinnah, when the Skeen Committee goes there.'

There could be another reason, apart from her urgent need to breathe freely, why she was in such a hurry to get to Paris, even before Jinnah could finish his work in England. Sarojini only discovered it by chance three years later, in 1929, when she ran into an acquaintance of Ruttie's in Paris. The lady, a princess and cousin of the queen of Italy, told Sarojini that 'Madam Zhinna' had been recklessly experimenting with drugs since her visit to Paris in 1924—'the long needle', as she put it, meaning morphine that had to be injected. And when this friend warned Ruttie that 'she was ruining her life with drugs and how all her beauty was being destroyed', she did not heed her. It was as if mere magnetizing and thought transference could no longer help her cope with the feelings that were threatening to overwhelm her.

Leaving him to his work of interviewing military experts for the Skeen Committee, she went ahead of him to Paris. Either because she was in such a hurry to get to Paris or because she was not ready to forget their quarrel, Ruttie did not visit Leilamani at Oxford as she had always done on previous visits. Leilamani was hurt. 'I have learnt that the less one exhibits one's inmost feelings to those one really loves, the less risk is run of being damnably misunderstood,' she wrote to her sister on 28 April 1926. 'That is also why I am not writing to Ruttie, though the news of her arrival in England makes me pathetically eager to see her.'

Jinnah joined Ruttie in Paris only when it was time for both to board the ship for their onward journey to Canada and America, where his committee was going to study the working of their military academies. Immersed in his work, he did not notice, or ignored, the signs, but Syud Hossain, their friend from better days who had now moved to New York as editor of the *New Orient*, could see at once that she was on some drug. 'He spoke to her very seriously about it,' as Sarojini was to learn from him only much later. Whether his talking to her helped or not, she seemed to have got a grip on herself by the time they returned home in the first week of August 1926.

Or at least she looked no different from when she had left four months ago.

Sarojini, who met Ruttie nearly ten days after they returned, found her 'looking very lovely but very drawn in the face and . . . *very* restless', she wrote to Padmaja on 18 August 1926. 'She has brought back thirty-five saris all more or less of the same kind, two Persian cats, some shoes, cigarettes, jewels and all sorts of beautiful gauds. The cats are really beautiful—one black and one blue gray.'

Kanji, who met her soon after, could see no change either, except for the better. It was to do with the jade he had magnetized for her before she left. When he went to dine with them soon after their return, Kanji says in his memoir of Ruttie, he asked her casually if she had attended any séances, and how she had reacted to them. 'She jumped out of her sofa and exclaimed: "Good God! What kind of thoughts [did] you put in that jade?" I said: "Well, why, what happened?"

Ruttie said she had made three appointments for attending séances, once she missed the train, the second time the medium did not come and so nothing happened and the third time she forgot all about the appointment. "Tell me, what thoughts you put in that jade?" she asked again. I told her what I had done. She felt grateful and I know that she never any more thought in terms of séances.' Jinnah, too, was relieved, according to Kanji, by her having finally put an end to 'her fruitless and dangerous pursuit'.

To Kanji, they must have appeared as devoted a couple as ever. Certainly, they were both equally glad to see him. Jinnah had rushed off to Delhi for the last session almost as soon as they got off the steamer, but he got back to Bombay by the last week of August, when Kanji dined with them. It seems they sat up talking till five in the morning. 'Have you made up the sleep you must have lost last Saturday,' Ruttie wrote to Kanji on 1 September 1926, inviting him to dine with them again the following Saturday. 'Five o'clock in the *morning* is an early hour at which to be out and barely respectable. If ever I have to be up by 5 am I generally don't go to bed at all, it hardly seems worth the while!' Adding: 'Anyhow do come, both J and I would feel so pleased.'

Fresh elections to the assembly and council had been announced, giving them plenty to talk about, and there was camaraderie and humour once again in their home. Jinnah, as usual, was far too confident of winning his reserved seat to be under any pressure, and it was a surprisingly relaxed time for him, having nothing much to do except support other candidates in their campaigning. His taking his voters for granted had become something of a joke between Ruttie and Kanji. And yet, beyond the teasing and laughter, there was something troubling her. There was no other sign except she kept falling ill again.

She was fine on 26 September when she and Jinnah went to dine with Sarojini, who again was having a birthday party for Jaisoorya in her rooms in the Taj. But having overindulged in the rich Hyderabadi food that Sarojini had once again got her sister's cook to make for the occasion, Ruttie had another attack of her old illness. As Sarojini wrote to Leilamani on 2 October 1926: 'On the 26th we celebrated Jaisoorya's birthday with a dastarkhan dinner to which Mr and Mrs Jinnah, Chagla, Doshi, Mrs Harker [Sarojini's friend, a psychic] and others came and *how* they all ate what Gunnu Auntie's cook had made. All Hyderabadi dishes.' And here, Sarojini makes that remark about Ruttie's self-destructive pattern of eating to fall sick: 'She is usually ill and when she gets better she starts over-eating to get ill again.'

The first week of October went into just being ill. As Sarojini wrote to Padmaja on 11 October 1926: 'Ruttie has had a bad week but is now much better.' She had turned away even more than before from human company and looked to her animals for solace. Not content with the two cats she had brought back from abroad, she acquired another dog as well, an Alsatian, which was still a rare breed in India. 'Ruttie nowadays is mad on her animals,' Sarojini wrote in her next letter to Padmaja on 13 October 1926. 'She has a magnificent new dog which had pups the other day. What excitement! what fun! What preparations!'

But after the excitement, again the sickness. 'Ruttie has not been well at all,' Sarojini wrote to Padmaja on 23 October 1926, and then, looking for something less monotonous to write about, changed the subject to the forthcoming elections. 'The elections are making me sick—this scramble for seats is bringing one to the lowest and nastiest traits of Indian character. They *can't* fight clean somehow!'

In November, with the elections due in a couple of weeks, Ruttie made an effort to ignore her illness and take more interest in Jinnah's concerns. Seeing how he steadfastly refused to do anything to promote himself with his voters, Kanji and other friends had pitched in with some campaigning on his behalf, but that was not something in which she could join in, being a woman and his wife. Other friends tried to help by sending their cars to him on voting day, to be used to ferry voters to the booths. Having been forced to keep out of it all because of the illness, she now stirred herself to some last-minute activity. Perhaps it was a stirring of her wifely sense of duty or maybe she could think of nothing else she could do for him, and wanting somehow to be a part of his big day, she decided to pack a picnic basket with his lunch and take it to him in the town hall, where he had been the whole day because the counting was going on. But that too ended badly.

Chagla, who was with Jinnah throughout the polling, recounts the incident in his memoir, *Roses in December*: 'There was a lunch interval between one and two in the afternoon. Just before one o'clock Mrs Jinnah drove up to the Town Hall in Jinnah's luxurious limousine, stepped out with a tiffin basket, and coming up the steps of the Town Hall, said to Jinnah: "J"! guess what I have brought for you for lunch." Jinnah answered: "How should I know?" and she replied: "I have brought you some lovely ham sandwiches." Jinnah, startled, exclaimed: "My God! What have you done? Do you want me to lose my election? Do you realize I am standing from a Muslim separate electorate seat, and if my voters were to learn that I am going to eat ham sandwiches for lunch, do you think I have a ghost of a chance of being elected?" At this, Mrs Jinnah's face fell. She quickly took back the tiffin basket, ran down the steps and drove away.'

If he was remorseful for having hurt her feelings, he did not show it. And less than half an hour later, it was Chagla's turn to get his head bitten off. Jinnah had apparently not quite resolved his dilemma on whether to be true to his real self before his orthodox Muslim constituency or to pander to their prejudices in order to be able to call himself a Muslim politician. After an awkward pause caused by his tiff with Ruttie, Jinnah took Chagla with him to eat at a well-known restaurant near the town hall. Since the place was famous for its pork sausages, they ordered some and were eating it when an old, bearded Muslim and his young grandson came to meet Jinnah. He asked them very politely to sit down and ordered a cup of tea and a cold drink for them. And as they were sitting at the table, Chagla writes, 'I then saw the boy's hand reach out slowly but irresistibly towards the plate of pork sausages. After some hesitation, he picked up one, put it in his mouth, munched it and seemed to enjoy it tremendously. I watched this uneasily, in a state of mind compounded partly of fascination and partly consternation. After some time they left and Jinnah turned to me and said angrily: "Chagla, you should be ashamed of yourself." I said: "What did I do?" Jinnah asked: "How dare you allow the young boy to eat pork sausages?" I said: "Look, Jinnah, I had to use all my mental faculties at top speed to come to a quick decision. The question was: should I let Jinnah lose his election or should I let the boy go to eternal damnation? And I decided in your favour."'

Chagla does not say how Jinnah responded, but it was doubtless contradictions like this within him that he refused to even acknowledge to himself that drove Ruttie even further away both from him and his politics. She grew depressed at the distance between them. All through those two months when he was at home in Bombay, she was down with her nameless illness.

And to add to her troubles, she accidentally stepped on a needle and did not notice it until her foot swelled up and had to be operated on. The swelling was so troublesome that it required two consecutive surgeries to remove the broken needle stuck in her foot.

Yet, she would not—could not—sit still. The uneasiness within her forced her to flee, seeking some diversion or the other outside the home. Her foot was so swollen that it would not fit into her shoe, and yet she went calling on her friends, and going to the cinema in the night in her bedroom slippers. But there was no peace to be found outside either.

She was not ready to admit that anything was troubling her. Instead, being closest to Kanji now, she began to imagine he was the troubled one, not her. 'Ever since the other night when you had pot luck with us,' she wrote to him in an undated letter, 'have I been obsessed with the idea that you are troubled. I have tried to put away this thought as just merely the disordered fancy of ill-health, but it persists and so I am being true to instinct—not without an effort, and writing this to you.'

She could feel his sadness as she could not feel her own, writing to him that: 'I suppose we all have our moments of melancholy and moments when everything seems to be impending and yet nothing happens—a sort of waiting mood, and one just waits and waits and grows distrustful of life.'

She would much rather watch over him, and try and help him than pay attention to whatever was troubling her and making her so restless and unhappy. 'But I feel you are troubled—troubled—troubled,' she wrote, making Kanji feel flattered with her concern for him, 'and I too begin to become restless and unhappy. Anyway you know that you can come and see me whenever you want and that I am always glad when you come. So don't please let any idea of my not being strong enough and well enough keep you away, if you feel the need of friendship that understands without explanation.'

When it came to Kanji, she roused herself from the numbing fatigue and sickness that was pulling her down. Apart from nurturing his interest in social work and boosting his self-confidence, she did those tender little things for him that she once used to do for

Jinnah—sending him, for instance, a gift of mangosteen because she wanted him to taste an exotic new fruit she thought he might like. Kanji had begun by being overawed by her beauty, glamour and intellect. But now, they were on such free and easy terms that she dared to invite him to dine alone with her at home. And wrote letters to him telling him he was such a dear that 'the more I think on it, I feel you had no business to be born into the world with "Dhoti". The correct setting for a nature of such fine sensibilities is a Sari!—or a Skirt as the case may geographically require.' Falling deeper into her depression, she leaned on him now without her earlier reserve. It was only when he was around that she could let go of her distrust of life and relax. Her distress had become so acute by now that even the sleeping pills stopped working. 'When I used to be with her,' Kanji recounts in his memoir of her, she used to say, 'I am very tired but I cannot sleep.' All that I had to do was to say: "Ruttie, sleep", and hardly had I said this she was fast asleep. Sometimes she would say: "Oh, if I sleep you will go away", I said: "I would not go, sleep, I will read a book", and the next moment I found her sleeping peacefully. When I was not with her she would ring me up late at night to say that she was tired and could not sleep. On the phone I would tell [her]: "Go sleep, you will sleep." Next morning she would ring me up and thank me.'

In November, Padmaja came to visit her mother. To Sarojini, who had seen Ruttie go through worse times, she seemed happier than she had seen her for months. 'She [Padmaja] and Ruttie and Ruttie's three dogs, seven puppies, four cats and four kittens are very happy together,' as Sarojini wrote to Leilamani on 12 November 1926. But Padmaja, who was seeing her after a long spell, was shaken. 'Ruttie is not at all well,' was her version when she wrote to Leilamani on the same day from her mother's rooms in the Taj, 'and is lonelier than ever except for her wonderful animals.'

But even her wonderful animals let her down. One of the seven Alsatian pups, which Ruttie had given to Padmaja as a birthday gift—named, symbolically enough, 'Spirit of South Court'—fell ill and died. Three days later, another pup died. It traumatized both Ruttie and Padmaja. As Sarojini explained in a letter to Leilamani on 4 December 1926: 'This has been a very bad week for poor Bebe. First of all her beautiful little Alsatian pup which Ruttie gave her on her birthday died after a week's illness. Which meant of course a great new strain for her and much commingling of grief with Ruttie in whose garden it was buried with due honours. Yesterday Ruttie's twin pup died—just three days after, and a similar procedure was repeated, with the result that both Ruttie and Bebe are prostrated and worn out with vigils and weeping and emotion.'

And that was not the end of it. The following week, yet another of the pups died, driving Ruttie and Padmaja to further paroxysms of grief and Sarojini to exasperation. 'Another dog tragedy has happened in the Jinnah ménage,' Sarojini wrote on 11 December. 'So Bebe has again been requisitioned as chief mourner and spent the night there washing, scenting and watching by a small puppy. It has become a morbid obsession now with both Ruttie and Bebe.'

Even Dr Naidu, usually so indulgent to the many foibles of his eccentric family, especially Padmaja's, was fed up. 'No more cats or dogs,' he warned Padmaja from Hyderabad, 'not even if they come from the great Ruttie. They may or may not give much—but they always ask for too much from us. In fact they take it—I am getting too old to stand shocks from loss of friends, especially animals.'

It was a fact that Padmaja could see for herself, revealing a side of Ruttie that she had not seen before. As she wrote to Leilamani on 5 December 1926: 'I see a good deal of Ruttie who is lonelier than ever and clings pathetically to us. I practically lived in her house for over two days as an adorable puppy that was one of her lovely birthday presents to me was very ill and she was looking after her for me. She died a few days ago in great agony but her illness and the exquisite care Ruttie took of her, sitting up night after night to watch over her, was an astounding revelation even to me who had always suspected the immeasurable depths of tenderness and gentleness and devotion that Ruttie is capable of.'

Less than two months into the New Year, Ruttie's resilience was once again put to test. Yet another of her dogs fell ill and died. This was a little spaniel named Inera, and Ruttie was far more attached to her than to the pups. It left her drained and lonelier than ever.

She was 'unfortunate', according to Kanji, when it came to her pets—they kept dying on her 'inspite of her kindness and care and she suffered terrible unhappiness as a result'. Sarojini, too, was inclined to believe that 'there is a curse upon little Ruttie'. She was in Delhi for the Hindu–Muslim talks when she received a wire from Ruttie about her dog. 'Poor Ruttie is so unhappy and alone in Bombay with Inera in a dangerous condition,' Sarojini wrote to Padmaja on 23 February 1927. 'I had a wire from her yesterday.' And a few days later: 'I had a sad and unhappy letter from Ruttie. The little dog who looked like a spaniel died in a few minutes. There seems a curse upon little Ruttie. Poor child, poor child! Write to her and send her a message of comfort.' Then Sarojini added a line that explains why she felt so responsible for Ruttie, highlighting the tragic loneliness of a life that had once been so full of promise: 'She has only us to love her and understand her.'

It was all Sarojini could do—comfort Ruttie and urge her children to do the same. The previous week, a few days before Ruttie's birthday, her twenty-seventh, knowing how alone and sad Ruttie must feel in Bombay, with no links to her family and Jinnah in Delhi too busy to bother about trivial things like birthdays, Sarojini had written to Padmaja, reminding her to wish Ruttie. 'I hope you will give Father a happy birthday on Sunday,' she wrote to Padmaja on 12 February 1927 and because Ruttie's birthday fell on the same day, 'and that you will remember lonely little Ruttie too on that day.'

Of course, Sarojini never brought up Ruttie's loneliness with the one person who was the cause of it. Quite apart from knowing how fiercely Jinnah resented anyone invading his privacy, Sarojini herself could not bring herself to interfere in her friends' personal affairs. Besides, she had far more important matters to discuss with Jinnah other than the state of his marriage, the most crucial of them being the Hindu–Muslim political agreement that was holding up the drafting of a new constitution. They were both in Delhi, Jinnah for the new legislative session and Sarojini arriving in mid-February and staying for over a month at M.A. Ansari's house while she held political meetings at all hours, 'literally lost in the negotiation for a possible Hindu–Muslim Settlement', as she put it. And when Jinnah was not busy in the House speaking on every piece of legislation that came up, he was trying to build a consensus among the Muslim League members in order to negotiate a political settlement with the Congress. Sarojini, too—though not as much as Jinnah—was 'night and day been obsessed by it', as she wrote to Padmaja on 22 March 1927 when at last there seemed as if there was a breakthrough, '*not because of the Hindus but because the Muslims have shown great courage and statesmanship and even against their own feelings and fears they have shown remarkable unanimity in supporting me'.

And while she refused to take sides with either of the Jinnahs, she could not resist the occasional sly dig at one or the other. 'Ruttie of course has not arrived,' Sarojini wrote to Padmaja on 12 February 1927, soon after she reached Delhi, 'and I am rather glad because the accommodation would have been entirely unsuitable for her zoological department!' A week later, after watching Jinnah in the assembly, she wrote again to Padmaja: 'Jinnah seems more and more isolated and his following is reduced to a few members and two in uniform from the Punjab, extraordinarily handsome.'

Sarojini's admiration for Jinnah at one time was so unalloyed that people had mistaken it for infatuation, but this became more ambivalent over the years. When Jinnah's junior lawyer, Chagla, published a tongue-in-cheek portrait of his famous boss, for instance, a few months later, she was unambiguously delighted. 'I have read with much interest and pleasure your frank and able exposition—or is it exposure—of your Chief,' she wrote to Chagla on 4 August 1927. 'You are a plucky "devil" (it is your own word) to "expound" or "expose" him with such wit and candour and courage! Someone I understand has called it "a libel" on the great M.A.J. but I consider it only a "label" of those obvious outer qualities that are like a crust hiding the real man of which (or should it be whom? Being so impersonal an entity my grammar gets rather mixed in relation to him!) you never get a glimpse.'

But something within her also caused her to spring fiercely to his defence. And it is with that characteristic mix of wit and loyalty—and generous use of pun that Sarojini championed Jinnah in her letter to Chagla: 'I think you have done a capital impressionist sketch of him,' her letter goes on, 'monocle, audacity and all—someday I hope you will find yourself transformed from being a "devil" to being a friend of the "lonely man" who habitually breathes the rarefied air of the "colder regions". There you will find—as those of us who are fortunate enough to know him intimately have discovered long ago—that the spiritual flowers that blossom within the colder regions have a beauty and charm denied to the flora that grows in the warmer valleys of the common human temperament! But I confess you *do* need a fur coat now and then in the course of your botanical expedition in this polar region!!'

But for the present, Jinnah had risen higher than ever before in Sarojini's esteem. He had against all odds and almost single-handedly brought about a near resolution to the Hindu–Muslim problem that she and other Congress leaders had been attempting to resolve for so long. Summoning a meeting of prominent Muslims, most of them legislators like him, he came out with a bold set of proposals—the Delhi Proposals, as they soon came to be called—that set the basis for a Hindu–Muslim political settlement. The relief at finding at last a near resolution to what had so far been a political impossibility, was so great, as Sarojini wrote to Padmaja, 'that I feel sick with it'. The letter, written from inside the assembly, was dated 22 March 1927, the very day when the Delhi Proposals were finalized. 'Jinnah has absolutely risen to his height and carried the better mind of the people with him,' she wrote. 'I am very proud of Jinnah.'

It was easy for her then to shut her eyes to what living 'in this polar region' was doing to Ruttie. And even when it became impossible to evade the fact that Ruttie was now on the verge of a breakdown, Sarojini resolutely refused to blame Jinnah for it. She met Ruttie in the end of April, not in Bombay but in Lahore, where Sarojini had gone to tend the wounds of a communal riot, one of the worst that year, 'with 105 casualties and blood flowing in the streets', as she wrote to Padmaja. Ruttie, on the other hand, was heading for Kashmir, determined to take that holiday which Jinnah had been putting off for so long even if it was by herself. But while in Lahore, Ruttie clung to Sarojini, begging her to spend at least a few days with her. Sarojini, unable to bear her distress, yielded even though she had to get to Bombay for an All India Congress Committee (AICC) session. She wrote to Padmaja on 3 May 1927: 'My going there [Kashmir] was purely accidental. Had I known that the AICC was postponed, I might have yielded to Ruttie's tears and stayed on at least till Jinnah went up but I had no intention of going at all. I only promised to go from Lahore to Rawalpindi with Ruttie—about five hours journey. But when we got there she insisted on breaking journey to spend a few days with me, which considering her nervous condition, her immense quantities of luggage, four utterly democratic servants, ice panee, and her cats (on ice!) I thought wholly unadvisable. So I offered to go up for three days to Kashmir and get back in time to travel to Bombay for the AICC on the 5th May.'

It was Sarojini's first time. 'Kashmir,' she writes, 'is only 200 miles from Rawalpindi, a beautiful drive which need not take nine or ten hours and Kashmir itself is a land of Romance and Dreams, quite in accordance with every legend one hears. And yet it is not more beautiful than many parts of India—certainly not so beautiful as parts of Africa nor even Switzerland. But it is quite lovely enough to make one intoxicated. The air from the snow mountains scented with the breath of spring flowers is divinely full of balm and healing. The meadows were purple with iris, the orchards were cloud white and cloud peach with cherry, pear and apple blossom. The gardens were aglow with lilacs and wistaria and tulips and narcissus, all the Persian flowers and the Italian flowers of the spring. The life on the Jhelum—crowded with houseboats and little boats called shikaras which ply over the water past the crazy huddled old houses on the other side of the banks. And *what* unsurpassed beauty of colour and form have the women and children—alabaster and rose and pearl and ivory and silver—exquisite, incredible beauty and what dirt!'

Ruttie, however, was too troubled to enjoy it all, prompting Sarojini to add: 'I loved my three days there but I wanted you with me. You and I would love the dream peace of Kashmir. But I doubt if restless Ruttie whose whole life is so artificial can respond to its real simplicity and charm. She carries town with her everywhere, poor child!'

Had Sarojini but known it, there had been a time when Ruttie's heart too had leapt to life with Kashmir's charms. In happier days, when she had not yet given up on J and herself, Kashmir was the haven she had planned for their getaways from Jinnah's political work. He had indulged her then, letting her spend 50,000 rupees—a fortune in those days—merely to do up their houseboat. It was going to be their base from where she dreamt of setting out with him on horseback to explore a Kashmir known to only the most intrepid of travellers. As preparation for these trekking holidays she was determined to take with him—rather like her aunt Hamabai—she bought and pored over a travel guide to Kashmir, possibly the first of its kind. *The Tourist's Guide to Kashmir, Ladakh, Skardu & c* was for the intrepid traveller giving details of Kashmir's most remote and scenic regions and the

SHEELA REDDY

mountain passes and pony tracks by which one could get there, written by an expert, a Major Arthur Neve, who had served as a surgeon in the Kashmir Medical Mission and was therefore familiar with the terrain. Ruttie's copy of the guide, in its thirteenth print run by 1923, is heavily underscored in pencil, marking all the treks she must have diligently planned for them, drawing lines to remind her of all the practical details such as the times of the year when the mountain passes were accessible and camping directions. But that dream too had passed away.

She broke down and wept when Sarojini was leaving. 'Poor child!' Sarojini wrote, moved despite her exasperation with Ruttie. 'How she cried when I left. How she pleaded for me to stay and for me to bring you in June. But we cannot make plans—until after Father has sailed.' Dr Naidu was setting out in a couple of months on a working holiday to Europe, his first trip abroad since he had graduated from Edinburgh's medical college. But by then something had broken in Ruttie's heart, and she never again thought of going to Kashmir, with or without her friends.

Disturbing though Ruttie's tears were, Sarojini was soon immersed in politics again. At the AICC meeting later that month, Jinnah's Delhi Proposals were discussed and accepted as they were. It was the 'ray of light' that Sarojini had been waiting for so long, and in her gratitude to him for having brought it about, she gave him a magnificent gift to mark the occasion. It was a jewelled gold casket with an inscription: 'To Mohammed Ali Jinnah, Ambassador of Unity, From his loyal friend and follower, Bombay, May 1927, Sarojini Naidu.'

* * *

Ruttie did not go with Jinnah for the new session in Simla. Instead of involving herself in the fate of his Delhi Proposals, which were by now rousing both Hindu suspicions and Muslim fears alike, she began pestering Kanji to take her along with him to the brothels of Bombay where he was conducting his investigations of their living conditions. 'When are you going to take me round so that I may see for myself the conditions existent and the life lived by those poor women?' she wrote to Kanji on 28 August 1927, insisting on visiting the seamier establishments. 'Mind, the places I want to see are those commonly called "brothels" and *not* where the girls work independently.' And with Kanji by her side, she toured round these brothels 'for hours together, visiting one brothel after another'.

There were other ways she found of distancing herself from Jinnah and his politics. One was her sudden missionary zeal to improve the living conditions in the city's animal shelters. It involved visiting the shelters, the '*pinjrapoles*', as they were called, many of them run by Parsi charitable trusts, including one headed by her father. The conditions were harrowing, as Sarojini discovered when she was roped in to visit one shelter. Both Ruttie and Kanji wanted her to write about it in the newspapers to publicize the issue. 'My visit three days ago to the Chembur Pinjrapole is one of my saddest memories and I am haunted by the pitiful wail of the wretched dogs in the last agonies of living death,' Sarojini wrote to Kanji on 9 September 1927, just before leaving for Simla to try and resolve the Hindu–Muslim differences that still persisted. 'Dante would have, I think, another corner in his Inferno had he heard that incessant cry of misery . . . the dogs were a terrible sight and a terrible commentary on our ideas of compassion.'

Having visited once, Sarojini had no desire to repeat the experience. But with Ruttie, it became a morbid preoccupation. Accompanied by the ever-faithful Kanji, she spent weeks going thoroughly into the conditions of the suffering animals. She dwelled in almost loving detail on the animals' neglect and suffering. 'We saw dogs with matter oozing from their skins in the last stages of violent eczema— dogs with wounds, which through dirt and neglect had decayed the flesh . . . causing sinuses which had eaten an inch deep into their flesh and which on the resident Vet's own admission he had not even noticed,' says a letter dated 2 September 1927 that she wrote jointly with Kanji and published in the *Indian Daily Mail*.

At the Chembur shelter, the letter says, they found dogs 'in the last stages of starvation. The drinking water was as foul as on our previous visits. The refuse, instead of being removed, was heaped in the enclosure and served as a magnet to myriads of flies, which would alternate between the open sores of the victims and the delectable mound of filth.' Describing the conditions at the shelters as 'death by slow torture besides which a slaughter house would pale into insignificance', the letter urged 'the public of Bombay to bestir themselves and whip these gentlemen into action'.

In her zeal to save the animals, she was freed of the usual conflicting pull of her duty to Jinnah and her need to be away from him. The work, though harrowing, had kept her so engrossed that she had put off going to Simla until it was almost too late, with Jinnah deciding to cut short his stay and return to Bombay even before the session closed. And when Jinnah wrote saying he might be back in Bombay earlier than expected, she felt, if anything, almost dismayed. 'J writes that he may be returning before the end of the sessions and that Simla is quite dull, but surely the Sandhurst Committee will be sitting to the end of September, won't it?' she wrote to Kanji in her letter dated 28 August 1927.

But in September, Jinnah was elected chairman of the Hindu–Muslim Unity Conference of legislators and other leaders to be held in Simla later that month to settle the differences and grievances between the two groups. It left Ruttie just enough time to join him in Simla at least for the remaining one week of the session. But her going there, with her cats and their various ayahs, was not worthwhile. The conference was not a success, and Jinnah was in a hurry to get back to Bombay. But just as they were leaving, one of her cats escaped from their hotel room. and while she refused to leave without it, Jinnah did not want to stay until it was found. In the end, he left, expecting her to make her own way back. Once again, it was Sarojini to the rescue. 'Darling,' Sarojini wrote on 26 September 1927 from the Cecil to Padmaja, 'All the turmoil and the shouting has died and the Captains [Dadabhai Naoroji's three granddaughters active in the freedom struggle] and the Haqs [Maulana Mazharul Haque, a prominent Congress leader from Bihar and his wife] have departed. But as for me, I am held up walking between Banton's where I was staying and Peterhoff where I am supposed to be staying on account of Ruttie. Jinnah left with the Captains and the Haqs but Ruttie remains for no purpose that I can see except to "will" the lost cat to return out of nowhere. But I must persuade her to go back to Bombay as soon as I can without fulfilling her hare-brained scheme of motoring through all the villages from Ambala to Delhi with her eight cats, two ayahs, one jewel box and cigarette case looking for the prodigal.'

The humour apart, Sarojini was seriously alarmed by Ruttie's condition. 'I don't think Ruttie coming was worthwhile,' she continued. 'She has hardly seen anyone. She scarcely comes out of her room before the afternoon—poor child. There is a turmoil in her mind and a turmoil in her spirit and she cannot rest or concentrate her life in any way.'

Sarojini, too, was in as much a hurry to get back as Jinnah, but not for work commitments like him. Padmaja had fallen seriously ill. 'But,' as she says in her letter, 'this motherless child needs me terribly now.'

Three days later, they were still in Simla. 'My darling, I have had such an anxious time with Ruttie who has been in a desperate state of tension and excitement,' Sarojini wrote again to Padmaja, on 29 September. 'At last I have persuaded her to go back to Bombay and leave the search for the cat in the hands of the police commissioner. And she has agreed on condition I take her back. So I am leaving with her direct for Bombay on the 1st. If I can I shall leave for Hyderabad on the night of the 3rd Oct from Bombay but don't build on that too much darling as I find some wretched things have been fixed up in Bombay with the SPCC [sic] for me on the 9th. I am trying to see if the date can be altered. In any case I am coming home. You'll see me over there a few days later. I am so anxious about you darling. But you have the whole of Hyderabad to look after you while this poor child whose mind seems to be hovering on the brink of madness and loneliness has no one and clings to me with a terrible need.'

Sarojini eventually reached Ruttie to her home and Jinnah, but she kept worrying about her. Throughout the next fortnight, as she shuttled from Simla to Bombay, and then a brief stopover in Hyderabad to see her ailing daughter and back again to Poona to address a women's conference there, she was haunted by the image of Ruttie on the verge of a breakdown. In her anxiety, she made a call from Poona to Ruttie to find out how she was. To her relief, Ruttie sounded more composed. 'I've just spoken to Ruttie over the phone,' she wrote to Padmaja on 16 October 1927 from Poona. 'She is better.'

Jinnah would have been surprised had he known how worried Sarojini was about Ruttie. When he noticed Ruttie at all, she seemed no different from what she had always been. He was back in Bombay now that the session had ended, and thanks to a British blunder, had bounced back right into the centre of the political picture. This was because the Simon Commission, a statutory commission for constitutional reforms in India, had managed to raise the hackles of all nationalists cutting across party lines because it did not include a single Indian among its eight members. Jinnah had earlier approached the viceroy personally to urge him to include at least two Indians in the commission to win over 'the better mind of India'. But when the government went ahead and announced the formation of the all-white commission, he was among the first to advocate a boycott and stood so firm that even the leaders in the Congress had to reluctantly accept his leadership of the popular anti-Simon movement. In control again of the national discourse, he was at his best, speaking at public rallies and leading the boycott campaign and simultaneously getting the Muslim League to work in tandem with the Congress on the issue. His chamber in the high court was once more buzzing with young men looking to him to lead the way and he had not been this mellow in a long time.

He held court, too, at home. At one dinner party, as Kanji recounts in *India's Fight for Freedom*, with Motilal Nehru, R.D. Tata and himself, 'Jinnah kept the table roaring with laughter,' giving an instance of how his independent party in the legislature had worked with the Swaraj Party to pass the Steel Industry (Protection) Bill, the main purpose of which was to bolster the infant Tata Iron and Steel Works at Jamshedpur and enable it to withstand foreign competition. At the table, Jinnah told the story of how the evening before the final voting, Ratan Tata rushed to his suite of rooms in Cecil Hotel in Simla, screaming that one member of the assembly, a Swaraj Party member, was asking for a big consideration to vote in favour of the bill and threatened to vote against it if he did not get a bribe. Despite the lateness of the hour, Jinnah sent for the member who was staying in the same hotel and told him: "R.D. Tata has complained to me that you have demanded Rs 10,000 for your vote. You will not get that money. You go to hell and now you get out of this room."' The crestfallen member got out quickly and the next day voted for the bill. It was a story that made them all laugh, including Ruttie. It felt like they were friends again.

Not only did he not notice any sign of her unhappiness, she, too, seemed to have grown almost fond in her forbearance with him.

In fact, the week that the Simon Commission was announced and Jinnah's boycott campaign was just taking off had been a time of unusual marital accord between them. There had been a happy event in South Court: one of Ruttie's Persian cats had a litter. For a while, the whole household revolved around the 'happy little cat hold', with Ruttie supervising their care and feeding. It was a picture of such reassuring domesticity that even Jinnah was taken aback at her strength of mind when she decided to part with one of the kittens— the finest of the litter, in fact—as a birthday present for Padmaja. This time Padmaja could not make it to Bombay for her birthday, so the kitten had to be sent to Hyderabad instead. 'I can't make up my mind which to part with and am taking two along with me,' Ruttie wrote to Padmaja on 15 November 1927, just before leaving for the station. 'But of them the one I intended for you is the most intelligent of the litter. The ayah is crying and J *actually* called me a fool for parting with little bright eyes.'

It was the hardest thing she had done in a long while. After shedding her own farewell tears over the kitten at the station, she packed it off without a 'trousseau' but with many minute instructions on its welfare, from telling Padmaja to let the kitten sleep in her bed ('It has never slept by itself in the whole of its little life and it will feel very lonely if it is expected to do so now') to how 'the fish is served boiled and the chicken is roasted and finely chopped (not minced)'. She waited to hear of its safe arrival but after two days could wait no more, sending Padmaja an urgent cable: 'Wire news of the little newcomer. Anxious.'

And then, after her tender mockery of J and her separation pangs over a mere kitten, and having survived a nervous breakdown, finding the resources within her to rise to his support yet again when the Muslim League split, accompanying him without a word of protest to Calcutta for the session of his half of the divided League, she finally mustered the strength on their way back to break out of that cycle of love and guilt and tell him that it was finally over. She told him to his face, in their first-class coupé, on the train back from Calcutta.

On 4 January 1928, they parted wordlessly at Victoria Station, she going to the Taj with Sarojini, who had been on the same train, while he went home alone, too proud and hurt to stop her. He had not seen it coming.

Chapter Twenty

~

At first, the relief was enormous. To think that it had cost her so much agony and anguish over so many years when it had been so simple all along—just shift into the room next to Sarojini's in the Taj and no one any the wiser for weeks to come. It was strange, as Sarojini observed, 'how *few* people have even an inkling of what has happened in the very heart of Bombay. Fortunately, everyone is used to seeing her here at all hours that no one suspects her being here with her cats and he at home alone.'

In fact, it was Sarojini who showed more distress than either of them. Everyone still believed that she had been instrumental in bringing about what was openly acknowledged as the worst mismatch in recent times, but Sarojini's conviction that 'Jinnah is worth it all' had never shaken. And what is more, despite their quarrels and differences of temperament, she had persuaded herself that the two loved each other as much, if not more, than when they first got married against such stiff opposition—had 'come to a better understanding' of each other, as she put it a few weeks later in her letter to Padmaja. It was not in Sarojini's nature to interfere in other people's affairs, especially matters of the heart, but this was too important to let things go their own way. The very shock of Ruttie walking out on Jinnah was enough to drive her frantic with worry. For a full two weeks after Ruttie came to her, she was unable to think of anything else, even forgetting to write her daily letter home to her children, something that was unthinkable for her even at the busiest of times. On the two occasions when she was able to pull herself sufficiently together to write a line or two, she either forgot to post the letter or sent it absent-mindedly to the wrong address. But by the end of the first two weeks, she had to admit that matters between the Jinnahs were beyond even her legendary peacemaking abilities. 'I don't know how to explain my long silence,' she finally wrote home to her two daughters from the Taj on 16 January 1928, after a fortnight's silence. 'I wrote a long letter to you in the train but forgot to post it. I sent a wire the other day but addressed it Station Road Bombay—so of course it never reached. All of which goes to show that my mind has been very distracted owing to various reasons. Ever since I put my foot on the station platform I have been in the thick of worries and anxieties not one of which belongs to me strictly speaking and though I have been longing to write or get home, I have literally not had one spare moment.'

'I am going to Calcutta on Friday,' the letter continued, 'and returning on the 27th. I've not made *one note* for the Kamala lectures. But I hope everything will take a turn for the better soon and I shall be less ground between the upper and nether millstone of other people's affairs.' And then, unable to restrain herself any longer, she burst out with the secret she had struggled to keep: 'I think I should tell you—but it is so far as I could keep it so—quite confidential, that Ruttie is in trouble. It has I suppose been due and was due for years. What exactly has brought it to a head I cannot tell. Some slight incident in Calcutta apparently . . .' And then, without elaborating on what that 'slight incident' might have been, she goes on to recount what happened when they got off the train from Calcutta, returning from the Muslim League session, with Jinnah and Ruttie travelling as usual in a separate first-class coach by themselves: 'But on the platform, when we reached here, she told me she was not returning to South Court but coming to the Taj—and she has been here since the 4th in the room next to mine. I have done my best and can do no more. There is a point beyond which friends cannot interfere. No two people who really love each other are unhappy and bitter and will not come to any understanding. It is extraordinary how *few* people have even an inkling of what has happened in the very heart of Bombay. Fortunately, everyone is so used to seeing her here at all hours that no one suspects her being here with her cats and he at home alone. I am hoping desperately that things will come right; but who knows? Meanwhile I don't think you should write to her about it. The less said the sooner mended. But you can imagine my great anxiety.'

Her concern about Ruttie did not lighten her worries about her own two daughters coping alone at home by themselves, ending her letter with: 'My darlings, my heart is also with you. If I cannot write you will understand. Please take care of yourselves. If I know that you are doing that I shall at least be relieved of one heavy care. I will write again in a day or so. I have a Murshidabad sari for each of you. Mother.'

But it was another four days before Sarojini could bring herself to write home again. Perhaps because her younger daughter was away from home, having left on an all-India tour in search of employment, Sarojini was able to write more openly about the Jinnahs' breakup, having more confidence in Padmaja's discretion. 'I feel so unhappy about leaving Ruttie here alone and going away,' she wrote on 20 January 1928, just before leaving for Calcutta on her speaking engagement, in a letter brimming over with sorrow and concern for her 'poor child' Ruttie, whose depths of anguish and despair she was just beginning to discover: 'Nothing is settled about her except that she will not have any reconciliation but will go away with her mother to Europe in April. There is *nothing* that any friend can do at the moment since it's not just a sharp bitter quarrel as I had at first imagined, to be healed by time, patience, a little mutual toleration and a little mutual pardon for faults of temperament. But even we who have been so close to Ruttie and loved her so well never knew or guessed the deep underlying current of mutual unhappiness that began from the first day almost and has been gradually gathering strength, intensity and bitterness . . . She says that several times it came to almost breaking point (when I was in Africa) and she never meant to return and now she says "Don't force me back into slavery. Let me be free. Let me be free." Poor child, she does not realize the price of such freedom! She is not unhappy now, only restless and longing to be free of all her shackles. She says her youth is going and she must live, that Jinnah cannot satisfy her mind and soul. He stifles her by his lack of understanding and his lack of the spirit of the joy of life. He has also an accumulation of grievances against her . . . She makes charges against him . . . and it is a story to which every one of the ten years has added a fresh chapter apparently. Latterly it seemed to me that both were settling down to a better understanding of each other and Ruttie herself felt that he was much more tender and tolerant and there were none of the bitter quarrels that had so disturbed and devastated the earlier years of their marriage. But I suppose with two such individual natures—fervent youth and rather dull middle age personified—the clash was inevitable. Jinnah is too old, she is too young and neither in spite of the real affection that has surely been between them, can make the necessary surrender with honour to ensure peace. Poor little Ruttie! I never knew then her brave spirit suffered *fear*. She never spoke and we never knew. I think it best that she should go away to Europe with her mother in April as already arranged. Jinnah too will be gone about the same time. And who knows—Time might after all be the great atonement for the years that these two have caused each other pain and misery through blindness of heart and vision.'

But even in her anxiety to get them back together as quickly (and discreetly) as possible, Sarojini was forced to admit that Ruttie's decision to leave was not entirely unwarranted, as she had first thought: 'Meanwhile, curiously enough, Ruttie is much more *normal* than I have ever known her since her childhood. She eats and sleeps well and almost at regular hours. She is natural and *herself* as she never was in her own home. She keeps on saying "I am free. I am free." She wants you to know all her reasons someday for leaving Jinnah, for feeling she cannot go back again, as she puts it, "under this marriage ice". But I told her that you should be spared the suffering it will cause you to learn—as I have only now learned—how difficult have been those ten years,' and here Sarojini alights on the real cause of what must have surely shaken her to the core, especially when she had so far assumed that Ruttie's unhappiness was of her own making, almost as if it was mere capriciousness on Ruttie's part and not to be taken seriously. The half a sentence is so casually inserted and then dismissed, as if not wanting to call attention to it, but there is no hiding the grave import of what she is saying: 'and how she even tried to put an end to herself deliberately . . .' And having said the dreadful words, Sarojini seems anxious to quickly change the subject without further elaboration, either because it was too painful a subject for her to dwell on or more likely, to spare Padmaja the details, knowing how it would affect her morbid and sensitive daughter: 'Well, Ruttie has only us really. Her own people are strangers to her. Her poor mother loves her but drives her distracted . . . She loves us and trusts us and so she comes to me for sanctuary, poor child. She feels safe here. Safe in her soul.'

In her general distress, Sarojini did something she had never dared before—tried to talk to Jinnah about it. It was a liberty she had never taken before throughout their long years of friendship, knowing how fiercely Jinnah resented any interference in his personal affairs. But her anxiety was too great to stop herself: 'Jinnah has grown so dumb. No one can even approach him. I think he is hurt to the core because she left him like that, almost without warning. In any case no one can interfere with him. He is too hard and proud and reserved for even an intimate friend to intrude beyond a certain point. All he says is, "I have been unhappy for ten years. I cannot endure it any longer. If she wants to be free I will not stand in her way. Let her be happy. But I will not discuss the matter with anyone. Please do not interfere." And he is I suppose like a stone image in his loneliness and Ruttie is, although reveling in what she believes to be the beginning of liberty for her—Liberty costs too dear sometimes and is not worth the price . . . I am writing a line to Papi today. Poor child. She must like Ruttie be clamouring for "freedom". This Freedom!!'

What troubled Sarojini even more than their stubborn refusal to compromise was that neither Ruttie nor Jinnah seemed properly upset by what had happened. 'The really tragic part of it,' as she pointed out to her friend Syud Hossain a few weeks later, 'is that both seem so *relieved.*'

But neither was really as unemotional as they pretended to be. There was certainly more behind Jinnah's assumed indifference and show of relief than he let on. And Sarojini's initial suspicion that he was hurt to the core by Ruttie's sudden desertion was not entirely unfounded. Outwardly, he stuck to his old routine, driving himself even harder with no leisure even to feel his rage and humiliation at her unexplained desertion. There was more than enough to keep him busy for the moment. First, he had the split within the Muslim League to try and patch up. This seemed more urgent than working on his marriage because it was threatening to undermine his only remaining asset as a national leader—being the undisputed leader of Muslims in the country. With the split, the dissident Leaguers had gone over to the government's side, leaving him with no Muslim support for either the boycott of the Simon Commission or to reach a Hindu–Muslim settlement with the Congress. Grabbing the chance to hit him now that the chink in his armour was exposed, both the government and his opponents in the Congress began deriding him as a leader without a base. Facing increasing isolation, he fought back grimly, his proud spirit refusing to bend in order to placate his opponents.

It was the same on his personal front—his pride would not allow him to find a mediator nor could he personally humble himself by talking to Ruttie. Hurt mortally by what he considered her betrayal, he retreated within his shell, rejecting all offers from friends to mediate on his behalf. Within a week of their parting, he had left for a meeting of Muslim leaders in Lucknow without expressing a word of regret or remorse to her. He refused to talk about it, to her or to anyone else. The campaign he was leading to boycott the Simon Commission became his sole mission now, ignoring the fact that it was only making him more unpopular among Muslims.

As for Ruttie, he did not see or speak to her for the two remaining weeks in Bombay before he left for the new legislative session in Delhi in early February. The choice was clearly left up to her: to either stay on at the Taj if she wished or to return home during his absence in Delhi and go on as if nothing had happened. He certainly was not going to say or do anything to influence the outcome; it was as if it had nothing to do with him, as if he did not care. And he threw himself with more than his usual vigour into his political life.

But even that unfailing source of his well-being seemed bent on betraying him now. The first blow was in the Legislative Assembly where his efforts had invariably yielded rewards. But as the first sign of the frustrations that lay ahead, the government, without giving any reason, shelved the report he had so assiduously prepared on the Sandhurst Committee's recommendations, consigning all his hard work to the trash bin. Even Padmaja, cut off from politics in her sickbed, could sympathize with what he must have gone through at that moment. 'Poor Jinnah,' she wrote in a letter to Chagla from her sanatorium, 'the pronouncement on the Skeen [another name for the Sandhurst Committee] recommendations must be a bitter disappointment for him. He was so tremendously keen on it.' With the insight born of distance, or perhaps out of her more passive temperament, Padmaja could see the futility of his methods of fighting the government. 'I suppose it is just one more of the many humiliations we still have to suffer—a million protest meetings won't make *any* real difference. I am really beginning to wonder if it would not be more dignified for us *not* to utter any protests when these situations arise. We weep and cry and rant and threaten and protest and the government listens quietly and then simply does what it intended to do. But politics is a dismal subject . . .'

Dismal or not, Jinnah nevertheless felt compelled to keep battering either at the doors of the government or trying to reach a political settlement with the Congress, pouring all his energy into resolving the political situation rather than addressing his personal problems. Within a week of the government shelving the Sandhurst Committee's report, Jinnah's Delhi Proposals which everyone, including himself, thought would finally resolve the never-ending Hindu–Muslim differences, came up against heavy resistance at the all-parties conference. The proposals, when he had made them a few months ago, were warmly welcomed by the Congress and no one doubted that they would be cleared by the conference without any difficulties, considering that the subcommitteee which had been set up to steer the proposal through the conference included two influential Congress leaders who were also his friends—Motilal Nehru and Sarojini Naidu. But even they were helpless, with the Hindu Mahasabha putting up a stiff resistance to every clause of Jinnah's deal. As Sarojini put it in a letter home on 13 February 1928: 'The political all-parties conference is driving me silly. Even at this critical juncture men will not relent . . . and haggle for small gains! I am sick with them and of them.' It was Jinnah who showed more patience than her, trying to get the members to see reason. But in the end, he too had to give up and walk out of the conference. Sarojini, watching helplessly from the sidelines as his Hindu opponents tore into his proposals, felt her heart going out to him, valiant till the last. 'The Delhi session was really Jinnah's session,' she wrote to Chagla after the conference had ended without conclusion. 'His personality dominated both the issues in the Assembly and in the All Parties Conference. Never have I admired him more than now. What dignity and courage in the midst of suffering—what patience, persuasion and real statesmanship he showed during the most trying period of the prolonged conference.'

Sarojini had arrived in Delhi a fortnight in advance of the all-parties conference in order to lay the ground for a consensus, and stayed another ten days while the talks were going on—almost a month without once going back to Bombay at a time when she badly wanted to be there for Ruttie's sake. But as with Jinnah, politics came first and last, with personal work relegated to the crevices of time in between political work and meetings.

The Petits had also come to Delhi, as was their custom every year at this time. In fact, the Delhi 'season' usually began with a grand party they hosted every year. But while they tried to go on as usual, it was clear they were shaken by this second blow from their daughter. They had obviously heard about it before anyone else, possibly from Sarojini who would have undoubtedly been anxious to rope in Ruttie's parents to deal with the crisis before the news got out, even if Ruttie wished to keep them out of it. And Lady Petit at least appears to have lost no time in reaching out to her daughter, even getting Ruttie to agree to join her on a trip to Europe for the summer. But her distress over her daughter's situation, especially her acute alarm over the child who was now living alone with the servants while Jinnah was away in Delhi and Ruttie staying with her cats at the Taj, had put a visible strain on Lady Petit. So palpable was the effect of the shock on her that the next time Sarojini met her, which was at the Petit's gala in Delhi, the usually elegant and very poised Lady Petit looked simply 'terrible', as Sarojini wrote to tell Padmaja the day after the party.

While leaving Bombay, Sarojini had promised Ruttie that she would be back to spend at least the few remaining weeks with Ruttie before she sailed for Europe with her mother. But there was a change of plans at the last moment. News arrived from home that Padmaja, whose health had steadily deteriorated over the past few months despite Sarojini's brisk remonstrations to shake off her weakness, was finally diagnosed with the dreaded tuberculosis. Dr Naidu decided to move her at once to a TB sanatorium in south India until they could somehow arrange the money for an extended treatment in Europe. For Sarojini, who had long abandoned all family duties in service of the national cause, this was a maternal call she could hardly ignore. 'Courage Darling', she wired home directly from the Delhi Council chamber, almost the minute she got the news. And without waiting for the high command to release her from her various duties, Sarojini cancelled all her engagements for the next few weeks and prepared to set off for home at once: 'Returning home soon to look after you and make you well with love and care,' her cable said.

But even in her state of worry for her own daughter, thoughts of Ruttie continued to trouble Sarojini. Knowing how eagerly Ruttie would be awaiting her return from Delhi, Sarojini did not have the heart to go directly to Hyderabad without seeing her. She decided to reroute her train journey to Hyderabad via Bombay 'literally for a day, in case I can't get back to say goodbye before she [Ruttie] sails', as she explained in a letter to Chagla.

There was nothing in Ruttie's appearance at least to make Sarojini anxious. In fact, she seemed vastly improved in looks after the separation. As Sarojini wrote in a brief note to Padmaja from the Taj on the day she arrived, 'Ruttie is looking very lovely again.' There was also a letter waiting from Leilamani, who had recently moved to Lahore to take up a teaching job in a women's college. Referring to Leilamani's complaint about Ruttie continuing to cold-shoulder her because of their old quarrel, Sarojini added: 'Poor Papi is very hurt that inspite of a letter she apparently wrote, Ruttie remains cold and indifferent.' Characteristically, Sarojini left it at that, changing the topic to: 'Ruttie will feel very sad at my not being able to say goodbye to her when she sets out on her journey and her new life of what she calls Freedom.'

Radiantly beautiful as Ruttie had again become, Sarojini nevertheless continued to be concerned about her. All through the activity and bustle of shifting Padmaja to the sanatorium by train and the round of farewells that preceded their departure from Hyderabad, she could not rid herself of a nagging worry about Ruttie. And as soon as she had settled down in the sanatorium with Padmaja, she wrote to Chagla to ask: 'Do you see Mrs Jinnah at all? I am very troubled about her.' And then, as if to reassure herself more than him, she went on to say in the letter dated 2 April 1928: 'I believe in the French poet's saying, *A chacun son infini* [Each to his own infinity] and she will solve her problem in her own headlong way—it is headlong and headstrong—but youth will be served.'

This philosophical tone was certainly an improvement after her earlier frantic attempts to stop the news of the breakup from spreading among their friends. She had even written to Chagla then, cautioning him to keep his mouth shut. 'Be *very* discreet in all your dealings and conversations in regard to the affair that is causing all of us so much concern,' she had written to him on 5 February, four weeks after Ruttie left Jinnah and came to live at the Taj. And to take the sting out of her warning not to gossip, she added kindly: 'I know *you* are very discreet.'

But her main purpose in writing to Chagla from the sanatorium was altogether different. She needed to get in touch with Jinnah urgently before he too sailed for Europe as he had been planning to for some time, though without actually deciding one way or the other. The all-parties conference had ended with no consensus in sight and she knew that no political settlement was possible during his absence. She had left Delhi so hurriedly that she had had no time to even discuss with him which tactic they should now adopt in order to push his proposals through the Congress. 'Please let me know when he [Jinnah] returns to Bombay,' urged Sarojini in her letter, 'and also, should he finally decide to go to Europe, on what date he sails. You know his aversion to writing so you will please do this urgent commission for me.' And to underline the urgency, she added: 'Please wire me if Jinnah has returned.'

As it happened, Jinnah had already returned to Bombay even before Sarojini had written to Chagla. Ruttie had not moved back to South Court during his absence as he had been hoping, thinking perhaps her friends would instil some sense into her. Instead, she had prevailed upon Kanji to help her shift some of her things from South Court to a suite in the Taj, which she rented on a monthly basis, following the example of Sarojini and many others who lived in the hotel. Sticking to the plan she had made with her mother, Ruttie sailed for Europe with Lady Petit on 10 April 1928. Jinnah did not stop her. He could not—or would not—bend to seek a compromise with her. As he later admitted to an old Parsi friend who had been trying to bring them together: 'It is my fault. We both need some sort of understanding we cannot give.'

But the emotional toll of the past three months had left its mark on him. When Sarojini next met him, only twenty days after Ruttie sailed, she could see the change at once. 'Jinnah is looking very thin and aged,' she wrote to Padmaja on 1 May 1928, having just arrived in Bombay after settling her daughter down in the sanatorium.

Four days later, on 5 May, after resisting the idea of a holiday alone, Jinnah, too, had taken off for Europe. The courts had already closed for summer three weeks ago, and his hopes of reaching a historic political settlement with the Congress on the Hindu–Muslim issues had been effectively dashed by the opposition within the Congress; even his talks with the viceroy were useless. Tired of the constant struggle to hold his own while others combined forces to isolate and push him off the political stage, he decided a trip to England might not be such a bad idea, after all. At least, he still had friends in the British government who would perhaps be more amenable to reason.

It was the kind of voyage that he used to enjoy as a bachelor. On board with him were at least three friends—fellow legislator and a former Congress president, Sir Srinivasa Iyengar, another lawyer and politician, Tulsi Goswami, and a young friend he was very fond of, Dewan Chaman Lal, who he had once hired as an editor for the *Bombay Chronicle* and was now in the legislature with him. The three, especially the young and admiring Chaman Lal, were an ample audience for expounding his views on current politics. And while he did talk of nothing but politics on board, engaging even strangers on deck in political conversation, he was clearly not in the best of spirits. In fact, according to Chaman Lal, he cut a very lonely and despondent figure on board.

Midway through their journey, he had a sudden impulse. As Chaman Lal recalled, as the ship approached Port Said, Jinnah remarked that although he had passed through the Suez Canal countless times, either on his way to Europe or back, he had never stopped to see Cairo. Then he came up with a suggestion that was most unlike him. Why not they hire a boat and go to Cairo for the day, returning to the ship the same night before it took off the next morning? There was so much enthusiasm for Jinnah's suggestion, not only among his three friends but other passengers as well, that eventually a very large party set off at the crack of dawn in a fleet of taxis to explore Cairo. It was a trip that Ruttie had always yearned to make with him, travelling to unexpected places and living in a spontaneous way, open to new experiences. But it was Chaman Lal who made that trip with Jinnah, not her.

There were other instances during the same trip in which Chaman Lal began to see the more human side of his great friend.

One memorable moment was when they stopped in the middle of the desert to relieve themselves. As Chaman Lal recounted: 'Suddenly the huge procession of cars stopped. The women went on one side and the men on the other; and we were standing easing ourselves side by side, Jinnah and myself, when a tiny little dog belonging to one of the ladies in this place came along from under the car, gave one look at this tall figure, Jinnah, he thought was a lamppost and started to utilize it for this purpose. Jinnah was as much flabbergasted as anybody!'

Another incident that stayed with Chaman Lal about that unscheduled trip to Cairo had to do with their guide. 'I was riding a donkey and Jinnah a camel, both very appropriate,' Chaman Lal recounted. 'Another Mohammed Ali was our guide, who took us round and suddenly he turned to me and to Jinnah and said, "Sir, you see that kite, he goes up, he goes up and goes up and one day that kite falls. That is the British Empire—goes up, goes up and goes up and one day it falls."' It was a political prophecy that impressed Chaman Lal at least very deeply.

One of the first things that Jinnah did when he landed was to get in touch with Lady Petit. If he was hoping to find Ruttie with her mother, he was in for a disappointment. She had already fled to Paris by herself, even before he reached London. Apparently, her idea of freedom did not include spending a summer alone with her mother. Jinnah had not spoken to Lady Petit since his marriage but it was different now. With her daughter's marriage in trouble and with no Sir Dinshaw to deter her (he had to stay behind in Bombay because of an extended strike in his textile mills), Lady Petit had no difficulty reaching out to her son-in-law. She had anyway always had a soft spot for him, charmed by his old-world courtesies, 'always so gracious to ladies', as her daughter-in-law once told Bolitho. And now with a grandchild she was eager to rescue from her unloved state, she would have seen no reason to keep him at a distance. It was to Lady Petit that Jinnah instinctively turned for both reassurance and news of Ruttie only a few weeks later when he heard that Ruttie was seriously ill in Paris. Later, he would trust her with the child as well, allowing her to go and visit her grandmother as often as she wished.

But for the present he had not yet worked through his anger against Ruttie. And instead of chasing after her to Paris to talk things out with her, he preferred to spend his time visiting men of influence in England and discussing the Indian problem with them, but the discussions were as fruitless as in Delhi. Then, instead of heading for Paris, he put it off some more by taking an extended tour of Ireland, where he hoped to gain some support for boycotting the Simon Commission. It was now four months since Ruttie had left him but he was yet to come to terms with what she had done. And whether it was out of denial or loyalty or just plain bafflement at what it was that she wanted out of him, he refused to talk about it, not even to Lady Petit or Fatima.

In fact, Fatima appears to have had so little idea about the breakup of her brother's marriage that she spent that summer while Jinnah and Ruttie were away searching for dental work outside Bombay. Her life as a single, independent woman had not been a success. In the six years since she graduated from dental college, she had found barely any work, although with Jinnah's help she had opened her own private clinic. But almost no one came to her clinic and she ended up spending the evenings working for free at a municipality-run clinic. With no friends or social life of any sort, her life in Bombay did not seem worth clinging on to, which is why Fatima spent the better part of the summer of 1928 searching for work in Hyderabad, hoping to make a new life for herself.

Once again it was Sarojini who provided all the support Fatima needed, both moral and material. She was, of course, not in Hyderabad to personally oversee Fatima's stay, being away at that time, first at the sanatorium nursing Padmaja and then back in Bombay immersed in political work. But knowing how timid and inhibited Fatima was, she urged her to stay at the Golden Threshold, where Leilamani could take care to see that she was properly fed and entertained while Dr Naidu would do the needful in putting new clients her way for a future practice. And he did, as he wrote to Padmaja on 21 May: 'I saw Fatima Jinnah yesterday and offered her the house and my office for her work during her stay here. I think she can do more business here and be more comfortable than at the hotel. Most begums will hesitate to go to Montgomery's for their teeth.'

Whether she got more work or not, Fatima certainly enjoyed the trip, blossoming under all this care and attention. 'I hear Fatima Jinnah is having quite a gay time in Hyderabad and some customers as well,' Sarojini wrote to Leilamani on 31 May from the Taj. And again on 6 June 1928: 'I hope Fatima will be comfortable and get enough vegetables. Take her out towards Sarurnagar if there is time.' And finally on 12 June, when Fatima left: 'I am glad little Fatima had such a happy time. I don't think ever before in all her life did she have the opportunity to be herself to such a degree. She has always been so repressed.' Adding as an afterthought: 'Did you give Fatima a piece [of snakeskin to make a pair of sandals with]?'

Meanwhile, in Paris, Ruttie with the last restrictions on her freedom finally falling away, was finding it hard to resist that inner void and an aching sort of yearning for the unattainable that she was all too familiar with. Within weeks of moving to Paris, all the aspirations and plans she had made for herself before she sailed from India had evaporated, yielding to an overwhelming urge for self-destruction. She fell sick again from unknown causes and had to be admitted to a private nursing home. When Lady Petit heard and threatened to descend upon her from London, she put her off by pretending that she was getting better.

She, no doubt, would have preferred to drift away like this—in an unknown place, unrecognized by anyone. But the clinic thought differently. Finding her slipping away, a desperate message was sent out to the only Indian acquaintance of hers they could locate in Paris—Dewan Chaman Lal. He had passed through Paris earlier, on his way to Geneva to attend a conference of the International Labour Organization as head of the Indian delegation, and had called on her. At that time, she seemed fine. Like all their friends, he knew about the rift between Jinnah and her, without ever daring to bring it up with either of them. He had always been a great admirer of hers as well as Jinnah's, saying, 'there is not a woman in the world today to hold a candle to her for beauty and charm'. To him, she 'was a lovely, spoilt child, and Jinnah was inherently incapable of understanding her'.

But by the time Chaman Lal returned from Geneva, there was a message waiting for him at his hotel to call at once at the clinic. The message was so urgent that he proceeded to the clinic in the same taxi in which he had arrived at his hotel, stopping only to leave his suitcases.

At the clinic he found Ruttie running a temperature of 106 degrees, and delirious. Chaman Lal does not mention what could have been causing her delirium or the high temperature—was it another suicide attempt? Or perhaps it was not a deliberate attempt to kill herself, but an accidental overdose of morphine? The symptoms could have been anything and Chaman Lal, like all other contemporaries who ever mentioned Ruttie's various illnesses, is silent about it, either out of consideration for her and Jinnah's reputation or what is more likely, genuine ignorance, with the doctors themselves unable to diagnose the many dreadful effects of severe depression on both the mind and the body. All Chaman Lal can say is that she was lying in bed, barely able to move but still holding a book in her hand. When she saw Chaman Lal, she handed the book to him, saying, 'Read it to me, Cham.'

He took the book. It was a volume of Oscar Wilde's poems, opened at 'The Harlot's House'. Ruttie repeated, in a whisper, 'Please read it to me, Cham.' Chaman Lal read aloud Wilde's poem of disillusionment and betrayal, a dozen stanzas about how his beloved was seduced by the tune playing in a whorehouse, leaving him on the street for the soulless men and women inside, pretending to dance and mimicking a life and passion they could not feel. And when he came to the closing lines,

And down the long and silent street,
The dawn, with silver-sandalled feet,
Crept like a frightened girl.

Chaman Lal looked up and found Ruttie had slipped into a coma. After hurrying out of the room to fetch the doctor, he returned to his hotel and put a call through to Jinnah in London. But Jinnah was still in Dublin and it took another two days before he could reach Paris.

Although Jinnah rushed to Paris as soon as he got Chaman Lal's message, his suspicions got the better of him once he reached Paris. He began to grill Chaman Lal, in order to make sure that his friend had not got him there on a false pretext simply in order to mend the breach between himself and Ruttie. As Chaman Lal recounted: 'At the [Hotel] George V, where he stayed, he said to me, "But Lady Petit tells me Ruttie is better." I said: "I have just come from the clinic and it seems to me she, with a temperature of 106 degrees, is dying." He sat still for a couple of minutes, struggling with himself and asked me to telephone the clinic which I did. He spoke to the nurse in charge who confirmed what I had told him. Thumping the arm of his chair, he said: "Come, let us go. We must save her."'

Chaman Lal took him to the clinic and waited outside at a nearby café for nearly three hours. When Jinnah finally emerged from the clinic, 'the anxiety had vanished from his face. He had arranged for a new clinic and a new medical adviser and all was going to be well.' Yet, despite his determination to make her well at any cost, Jinnah was unwilling to delve too deep into what might be driving Ruttie to destroy herself. For the next few weeks, he poured all his self-determination into restoring her health, letting nothing stand in the way. For over a month, he did not leave her side, staying with her at the nursing home, devoting himself to nursing her and even eating the same food as she did, as Ruttie later told Kanji.

But there was an even bigger sacrifice he was making than just sharing her bland food that Ruttie didn't know about. Back at home, his absence was being acutely felt, holding up an exciting new possibility of finally working out a political settlement that all parties could agree upon. In fact, his presence was considered so vital for any political settlement to be reached between Hindus and Muslims that at first many leaders in the Congress suggested adjourning the proceedings of the all-parties meeting until his return. But the younger Congressmen, particularly Jawaharlal Nehru, who had a very low opinion of Jinnah's worth, both politically and personally, insisted that they go ahead with the meetings without him. And with the Nehru Commission formed to draw up a new constitution as a challenge to the Simon Commission, Jinnah began to receive more and more urgent appeals from his friends within the Congress to return home at once to participate in the drafting of the Nehru Report. 'Have you any news of our local Sir John Simon from abroad?' Sarojini inquired of Chagla on 1 July 1928, meaning Jinnah who had been described in a London paper as the 'Indian Sir John Simon'. 'Do let me know if that Sphinx has ever indicated any of his secrets about his plans.' But even the combined entreaties of Sarojini, Chagla and Motilal Nehru could not persuade Jinnah to leave Ruttie in her critical condition to participate in the talks.

Chagla, who had used Jinnah's absence to claim for himself the role of the Muslim League's spokesman and had been enthusiastically participating in the drafting of the Nehru Report, wrote to Jinnah in July urging him to return soon in order to discuss a possible compromise with Motilal Nehru before he presented the report to an all-parties conference that had been called in Lucknow the following month. Adding his urgent entreaty to Chagla's was Motilal Nehru himself. He mailed Jinnah a draft of the report on 2 August, assuring him that the commission was still open to any suggestions he might have, and pressing him to return in time to attend the Lucknow conference beginning on 27 August. And if Jinnah could not make it back by that date, he was still urged to try and reach at least by 29 August evening. One reason why Motilal and others in his committee were so desperate to get Jinnah back to India on time to attend the conference was because they realized that without his support, the report would never be accepted by the majority of Muslims. Right now they were evenly divided into pro- and anti-Nehru Report camps, with the report's recommendation to cut Muslim representation in the central legislature from the one-third that Jinnah had asked for in his Delhi Proposals to just a quarter, the abolishing of separate electorates being particularly unpopular. Motilal was hoping that since Jinnah was such a staunch nationalist and a good friend as well, he would somehow prevail upon Muslims to accept the report as it was. But he disappointed the Congress. As Sarojini astutely observed in a letter to Padmaja on the eve of the conference, on 22 August: 'Poor Ruttie is very critically ill and Jinnah has not been able to come as expected although in his absence the Mussalmans will come to no conclusion!'

Like Sarojini, Jinnah, too, was certain that the Congress could not reach any political settlement without him. He felt sure he could afford to wait to address the political situation until Ruttie was better and they could go home together. But the first blow to his confidence came when Ruttie insisted on going back to Bombay with her mother, without even waiting until she had fully recovered.

She left so suddenly that all their friends, who had assumed reasonably enough that the rift between them was healed, were caught by surprise. Sarojini, who was on her way to America on an extended tour but stopped in Paris for two days only to see 'poor little suffering Ruttie', was surprised to find Jinnah alone. 'I think Jinnah tried very hard to get her to come back,' Sarojini wrote to Padmaja after she arrived in Paris on 10 October, five days after Ruttie's departure, repeating what she had heard from a common friend. 'But Ruttie is, so I am told, beyond all appeal. Her health is still very precarious. But I have had no talk with Jinnah as yet.'

But the next day, when Sarojini did manage to meet him, Jinnah did not want to talk about his personal problems. Instead, they discussed the Nehru Report. He was so pessimistic about the report that Sarojini was convinced that his view was coloured by his personal situation. 'I have had long talks with him in Paris . . . He has had to endure such incalculable personal troubles lately that I do not wonder that he is shaken and uncertain about vital public problems,' she wrote to Chagla on 25 October 1928, on board the ship to America.

Chaman Lal, too, returned to Paris after a few days' absence to find Jinnah alone. He was surprised, having assumed that they were now reconciled, considering that Jinnah had not only taken charge of Ruttie's medical treatment but even moved into the nursing home with her. Wondering what had happened and yet not daring to ask, Chaman Lal finally plucked up the courage after spending the whole day with him to ask Jinnah: 'Where is Ruttie?' Jinnah's answer was curt: 'We quarreled; she has gone back to Bombay.' And, as Chaman Lal writes, Jinnah 'said it with such finality that I dared not ask any more'.

But in fact they had not quarrelled. It had been the tenderest of farewells, at least on Ruttie's part. As she tried to explain in a letter she wrote to him as soon as she boarded her ship to Bombay, 'had I loved you just a little less, I might have remained with you'. And far from responding in the heat of the moment, Ruttie had actually taken time to think over what she would say to him, something that was alien to her spontaneous temperament, trusting as she did wholly to what her instinct produced in words. But now, for the first time in her life, she had torn up the letter she had previously written to him in Paris, writing him a fresh letter after boarding her ship in Marseilles. 'I had written to you at Paris with the intention of posting the letter here (Marseilles, on board the S.S. Rajputana),' as she says in the postscript, 'but I felt that I would rather write to you afresh from the fullness of my heart.'

It was a letter almost frightening in its absence of all hope and future, drained of all life and passion, and yet filled with great tenderness and sorrow, as if her only concern now was how best to protect his 'over-tuned' feelings from the hurt she was about to deliver by deliberately putting an end to their 'tragedy'.

'Darling,' it begins, her bold, clear hand unchanged by the recent weeks of her illness, her words flowing without faltering—only one word in the entire letter scratched out and replaced—'thank you for all you have done. If ever in my bearing your over-tuned senses found any irritability or unkindness, be assured that in my heart there was place only for a *great* tenderness and a greater pain—a pain my love without hurt. When one has been as near to the reality of Life— (which after all is Death) as I have been, dearest, one only remembers the beautiful and tender moments. And all the rest becomes a half-veiled mist of unrealities.'

Even her reproach seems that of a dying woman, all the more terrible because it was drained of all anger or resentment: 'Try and remember me beloved as the flower you plucked and not the flower you tread upon. I have suffered much, sweetheart, because I have loved much. The measure of my agony has been in accord to the measure of my love.'

She ends with what she could have never said to his face, a heart-wrenching plea not to drag her down any more: 'Darling, I love you. I love you—and had I loved you just a little less I might have remained with you. Only after one has created a very beautiful blossom one does not drag it through the mire. The higher you set your ideal, the lower it falls. I have loved you my darling as it is given to few men to be loved. I only beseech you that our tragedy which commenced with love should end with it. Darling, Good night and Goodbye, Ruttie'

A week later, Jinnah boarded the next available steamer for Bombay. There was nothing now to hold him back from the work that was calling to him with increasing urgency. In fact, he did not even wait to land in Bombay before getting down to political business, using his time on board to read and catch up on his mail, including a long-delayed response to Motilal Nehru's letter seeking his support for his committee's report. Jinnah was aware, of course, that his return was being awaited eagerly by both the supporters and opponents of the Nehru Report and that much depended on what he had to say on it. But he had no intention this time, unlike during the Simon Commission's boycott, of rushing into a commitment one way or another, only saying to Motilal in his letter that he had not read through the whole report, and, in any case, 'much water has run down the Hooghly' since its publication.

But even before he disembarked, he faced his first frustration. And unusually for one of his customary iron control, he lost his temper. It was Chagla who became the target of his fury. Having taken his role as the Muslim League's secretary more seriously than Jinnah had intended, Chagla had taken it upon himself to publicly accept the Nehru Report on the League's behalf. He had not thought to consult Jinnah on the matter before going ahead and doing what he thought was right. Jinnah must have read about it in the papers just before Chagla went on board to greet him ahead of the ship docking in Bombay. Jinnah was in his cabin 'in a furious temper'. He shouted at Chagla: 'What right did you have to accept the Nehru Report on behalf of the Muslim League? Who authorized you?' Terrified that Jinnah might contradict him as soon as he landed, consigning all his work to the dustbin, Chagla pleaded with him: 'Please don't rush to the press, and issue a statement rejecting the report out of hand. Listen to what I have to say first, and then decide.' And to his relief, the flash of temper was gone in a moment, and Jinnah was his usual impassive self once more. Clearly, he had no intention of giving in to his feelings and risk ruining the political work ahead. As Chagla later recounted in his memoir, 'After thinking for a moment he said: "All right. I will reserve judgement and we will consider the report at a regular meeting of the League."'

Sarojini had, in fact, anticipated how Jinnah would react, as she wrote in her letter to Chagla on her way to America. 'Tomorrow when you meet your chief after all these months, the first question you will both discuss will inevitably and properly be the Lucknow conference and by the time this letter reaches you, you will have realized all the implications—and dangers if I might use such a violent word—of his general uncertain and pessimistic attitude and his real conviction that things were bungled in his absence in regard to the Muslim rights or demands.'

'But,' she added somewhat more reassuringly, 'I am also sure that with his very quick perception and clear analysis of the situation as it will present itself to him not at the distance of six thousand miles, he will grasp the real issues and revise his impressions . . . and Jinnah who would, I really believe, give his soul to have the Hindu–Muslim question settled must be made to understand that he holds the scales . . . he must be made to realize the terrible responsibility that is his in his unique position and that he must accept the challenge and the opportunity to prove the worth and wisdom of his leadership not as a communal politician but as a statesman of wider vision and indomitable courage.'

Neither his unique position nor the golden opportunity to prove his worth was lost on Jinnah and for the next eight weeks, he plunged into politics again with no time for anything except to work out how best to rally the dispersed Muslim points of view under his leadership and how best to work out a compromise that all sides could agree upon.

Ruttie, on the other hand, had little to distract her from her troubled self. It was true that the lives of nearly everyone she knew of her own age or younger seemed to be falling apart, and suffering from depression or the 'Blue Devil', as common as the flu: Padmaja reduced to invalidism, her dreams of an active life and love crushed; Leilamani struggling to keep afloat as a single woman, teaching in faraway Lahore and getting addicted to drink, like their brother, Ranadheera; while the older brother, Jaisoorya, studying medicine in Berlin, actually admitted himself into a sanatorium to be treated for depression. But at least they had parents who supported them both financially and emotionally. Dr Naidu especially, although living alone in Hyderabad while his family had scattered to various parts of India or abroad, was a pillar of strength, invariably sending words of encouragement along with the gifts of cash that kept each of them going.

With Ruttie, however, her isolation was near-total. As Sarojini put it a few months later, 'She was so utterly defenceless and alone in the midst of the world's plenty.' Her estrangement from her father and brothers had not changed despite her now single status, and the gates of Petit Hall were still barred to her. The only relative who did visit her occasionally was Lady Petit, but since her mother's visits usually left Ruttie feeling even more irritable and depressed, that hardly helped. The only person who could perhaps have lifted her morale was Sarojini, but she, of course, was away on her protracted

tour of North America and would not be back for another six months
at least. But by now it hardly seemed to matter to Ruttie, her spirits
having sunk so low that she did not even care enough to pick up pen
and paper to write to Sarojini. In her despair and numbness, she made
no effort to reach out to Padmaja either. But in any case, Padmaja was
unavailable just then—when she was not lying in bed recovering from
her tuberculosis, she was either thinking of getting a job in Madras or
going to Calcutta to attend the Congress year-end session because she
felt 'a great need for contact with great surging crowds after a year of
utter inaction'.

Only Kanji was still around, putting his home, his time and
occasionally even his wife at her disposal, which the long-suffering
woman did not seem to mind (or if she did, Kanji does not mention
it). He called on Ruttie every day at the house where she was now
living, going there sometimes more than once a day if his busy official
duties permitted. She seems to have moved out of the Taj after her
return from Europe and Kanji's account suggests she settled into an
independent house of her own. Throughout January and February
1929, Ruttie continued to be ill, according to him, and this depressed
her. With so little known about depression then, it did not occur to
him that it might have been the mental agony that was the real cause
of her phantom illness. Watching helplessly as she deteriorated before
his eyes, Kanji tried to lift her spirits as best as he was able. Since
she had stopped going out altogether, he persuaded her to take short
walks with him. He tried to revive her interest in spiritualism and
took his theosophist friends, including J. Krishnamurthy, to visit her,
hoping they would cheer her up. Her guests certainly took to her—in
a letter to Kanji on 30 November 1928, Krishnamurthy repeatedly
hopes Ruttie is very much better and asks Kanji to give her 'my love,
if she will have such a thing from me. Also please tell her that I am
thinking of her constantly.' But somehow, Ruttie's heart was no
longer in spirituality—or anything else for that matter.

Not all Kanji's deep devotion and concern for her could stop her
from sinking further each day into depression, her pain and despair so
overwhelming that only her sleeping pills could provide some relief.
But the pills, the only known barbiturate of that time marketed under
the brand name Veronal, had their lethal side effects which nobody
suspected then—that fatal cycle of dependency and overdose, and

untold damage to liver and other internal organs that was detected only half a century later. Her condition became so precarious that he was afraid to leave her alone even for a few days, taking on his own shoulders all the responsibility for checking on her night and day. Jinnah was there but he may as well have not been. When he was in town he came regularly every evening to see her, but failed to notice how sick she was. For the hour or so that he sat with her, the three of them—Kanji, Ruttie and Jinnah—'kept on talking as in the old times', as Kanji put it. Jinnah's entire time and attention at this time was taken up with meetings and discussions on the Nehru Report, which was coming up for discussion at the all-parties conference called by the Congress in Calcutta. It did not strike Kanji—and certainly not Ruttie—that Jinnah was quite unconcerned about her ill-health. Instead, the mere fact of Jinnah dropping in every day at Ruttie's home for a pleasant chat appeared to Kanji as a clear sign of Jinnah's devotion to her from which he drew the inference that the two would get back together very soon.

As for Kanji himself, he felt so responsible for Ruttie that he did not want to go to Calcutta for the all-parties conference because it meant leaving Ruttie alone for a few days. But his leader, Annie Besant, insisted he come and Kanji had to obey her, setting aside his apprehension.

Surprisingly, when Kanji returned from Calcutta, he found Ruttie much better than when he left her. She looked so much improved that J. Krishnamurthy, who dropped in on her during his next visit to Bombay, thought she would get well soon. Funnily enough, her recovery, although only partial, coincided with Jinnah's collapse, both emotional and physical, immediately after he returned from the all-parties meet in Calcutta. It was as if she had dredged out her waning life force now that he needed her again.

He had had a harrowing time there. After an acrimonious debate that lasted till 2 a.m., the Muslim League at its session in Calcutta finally decided to accept the Nehru Report with six amendments. But the next morning, when Jinnah took the amendments to the all-parties conference called by the Congress, expecting at least a reasonable hearing, he was shouted down and attacked viciously, especially by Hindu Mahasabha associates such as M.R. Jayakar. Instead of discussing the amendments, Jayakar mounted a personal attack on Jinnah, questioning his credentials as a Muslim leader. Even the Liberals who were for accepting the League's amendments were hostile, with Tej Bahadur Sapru, co-author of the Nehru Report, calling Jinnah 'a spoilt child'. But deeply offended as Jinnah was, he still managed to keep a leash on his temper and appealed to the convention again and again—'not as a Mussalman but an Indian'—to accept these small concessions that Muslims were demanding for the sake of unity. And when all his persuasion and conciliatory speech failed to convince the Hindus and Sikhs to accept the amendments, he still appealed to the convention to 'let us part as friends' and avoid 'bad blood'. But it fell on deaf ears, and with Jayakar calling him a 'communal zealot', Jinnah abruptly left the conference.

He was so unnerved by the abuse heaped on him that the next day when he left Calcutta, he broke down and wept. It was the first time anyone had seen him cry. As his friend, Jamshed Nusserwanjee, later told Jinnah's biographer, Hector Bolitho: 'It is a fine thing that he did, pleading as a great man for his people.' Jamshed was referring to Jinnah's role in the conference. 'His demands were rejected. One man said that Mr Jinnah had no right to speak on behalf of the Muslims— that he did not represent them. He was sadly humbled and he went back to his hotel.'

'About half-past eight next morning, Mr Jinnah left Calcutta by train,' Jamshed recounts, 'and I went to see him off at the railway station. He was standing at the door of his first-class coupé compartment, and he took my hand. He had tears in his eyes as he said, "Jamshed, this is the parting of the ways."'

Jinnah did not go back directly to Bombay. He stopped at Delhi to attend the All India Muslim Conference organized by Muslim hardliners. He had no plans initially of attending the conference but after his all-parties failure, he decided to put in an appearance at their open session, raising hopes among the hardliners that they 'had at last won him over to our view'.

But shaken though he was by the way he had been treated in Calcutta, he could not think of crossing over to the hardliners' camp. He returned instead to Bombay, heart-sick. He would have given, as Sarojini said, his soul for Hindu–Muslim unity and instead, he'd just been shown the door again by the Congress. It was in this moment of utter desolation that he once more reached out to Ruttie, needing her at least to talk to and comfort him. Even his health broke down, and it seemed as if he had lost his will to fight back. And, of course, she could not bear to see him like that, summoning all her remaining strength out of sheer force of her will, in order to be there for him. All of January 1929 Jinnah dropped in on her every day, and she unfailingly rose out of her sickbed to receive him, and cheer him up with talk 'like in old times', with Kanji also there to keep the conversation going.

And cheering him up was seemingly good for her as well. Or so Kanji must have thought when he saw Ruttie's renewed interest in people and social life. Hearing that Krishnamurthy was coming to Bombay, she asked Kanji to bring him over for tea. She had not invited anyone over to her house for weeks now. They all had such a good time together that after spending almost two hours at Ruttie's house, Krishnamurthy invited her for dinner the very next day at his host's house. She accepted with alacrity and took Kanji along as well and it was yet another pleasant evening that they spent together.

With this renewed interest in life and people, Ruttie looked, as Krishnamurthy remarked in another letter to Kanji, as if she was getting better. In fact, it was Jinnah who got sick now, something that seldom happened to him. He had become weak enough to force him to skip the opening of the new legislative session. But, of course, with his willpower, he was able to shake it off soon enough. By 6 February 1929, he was back to his usual self, as his telegram to the Muslim League's assistant secretary in Delhi amply demonstrates: 'Thanks am better. Shall reach Delhi soon. Please call Council meeting end Feb. Consult Kitchlew.' Five days later, he was back on the floor of the legislature, the 'Lion of the House' once again, harrying the government with his indefatigable questions, from the racial discrimination in grants of overseas allowance to bank and railways employees to interventions on the trade disputes bill, and ending the day by being chosen to work on the select committee.

But once he left Bombay, Ruttie's will to get better also seems to have vanished and her health began to deteriorate again. She was fine for the first couple of days after Jinnah left for Delhi, even going to the cinema with Kanji and his wife for an after-dinner show. But within a few days of Jinnah leaving and Kanji also getting caught up in other things, Ruttie sank deeper into depression than before.

The Bombay riots were on, as Kanji recounts, and as an honorary magistrate, he had night duty in the outlying Byculla on the night of 16 and 17 February. The next morning, Annie Besant arrived for a day's visit, and Kanji could not go to see Ruttie because he had to receive Mrs Besant at the station. Since Mrs Besant's visits to Bombay were invariably very brief—she usually arrived by the morning train and returned to Madras the same evening—Kanji was expected to spend the entire day with her until she left Bombay. He stayed with Mrs Besant till lunch but after that, when he went home for a short while, Ruttie came there, 'terribly depressed and unhappy'. So Kanji had to spend the next four hours with her in his flat, and eventually he took her back to her place. Mrs Besant had asked him to come in time for tea, and he hoped to keep that engagement. But once she got to her house, Ruttie called him in and made him some tea and he found he could not leave her in 'that condition of terrific depression'. So he skipped the tea appointment with Mrs Besant, something he had never done before, and stayed with Ruttie till seven in the evening, only able to leave her after assuring her that he would be back by 10.15 in the night, after seeing Mrs Besant off at the station.

When Mrs Besant heard what had kept Kanji from meeting her earlier, she understood, telling him to look after Ruttie. But short of admitting her in a hospital, with all its attendant stigma, there was little Kanji could do to save her. By the time he got back, she was almost gone. 'I discovered to my horror that she was unconscious,' Kanji writes in his book on Ruttie, again, like Chaman Lal, maintaining a discreet silence on what clearly appears to be another suicide attempt by an overdose of sleeping pills. He spent the night trying to revive her—perhaps because calling in a doctor without her permission would be taken by Ruttie as a breach of trust—and eventually she woke up. Kanji went home after that, undoubtedly exhausted, but did not get any sleep. Early the next morning, Ruttie was on the phone, asking him to see her on his way to office. She was still 'most depressed', according to Kanji. He tried his utmost to comfort her but it was of no use. Knowing her, it would have been futile for him to suggest calling in a doctor or even her mother. Neither in any case would have been of much help, with her compulsion to kill herself becoming more overwhelming by the hour. As he was leaving, he said: 'I'll see you tonight.' Her reply was ominous: 'If

I am alive. Look after my cats and don't give them away.' He had a dinner engagement that night but his anxiety drove him to visit her after that, reaching Ruttie's house at 11.15 p.m. He found her fast asleep. Instead of being alarmed, he felt relieved and went back home, wanting to catch up on the sleep he had not had for two nights in a row.

But by the next afternoon, Kanji writes, 'I was informed by telephone that she was unconscious again and there was very little hope of her living.' He does not say who gave him the news, whether it was one of her servants or perhaps Ruttie's mother or brother who might have been summoned to the house by the servants when they realized that she was sinking. He went immediately to her house, but either because she had been taken to the hospital or her parents had arrived and taken charge, he could not see her. On the following evening, 20 February 1929—her twenty-ninth birthday—she passed away. There is no medical record stating the official cause of her death, but nearly half a century later, Kanji did come out with the truth. In an interview he gave to an Urdu author close to the end of his life, Kanji unequivocally declared that Ruttie had killed herself by taking sleeping pills that were always by her bedside. 'She chose to die on her birthday,' Kanji told the Pakistani writer, Syed Shahabuddin Dosnani, who met the ageing but very alert Kanji in his apartment in Bombay on 16 February 1968.

It was not Jinnah's practice to call and wish Ruttie on her birthday, or he might have heard sooner. As it was, he was sitting with Chaman Lal in Delhi's Western Court late that evening, unaware of what was going on with Ruttie, when a trunk call was put through to him from Bombay. Chaman Lal heard Jinnah say calmly over the phone that he would leave that night, and then, putting down the phone, he walked towards Chaman Lal, saying: 'Ruttie is seriously ill. I must leave tonight.' There was a pause, after which he said: 'Do you know who that was?' And not waiting for Chaman Lal to speak, answered his own question: 'It was my father-in-law. This is the first time we have spoken to each other since my marriage.'

Chaman Lal suggested that Jinnah leave by the Frontier Mail next morning—because in any case the night train would not get him to Bombay any quicker. Jinnah, all reason as usual, agreed, not knowing until the next morning that Ruttie was already dead. The news was broken to him on the train via the telegram of condolence that came from the viceroy. If he broke down when he was alone in his first-class compartment for the twenty-four hours he spent on the train, no trace of it was visible when he got off at Grant Road station on 22 February morning. Kanji, along with a colonel and Mrs Sokhey, received him at the station and found him his usual self, well fortressed against any talk of a personal nature. Arrangements for the funeral ceremony had already been made while he was on his way from Delhi. The Petits would have liked no doubt to take over and give her a Parsi funeral, at least reclaiming their daughter in death. But that would be at the risk of excommunication of the entire Petit family, according to the ruling of the Parsi panchayat after her marriage. Instead, the arrangements had been turned over to strangers, including a Haji Daudbhai Nasser and Rajab Alibhai Ibrahim Batliwala. The funeral prayers were to be held according to Muslim rites at Pala Galli mosque from where the body was to be taken in a buggy to Arambagh, the Khoja cemetery at Mazagon belonging to the breakaway sect of Khoja Shia Isnaashari Muslims to which Jinnah and his father had affiliated themselves nearly thirty years ago.

To her friends, though, it seemed the ultimate irony of Ruttie's life. 'Irony of ironies,' as Sarojini put it later, 'that Ruttie's beautiful, suffering body should be put to sleep in a Khoja graveyard among Muslims whose days were measured by tape measure and in the scales with silver and copper coins . . .' Kanji must have felt so too, because he brought it up with Jinnah even as they drove off from the station, telling him that Ruttie would have liked to be cremated, not buried. But Jinnah, possibly too numb to care, let them go ahead with the Islamic rites.

The funeral was unusual for the large turnout of ladies and gentlemen from all communities, friends of both Jinnah and Ruttie. Throughout the five hours of the funeral ceremony, Kanji sat beside Jinnah, watching him struggle to keep a tight leash over his emotions, distancing himself by talking only politics. 'Jinnah put up a brave face,' Kanji recounts, 'and after a tense silence, he began to talk hurriedly of his work in the Assembly a week before, and how he helped Vithalbhai Patel, the Speaker, out of the tight corner the latter had got into with [the] Government.' Then, as Ruttie's body was lowered into the grave and he was called as the nearest relative to be the first to throw the earth on her grave, it finally sank in. 'He broke down suddenly and sobbed and wept like a child,' Kanji writes. The emotion lasted only a few minutes and Jinnah was his reserved self once more. But the momentary breakdown left a lasting impression on all those who attended the funeral. Even Chagla, who was fond of taking potshots at Jinnah's cold and unfeeling temperament, was forced to admit that 'there were actually tears in his eyes', saying it was 'the only time when I found Jinnah betraying some shadow of human weakness'.

Reaching home, Jinnah could no longer keep his feelings on hold. He had asked Kanji to meet him at home the next evening and Kanji thought Jinnah probably wanted to know about Ruttie's last days, since Kanji had been with her all the weeks prior to her death. But it was not for this that Kanji had been summoned. Instead, as Kanji writes, 'he screamed his heart out, speaking to me for over two hours, myself listening to him patiently and sympathetically, occasionally putting a word here and there.'

Watching Jinnah break down and weep like that, Kanji had a sudden flash of understanding about his friend that gives a profound insight into Jinnah's very soul: 'Something I saw had snapped in him. The death of his wife was not just a sad event, nor just something to be grieved over, but he took it, this act of God, as a failure and a personal defeat in his life.' Kanji did not know then, or ever, of Ruttie's piteous appeal to Jinnah to 'Try and remember me beloved as the flower you plucked and not the flower you tread on.' Jinnah had no means of escaping from those wounding words now.

And yet, he would not face this biggest defeat of his life, trying to go on in his old work-addicted way. For the week he remained in Bombay after the funeral, he kept himself busy with intensive negotiations, preparing the ground for the Muslim League Council meeting he had scheduled in Delhi for the following week. In an effort to shut off his memories, he packed away everything that reminded him of her—her photographs, her dresses, her beautiful collection of jades, rare objets d'art and first editions—and left Bombay in time for the Muslim League meeting on 3 March. He never mentioned her name or referred to her ever again. But none of this really helped, as Kanji points out: 'He never recovered right till the end of his life from this terrible shock.'

Had he looked into her books before he shut them up into boxes, Jinnah might have discovered even more to torment him. Unlike the books she bought later—light Edwardian comedies of manners, old-fogey husbands struggling with new-age modern wives—these books that she had gathered around her in the last months of her life were all favourites from her girlhood years, plucked from Petit Hall where they must have gathered dust all these years, signed with her maiden name with a fountain pen. It was a curious set of books she chose to plunder from her shelves at Petit Hall—*Eugenie Grandet* by Honoré de Balzac, the story of a young heiress disinherited for marrying the wrong man, for loving him with 'that love which was her doom'; or *Twenty Years After* by Alexandre Dumas, revolving around the leader of the Three Musketeers, D'Artagnan, finding himself very isolated while his friends have moved on, reflecting that he was one of those 'who remain, whether by chance, by bad fortune, or by some natural impediment, stopped mid-way in their course towards the attainment of every hope'. Or another of Dumas's novels in first edition, *Louise de la Vallière* (volume 3 of *The Vicomte de Bragelonne*), with its story of being locked irretrievably in an unhappy relationship.

And some of the margin markings were certainly not of the girl she used to be at twelve or thirteen. On the front page of *The Count of Monte Cristo* (volume 2), for instance, under the 'Rutty D. Petit' written in pencil, is a new marking in fountain pen, saying only: 'Page 720'. And turning to page 720, no one can miss the paragraph highlighted with a line drawn down its entire length, not once, but six or eight times. It reads: 'You have spoken truly, Maximilian, according to the care we bestow upon it, death is either a friend who rocks us gently as a nurse, or an enemy who violently drags the soul from the body. Some day, when the world is much older, when mankind will be masters of all the destructive powers in nature, to serve for the general good of humanity; when mankind, as you were saying, have discovered the secrets of death, then that death will become as sweet and voluptuous as a slumber in the arms of your beloved.' Why was this 'Blue Flower' he had plucked only ten years ago yearning so desperately for death? It was not a question that Jinnah would ever want to face.

It meant looking deep into the dark corners of his own heart and confronting the truth. How did he 'tread upon' this Flower he had plucked, just as she had accused him of? How much of it was to be blamed on his own harsh intransigence, chipping away at her self-worth and pushing her further down the spiral of her dreadful disease of despair and anguish? Or was that only one small part of the inexorable train of circumstances? First had come her exile from her family and community for marrying him, losing everything, including her inheritance and identity. Then came the second exile, more terrible even than the first because it condemned them to stand apart, hated and reviled, only because he refused to follow Gandhi blindly. Finally, so much more vulnerable than him, without his carefully built-up defences, Ruttie had become prey to her own mind's darkness. Yet, somewhere in his fortressed imperviousness, her reproach in that last letter must have pierced him, for he did confess to a friend's wife, many years later: 'She was a child and I should never have married her. The fault was mine.'

Her friends, too, struggled with the guilt and pain, trying to make sense of it all—sometimes in vain, as in Padmaja's case. She had not been in touch with Ruttie for months but, as she wrote in a letter to Chagla, 'though we were so utterly different in every way imaginable, we were very close to each other and between us was a bond of understanding that had long ago grown beyond all need of speech'. And on the night that Ruttie died, Padmaja recounts in the letter, 'I was seized with such a terrible restlessness and fear that I could not sleep or even lie down and I spent the whole night wandering alone in the garden thinking of Ruttie and shaking with a nameless fear to which I had no clue until I heard twenty-four hours later of Ruttie's death. By that time I was myself very ill having caught a terrible chill in the garden.'

Four months after Ruttie's death, Padmaja was still lying in bed, worn out in body and spirit by her loss. 'I have not yet grown reconciled to it,' she writes in a letter to Chagla dated June 1929. 'It is foolish and futile I know and yet somehow I resent it still. It is not that I fear Death for those I love—Death can be a very beautiful and merciful thing I know and I have been praying every moment for the last two months that it may come to a dear, dear friend of mine who is in agony—but in Ruttie's case I am bitter because it seems like the wanton destruction of a beautiful thing that was still unfulfilled. What a tragedy of unfulfillment Ruttie's life has been—she was so young and so lovely and she loved life with such passionate eagerness, and always life passed her by leaving her with empty hands and heart.'

Sarojini, too, was in extreme shock when she first heard the news. It took her almost a month to find out, with her family and friends shielding her from the truth because she was so far away on her American lecture tour. But the news did eventually reach her, 'casually over the telephone, told me by someone as a piece of Indian news just come by the mail that "Jinnah's wife" had died', as Sarojini put it in a letter to Padmaja from New York on 19 March 1929. 'He did not know that it was not Jinnah's wife but someone unutterably dear and cherished.' The shock was so severe that it felt 'as if the sun and the springtime had suddenly died out of the world'. But like Jinnah, she belonged to a generation where work came before feelings, always: 'And yet, I had to go on into crowds and speak when all my thoughts and tears were around a grave in a Muslim graveyard.'

But work could not distract her from her grief, as she says in the letter: 'For the first time since I came to the New World have I felt desolate and deserted with an overpowering sense of weariness, loneliness and pain. I did not know that one lovely face hidden in the ground with the earth lying heavy upon its beauty would or could hurt me and cripple all my life forces like this. When Umar died, it was a deep sorrow that cannot be forgotten. But with Ruttie dead, it is as if some intimate, integral part of oneself had gone into the Great Silence.'

Like her daughter, Sarojini, too, felt a strong sense of foreboding on the day of Ruttie's twenty-ninth birthday. 'Strangely enough, on the very day she died I was overcome with a dreadful sense of foreboding and loss. But I resisted my insane impulse, as it seemed, to cable and find out if all were well. It was not an insane impulse. It was the instinct and foreknowledge of love, because I loved little Ruttie with a strange passion of protection . . .' Sarojini says in the letter.

And yet, under the protective passion, Sarojini could still be harsh in her judgement of Ruttie, holding her somehow to blame for her own destruction. Death was the only way out for Ruttie, as Sarojini wrote to Padmaja, trying to console her: 'Somehow I suppose life will not be the same again. Out of the day and night a joy has taken flight—and yet, I know that there was no other solution to her problem. Death was the sole, the supreme compassion for that broken life, for the shattered body, that clouded mind, those ruined and degraded nerves that had become the victims of every poison that could destroy the fineness, the nobility, the lucidity, the loveliness of the once radiant spirit. Had she lived, it would have been both unspeakable grief and maybe unspeakable shame too for those who loved her. She could not have been salvaged from the causes and effects of her own folly and fantasy of life. Far better for her and for all who loved her that she should pass out on the high crest of her youth, and be remembered for what she really was—beyond and behind the clouds that had begun to throw the sinister shadows across her soul. For the shadows had already begun to gather and grow two years ago. And last year, when I came to you at Arogyavanam, there was already doom written upon every line of her being—poor fatal child.

'But in the midst of such unhappiness, disillusion, suffering, the extravagance of her caprice, her wayward and stubborn self-destruction, she was a spirit of flaming beauty and purity. In her there was nothing intrinsically small or mean or unclean. She had valour and vision, magnanimity, loyalty and a passionate sense of truth and incomparable tenderness towards dumb things.

'Let us remember her always as that radiant spirit of delight, unstained by a single shadow, unsullied by a single flaw which after all were incidental and not integral parts of the Ruttie we loved and the Ruttie who loved us. You she loved with a deep, clinging love that held in it trust and admiration and a soul of worship for the beauty of your spirit. Let us offer a prayer of thanksgiving for the supreme compassion of her death. Her body will become dust but for you and me she will be a flame of gold and an illumination of immortal loveliness.'

She ends her long letter with: 'Goodnight my darling. I have yet to write to her mother, her husband and her child—but we loved her more than they and knew her better.'

In the following week, Sarojini found out more to reinforce her conviction that death was the only reprieve for Ruttie's troubled life: 'Today I was lunching with Princess Journevitch, whose husband is a famous Russian sculptor,' Sarojini wrote to Padmaja from New York on 25 March 1929. 'In the course of lunch she casually mentioned having known a Madam "Zhinna" four years ago in Paris and how she was ruining her life with drugs and how all her beauty was being destroyed. And how she had heard that Madame Zhinna was in Paris very ill and separated from her husband. But what would you? said the Princess. And when I told her that "your friend is dead", she said "La! La! Of course. The long needle . . ." I was startled. But Syud Hossain tells me that when the poor little thing was in America it was the same and he spoke to her very seriously. And a dear old lady here Mrs Fud who admired her beauty said there was death already on her face. Well! As Cousins said to me only last night, "I think it is the mercy of God." "Why?" I asked. "Sarojini Devi, when we saw her in Kashmir something had already broken in her brain." Poor little child. If all the world knew, it was better for her to have passed away into the Silence in the spring time. In a little while people will remember only the beauty and radiance and not the gathering cloud and shadow upon that beauty and radiance . . .

'It was as long ago as 1920 mad Mrs Harker foretold her sudden death either on her 28th or 29th birthday. I had forgotten that prophecy but how strange and true it was! I wonder if she has found all her beloved dogs and cats awaiting her coming in the world to which she has gone—Nere, Dono, Loafer, Zippie—it would be so lonely for her without them.'

By the following week, Sarojini had come to terms with her own guilt and pain and loss, ending her mourning process. 'For the last fortnight I haven't slept, since I heard in such a crude and casual manner about little Ruttie's death—but I have now realized that it *was* indeed a release from all the many forces of bondage she endured by the very fact of being alive,' she wrote to Padmaja on 30 March 1929 from Pennsylvania, USA. 'Somehow she seems very near and I have now faith that she is happy and *sane* . . . she had departed from all sanity on earth long ago but now I know that she is *herself* in that region of liberty once more a brilliant flame and not a broken and flickering ember of a bright and shattered fire. It will be very sad for me to return to Bombay and find no Ruttie . . .'

Strong as ever, she was able to console her still-grieving daughter: 'Darling, I know how much you have felt her death and yet you must realize that she *could not* stay. There was nothing for her to cling to because she herself had not the power to hold on to anything. And so it is best that she has gone back to the first Light of spring. There are two cats in the house, for all the world they reflect of Ruttie's grey cat and black cat. But not so beautiful as Ibn-e-Shapur, on whom be peace!'

A lover of nature and all good things on earth, for Sarojini there was always some cure at hand for her sorrow. In Pennsylvania, as she wrote the next day to her younger son, Ranadheera: 'I am staying with a lovely woman. Her house is 12 miles from Philadelphia set in a wood and bordered by a river. And today the woods held a real celebration of beauty. It has brought me great refreshment. I was *so* worn out after the shock and sorrow of Ruttie's death. But now I am no longer sad. I *know* she has found deliverance and is at rest.'

And again the following week, in a letter to Padmaja on 7 April 1929 from Montreal, Canada: 'There is the radio playing—all the way from New York comes the music upon the waves of air. What is distance, what is the menace of sea and land to the conquering force of knowledge. And by the same token it is wondrous and yet how proper and natural that one does not realize the menace of death or the challenge of distance when one lives truly and with understanding. So darling you are very very close to me, closer than the music that comes across so many hundreds of miles . . . and now little Ruttie is even nearer to me than she was in life when her poor lonely pitiful hands and heart clung to me for affection and shelter—from life, from *herself* most of all, poor little Ruttie!'

But there was one more shock in store. Stopping in England on her way back to India, she met an acquaintance—two, in fact—who confirmed what a psychic in New York had told her about Ruttie's death. 'But nothing amazes me any more really,' Sarojini wrote to Padmaja on 6 May 1929 from Lyceum Club, Piccadilly, 'since a woman I met in New York told me—not knowing my name or anything else about me—a reclusive woman—that a young friend of mine had suddenly passed away lately *having after much preliminary consideration taken an overdraught of a sleeping draught and left a letter to say so . . . and that I would know of it after leaving the States.* And last night Lady L [illegible] told me and today [illegible] guardedly corroborated the fact that poor little Ruttie had taken an overdraught of veronal! And almost to the letter what Lady L told me . . . it was all inexplicable.' Sarojini did not forget to remind her daughter to be discreet about what she had just passed on: 'But, darling, you realize of course that this is not the official version.

I suppose there was no other end possible . . . poor mad little suffering child. Maybe she'll find the peace that she was denied—or denied herself on earth . . .'

But she need not have worried about the gossip getting around. By the time Sarojini reached Bombay, five months had elapsed since Ruttie's dramatic end and no one seemed to care to even talk about it. Sarojini herself was instantly plunged into political activity, dragged against her inclination to Allahabad on Congress committee work. 'This is the *first* moment since I arrived the day before yesterday that I am actually alone and able to write a line to you,' she wrote to Padmaja on 24 July 1929 from the Taj in Bombay. 'You can understand that I have been literally *drowned* since I returned in floods upon floods of welcome letters, telegrams and the aftermath of all the communal quarrels that have broken out during my absence. I wanted to revolt against Congress and not go to Allahabad but the combined appeals from Panditji [Motilal Nehru] and [M.A.] Ansari are more than I can resist. Not because of the stupid AICC but because of the Hindu–Muslim situation. I don't want to go but I must and so I am going tonight.' Adding: 'Of course the day I arrived I went and saw Ruttie's grave and put all my garlands upon it. She is not under that mound of earth. You can begin laying down a red rose plant to be placed among the other flowering plants round her grave. She loved red roses.'

It was a whole month later before she met Sir Dinshaw and Lady Petit. They had aged visibly since she last saw them a year ago. As Sarojini wrote to Padmaja in her letter of 22 August 1929: 'I am sending you a photograph of Ruttie which Lady Petit has given me for you with a special inscription. I saw her for the first time today as she has been away. She is old and perfectly white-haired. The old man is an even more pitiful sight and he broke down when he saw me quite frankly. Lady Petit was very pleased when I said you were going to send a red rose tree from our garden for Ruttie's grave.'

Two days later, she left for Simla on her political work, where she met Jinnah and Fatima, who had moved in with her brother. 'Jinnah and Fatima dined here last night,' she writes in her letter dated 24 August 1929 (from Mount Stewart, Simla). 'Jinnah looked very worn and gray but Fatima full of society and new clothes and self-assurance living with her brother.'

Despite looking so worn, Jinnah was resolved to carry on as before, firmly shutting out all memories of Ruttie. But there was a part of him that had changed forever, and the next time Sarojini met him in Bombay, he surprised her by exposing a new side of him. 'Jinnah has acquired three magnificent dogs of the special breed that Paleale [illegible] produces,' she wrote to Padmaja on 1 September 1929, from the Taj, Bombay. 'He has come up with idiotic names like Edith, Assie and Montford. How Ruttie would have adored them! But Jinnah seems to have taken heartily to them himself and I think it will humanize him!'

But he did not go with her to visit Ruttie's grave. Returning from the Congress session in Lucknow, Sarojini made another trip to the Khoja cemetery in Mazagon, this time carrying the special rose bush Padmaja had sent from Hyderabad to be planted there. 'Yesterday I visited Ruttie's grave to take your rose-tree and put it near her head,' she wrote to Padmaja on 21 October 1929. 'Dr Masson went with me. It's been eight months exactly since she passed away. I miss her terribly, now and more I think as time goes by.'

Curiously enough, the child is not mentioned anywhere in either Sarojini's correspondence or that of her daughters for almost another year. This may have had something to do with Lady Petit stepping in and taking charge of the child, now nine, and suggesting to Jinnah that since he was mostly away in Delhi or Simla, she would be better off in a boarding school than at home alone. She even recommended the right convent school for her in the nearby hill station of Panchgani, where all Bombay's fashionable families sent their children. Jinnah not only submitted docilely to her suggestions, but was relieved to have the decision taken out of his hands, trusting Lady Petit henceforth with all major decisions regarding the raising of his only daughter. Although Lady Petit had not met her granddaughter till Ruttie's separation from Jinnah, the bond between grandmother and granddaughter was close and lasting. Still nameless, the child decided on her own to take her grandmother's name, Dina. And to this day, Dina tells her friends of how much she loved her grandmother and her deep gratitude for the way 'she took over completely and brought me up' after her mother's death.

By the following year, when Leilamani visited Panchgani and went to see her at her boarding school, Dina appears to have happily settled into her new life. On her first visit to the school, Leilamani could not meet Dina. 'Dina Jinnah is away for a couple of days but I will surely see her before I go or else have her here to spend the day,' Leilamani wrote to Padmaja on 9 September 1930 from Rasheed Manzil, Panchgani, the summer home of a family friend, Lady Abbas Ali Baig. The following week, on 15 September, in a postscript to another letter to Padmaja, she adds: 'Dina Jinnah spent the day here yesterday. She makes me nervous to look at her cos she's so much like Ruttie.'

But in temperament, Dina was nothing like her mother. Instead of killing herself trying to break through the icy walls of her father's reserve, Dina very soon learnt how to handle her 'Pop' without looking for anything more than he could give her. He was an indulgent father, denying her nothing except his time and of himself, but she did not seem to mind, describing him later in her life as 'affectionate but undemonstrative'. Two years later, when he moved to England with Fatima and set up home in Hampstead, Dina, too, moved with him but not to live at home with them. He had found a small private school for her in Sussex, run by a Mrs Frances Browne, where she quickly settled down, spending five happy but academically unsuccessful years—she failed the school certificate examination but learnt 'some self-reliance and poise'—until she had to leave suddenly, much to her distress, because the school abruptly closed down on account of Mrs Browne's health and financial problems.

But while Dina was at Mrs Browne's, she did spend her holidays with her father, who if he did not give her time, did give her the freedom to tease him. Dina took to calling him 'Grey Wolf' because of a book he was much taken with around this time—*Grey Wolf: An Intimate Study of a Dictator* on the life of Mustafa Kemal Ataturk. The story of Ataturk, born around the same time as Jinnah and rising from similar circumstances to create an independent Turkey, resonated so deeply with Jinnah that he could talk of nothing else but Ataturk for days and he even thrust the book on Dina, who at thirteen knew her own mind. She began chafing him about his passion for Kemal and nicknamed him 'Grey Wolf', and then 'cajole[d] him into putting a brief aside, with the plea, "Come on, Grey Wolf, take me to a pantomime; after all, I am on my holidays."'

But that was about the only time in their life that he had the leisure to bond with her in whatever limited way. When they returned to India, Jinnah having sold his house in Hampstead and wound up his practice in London, he was again full of his great mission, and she was relegated once more to the margins of his life, allowed to do as she pleased, so long as she did not distract him at his work. At fifteen, alone at home with an aunt she did not get along with and no one to talk to except the servants, she spent her time visiting her grandmother, often staying overnight. Sir Dinshaw had died while they were in England, removing the last of any restrictions that Lady Petit might have had in receiving her granddaughter in her home. And when Dina was not at her grandmother's, she was out shopping— 'roamed from one shop to the other for hours'. When she returned, Fatima used to take the driver aside to find out where she'd been and what she had bought. But Jinnah let her do as she pleased and spend as much money as she liked, his only restriction being to try and stop her from driving the car, which she did on the sly.

The only time father and daughter had a falling out was when she announced her decision to marry Neville Wadia, born into a Parsi family and heir to a fortune in textile mills, who had converted to Christianity. To have his only child marry a Parsi Christian would be a serious political embarrassment for Jinnah, and he tried to dissuade her. But finding her adamant, he then threatened to disown her. Instead of relenting, it only made her more stubborn and she moved into her grandmother's home, determined to go ahead with the marriage even at that cost. He collapsed under the emotional strain, succumbing to one of his rare bouts of sickness. 'For two weeks,' one of his drivers later recounted to Urdu writer Saadat Hasan Manto, 'he would not receive visitors. He would just keep smoking his cigars and pacing up and down in his room. He must have walked hundreds of miles in those two weeks.'

But soon he was back in control. 'After two weeks he resurfaced,' the driver said. 'There was no sign of grief on his face, nor any tension.'

But something about this quarrel with his daughter seems to have reopened his old wound which he still refused to examine. At such times, the only thing that gave him some relief, according to the driver, was to 'ask for a certain metallic chest to be brought to his room and unlocked'. It was full of Ruttie's clothes. 'The clothes would be taken out and sahib would gaze at them without saying a word. His gaunt, transparent face would become clouded. "It's all right, it's all right," he would say, then remove his monocle, wipe it and walk away.'

But there was no walking away for him, ever. In fact, according to Kanji, her death left such a deep wound that he changed completely, turning from a 'cheerful, pleasant and social friend with a dry sense of humour' to someone 'egocentric and sensitive to criticism'. He reacted to his wife's death so severely that he not only never mentioned her name ever again, but became so bitter that 'he could not stand abuse, ridicule, misunderstanding and misrepresentation of his actions and never forgave those who, unwisely and unjustly indulged in them'. It was Jinnah's bitterness, born out of his personal loss and disappointment, which travelled into his political life. 'This, I feel,' writes Kanji, 'is the correct analysis of Jinnah's political bitterness which lasted throughout the nineteen years he lived after his wife's death, and influenced his political life and opinions.' If Ruttie had been alive, Kanji was convinced, Jinnah would never have turned communal. Chagla, while agreeing to a certain extent—that Ruttie 'kept Jinnah on the right track so long as she was alive'—goes one step further in his memoir by holding Fatima at least partly responsible for Jinnah's transformation. 'She [Fatima] enjoyed Jinnah's diatribes against the Hindus, and if anything, injected an extra dose of venom into them.'

It was true, of course, that Jinnah leaned on Fatima for everything—even while playing billiards, according to the driver who spoke to Manto. Whenever Jinnah felt the urge to play this only indoor sport he enjoyed, Fatima had to come into the room with him to watch him play. 'If the shot went through as planned, he would smile triumphantly at his sister.'

But even Fatima was powerless when it came to influencing Jinnah's opinions. Once his mind was made up, as Chagla himself points out elsewhere, nothing in the world could divert him from his chosen objective: 'No temptation, no bribe, no pressure had the slightest effect.' He had taken up the cause of the Muslims as his mission and stopped only after he won. The effects of what he had done only sunk in later. Jinnah wept when he saw the refugees in the country he had just created almost single-handedly. But the tears were less for the refugees than for what he had just done—destroyed yet again that which he loved the most.

Acknowledgements

~

This book would probably have never seen the light of day without the generous and selfless help that I gratefully accepted from innumerable friends, and strangers who became friends in the four years it took in its making. I could not have begun, first of all, without the passion and diligence of Padmaja Naidu who spent the last years of her life building up the Nehru Memorial Museum and Library, and had the foresight and imagination to collect and preserve her family's vast and lively correspondence, a treasure trove of rich source material, and put it at the disposal of the curious in the NMML archives.

I owe much also to Ameena Saiyid for her generous hospitality, and for making my month-long research visit to Pakistan both joyful and productive, putting me in touch with anyone and anything of use to me in my pursuit of the elusive Jinnahs, and overwhelming me with lists of contacts and books. Among the many friends who translated from Urdu and put books and papers my way were the staff of the Karachi University Library and the Quaid-i-Azam Academy, Karachi, besides the librarian of the *Dawn* newspaper. Among the many authors and scholars on Jinnah who shared of their valuable time and knowledge, my special thanks to Sharif al Mujahid, Khwaja Razi Haider, Riaz Ahmad and Naeem Qureshi.

In Bombay, Cyrus Gazdar was tireless in helping me track down elusive persons from the Parsi community and for magically opening doors that were firmly closed to me, and Syloo Mathai for shedding some light on Ruttie's family tree and background. The librarian of the Cama Oriental Institute was of invaluable help in locating material on the Parsis. Sunita Narain and Wendy of the *Taj* magazine were also of help in pulling out books from their archives and copying files for me. In Hyderabad, a temple trustee helped me locate Padmaja Naidu's forgotten papers and photographs, gathered in a cloth bundle and locked up in a dusty cupboard inside a dharmashala in a *sabji mandi*.

Nor would this book have been possible without Khushwant Singh, friend and mentor and indefatigable nagger, and Vinod Mehta, who until the end, did not allow me to lose hope or cut corners. And equally impossible without my editor, Ranjana Sengupta, the deftest of midwives whose searching questions enabled me to look deeper, and Shanuj V.C., who kept me from panicking with his calm competence. Thank you, both.

This book owes a lot too to the unwavering support of my sisters, Usha, Asha and Shobha, whose love and faith carried me through, and my cousin Malini in Bombay for sending me off every morning to do my research with a packed tiffin box, and Madhavan, who thought the book was a good idea worth pursuing, and Ruchira for her prayers.

Most of all, thank you to my daughter Minna for believing that I could write this book, no matter how despairing I got, and her partner, Kian, for holding my hand through countless late-night computer disasters.

Notes

~

Chapter One

Details of Sir Dinshaw Petit's ancestry and family history and wealth, from *Memoir of Sir Dinshaw Manockjee Petit—First Baronet* by S.M. Edwardes (printed by Frederick Hall at the Oxford University Press, 1923).

Ibid for the history of Petit Hall with photographs.

An account of Sir Dinshaw's private estates and portrait of his son and heir in *Dropping Names* by Manohar Malgonkar (New Delhi: Roli Books, 1996).

Sir Dinshaw's resume, including business, year of marriage and accession to title, charitable works and membership to clubs, from *Indian Year Book 1930*.

Lady Petit's family tree and history, from *Jamsetjee Jeejeebhoy: The First Indian Knight and Baronet* by Jehangir R.P. Mody (published by Jehangir R.P. Mody, Bombay, 1959), and monograph on his successors at the K.R. Cama Oriental Institute, Mumbai.

Jinnah's role in the famous 'Extortion Case' filed by Sir Dinshaw (before he succeeded his grandfather to the title) is taken from *The Works of Quaid-i-Azam 1893–1912*, vol. 1, edited by Riaz Ahmad (published by 'Chair on Quaid-i-Azam and Freedom Movement', 2002).

Ibid for Sir Dinshaw's alleged vanity, on which a British member of the Bombay municipal committee had this to say on the witness stand: 'I think it was vanity. Sir Dinshaw felt slighted because we asked the eldest sons of Sir Jamsetjee and Sir Jehangir Cowasji first (to join the British-approved list of representatives for the municipal elections). Sir Dinshaw would have gladly joined if we had asked him earlier.' Cited in 'Justices' Election Case—Three Petitions (17 March–6 May 1907)', *Bombay Gazette Summary*.

Sir Dinshaw Eduljee Wacha's comments on Sir Dinshaw Petit, from *Enduring Legacy—Parsis of the Twentieth Century*, edited by Nawaz B. Modi (published by Nawaz B. Modi, 2005).

Sarojini Naidu's remarks on Petit Hall, from her letters dated 3 and 15 March 1917. Sarojini's correspondence found in *Padmaja Naidu Papers* in Nehru Memorial Museum and Library (NMML) archives.

Sir Dinshaw's schooling at the Fort High School, Bombay, finds mention in *Representative Men of the Bombay Presidency* (published by C.B. Burrows).

On the navjot ceremony among modern Parsis, Sarojini Naidu's comment in her letter of 9 March 1917 is illustrative: 'Tomorrow there is a friend's Navjot ceremony for his little daughter [and] the whole world seems invited, about 800 people!'

Details of R.D. Tata's marriage to French Soonibai are noted in *Beyond the Last Blue Mountain: A Life of J.R.D. Tata* by R.M. Lala (New Delhi: Viking, 1992).

Court case filed by Dinshaw Petit on the right to conversion is cited in *Zoroastrianism in Judgements—Petit vs Jeejeebhoy 1908* (Mumbai: Parsiana Publications, 2005).

Account of Jinnah's marriage proposal, from *Roses in December: An Autobiography* by M.C. Chagla (New Delhi: Bharatiya Vidya Bhavan, 1973).

Chapter Two

All quotes of Kanji Dwarkadas on Jinnah and Ruttie in this chapter are taken from his *Ruttie Jinnah: The Story of a Great Friendship* (published by Kanji Dwarkadas, 1963).

Jaisoorya Naidu's comments on Ruttie are from his letters of 19 August 1917 and 30 December 1917 to Padmaja Naidu, found in *Padmaja Naidu Papers* (NMML archives).

Sarojini Naidu's description of Jinnah, from *Mohomed Ali Jinnah, An Ambassador of Unity: His Speeches and Writings 1912–1917* (Madras: Ganesh & Co., 1918).

From K.H. Khurshid's *Memories of Jinnah* (Karachi: Oxford University Press, 1990). The episode about the hot-water bottle appears in the same as told to him by Jinnah as happening to a fictitious young man newly arrived in England.

In response to a question if he had once acted on the English stage, Jinnah 'stretching his long legs to the full limits of comfort, said smilingly in slow, measured and dramatic tones, as always: "Yes I know that part of my life has been widely publicized but the real truth about it is not told yet."' Quote taken from *Jinnah and His Times* by Aziz Beg (Lahore: Allied Press, 1986).

Sarojini Naidu's letter to Chagla, from *Sarojini Naidu: Selected Letters* by Makarand R. Paranjape (New Delhi: Kali for Women, 1996).

Horniman's defamation case, from *Bombay Chronicle*, 2 April–11 May 1916, cited in *The Works of Quaid-i-Azam Mohammad Ali Jinnah 1916–1917*, vol. 3, edited by Riaz Ahmad (published by 'Chair on Quaid-i-Azam and Freedom Movement', 1997).

Ruttie's letters and poems, from the Padmaja Naidu and Leilamani Naidu papers (NMML archives).

Details of Sarojini's marriage and courtship, and Edmund Gosse's quote, from *Sarojini Naidu: A Biography* by Padmini Sengupta (Bombay: Asia Publishing House, 1966).

From the Oral History Transcript of K.L. Gauba (Account No. 76, NMML archives).

On the appropriate age for girls to switch over to saris, Sarojini writes to her girls, aged fifteen and a half and thirteen, on 13 May 1916 (from the *Padmaja Naidu Papers* in the NMML archives): 'I hope you girls will wear your saris for every big occasion like the Fancy Sale and the Prize-giving.'

Ruttie's books with marking in pencil from Jinnah's collection, now in the Karachi University Library.

Chapter Three

For Jinnah's undisputed position as the foremost leader of Congress, see, among other newspaper reports, Gandhi's speech at the Bombay provincial conference proposing Jinnah for president of the conference because he was 'the right man for the right post' and the editorial in the *Bombay Chronicle* of 23 October 1916 (cited in *The Works of Quaid-i-Azam 1916–1917*).

Sarojini Naidu's letter to Padmaja, dated 19 May 1916, from the *Padmaja Naidu Papers*, in the NMML archives.

On the random education given to girls even from rich and progressive homes, *The Scope of Happiness: A Personal Memoir* by Vijaya Lakshmi Pandit (New York: Crown Publishers, 1979) is insightful: '. . . there was no supervision and no plan. Studies were haphazard, and because there was no competition they were also rather dull. Beginning with a governess, lessons were later conducted by a series of tutors . . . I knew more than the average school-going child of my age, but there were subjects with which I had only the slightest acquaintance. The mental discipline which a formal education imposes was lacking and I am always conscious of what I missed.'

Some of Hamabai Petit's biographical details and that of her husband, Jehangir K.B. Mehta's, from *Parsi Who's Who*.

On Hamabai Petit's riding prowess, see Sarojini Naidu's letter to Padmaja on 15 March 1917 from Petit Hall (*Padmaja Naidu Papers*, NMML archives). In the same letter: 'Ruttie has gone out to her ride. She rides astride and looks very nice in her habit.'

Jinnah is quoted in Gauba's oral history transcript (Account No. 76, NMML archives) as saying: 'Gauba, I am a Rolls Royce. Anybody who wants a Rolls Royce must pay the price of a Rolls Royce.'

Kanji's reminiscences of the two Miss Petits on the train to Lucknow accompanied by senior Parsi barrister D.N. Bahadurji are based on *Ruttie Jinnah: The Story of A Great Friendship*.

A somewhat garbled version of Hamabai's first meeting with Jinnah in Nice appears in *In Quest of Jinnah: Diary, Notes and Correspondence of Hector Bolitho* (Oxford: Oxford University Press, 2007), edited by Sharif al Mujahid. In the introduction, Mujahid writes that Hamabai was doing her baccalaureate in Nice along with her 'younger sister' Ruttie (who, being seventeen years her junior, was not even born when Hamabai was in school), and that they both met Jinnah at the railway station in Nice while Jinnah was on his way to England to appear before the Privy Council in 1913.

The incident of the coachman threatening Jinnah is cited in the *Bombay Gazette* of 17 November 1906; it's reproduced in *The Works of Quaid-i-Azam Mohammad Ali Jinnah* 1893–1912, vol. 1, edited by Riaz Ahmad.

The description of a railway station in British India is from *Inside India* by Halide Edib (New Delhi: Oxford University Press, 2002).

The reception to Jinnah when he arrived in Lucknow as president-elect of the All India Muslim League (AIML) is narrated in the *Bombay Chronicle* of 25 December 1916, and reproduced in *The Works of Quaid-i-Azam 1916–1917*, vol. 3, edited by Riaz Ahmad.

Aziz Beg in *Jinnah and His Times: A Biography* (Lahore: Babur and Amar Publications, 1986) gives an account of how Jinnah got his first Turkish cap and wore it throughout the Lucknow session.

Sarojini Naidu's letter to Syed Mahmud, dated 28 April 1918, in *Sarojini Naidu: Selected Letters* edited by Makarand Paranjape.

'Here [at the Lucknow session] Jinnah was observed travelling in Sir Dinshaw Petit's car with Lady Petit [*sic*] and Ruttie, who was present throughout the conference,' writes Khwaja Razi Haider in *Ruttie Jinnah* (Karachi: Oxford University Press, 2010).

Khwaja Razi Haider also quotes from Stanley Wolpert's *Jinnah of Pakistan* (New Delhi: Oxford University Press, 2005) asserting that Jinnah's marriage proposal came after the Lucknow session: 'Jinnah's triumph was unmarred. The complete contract he had written was accepted by both parties. Now he was ready to put it to the acid test of personal application. He found a way to unite the two subjects uppermost in his mind and approached Sir Dinshaw Petit . . . informing his old friend that he wanted to marry his daughter.'

Meston's letter to Chelmsford, dated 11 January 1917, is from the Chelmsford Papers, and quoted in *The Works of Quaid-i-Azam 1916–1917*, vol. 3, edited by Riaz Ahmad.

On Ruttie proposing to Jinnah, see *In Quest of Jinnah: Diary, Notes and Correspondence of Hector Bolitho*, edited by Sharif al Mujahid. In the introduction, Mujahid writes: 'He [Jinnah] excited her young imagination as no one else had, and she hero-worshipped him. Not inexplicably, therefore, it was she who asked him to marry her. Reportedly Jinnah answered, "It seems to be an interesting proposition!"'

Undated page of Ruttie's letter (with pages missing at beginning and end) written on letter paper, printed with 'Mount Pleasant Road, Malabar Hill, Bombay', says: 'J for his part is growling because I won't let him [illegible] [cut?] his hair—you will perhaps [illegible] how that is possible—it was one of the terms on which I accepted him i.e. that he couldn't touch his hair without my previous sanction.' Cited in the *Padmaja Naidu Papers* (NMML archives).

Ruttie's letters of 3 January and 20 January 1917, from the *Leilamani Naidu Papers* (NMML archives).

Ruttie's letters of 7 January and 27 January 1917, from the *Padmaja Naidu Papers* (NMML archives).

Chapter Four

Details of the Nehru home and upbringing from *The Scope of Happiness: A Personal Memoir* by Vijaya Lakshmi Pandit (New York: Crown Publishers, 1979).

On Vijaya Lakshmi Pandit's previous betrothal being called off by Raja Narendra Nath, from K.L. Gauba's Oral Transcript Account No. 76, NMML archives.

Sarojini Naidu's letter from Lyceum Club, 138 Piccadilly, W.1, 2 March 1920 (*Padmaja Naidu Papers*, NMML archives): '. . . cannot stand such a galvanic gallery of shocks . . . the Khilafat Deputation and on it a Syud married in some strange uncertain [way] and may be *not* permanent fashion to the little Sarup Nehru . . . Syud has behaved splendidly but you know the course of true love runs over difficult courses.'

Gauba's reference to Motilal Nehru's daughter's elopement, from *Friends and Foes: An Autobiography* by K.L. Gauba (New Delhi: Indian Book Company, 1974).

Sarup's experience of Gandhi and his ashram, from *The Scope of Happiness* and a letter to Padmaja from Anand Bhavan on 13 March (year not stated), from the *Padmaja Naidu Papers* (NMML archives).

Vijaya Lakshmi's courtship and marriage to Ranjit Sitaram Pandit, from *The Scope of Happiness*.

K.L. Gauba on his inter-communal marriage, from his Oral Transcript (NMML archives).

Aziz Beg in his *Jinnah and His Times* refers briefly to Sir Dinshaw Petit's first court case against Jinnah: 'In 1916, Sir Dinshaw filed a petition preventing Jinnah from marrying Ruttie or having any contact with her as she was a minor.'

Jinnah's diary of political and other engagements carried in the *Bombay Chronicle*, which is also cited in *The Works of Quaid-i-Azam*, vols. 3 and 4.

Sarojini Naidu's letter, from *Leilamani Naidu Papers* (NMML archives).

Sarojini Naidu's family background narrated in *Sarojini Naidu: A Biography* by Padmini Sengupta (London: Asia Publishing House, 1966).

Chapter Five

Quotes in this chapter unless otherwise stated are from *My Brother* by Fatima Jinnah, and edited by Sharif al Mujahid (Karachi: Quaid-e-Azam Academy, 1987).

Aziz Beg quotes Jinnah's sister Shirin Bai on the birthmark on the sole of his right foot for which his sisters made him take off his shoes and socks in order to examine. Cited in *Jinnah and His Times*.

Another incident relating to Jinnah's very English habits is related in *Memories of Jinnah* by K.H. Khurshid, and edited by Khalid Hasan (Karachi: Oxford University Press, 1990): 'Everyone was seated on the floor and it had not occurred to the hosts to provide cutlery as rice is always eaten with one's fingers in the traditional way. Mr Jinnah felt rather embarrassed but then the situation was saved when someone produced a spoon with which [he] helped himself to some rice, washing it down with a glass of soda water.'

Quote of the young cousin on Jinnah's late-night studies, cited in *Jinnah: Creator of Pakistan* by Hector Bolitho (Karachi: Oxford University Press; reprinted from John Murray, London, 1954).

Cicero's *'Offices': Essays on Friendship and Old Age and Select Letters* (London: J.M. Dent, 1911 reprint) is among Jinnah's collection of books in the Karachi University Library.

Bolitho in *Jinnah: Creator of Pakistan* describes Jinnah's first mentor: 'At that time when Jinnah finished his schooling, there was an Englishman, Frederick Leigh Croft, working as an exchange broker in Bombay and Karachi. He was heir to a baronetcy—a thirty-two-year-old bachelor, described by a kinswoman who remembers him as "something of a dandy, with a freshly picked carnation in his buttonhole each morning; a recluse and a wit, uncomfortable in the presence of children whom he did not like." But he liked Mohammed Ali Jinnah, and was persuaded by his talents.'

The astrologer's prediction that the boy Jinnah would grow up to be a king is cited in Bolitho's *Jinnah: Creator of Pakistan*. Also, Ahmedali Jinnah's letter to his brother on 11 July 1947 from Bombay (Pakistan National Archives, Islamabad): 'You will remember telling father that an astrologer had predicted that you would one day be the uncrowned king of India. His words came true.'

Emibai's age at the time of her marriage was sixteen years, according to Aziz Beg's *Jinnah and His Times*, which is highly unlikely considering the average age of both Hindu and Muslim brides at that time was well below twelve years, and Jinnah himself had barely turned sixteen by then.

Although Jinnah's home in Karachi was a modest two-room tenement in a narrow lane of a crowded bazaar, Fatima Jinnah in *My Brother* portrays the family as being very affluent, with her father owning several carriages and 'a number of fine horses' in his stable.

The story of the young man who arrived in an English lodging house and the hot-water bottle in his bed that he mistook for a snake, as related by Jinnah, appears in *Memories of Jinnah*. Among the other stories Jinnah shared with Khurshid that appear in the book are his fondness for cold-water baths and learning to be orderly.

Jinnah's curt view of his first few months in London is mentioned in the draft note 'Some Questions for Mr Jinnah' sent by Sir Evelyn Wrench on 16 February 1944 (F1190, Pakistan National Archives, Islamabad): 'To a question as to what were the things that he liked best when he was in England and the things that he liked least, Jinnah responded: "Roast beef and apple tart and flowers and fruit. I liked fogs the least." And on what were his chief ambitions as a boy, he replied: "Went to the Court with father and saw a barrister with gown and bands and enquired who this person was." On being told he was a barrister, he immediately said: "I want to become one," and, in fact, he did become one, and his dream of boyhood came true. He began taking an interest in politics as a boy of 17 studying in London.'

Jinnah's Latin textbook, *Sallust Catiline*, in his collection of books in the Karachi University Library; edited by T.M. Neatly and B.J. Hayes (University Correspondence College Press/University Correspondence College Tutorial Series). It's signed M.A. Jinnah, for the first time since he changed his name, on two separate pages. Heavily marked till two-third of the book until chapter twenty with notes especially in the section marked 'Vocabulary', and sometimes even English words explained such as 'gait=manner of walking'.

The only poem that struck a chord with Jinnah was a verse from Dante quoted in *Sesame and Lilies* by John Ruskin (George Allen, 1899—from Jinnah's collection of books in the Karachi University Library). The lines are underlined with pencil on page 100: 'But on thee dwells my every thought and sense; / Considering that from thee all virtues spread / As from a fountain head, / That in thy gift is wisdom's best avail, / And honour without fail.' And the second stanza has been underlined twice, as if for double effect: 'A man from a wild beast / Thou madest me, since for thy love I lived.'

On Jinnah's short career on the stage, Aziz Beg in *Jinnah and His Times* quotes a former diplomat, Malik Wahedna, who asked Jinnah about his acting career and received the following reply: 'I used to read out Shakespeare before my friends. Soon the news got around. "Jinnah reads well." After I was called to the Bar, I was taken by some friends to the Manager of a theatrical company, who asked me to go up to the stage and read out pieces of Shakespeare. I did so. His wife and he were immensely pleased and immediately offered me a job. I was exultant, and I wrote to my parents craving for their blessings . . . My father wrote a long letter to me, strongly disapproving of my project; but there was one sentence in his letter which touched me most and which influenced a change in my decision: "Do not be a traitor to the family." I went to my employers and conveyed to them that I no longer looked forward to a stage career. They were surprised, and they tried to persuade me, but my mind was made up. According to the terms of the contract I had signed with them, I was to have given them three months' notice before quitting. But you know, they were Englishmen and so they said: "Well, when you have no interest in the stage, why should we keep you against your wishes for three months with us?" My stage career, therefore, was very short.'

On Jinnah's straightforwardness and refusal to pull strings, Bolitho writes in *Jinnah: Creator of Pakistan*: 'Early in 1900, there was a vacancy for a Presidency Magistrate in Bombay—an office that required generous recommendation. Jinnah was hopeful; and he was also enterprising. He sat, 'gazing through a window . . . smoking a cigarette, wondering what he could do; a cab passed by and an idea struck him: he jumped into the cab and drove straight to the office of Sir Charles Ollivant, the then Member in charge of the Judicial Department.' Jinnah went in and asked for an appointment. He obtained the necessary recommendation from Sir MacPherson, and within a few weeks, he became a temporary presidency magistrate.

Bolitho in *Jinnah: Creator of Pakistan* quotes the Muslim barrister who spoke to him on Jinnah's unpopularity at court, as also saying: 'I think his apparent rudeness was linked with his deep honesty.'

The Story of My Heart: My Autobiography by Richard Jefferies (among Jinnah's collection of books, Karachi University Library). Inscribed as M.J.A from H.G.A, 1916.

Chapter Six

Sir Dinshaw's official engagements, from the *Times of India*, April 1918

Advertisements from agencies supplying servants appeared regularly in English-language newspapers, like this one from the *Times of India*: 'Domestic Servants Agency (Estd. 1890). The only original firm that supplies highly efficient and absolutely reliable High Class servants, such as cooks, Kit Bearers, Ayahs and travelling Servants etc. A Good Servant is a source of pleasure to everyone and the nature of our offers is such as to make it Easy for you to have a REAL GOOD SERVANT in place of one that is only a source of annoyance. Hundreds of Testimonials. Osborne & Co, 101 Esplanade Road, Bombay.'

Even a generation later, the style and scale of Petit Hall's meals were legendary: '. . . Petit Hall food, than which there was no better in the world: Mughlai, Parsi or Continental dishes concocted by a succession of gifted cooks . . . there were seldom less than a dozen people for meals.' Cited in *Dropping Names* by Manohar Malgonkar.

Ibid. 'The marble staircase from the old Petit Hall today adorns the foyer of the Tata Centre for Performing Arts (Bombay), and the Grecian pillars that give the large dining room at the Taj Mahal hotel in Bombay its Edwardian elegance, have been lifted from his house (Petit Hall), which sadly had to be demolished in the sixties . . . (and) the vast park surrounding it . . . are now half a dozen developers' dreams: Malabar Apartments . . . To be sure, there is a new Petit Hall too; not quite a palace but not a bungalow either, a mansion, perhaps, much closer to the sea and surrounded by its own trees and a garden . . . still one of the most luxurious, most spacious, private houses in Bombay.'

In the *Bombay Chronicle*'s issue dated 19 April 1918, page 13: 'Ganesh & Co's New Publications. Speeches of Mohamad Ali Jinnah. The latest addition to the Indian Political literature is the publication of a handsome volume containing the speeches of the Hon. Mr Mohamad Ali Jinnah, which cover all topics of the day and the volume opens with a foreword by the Raja of Mahmudabad together with a biographical appreciation by Mrs Sarojini Naidu. The Hon. Raja of Mahmudabad writes: "The speeches reveal a study, in a spirit of abiding and indistinguishable faith of the problems affecting the political destiny of India, of which no other worker among the Indian Mussalmans has so far given proof in an equal degree." Mrs Sarojini Naidu writes: "These valuable speeches which now collected for the first time cannot fail to arouse profound and vivid interest in the minds of all who are concerned with the vital issues of contemporary political events and activities in India." Over 320 pages printed on Antiue paper and attractively bound with a Portrait and Index. Price: Two rupees.'

Sarojini's close friendship with Jinnah, especially her warm defence and admiration of her friend expressed on all occasions in public and private, gave rise to some speculation even in her own lifetime, with the gossips insisting that she had either nursed an unrequited passion for Jinnah or had been displaced in his affections by Ruttie. She first met him in 1910 at the Calcutta legislative session and was instantly enamoured of him, recommending him warmly to B.R. Gokhale. But Chagla, who had known and worked closely with both, comes nearest to the truth of their relationship: 'He (Jinnah) treated her in a rather cavalier fashion as a poet but with no political sense. But on her side, she had great admiration for Jinnah, and she was anxious that the quality of leadership and the undoubted talent that he possessed should be harnessed to the service of the country.'

According to Khwaja Razi Haider in *Ruttie Jinnah*: 'Having sought counsel from his friends, in particular Mohammad Umer Sobhani, Jinnah took Ruttie to the Jamia Mosque where she converted to Islam . . . in front of a great religious scholar, Maulana Nazir Ahmad Khujandi . . . (who) was a renowned alim and performed Imamat at the Jamia Masjid in Bombay. He also took an active part in Indian politics. He was, from the very beginning, a member of the All India Muslim League, a good orator and journalist. In 1946, he composed a poem about Jinnah and recited it at a birthday function held for him in Bombay.'

All Ruttie's quotes in this chapter are from her letters and poems written during 1916–17. They are now in the *Padmaja Naidu Papers* and the *Leilamani Naidu Papers*.

Sarojini's letter to Syed Mahmud from Hyderabad dated 28 April 1918, from *Sarojini Naidu: Selected Letters* by Makarand R. Paranjape.

The Scope of Happiness: A Personal Memoir by Vijaya Lakshmi Pandit.

Celibates by George Moore (London: Walter Scott, 1895).

Novels by Eminent Hands by William Makepeace Thackeray (London: Collins Clear Type Press, 1859).

'Powvala, Kavashaw Sorabjee' is listed in the *Times of India Directory* of 1918 with two addresses, one presumably his office: 'Landed Proprietor, 237, Hornby Road, Rydal Mount, Mount Pleasant Road, Malabar Hill'.

'I have had such a ripping time with you all in Hyderabad that I am quite spoilt for this fun-forsaken place,' Ruttie wrote in a letter dated 9 February 1920 (*Padmaja Naidu Papers*, NMML archives).

According to Urdu biography *Quaidi Ibtidai Tees Saal* (Quaid's Early Thirty Years) by Rizwan Ahmad (Karachi: General Knowledge Academy, 1977), Jinnah shifted from his first-floor apartment in Colaba 'because it was very noisy outside with children playing and ayahs gossiping' and moved to a house he rented from Justice Ranade on Mount Pleasant Road 'which suited him better, being quiet and pleasant'. However, 'Mohdali Jinah, Hon'ble Mr. Barrister', begins appearing as a homeowner in the *Times of India Directory* from 1912 onwards, and the address: Mount Pleasant Road, Malabar Hills. At that time, only four other Muslims owned houses on Malabar Hill, including the Aga Khan.

By the time K.H. Khurshid went to live in Jinnah's house, it had been razed and rebuilt into a grand marble mansion but the locale was unchanged: 'About a 100 yards down Mount Pleasant Road, from the point where it branches off from Gibbs Road, lay the house, perched on the eastern slopes of Malabar Hill, which project into the Arabian Sea over a tiny peninsula. As you entered through the main gates, the road went down a slope and round a big papal tree which overlooked the front porch of the house, some of its branches almost touching the windows on the balcony above . . . The rooms were sparsely but tastefully furnished. There were hardly any decorations on the wall.' Cited in *Memories of Jinnah*.

On Jinnah's very modest household arrangements as a bachelor, G. Allana writes: 'Before Ruttenbai married the Quaid, his house was being run by a well-trusted and devoted servant, Visan, who served the

Quaid-e-Azam for very many years. He was his valet, his cashier for running the household budget, his bearer, the servant in charge and in command of the entire household staff—rolled into one.'

Syed Nabiullah's letter to Padmaja, undated, from the *Padmaja Naidu Papers* (NMML archives).

Chapter Seven

Raja Amir Ahmed Khan's memories of Ruttie from *Ruttie Jinnah* by Khwaja Razi Haider. Haider also writes of the Raja's second meeting with Ruttie at the Maidens Hotel in Delhi as a boy of nine: 'On this occasion she gave him five hundred rupees, a great deal of money at that time, to buy himself some toys.'

On the maharaja of Mahmudabad's legendary hospitality, Chagla writes of his experience dining in his palace in Lucknow for the drafting of the Nehru Report in 1928: 'I remember the first evening when we sat down to dinner. Our host was the Maharaja of Mahmudabad, a prince famed for his hospitality. I believe Montagu, who was Secretary of State for India, reports in his diary that when he dined with the Maharaja of Mahmudabad he served him a dinner which had 42 courses. We were almost as liberally treated at Kaiser Bag as Montagu was. I remember the first dinner—we started with Western food—soup, fish, meat and so on. Then came Muslim food—Murgh Mussalam, Biryani, and all the famed dishes of the North, and finally Hindu food with puris and vegetables and then Hindu sweets. When I started I thought the dinner consisted only of the English courses, and I ate my fill. When the Muslim and Hindu dishes arrived, I could only sit and watch. Motilal Nehru and Tej Bahadur Sapru, who were relatively old men, kept pace, however, and did full justice to whatever was served at the dinner. I still remember Motilalji telling me: "Young man, how will you fight for your country if you don't know how to eat?"'

See the issues of the *Bombay Chronicle* of April 1918 for the build-up and proceedings of the Delhi War Conference, held from 27 to 28 April 1918.

Ruttie's remark on Maidens Hotel in Alice Reading's letter dated 13 February 1924, quoted in *Jinnah and His Times*.

The Delhi War Conference, an attempt to demonstrate Indian support to the British government, was characterized as 'a sad fiasco' in a letter from Willingdon to Montagu, 30 April 1918, cited in *Ambassador of Hindu–Muslim Unity: Jinnah's Early Politics* by Ian Bryant Wells (New Delhi: Permanent Black, 2005).

Whether Jinnah intended it or not, Ruttie's conversion to Islam became of strategic importance to him later in his political career, especially in his election campaign of 1945 when his Muslim rivals openly levelled allegations about his un-Islamic marriage to undermine his credibility as a Muslim leader.

Gauba who converted to Islam in 1933 describes the reaction of Lahore's Cosmopolitan Club members to his conversion: 'It was a sort of, that I had really committed suicide, socially and politically.' Cited in the Oral History Transcript of K.L. Gauba (Account No. 76, NMML archives).

Paisa Akbar, Lahore, 22 April 1918, quoted in Khwaja Razi Haider's *Ruttie Jinnah*.

See *In Quest of Jinnah: Diary, Notes and Correspondence of Hector Bolitho*, edited by Sharif al Mujahid, for details on Jinnah's 'almost tiresome celibacy' and his 'mental and moral celibacy'. Bolitho writes in a later expunged passage: 'A contemporary who knew him well told me: "Jinnah was a cold fish—much too formal ever to be a good lover.' Khurshid, Jinnah's private secretary, is also quoted as saying: 'He was by nature celibate. Marriage was alien to his nature." Also, Ruttie's words as reported by Sarojini Naidu in her letter to Padmaja (see chapter twenty) about the 'unhappiness that began from the first day almost' and feeling stifled because of 'his lack of the spirit of the joy of life'.

On Jinnah's need for the female gaze, Urdu writer Saadat Hasan Manto provides an insight in his essay, 'Jinnah Sahib', based on an interview with Jinnah's chauffeur: 'The only indoor sport the Quaid-e-Azam liked was billiards. Whenever the urge to play came upon him, he would order the billiards room to be opened and although it used to be cleaned and dusted every day, the servants would still take one extra look at everything on such days to be sure that all was spick and span. . . . Twelve balls would be placed in front of the sahib and he would carefully choose three and then begin playing. Miss Jinnah would often be there too. Sahib would place his cigar between his lips and study the position of the ball that he planned to hit. This would take several minutes, as he would examine it from every angle. He would weigh the cue in his hand, run it over his long and slim fingers as if it was a bow he was going to play a stringed instrument with, take aim and then stop short of executing the stroke because he had thought of a better angle. He only played his shot when he was fully satisfied that it was the right one. If the shot went through as planned, he would smile triumphantly at his sister. From *Bitter Fruit: The Very Best of Saadat Hasan* Manto, edited and translated by Khalid Hasan (New Delhi: Penguin Books India, 2008).

Ruttie Jinnah's letter to Syed Mahmud dated 15 May, Galloway House, Naini Tal, from Syed Mahmud's correspondence with Jinnah (NMML archives).

Syed Mahmud (1889–1971), barrister and a doctorate holder from Munster University, Germany, belonged to a rich zamindar family in Bihar, and was a friend of Sarojini Naidu and Jinnah.

Chapter Eight

Among Ruttie's book collection is *The Complete Works of Alfred Lord Tennyson* bearing the inscription: 'To dear Rati from her loving Papa. 14th December 1911.' The date of the birth of her little brother, Jamshed. The facsimile of the front page, the table of contents (signed Rutty Petit) and front-page etching of 'The Lover's Library' in large font are reproduced in *Some Aspects of Quaid-i-Azam's Life* by Syed Sharifuddin Pirzada (Islamabad: National Commission on Historical and Cultural Research, 1978).

Lady Petit's daughter-in-law (also Lady Petit) is quoted as telling Bolitho: 'He [Jinnah] was always so gracious to ladies. He would compliment us on our saris. The other politicians were grand and swept one aside.' Cited *In Quest of Jinnah*.

The proceedings of the Bombay Provincial War Conference, 10 June 1918 (India Confidential Proceedings, India Office Records and Private

Papers), vol. 36, cited in *The Works of Quaid-i-Azam 1917–1918*, vol. 4, edited by Dr Riaz Ahmad.

Shantaram Chawl, situated in the heart of Bombay populated by industrial and government workers, was a popular venue for public meetings for the nationalists partly because of its large compound and adjacent buildings which could accommodate a crowd of up to 10,000. Special permits had to be obtained from the police commissioner to hold these open-air meetings at the chawl. Later, in the 1920s when public meetings began to draw crowds in lakhs instead of thousands, political meetings began to be held on the Chowpatty beach.

On the second court case filed by Sir Dinshaw against Jinnah, Aziz Beg writes in *Jinnah and His Times*: 'Sir Dinshaw Petit filed another suit saying that Jinnah had abducted his daughter. Before Mr Jinnah could reply to the court's query, Ruttie stepped forward and said: "Sir, Mr Jinnah has not abducted me; in fact I have abducted him; so there is no case and he should be immediately exonerated of all charges." The court was surprised, the father was angry, Ruttie's mother flabbergasted and Jinnah was just smiling.'

A report carried in the *Times of India* of 28 May 1918: 'A meeting of the Parsi priests of Bombay was held on Sunday at the Dady Seth's Fire Temple, Agiari Lane, Bombay, to express its disapprobation of marriages of Parsi women with non-Parsis. Shams-ul-Ulma Dastur Darab Peshotan Sanjana was voted to the chair. In opening the proceedings, the Chairman stated that during the past few months the Parsi community had been greatly grieved by marriages of Parsi girls with non-Parsis such as Christians, Hindus and Mohamedans and this feeling of grief was particularly noticeable among the priestly class of the community. They considered that some steps should be taken to prevent such unions in the future. Unions such as these were to be highly deprecated in the interests of the community and he exhorted Parsi parents not to allow their daughters to mix with non-Parsis until they had received sufficient instructions according to the tenets of the Zoroastrian religion. Dastur Dinsha J. Garda then moved a resolution condemning marriages of Parsis with non-Parsis, and particularly marriages of Parsi girls with non-Parsis, and calling upon the Parsi community to adopt measures to prevent such unions, one of these being to give their children religious instructions and to teach them to follow in the footsteps of their great forebears who had left their mark on their ancient history. The resolution was carried. In the next resolution it was affirmed that when a Parsi woman married a non-Parsi, she left her fold, and therefore when she died, or when any Parsi, man or woman, who lived with such a woman died, no Parsi priest should perform the funeral ceremony in connection with their deaths. The resolution would also apply to a Parsi woman who professed to follow Zoroastrianism even after marrying a non-Parsi.'

Five years younger than Sir Dinshaw Petit, Sir Jamsetjee Jeejeebhoy the Fifth was not only president of the Parsi panchayat's board of trustees, like his father before him, but also the sheriff of Bombay in 1915. In June 1917, he started a drive to extend Lord Willingdon's term as governor, which was expiring the following year.

The proceedings and resolutions passed by the Parsi panchayat in meetings held on 21 July 1918, 28 July 1918 and 2 February 1919, reproduced from reports in *Kaiser-e-Hind* (2 June 1918, 28 July 1918 and 23 March 1919), and in *Jam-e-Jamshed* (26 May 1918 and 4 February 1919), quoted in *Parsee Prakashan Daftar* (No. 5, Part 5, 1919).

Chapter Nine

Orient Club was one of the many clubs started by educated Indians to counter the racial discrimination they faced in joining the Gymkhana clubs. It was opened on 1 May 1900, and according to the *Times of India Directory and Yearbook*, 1918, 'owes its origins to a desire to provide a first class Club, managed on European lines, to which gentlemen of culture and position could be admitted irrespective of race, creed or politics, on terms of social equality. The immediate object is to encourage more intimate and friendly relations between the Leaders of Native Society and European gentlemen. Provision to admit Ruling Princes as members without ballot. Jinnah was on the management committee but according to Kanji Dwarkadas (*Ruttie Jinnah: The Story of a Great Friendship*), he resigned from the club after his marriage. He used to go there to play Chess and Billiards but never cards because "he abhorred every kind of gambling and all games of chance".'

Jinnah's unsuccessful attempt to be elected to the Western India Turf Club and that he was unable to find anyone prepared to propose him for membership appears in the Bombay Police Secret Abstract, 1918, with the Bombay Police suggesting that Jinnah's personal antagonism towards the Bombay governor, Willingdon, stemmed from this. According to the police, Jinnah attributed his failure to get in to the club to the influence of Willingdon. Cited in *Ambassador of Hindu–Muslim Unity: Jinnah's Early Politics* by Ian Bryant Well (Lahore: Vanguard Books).

From Gauba's Oral History Transcript: 'You see, we were so important in Lahore society at that time that my wife's invitation was a bigger command than even the Government House's command. Nobody would venture to refuse an invitation from her. But yet, there was not that mingling that you could say that the prejudice was over . . . Of course she had her own entertainments and her own friends and she and Kanwarani Dalip Singh dominated Lahore society . . . She was unusual in the sense that she kept a beautiful home and she made our home one of the most attractive homes in Lahore. She started a fashion in Lahore, the fashion of modern houses. She was the mainspring of ideas of the new life and new living . . . But the prejudice did not quite disappear. These things are not decided as matters of reason, but as matters of feeling.'

Jinnah's speech on the floor of the House on the Hindu Marriages Validity Bill, 5 September 1918, cited in the *Proceedings of the Indian Legislative Council April 1918 to March 1919*, vol. LVII, Calcutta, 1919; quoted in *The Works of Quaid-i-Azam, 1917–1918*, vol. 4.

For a portrait of Ruttie's brother Fali who succeeded his father to the baronetcy, see 'Third Baronet: Sir Dinshaw Petit' in *Dropping Names*.

References to Jinnah's Jeeves, Visan, in *Quaid-e-Azam Jinnah: The Story of a Nation* by G. Allana (Lahore: Ferozsons, 1967), and *Quaidi Itbidat Tees Saal* by Rizwan Ahmad.

'The haven and refuge for briefless barristers who were waiting for their brief was that great institution—the Bar Gymkhana. I did not leave the chamber at the end of the day until Jinnah had finished his conferences and was going home. He would then take me along and drop me at the Bar Gymkhana. We members used to sit there playing bridge and poker and I must confess also drinking . . . Friday evening was a great occasion at the Bar Gymkhana, as the day after was Saturday and not a court day. We used to have dinner at the Bar Gymkhana and Azad, as the most affluent member in the company, would send his car to fetch the most delectable food which we enjoyed while we carried on with our game that lasted till midnight and even later. Sunday morning used to be what was known as Sir Jamshed Kanga's durbar. He would come at about 10 and stay on till about noon, and treat us all to beer.' From *Roses in December*.

Bolitho writes in *Jinnah: Creator of Pakistan*: 'When another old friend of this time was asked, "But was Jinnah absolutely without passion?" he answered, "It may sound ridiculous but I believe his only passion was for newspapers. He had them sent from all over the world: he cut pieces out of them, annotated them, and stuck them into books. He would do this for hours—all through his life, he loved newspapers."'

'Dear Mr Mahmud,' begins Ruttie's letter from Mount Pleasant Road, Malabar Hill, on 5 January (year not mentioned), inviting Syed Mahmud to dinner. 'We are so sorry not to have seen you when you called yesterday. I don't know whether you are stopping in Bombay or just a bird of passage. Anyhow if Saturday still finds you here—will you come and dine with us—quietly, perhaps another friend or two. Yours sincerely, R. Jinnah.' Syed Mahmud's correspondence with Jinnah (NMML archives).

Nowhere is the transformation in Jinnah's style of dressing after his marriage better illustrated than in this anecdote related by G.L. Mehta, who saw Jinnah for the first time in 1913 when both of them were travelling on the same steamer. Mehta, who was only thirteen then, says he was very struck by Jinnah's carefully cultivated dress code. 'What was most amusing was that at about 5 pm when he would come out on the deck after his nap and tea, he would put on an evening cap even on the steamer! Nobody used to put on that kind of cap, and even in England I saw only workers wearing that kind of cap.' (G.L. Mehta, Oral History Transcript, Account No. 47, NMML archives). After Ruttie came into his life, he never made that kind of sartorial mistake ever again, wearing custom-made silk suits and shirts tailored in Paris and London.

Ruttie's physical appearance and charm were universally acknowledged among her friends as irresistible, as this letter from Sarojini Naidu to Padmaja Naidu, dated 6 August 1922, shows: '*Who* do you think came to see me yesterday—the daintiest, naughtiest, darlingest of all my many visitors, smarter too, all in tawny gold with tricky little ways and full of sparkling mischief. Guess once, twice and three times—No, not Ruttie, but a doggy counterpart of Ruttie—a little Pom belonging to Janakidas.' From the *Padmaja Naidu Papers* (NMML archives).

Margaret Monck, daughter of Viceroy Lord Chelmsford, recounts Indian ladies making their curtsey before the viceroy and his family: 'In early 1919, they used to have drawing rooms like the ones at Court [in England] and the Viceroy and his family sat on a dais where the ladies of Simla used to come and make their curtsey. They were very nervous and they used to make their curtsey and very often would faint. The Viceroy's butler named Jordan would stand behind them, sort of ready to catch them in case they fainted . . . they came dressed in their best clothes, even the children in beautiful organdies and silks.' Cited in Oral History Transcript (Account No. 225, NMML archives).

Lady Curzon's letter, cited in *Lady Curzon's India: Letters of a Vicerine*, edited by John Bradley (New York: Beaufort Books, 1986).

Lady Reading's letters, one dated 13 February 1924 and the other undated, quoted in *Some Aspects of Quaid-i-Azam's Life* by Syed Sharifuddin Pirzada (Islamabad: National Commission on Historical and Cultural Research, 1978).

Hector Bolitho writes *In Quest of Jinnah*: 'Lady Willingdon is a very silly woman. She should have known better. It is a pity, because Lord Willingdon was a great gentleman. It is a question, you know—how much were the wives of Britons appointed to India responsible for our losing her. Wives of senior army officers often lose the battles their husbands have won.'

'I saw Ruttie yesterday looking very ill but quite happy,' writes Sarojini Naidu to Leilamani Naidu, in a letter dated 21 August 1918 from Taj Mahal Hotel, Bombay. From the *Leilamani Naidu Papers* (NMML archives).

Chapter Ten

Vicereine Alice Reading wrote in a letter dated 13 February 1924: 'Mostyn-Owen, one of our Aides, who is rather a good young man, said to her [Ruttie] that the hotel where she is living was "nice and quiet at night", to which she replied, "I don't like nice, quiet nights, I like a lot going on."' Quoted in *Jinnah and His Times*.

Ruttie's fantasizes about her role in public life in her letter to Padmaja Naidu, dated 7 January 1917, cited in the *Padmaja Naidu Papers* (NMML archives).

Public demonstrations, speeches and events leading up to the meeting in the town hall and after, from the *Bombay Chronicle*, 8–28 December, reproduced in *The Works of Quaid-i-Azam 1917–1918*, vol. 4.

Jinnah's recollection of his mentor and patron, Sir George Lowndes, quoted in *Secular and Nationalist Jinnah* by Ajeet Jawed (New Delhi: Oxford University Press, 2009).

Pencil markings in Jinnah's copy of Cicero's *'Offices', Essays on Friendship and Old Age and Select Letters*, from Jinnah's collection of books in the Karachi University Library.

In 1915, Jinnah brought the Muslim League close to the Congress by holding its session at the same time as the Congress's in Bombay, but the proceedings were disrupted by a large group of dissidents with tacit support from the government, which did not approve of the two organizations coming together. After its president was abused by the dissidents for his English way of dressing and conducting the proceedings in English instead of Urdu, the sitting was adjourned and reassembled the next day in the Taj Mahal Hotel, with only League members and the press allowed to enter the closed-door meeting.

Years later, Sir Cowasji Jehangir told Bolitho: 'I was fond of him [Jinnah] because of his sense of justice and because, with all the differences and bitterness of political life, he was never malicious. Hard, maybe, but never malicious.' Cited *In Quest of Jinnah*.

Kanji Dwarkadas writes: 'At a Committee meeting of the Home Rule League in March 1918, where Mrs [Annie] Besant was present by special invitation, Jinnah, pointing at me, told her, "Mrs Besant, this is my best worker in the whole Committee. He works, the others make speeches." This was overheard by one of our colleagues, who resented the remark and felt that Jinnah was running him down.' From *Gandhiji through My Diary Leaves 1915–1948* by Kanji Dwarkadas (published by Kanji Dwarkadas, Bombay, 1950).

Miss Agatha Harrison, one of the speakers at a memorial meeting for Jinnah at Caxton Hall, London, on 14 September 1948, is quoted as saying: 'When Jinnah was a student in London [1892–96] the suffragette movement was gathering momentum; but we had very few sympathizers and supporters. Young Jinnah always came to our meetings and spoke in defence of vote for women. Even then he was not afraid of championing an unpopular cause.' From *The Jinnah Anthology*, edited by Liaquat H. Merchant and Sharif al Mujahid (Karachi: Oxford University Press, 2010).

Chapter Eleven

According to Sir Purshotamdas Thakurdas, eminent lawyer and politician, 'Jinnah was at once a hero, admired, honoured, praised, nay, loved by all. Public addresses were presented to him, garden parties were held in his honour, and every one suggested that this unique service rendered by him to his people should be commemorated.' Another colleague who later turned into Jinnah's political foe, M.R. Jayakar, said: 'The public sentiment created by the agitation was so strong that Jinnah received the gift of a public fund, called the People's One Rupee Fund, out of the proceeds of which was raised a memorial to him, called "the Jinnah's People's Memorial Hall" in Bombay.' Quoted in *Jinnah and His Times*.

J.N. Sahni writes in *The Lid Off: Fifty Years of Indian Politics* (New Delhi: Deep Publications, 1972) about his first meeting with Jinnah. Sahni was a volunteer at the Amritsar session of the Congress (26–30 December 1919): 'At this time Railway Porters went on strike. We were suddenly commissioned to transport the loads of luggage of an unending stream of incoming passengers. One of these, more striking than the others, emerged from a first-class compartment dressed like a fashion-plate model—tall, slim and commanding. His attendant poured out several fancy pieces of luggage and insisted that each piece be carried separately. He himself undertook to carry the tiffin carrier and a silver-knobbed walking stick of the "master". We felt proud of the commission since the gentleman in top coat, sola topee, gloves and spats was the famous M.A. Jinnah.' Quoted in *Secular and Nationalist Jinnah*.

The Jinnahs usually travelled in a first-class coupé attended by several servants who travelled in a separate coach and whose duty it was to come to their carriage at every station to see if anything was required of them by their master and mistress.

Jinnah's speeches on the floor of the House on the Rowlatt Bills, cited in the *Proceedings of the Indian Legislative Council from April 1918 to March 1919*, vol. LVII, Calcutta, 1919; also quoted in *The Works of Quaid-i-Azam 1919–1920*, vol. 5.

George Lloyd's letter to Montagu, 4 July 1919, in the *Montagu Papers*, vol. 24, and cited in *Ambassador of Hindu–Muslim Unity* by Ian Bryant Wells.

The plan to arrest Jinnah and Gandhi along with four others had gone far enough for the viceroy to wire to the governor of Burma on 12 April 1919: 'It is probable that I shall deport in the immediate future some six persons from Bombay area. I hope you will assist by accepting charge of them.' From *India's Fight for Freedom*.

Ibid. On Jinnah's close friendship with Sir Pherozeshah Mehta, Gauba recounts in his Oral History Transcript: 'It was said these three men (Sir Pherozeshah Mehta, Horniman and Jinnah) more or less bachelors, artificially bachelors, in their youth painted Bombay red.' The friendship between Horniman and Jinnah goes even further back, as Diwan Chaman Lal recounts in his oral history transcript (Account No. 220, NMML archives): 'Benjamin Horniman told me that he and Jinnah, when Jinnah was in need of funds in England, both began on jobs in some play or other, in a theatre. They were both supernumerary in the theatre. Horniman told me the story that he himself was on the stage doing a job when Jinnah applied to be taken on and their friendship goes back to those early days of this century.'

Sarojini Naidu's quotes from her letters to Padmaja Naidu, dated 13 and 25 February 1919 and 20 March 1919 (*Padmaja Naidu Papers*, NMML archives). Sarojini's letters to Leilamani Naidu, dated 28 February 1919 and 20 April 1919 (*Leilamani Naidu Papers*, NMML archives).

Ruttie's silent dismay at the approaching arrival of her baby became pronounced enough to elicit comments from her friends and mother, but only after the birth of the child. As for how lonely and estranged Ruttie felt at this time while pretending to be in good spirits, she was to confess this to Sarojini only nine years later, as Sarojini's letter to Padmaja Naidu, dated 20 January 1928, reveals.

On Sarojini's soirées in her Taj Mahal Hotel suite, one visitor, journalist G. Venkatachalam, had this to say: 'Sarojini Naidu was then almost a permanent resident at the Taj, and her rooms at the hotel were always crowded with visitors of all sorts, from princes to paupers, and she played the hostess in the most princely way. All were welcomed and all were treated to drinks and food whenever they came. Even before you sat down, her first question would be: "What will you have?" If it was lunch or dinner time, she never asked you if you would care to share the meal with her; it was always a command: "Stay on and let us see if this poverty-stricken hotel would give us some decent food." How she managed to produce that variety of appetizing food in a hotel like the Taj has always been a wonder to people! An invitation to dinner by Akka was always a social event, for you met at her table many interesting personalities, hobnobbed with the big and the small, ate and drank merrily in her genial company.' Quoted in *The Taj at the Apollo Bunder* by Charles Allen and Sharada Dwivedi (Mumbai: Pictor, 2011).

Nellie Sengupta (born Edith Ellen Gray) met her future husband, Jatindra Mohan Sengupta, as a student lodger at her parents' home in Cambridge where they fell in love. Sengupta, a zamindar's son from Bengal, nearly returned home after his graduation in law without her but midway through the journey, at Port Said, he changed his mind and went back to marry her and bring her home with him. He started a successful career as a lawyer which he gave up to join Gandhi's non-cooperation movement of 1921 along with his wife, Nellie. They were both good friends of Sarojini Naidu's.

After the trend of commissioned portraits in oil, portrait photography impressed the Indian gentry, especially the Parsi community, who became important patrons of the art from 1850 onwards. By 1875, it became so popular that a number of studios sprang up in Bombay, where the fashion-minded went to be recorded for posterity on film. The technique largely depended on daylight, and gas lamps were used to work after sunset. Large-format cameras and large-format paper negatives were in use then, and while the technique improved considerably by the twentieth century, it was still a time-consuming and unwieldy business to have your portrait taken.

According to Kanji Dwarkadas, before Gandhi came into the political arena, 'There was universal opposition to the Rowlatt Act from all over India, from all shades of political opinion. By his talk of passive resistance and civil disobedience, Gandhiji split the united opposition to the Rowlatt Act into two and those who did not join Gandhiji's movement were dubbed traitors and cowards.' Annie Besant, who was against Gandhi's mass civil disobedience scheme, warned him that it would lead to every kind of violent upheaval but Gandhi did not agree. Cited in *India's Fight for Freedom*.

Jinnah's correspondence with the Bombay government regarding the *Bombay Chronicle* of 26 April–8 May 1919, from *The Works of Quaid-i-Azam 1919–1920*, vol. 5.

Chapter Twelve

In a letter to Gokhale on 18 April 1913, Sarojini Naidu wrote: 'Mr Jinnah is travelling with you, one of the reasons I believe for his doing so is to discuss freely and fully with you problems that are as dear to me. Please have confidence in my judgement and conviction—about him—and use your great influence to make him realize that he is the man for whom great work is waiting. I believe if you confer together, you will gain a new hope and a colleague uniformly worth having. You are the only two men in whom I have faith . . .' Cited in *Jinnah and His Times*.

About the long period of limbo the First World War cast young people into, unable to plan their career or future, Shankarlal G. Banker, a former Home Rule League office-bearer who joined Gandhi's Charkha Sangh, recounted: 'No one foresaw the First World War coming and those caught in London colleges like me found the work at college becoming disorganized. No one could foresee how long the war would last.' Cited in the Oral History Transcript of Shankarlal Banker (Account No. 153, NMML archives).

In the world of rich Parsis that Ruttie came from, being widely travelled was an important element of good living, with books on eminent Parsis of Bombay's high society listing among their many accomplishments the number of far-flung places across the world that they had visited. For example, a member of Bombay's Society, a businessman and agent for Singer sewing machine, is described in one of these compendiums of successful Parsis in the early 1900s, as having visited, along with his wife, 'all parts of Europe, America and the Continent'. In India, this couple laying claim to being the most-well travelled of a community that spent all its leisure exploring new places went 'up to Peshawar and has even crossed the Frontier and visited Quetta, Chaman, Kandahar and the Khyber Pass, Lundi, Kotal and Ali Masjid and down South to Tuticorin and Ceylon as well as Karachi and Burma'.

According to Kanji Dwarkadas, Annie Besant first tried to persuade Gandhi to join her delegation to give evidence before the Joint Select Committee on Indian Reforms. 'Gandhiji said he would only go as an independent member. Mrs Besant immediately accepted the condition and added: "We can take you as an independent member. Why don't you join our Home Rule League deputation?" But he eventually turned it down, and at the same time, also shot down sending a Congress deputation 'because the men whom the Congress had selected would bring discredit to India'. Cited in *India's Fight for Freedom*.

Sarojini Naidu's letter from on board the steamer *Maskara* to Leilamani Naidu, dated 15 June 1919, from the *Leilamani Naidu Papers* (NMML archives).

Jinnah's letter to S.A. Brelvi, dated 20 June 1919, in the *S.A. Brelvi Papers* (NMML archives).

Jinnah's distrust of Syed Abdullah Brelvi, who took Horniman's place as editor of the *Bombay Chronicle*, was not unfounded as future events revealed. Kanji Dwarkadas writes of Brelvi's role in the crusade to dub Jinnah a communalist in 1927 when the latter was making a 'valiant' effort to build Hindu–Muslim consensus: 'As regards the Bombay Chronicle . . . with an amiable and mild editor, Syed Abdullah Brelvi, it started a crusade against Jinnah, dubbing him a rank communalist. Jinnah, I submit, was not a communalist, but Brelvi, to curry favour with the Congress High Command, attributed all kinds of base motives to Jinnah and created suspicion against and hatred of him. I know Jinnah rightly resented these false aspersions against him. The consequences were, however, what the reactionaries on both sides, and the Government wanted. And these misunderstandings and misrepresentations went on for years and years.' Quoted in *India's Fight for Freedom*.

Jinnah–Gandhi correspondence, dated 2 June 1919, from *The Collected Works of Mahatma Gandhi*.

As Ian Bryant Wells writes: 'Jinnah's attempts to have Horniman's passport returned to him proved unsuccessful. Similarly, his hopes that Montagu would overturn the Rowlatt Act failed to bear fruit, partly due to the fact that by 1919 official opinion of Jinnah had begun to sour. Both Lloyd and Willingdon had done their best to undermine Jinnah's position with Montagu, with Lloyd writing to warn him of Jinnah's unreliable character . . . Jinnah's confidence in Montagu proved ill-placed. By 1919 Montagu's star had begun to wane.' Cited in *Ambassador of Hindu–Muslim Unity: Jinnah's Early Politics*.

Diwan Chaman Lal's reminiscence on visiting Jinnah in London, from *Tributes to Quaid-i-Azam* edited by Muhammad Hanif Shahid (Lahore: Sang-e-Mell Publications, 1976).

Chagla's quote, from *Roses in December*.

Jinnah's evidence before the Joint Select Committee, from the Report of the Joint Select Committee on the Government of India Bill (London) published by His Majesty's Statutory Office as ordered by the House of Commons on 17 November 1919. Reproduced in *The Works of Quaid-i-Azam 1919–1920*, vol. 5.

B.G. Telang's letter, dated 7 August 1919, from India's *Fight for Freedom*.

Shankerlal G. Banker relates how spinning classes were started at his home in Gamdevi where all the prominent ladies of Bombay came to learn spinning. A former Home Rule League member, when Banker joined Gandhi's Swadeshi Sabha, set up in Bombay after the suspension of the movement for the repeal of the Rowlatt Act in 1919, he was given the job of finding a lady instructor to teach society ladies how to spin yarn. After searching high and low, he finally discovered his mother used to spin in her childhood and could teach others. Cited in Oral History Transcript (Account No. 153, NMML archives).

Sarojini Naidu's letter from London to her son Ranadheera, dated 13 August 1919: 'I gave my evidence [before the Joint Select Committee] and apparently has caused a great stir throughout the country as I find all the journals devoting special space to it and I am dogged by photographers, interviewers and what not. I also took my deputation of men and women to wait on the Secretary of State—all this has meant hard work for me besides the almost daily sittings of the Parliamentary Committee . . . C.P. [Ramaswami Aiyer] is going back to India very shortly as also some other members of deputation who can get passages. I have to stay sometime longer both for my treatment and for further work.' Cited in the *Ranadheera Naidu Papers* (NMML archives).

Chapter Thirteen

Ruttie's letter to Kanji Dwarkadas on 25 September 1922: 'On Thursday we are due to reach Aden, and as I find your name among those heading my list, you can understand the date that tops this letter. Not that I have such a formidable budget to get through—but while riding the seas I drop my characteristics and become cautious. As many of you who have known me on sea times can ever imagine—for my intestine is ever on the defensive against the surging surface.' Quoted in *Ruttie Jinnah: The Story of a Great Friendship*.

Notice of Mr and Mrs Jinnah's arrival in Bombay in the *Bombay Chronicle* of 15 November 1919. Cited in *The Works of Quaid-i-Azam 1919–1920*, vol. 5.

Jinnah's interview under the headlines—'Sooner Lord Chelmsford Is Recalled The Better'; 'Fate of Poor Turkey Almost Sealed'; 'No Home Rule Without Power To Defend Homes'; 'Mr Jinnah On Essentials of Indian

Renaissance'—appeared in the *Bombay Chronicle* of 17 November, and is quoted in *The Works of Quaid-i-Azam 1919–1920*, vol. 5.

Ruttie's worship of spontaneous expression and loathing for any premeditated act of communication is reflected in her letter to Padmaja Naidu, dated 4 July 1916: 'Strange isn't it? But I also never re-read my letters once they are written. I don't know why but somehow it would be unlike me to do so. There is something too tame and calculative about the idea.'

Jinnah's habit of reticence at home when there were no guests at the table is illustrated in this anecdote related in a biography of his sister, Fatima Jinnah, by Agha Hussain Hamdani: *Hayat Aur Hidmat* (Life and Work). Jinnah loved discussing politics at the breakfast table with Fatima but did not appreciate her asking him any probing questions. Once when she tried to find out from him what had happened in the (Muslim League) working committee's meeting, he fobbed her off by responding with a smile: 'Ask your representative. I'm not your representative.' And when Fatima complained that her representative, a person known to her called Begum Mohammed Ali, doesn't tell her anything, Jinnah responded: 'Good. It is unusual for a woman to be quiet.'

It was common among rich and anglicized Indian families to adopt the prevailing custom of the British memsahibs to hand over their children entirely to the hands of a large staff of trained personnel, while they accompanied their husbands to different locations on work. The 'Wanted' columns of English newspapers like the *Pioneer* were full of advertisements such as this one on 18 April 1918: 'Wanted an experienced English Nurse to take baby from the month of August to Srinagar. Ayah kept.'

'Do you know,' Ruttie writes in a letter to Padmaja on 3 March 1920: 'I ordered a sari in November, just a day or so after my return from England, and I haven't yet received it.' Cited in the *Padmaja Naidu Papers* (NMML archives).

The proceedings of the Muslim League and Congress sessions in Amritsar, from the *Bombay Chronicle*, 27 December 1919–January 1920, reproduced in *The Works of Quaid-i-Azam 1919–1920*, vol. 5.

The Ali brothers, Shaukat and Mohammed Ali, made their first public appearance after their release from prison at the Amritsar session of the

Muslim League (29–31 December 1919), and the regular proceedings were disrupted amid emotive scenes.

Ruttie's letter describing the Hyderabad 'I have never seen, only dreamt of', to Leilamani Naidu, dated 24 November 1916.

Padmaja's letter to Ranadheera 'Miniman' Naidu (undated): 'Ruttie has been staying here for over a fortnight and how the poor kid has been enjoying herself. Jinnah has been writing and begging her to return . . .' Cited in the *Padmaja Naidu Papers* (University of Hyderabad).

The phrase 'your over-tuned senses' is from Ruttie's letter to Jinnah on 5 October 1928 (National Archives of Pakistan, QAP-F-890).

From Sarojini Naidu's letter to Padmaja, 20 January 1928: '. . . she says "Don't force me back into slavery. Let me be free. Let me be free . . . Poor child . . . restless and longing to be free of all her shackles. She says her youth is going and she must live . . .' Cited in the *Padmaja Naidu Papers* (NMML archives).

Chapter Fourteen

K.H. Khurshid, who worked as Jinnah's personal secretary in the 1940s, asserts he never saw Jinnah angry but he could be irritated sometimes. And he gives an example: 'The power supply suddenly went off, plunging his room into darkness. Gul Mohammed, the watchman, must have done something while trying to fix the fuse because suddenly the entire house went dark. Mr Jinnah, who was waiting for the light to come back, on noticing what had happened, got angry. His anger was controlled. In Urdu, he said to Gul Mohammed: "*Tum gadha hain. Tum bewakoof hain. Tum tumhara kaam kahe ko nahin karta?* (You are an ass. You are a fool. Why don't you do your work?)" He said this twice and then returned to his dark room.' Quoted in *Memories of Jinnah*.

Description of the Naidu's home by Margaret E. Cousins, author and a friend of Annie Besant's, who broke her journey from Poona to Madras in June 1916 to spend a few days with Sarojini Naidu at 'The Golden Threshold'. Quoted in *Sarojini Naidu: A Biography* by Padmini Sengupta.

On the Golden Threshold's garden, as M.G. Naidu wrote to Padmaja in a letter dated 12 April 1914: 'I like to see a garden well filled with the most beautiful flowers and shrubs and then allowed to relapse into wildness . . . I have no fancy for well-trimmed lawns, for terraces made to measure and flower beds in geometrical patterns.' From the *Padmaja Naidu Papers* (NMML archives).

M.G. Naidu's views on discharging one's responsibilities were very strict, as this letter of 16 July 1918 to Padmaja shows: 'Your mother's devotion to the cause of her country does I fear often lead her to the neglect of her other duties . . . We are born into the world with certain responsibilities—these we cannot evade. Others we incur after we are born. Once incurred it is but right—nay it is imperative—that we should discharge them at all costs.' Quoted in the *Padmaja Naidu Papers* (NMML archives).

My Own Story by Emmeline Pankhurst (Eveleigh Nash, 1914), part of Jinnah's collection of books (Karachi University Library).

Dr M.G. Naidu's letters to Jaisoorya Naidu, 20 and 27 January 1920, from the *Jaisoorya Naidu Papers* (NMML archives).

Undated letter from Padmaja Naidu to Ranadheera Naidu on Ruttie's visit to Hyderabad, from the *Padmaja Naidu Papers* (University of Hyderabad).

Ruttie's letters to Padmaja Naidu dated 9 and 25 February and 3 March (1920), from the *Padmaja Naidu Papers* (NMML archives).

Jinnah did not like dogs to touch him but they loved him. As Khurshid writes: 'They never took liberties with him, but always liked to be near him without actually touching him.' Quoted in *Memories of Jinnah*.

Ruttie's letters to the Naidu girls up to 1920 are liberally sprinkled with quotes from 'De Profundis', a long letter from prison written by Oscar Wilde, an author she seems to have admired for his modern, epigrammatic style, and whose other books too she read but none that left as deep an impression on her as 'De Profundis'.

Begum Liaquat Ali Khan said of Jinnah: 'It was his clearness that stirred one's astonishment and admiration—his complete lack of humbug. I seem to remember someone writing about "twin lamps of truth". Jinnah's eyes were "twin lamps of truth". Only the honest could look him straight in the eye.' Quoted in *Jinnah: Creator of Pakistan*.

Jinnah could be exasperatingly penny wise over small things—the rationing of tea to his staff, the price of a tie, the amount of petrol used in his car—but there was no rancour or pettiness in his heart, as Bolitho writes in *Jinnah: Creator of Pakistan*.

Chapter Fifteen

Sarojini Naidu's quotes on Fatima Jinnah are taken from her letters to Padmaja from 17 Park Lane, London, dated 27 January 1914 (*Padmaja Naidu Papers*) and to Leilamani, dated 6 June 1928 (*Leilamani Naidu Papers*, NMML archives).

Ruttie's copy of Charlotte Bronte's *Shirley* (New York: Thomas Y Cromwell & Co.) is inscribed: 'To dear Ruttie from Manek, Feb. 18, 1912'. Quoted in *Ruttie Jinnah: Life and Love* by Shagufta Yasmeen (Islamabad: Shuja Sons, 1997).

Ruttie's letter to Padmaja on 3 March 1920.

Details of Jinnah's early life and family details, from Rizwan Ahmad's *Quaidi Ibtedai Tees Saal*.

Jinnah's mother gave birth to four sons but two died, one in infancy and the other at birth, according to Rizwan Ahmad's biography of Jinnah, *Quaidi Ibtedai Tees Saal*. Ahmed Ali, born in 1886, was his only surviving brother. He had four sisters—Rahmat (b. 1878), Maryam (b. 1882), Shirin (b. 1888) and Fatima (b.1893).

Apollo Hotel, where Jinnah stayed in his early years in Bombay, also ran a provision store, Apollo Hotel Stores, 'entirely under European management', where cuts of ham, bacon and cheese brought in 'fresh consignment by the through fortnightly mail' were sold. (From an advertisement in the *Times of India*, 3 April 1917.)

Sir Cowasjee Jehangir, eminent Parsi millionaire, recounted to Bolitho: 'I knew Jinnah as far back as early 1901. He was poor then, but his clothes already had distinction. He was a member of Orient Club and I used to see him there. He was even more pompous and independent during those lean years than later on.' Quoted in *In Quest of Jinnah*.

While the Muslim community was scandalized by Jinnah's decision to put Fatima in a convent boarding school, he nevertheless seems to have made it fashionable among a certain small Muslim elite in Bombay to send their girls to the convent school run by Belgian nuns. By 1906, St Joseph's Convent, Bandra, had not only become 'one of the most celebrated and successful schools in the Bombay Presidency', an 'admirably built and appointed school with its spacious grounds near the seashore', but also boasted of several Muslim students among its 120 boarders and day school students belonging to all communities—Catholics, Protestants, Parsis, Mohammedans, Hindus and Jews, with an assurance that 'no religious belief be interfered with'. Cited in the *Times of India Directory and Yearbook*, 1906.

About Fatima Jinnah's early life and schooling, and living with her brother, from *Fatima Jinnah: Hayat-o-Khidmat* by Agha Hussain Hamadani (National Institute of Historical and Cultural Research, Pakistan).

Mohammed and the Rise of Islam by D.S. Margoliouth (G.P. Putnam & Sons, 1905), signed 'M.A. Jinnah'. Some words on the first page are heavily marked with pencil: 'anathematized', 'sterater', 'doughty' and 'courage'.

Gauba recounts how he invited Jinnah to pray in a mosque for the first time, in 1936. When Jinnah demurred that he would 'not know how to act in a mosque', Gauba said: 'Just follow others.' Cited in the Oral History Transcript of K.L. Gauba (Account No. 76, NMML archives).

Jinnah came into the lounge of the Cecil Hotel in Simla, accompanied by Sikander Hayat Khan and a moulvi with a long beard. They sat down and were offered a drink by Diwan Chaman Lal. Jinnah asked for a whisky soda while Sikander, keeping one eye on the moulvi, asked for a lemonade. Jinnah then turned to Chaman Lal and said: 'You know, I am not the religious leader of the Muslims. I am only their political leader.' Cited in the Oral History Transcript of Diwan Chaman Lal (Account No. 220, NMML archives).

Sarojini Naidu, in a letter dated March 2 1920 to Padmaja, complained of the several shocks 'too hard to bear for a forty-one-year-old mother with a weak heart', one of them being 'Ruttie and Arlette—minus Jinnah and Baby' arriving with Leilamani to England. Cited in the *Padmaja Naidu Papers* (NMML archives).

Kanji Dwarkadas writes of Jinnah closeted in a meeting with Annie Besant for several hours and emerging exhausted. When asked how the meeting had gone, he replied: 'My dear fellow, never argue with a woman!' Cited in *India's Fight for Freedom.*

Ruttie's letter to Leilamani from West End Hotel, Bangalore, dated 18 April 1920, saying she is on her way up to Ooty. Cited in the *Leilamani Naidu Papers* (NMML archives).

Chapter Sixteen

'Mr and Mrs Gandhi Entertained By Gurjar Sabha-Jinnah On South African Problems', from the *Bombay Chronicle*, 15 January 1915, and reproduced in *The Works of Quaid-i-Azam 1913–1916*, vol. 2.

Gandhi himself admitted later that Jinnah was shocked when in his reply to the address of welcome, he described Jinnah as a fellow Muslim Gujarati and not as an Indian. Cited in *The Collected Works of Mahatma Gandhi*, vol. XIII, and quoted in *Secular and Nationalist Jinnah.*

Hansa Mehta, who later became a devoted disciple of Gandhi, recalls how unimpressed she was by Gandhi when she first saw him at the Bombay Congress session in 1915: 'He spoke in a very low voice and his dress was peculiar—turban and all that. He did not interest me then.' Cited in the Oral History Transcript of Hansa Mehta (Account No. 43, NMML archives).

Kanji Dwarkadas writes: '[We] approached Gandhi for assistance to get Mrs Besant out. Then Gandhi started his first talk of Passive Resistance and suffering in India. He wanted 100 volunteers, true and faithful, to walk from Bombay to Coimbatore . . . where Dr. Besant was interned and he said this would help in her release . . . After his return from Champaran in October 1917, Gandhi was asking for volunteers to go to

Champaran for social work, which included removal of night soil from the streets.' Cited in *Gandhiji through My Dairy.*

Letter from Gandhi to Jinnah dated 4 July 1918: '"Can you not see that if every Home Rule League became a potent Recruiting Agency, whilst at the same time fighting for constitutional rights, we should ensure the passing of the Congress–League Scheme . . ." Seek ye first the Recruiting Office and everything will be added unto you.' Cited in *The Collected Works of Mahatma Gandhi*, vol. 17.

Ian Bryant Wells writes: 'During the War years he [Gandhi] had actively recruited for the British, while Jinnah's view was that if the British wanted Indians to join the army they "must make the people feel they are citizens of the Empire, and the King's equal subjects". Gandhi placed no such restrictions on his loyalty to the British war effort, and Jinnah had been shocked by Gandhi's suggestion that support of the recruiting programme would bring political reforms for India.' Cited in *Ambassador of Hindu–Muslim Unity: Jinnah's Early Politics.*

In November 1917, Montagu travelled to India to meet leaders of the various political parties and wrote of them in his diary. On Gandhi, he wrote, 'A social reformer with a real desire to find grievances and to cure them, not for any reasons of self-advertisement, but to improve the conditions of his fellow men.' On Jinnah, he wrote: '. . . young, perfectly mannered, impressive looking, armed to the teeth with dialectics, and insistent upon the whole of his scheme . . . Jinnah is a very clever man, and it is, of course, an outrage that such a man should have no chance of running the affairs of his own country.' Cited in *Jinnah: Creator of Pakistan.*

According to Ajeet Jawed, 'Gandhi sat on a platform without chairs and asked Jinnah to sit down next to him. Jinnah who was dressed in his Western suit and had long legs reluctantly sat hanging his legs over the edge of the platform. When Jinnah started speaking Gandhi interrupted him. He protested against the use of English in a Gujarati gathering and asked Jinnah to speak in Gujarati, a language Jinnah did not know . . . Jinnah felt humiliated and "considered this a rude request and an unkind cut". Perhaps this was the beginning of the rift between the two as Gandhi himself admitted later that Jinnah never forgave him for this and took it as a personal insult.' Cited in *Secular and Nationalist Jinnah*.

Jinnah voiced his view on English versus Indian language during a speech he gave to students in Bombay on 14 March 1920. As reported in the *Bombay Chronicle* of 17 March 1920: 'He said, personally, he would be glad to speak in Urdu or any other national language instead of a foreign one. But under the present circumstances they could not help it. However, if they had to speak in English and if they had to conduct their proceedings in English they must speak as good English as an Englishman might speak.' Quoted in *The Works of Quaid-i-Azam 1919–1920*, vol. 5.

Jinnah was not the only leader to buck at Gandhi's orders to conduct public meetings in an Indian language. Sarojini Naidu's biographer Padmini Sengupta relates how in 1917, at the Bihari students' conference in Bhagalpur, when Sarojini was asked by Gandhi to speak in Hindustani, she said in an aside to one of the organizers: 'Gandhiji does not want English to be spoken. I don't know how I am going to speak in Hindustani. I tell you what, when I get up, ask the students to shout "English! English!"' But Sarojini, who had been educated in the Nizam's state of Hyderabad, where the medium of instruction was Urdu, ended up speaking in high-flown Persianized Urdu. Cited in *Sarojini Naidu: A Biography*.

Letter to M.A. Jinnah dated 28 June 1919, in *The Collected Works of Mahatma Gandhi*, vol. 18.

Letter to Mrs Jinnah dated 30 April 1920, in *The Collected Works of Mahatma Gandhi*, vol. 20.

The All-India Muslim League session and the Khilafat Conference, Amritsar, from the *Bombay Chronicle* (30–31 December 1919, 1–2 January 1920 and 5 January 1920), and mentioned in *The Works of Quaid-i-Azam 1919–1920*, vol. 5.

Young India, 12 May 1920. Also in *The Collected Works of Mahatma Gandhi*, vol. 20, 1999.

Letter from Jinnah to Syed Zahur Ahmad, joint secretary of the All-India Muslim League, dated 1 May 1920, from the AIML Papers Council Meetings, cited in *The Works of Quaid-i-Azam 1919–1920*, vol. 5.

Letter from Zahur Ahmad to Jinnah dated 27 May 1920, from the AIML Papers Council Meetings.

Letter from Jinnah to Brelvi dated 19 May 1920, from the *Bombay Chronicle*, 12 June 1920.

Padmaja's quote on Ruttie from her letter to Chagla dated June 1929, from the *Chagla Papers* (NMML archives).

The journey and events in the Calcutta special session of the Congress in September 1920. Cited in *India's Fight for Freedom*; *Ruttie Jinnah: Story of a Friendship*; Mahadev Desai's diary, *Day to Day with Gandhi*, vol. 3 (Ahmedabad: Navajivan Publishing House); the *Bombay Chronicle*, 6 September 1920, cited in *The Works of Quaid-i-Azam 1919–1920*, vol. 5; and *Ambassador of Hindu–Muslim Unity: Jinnah's Early Politics*.

Jinnah's protest over the revision of the Home Rule League's constitution and his open letter to Gandhi (signed by nineteen others), from the *Bombay Chronicle* (5 October 1920 and 7 October 1920), and cited in *The Works of Quaid-i-Azam 1919–1920*, vol. 5.

The events during the Nagpur Congress session and after, from the *Bombay Chronicle*, 29–30 December 1920, and cited in *The Works of Quaid-i-Azam*; as also in the Oral History Transcript of Shankerlal G. Banker (Account No. 153, NMML archives).

V.R. Bhende, member of the Home Rule League and secretary to Vithalbhai Patel, relates how Ruttie was thrown out of the Congress session in Nagpur, because she was Jinnah's wife: 'Some Madrasi delegates sent a chit to the president of the session, C. Vijayaraghavachariar, objecting to Ruttie's dress [although] she was wearing a beautiful saree and an armless blouse. The president passed on the chit to Mr Jinnah and Mrs Jinnah had to withdraw [from the session].' Cited in the Oral History Transcript of V.R. Bhende (Account No. 158, NMML archives).

Chapter Seventeen

Letter to the editor titled 'Non-Cooperation in Practice' under the initial 'R' in the *Times of India*, 13 January 1921.

A Gujarati magazine in Bombay, *Vismi Sadi*, put a list of eight questions to Jinnah which he answered in his own hand in Gujarati, and appeared in the May 1916 issue of the monthly. The questions and answers: 1) What quality is admirable in a man? Independence; 2) What quality is admirable in a female? Loyalty; 3) What do you believe is the success of life? To acquire [the] love of masses; 4) What do you like for recreation? Riding a horse; 5) Which flower do you like? Lily; 6) Which writer do you like? Shakespeare; 7) Which book do you like? Monte Cristo [*sic*]; and 8) What is your motto? Never to be disappointed. Cited in the *Rare Speeches and Documents of Quaid-i-Azam* edited by Yahya Hashim Bawany, and quoted in *Ruttie Jinnah* by Khwaja Razi Haider.

Umar Sobhani, Jinnah's loyal lieutenant who went over to Gandhi's side, wrote on his disillusionment with Jinnah in a letter to Padmaja Naidu dated 3 October 1920: 'I wonder if you have heard of Jinnah's antics. Few months ago, I would have knocked off the head of the man who would have dared to suggest that Jinnah could be so petty. What disillusionment. If you have not heard about him, I shall not enlighten you at present but some day I shall give you an account of the whole business.' Cited in the *Padmaja Naidu Papers* (NMML archives).

Hector Bolitho met the broker in charge of Jinnah's investments who said about Jinnah: 'At the time of Partition his fortune must have been from six to seven million rupees. Although he was thrifty, he never pursued money in a cheap way. One instance of this. A client was sent to him and he told Jinnah that he had limited money with which to fight his case. Jinnah took it up and lost. But he believed in the case and that it should be taken to the Appeal Court, so he promised to fight the case, without being paid. He won, and when the client offered to pay, Jinnah refused; he had agreed to take no fee and he would not have the conditions changed just because he had succeeded.' Cited in *In Quest of Jinnah*.

Ruttie's quote from her letter to Kanji Dwarkadas, dated 25 September 1922. On Ruttie, Kanji wrote: 'She was always with him, and though she was much younger than he, she without him realizing it, looked after him and made his life in all its aspects, pleasant, carefree and well worth living.' Cited in *Ruttie Jinnah: The Story of a Great Friendship*.

One of Jinnah's young friends, M.A.H. Ispahani writes: 'If he decided . . . not to take more than a quantity fixed by him of food or other refreshment, no amount of persuasion and no temptation would wring a change in his resolve. He had so disciplined himself that he could, without stress or strain, resist all temptations and pleading.' From *Quaid-i-Azam Jinnah As I knew Him* by M.A.H. Ispahani (Karachi: Forward Publications Trust, 1967).

Sarojini Naidu's letter to Padmaja, dated 28 January 1928, on Ruttie's confession about the state of her marriage, from the *Padmaja Naidu Papers* (NMML archives).

Jinnah attends the public meeting of the Ali brothers on 21 January 1921, and his speech at Gokhale's sixth death anniversary on 19 February 1921. Cited in the *Bombay Chronicle*, and reproduced in *The Works of Quaid-i-Azam 1921–1924*, vol. 6.

Meeting at the Excelsior Theatre, from *India's Fight for Freedom*.

Padmaja Naidu's letters to Leilamani dated April 1921 and June 1921, from the *Leilamani Naidu Papers* (NMML archives).

Sarojini Naidu's letter to Leilamani dated 11 June 1921, from the *Leilamani Naidu Papers* (NMML archives).

Sarojini Naidu's letter to Padmaja (undated); her letter to Leilamani dated 5 July 1921; and her letter to Padmaja dated 20 January 1928; from the *Padmaja Naidu Papers* (NMML archives).

The incident of Jinnah leaving the ballroom after the band struck up, from M.A.H. Ispahani's recollections in *Quaid-e-Azam Jinnah As I Knew Him*.

Jinnah recounted the anecdote of finding shirts after the War at pre-War prices to K.H. Khurshid, from *Memories of Jinnah*.

On Jinnah's fastidiousness, Diwan Chaman Lal writes: 'I reminded him of the day we spent together in Paris . . . roaming the shops to buy ties and shirts. After seeing hundreds of ties he at last chose one . . .' From *Tributes to Quaid-i-Azam* edited by Muhammad Hanif Shahid (Lahore: Sang-E-Meel Publications, 1976)

Leilamani Naidu's letters to Padmaja dated 6 July 1921 and 15 July 1921, from the *Padmaja Naidu Papers* (NMML archives).

Jinnah's letter to Montagu from Paris dated 8 August 1921, from *The Works of Quaid-i-Azam 1921–1924*, vol. 6.

Sarojini Naidu's letter to Leilamani dated 10 August 1921 and 14 December 1921 from the *Leilamani Naidu Papers* and her letter to Padmaja (undated), from the *Padmaja Naidu Papers* (NMML archives).

Sarojini Naidu's letter to Syud Hossain dated 9 September 1921, from the *Sarojini Naidu Papers* (NMML archives.)

Sarojini Naidu's letters to Padmaja dated 19 September 1921, 4 October 1921 and 8 November 1921, from the *Padmaja Naidu Papers* (NMML archives).

A short biography of Anita Delgado in *Wicked Women of the Raj* by Coralie Younger (New Delhi: HarperCollins India, 2003).

Rushbrook William's article quoted in *Ruttie Jinnah* by Khwaja Razi Haider.

Chapter Eighteen

Kanji Dwarkadas's all-night political discussion with the Jinnahs on 2 and 3 January 1922, from *Ruttie Jinnah: The Story of a Great Friendship*.

Ruttie's letter to Padmaja, dated September 1915, refers to her bilious complaint: 'I have had *that*—sweet things make you bilious—*so much* dinned into me . . .' Cited in the *Padmaja Naidu Papers* (NMML archives). Jinnah smoked fifty cigarettes a day (his brand was Craven A), and according to his physician, could live on 'will-power, whisky and cigarettes'.

Sarojini's letters to Padmaja dated 9 and 13 January, 1922; 20 and 26 March 1922; 16 May 1922; 22 June 1922; 20 January 1928; 1 and 28 July 1922; 7 and 12 September 1924; 2 December 1924; 30 January 1925; 5 and 21 February 1925; and 25 March 1925; from *Padmaja Naidu Papers* (NMML archives).

Fatima Jinnah relates her brother's aversion to doctors, 'thinking he could will his way to health . . .' and also the story he told the doctor about a woman who would not leave her bed despite the doctor assuring her that she was all right in *My Brother*.

Sarojini's letters to Leilamani dated 2 February 1922; 20 April 1922; 2 June 1922; 29 July 1922; and 5 June 1923; from the *Leilamani Naidu Papers* (NMML archives).

Leilamani's letters to Padmaja dated 22 February 1922; 14 June 1923; 26 and 20 November 1924; 16 January 1925; and 15 February 1925; from the *Padmaja Naidu Papers* (NMML archives).

Ranadheera Naidu's letter to Leilamani dated 25 April 1922, from the *Leilamani Naidu Papers* (NMML archives).

Padmaja's letters to Leilamani dated 20 April 1922; 12 November 1926; 5 December 1926; from the *Leilamani Naidu Papers* (NMML archives).

On Jinnah's carefulness with money but his good humour in putting up with being teased about it, Kanji Dwarkadas recounts how Ruttie and he ribbed Jinnah about the note he left in the suggestion book of the Orient Club in 1906 asking for a reduction in charges paid for losing at billiards by six annas a game: 'Jinnah replied [that] six annas was very much six annas and in those days when his legal practice was not bringing a good income, he could not afford to pay twelve annas a game.' Cited in *India's Fight for Freedom*.

Ruttie's letters to Kanji Dwarkadas dated 25 September 1922; and 21 November 1924; from *Ruttie Jinnah: The Story of a Great Friendship*.

Madame Bhikhaiji Cama by Khorshed Adi Sethna (Builders of Modern India Series, Ministry of Information and Broadcasting, Government of India, 1987).

Jaisoorya Naidu's letter to Leilamani dated 10 November 1926, from the *Leilamani Naidu Papers* (NMML archives).

Leilamani Naidu's letter to her father dated 19 June 1923, from the *M.G. Naidu Papers* (NMML archives).

Ruttie's letter to Leilamani dated 22 June 1923, from the *Leilamani Naidu Papers* (NMML archives).

Jinnah's election manifesto in the *Bombay Chronicle* (20 September 1923), cited in *The Works of Quaid-i-Azam 1921–1924*, vol. 6.

Jinnah's remark on Pandit Motilal Nehru, from *Alva, Leaders of India*, quoted in *Secular and Nationalist Jinnah*.

Jinnah's quotes on his marriage and Ruttie, from *In Quest of Jinnah*.

Ruttie's poem and note to Padmaja dated 9 January 1925 and letter dated 2 January 1925, from the *Padmaja Naidu Papers* (NMML archives).

Sayyada Badrunnisa's article on her visit to the Jinnahs' home quoted in Khwaja Razi Haider's *Ruttie Jinnah*.

Jazz music and dance in Bombay, from *The Taj at Apollo Bunder* by Charles Allen and Sharada Dwivedi.

Kanji Dwarkadas's interview with Shahabuddin Desnavi in his autobiography, *Deeda-o-Shuneeda*.

Napoleon—Lover and Husband by Frederick Masson, translated by J.M. Howell (Ohio: Saalfield Publishing Co, 1907), is among Jinnah's personal collection of books in the Karachi University Library.

Dr M.G. Naidu's letter to Padmaja dated 28 July 1918, along with newspaper clipping on spinal bath, from the *Padmaja Naidu Papers* (NMML archives).

Sarojini Naidu's letters to Ranadheera (wrongly) dated April 1921; 23 March 1925; from the *Ranadheera Naidu Papers* (NMML archives).

Ruttie's letters to Kanji Dwarkadas, undated (on Khannum's visit) and dated 1 May 1925, from *Ruttie Jinnah: Life and Love* by Shagufta Yasmeen.

Reminiscence of Ruttie in Simla by Nawab Yameen Khan in his memoir *Nama-i-A'amal*, and cited in Khwaja Razi Haider's *Ruttie Jinnah*.

Ibid for Jahan Ara Shahnawaz's recollection of Ruttie.

Chapter Nineteen

Sarojini's letters to Padmaja dated 10 April 1925; 1 and 27 September 1925; 7, 13 and 27 February 1926; 8 April 1926; 18 August 1926; 11,

13 and 23 October 1926; 12 and 23 February 1927; 22 March 1927; 3 May 1927; 26 and 29 September 1927; and 16 October 1927; from the *Padmaja Naidu Papers* (NMML archives).

Sarojini's letters to Leilamani dated 3 October 1925; 21 and 29 January 1926; 23 February 1926; 3 March 1926; 10 April 1926; 12 November 1926; and 4 and 11 December 1926; from the *Leilamani Naidu Papers* (NMML archives).

Ruttie's letters to Kanji Dwarkadas dated 28 December 1924; 7 and 12 April 1925; 5 June 1925; 31 March 1926; 1 September 1926; two undated letters; and 28 August 1927; from *Ruttie Jinnah: The Story of a Great Friendship*.

Ruttie's letters to Kanji Dwarkadas, undated (on Khannum's visit) and dated 1 May 1925, from *Ruttie Jinnah: Life and Love* by Shagufta Yasmeen.

Sarojini's letter to M.C. Chagla dated 22 March 1927; 4 August 1927; from the *Chagla Papers* (NMML archives).

The Tourist's Guide to Kashmir, Ladakh, Skardu & C edited by the late Major Arthur Neve, surgeon to the Kashmir Medical Mission. This was printed at the Civil and Military Gazette Press in 1923, and is among Jinnah's personal collection of books in the Karachi University Library.

Sarojini's letter to Kanji Dwarkadas dated 1 September 1927, from *Ruttie Jinnah: The Story of a Great Friendship*.

Ruttie's letter to Padmaja dated 15 November 1927 and wire dated 17 November 1927, from the *Padmaja Naidu Papers* (NMML archives).

Chapter Twenty

Sarojini Naidu's letters to Padmaja dated 16 and 20 January 1928; 12 February 1928; 14 March 1928 (cable); 2 April 1928; 1 May 1928; 22 August 1928; 10 October 1928; from the *Padmaja Naidu Papers* (NMML archives).

Sarojini Naidu's letter to Syud Hossain dated 26 July 1928, from the *Sarojini Naidu Papers* (NMML archives).

Padmaja Naidu's letters to M.C. Chagla dated March 1928, from the *M.C. Chagla Papers* (NMML archives).

Sarojini Naidu's letters to M.C. Chagla dated 5 February 1928; 2 April 1928; 1 July 1928; 25 October 1928; from the *M.C. Chagla Papers* (NMML archives).

Jinnah returned from Delhi on 30 March 1928 and 'found that Ruttie had moved from their home to Hotel Taj Mahal, renting a suite there by month. Kanji Dwarkadas helped Ruttie in shifting herself to [the] hotel.' Cited in *Quaid-i-Azam and His Times: A Compendium* edited by Sharif Al Mujahid (Karachi: Quaid-i-Azam Academy, 1990).

Jinnah's remark to Parsi friend, from *Jinnah: Creator of Pakistan*.

Diwan Chaman Lal's reminiscence of Jinnah on board the ship and the one-day tour of Cairo, from his Oral History Transcript (Account No. 220, NMML archives).

Sarojini Naidu's letters to Leilamani dated 31 May 1928; and 6 and 12 June 1928; from the *Leilamani Naidu Papers* (NMML archives).

M.G. Naidu's letter to Padmaja dated 21 May 1928, from the *Padmaja Naidu Papers* (NMML archives).

Diwan Chaman Lal's recounting of Ruttie's illness in Paris and their parting after a month, from *Jinnah: Creator of Pakistan* and Lall's article, 'The Quaid-i-Azam As I Knew Him', cited in the *Pakistan Times*, and quoted in *Tributes to Quaid-i-Azam*.

Motilal Nehru's letter to Jinnah dated 2 August 1928 and Jinnah's reply to Motilal Nehru dated 20 October 1928, from *Quaid-i-Azam and His Times: A Compendium*.

Ruttie's letter to Jinnah dated 5 October 1928 (QAP-F-890, National Archives of Pakistan).

While some historians state that Ruttie went to live in the Taj Mahal Hotel in Bombay after returning from Paris, there is no evidence to support it. On the contrary, Kanji Dwarkadas's memoir, *Ruttie Jinnah: The Story of a Great Friendship*, makes frequent references to Ruttie's 'house' and not a hotel suite. According to G. Allana's *Quaid-E-Azam Jinnah: The*

Story of a Nation, 'When she returned to India, Mrs Jinnah went to live with her brother in Bombay.' And according to Syed Sharifuddin Pirzada's *Some Aspects of Quaid-i-Azam's Life*, she went to live with her mother. But the Petits' with their vast estates are more likely to have set her up in an independent house, which is what Ruttie would have no doubt preferred rather than living as a dependent on either her brother or mother.

J. Krishnamurthy, in his letter to Kanji dated 1 April 1929, wrote: 'I thought she would get well, when we last saw her [on 2 February 1929]. She looked so much better.' Cited in *Ruttie Jinnah: The Story of a Great Friendship*.

Quotes from Jinnah's speech at the all-parties conference in Calcutta on 28 December 1928, from *Quaid-i-Azam and His Times: A Compendium*.

Ibid. Jinnah's cable to the All India Muslim League assistant secretary, dated 6 February 1929.

Jamshed Nusserwanjee's recollection of Jinnah after the all-parties conference in Calcutta, from *Jinnah: Creator of Pakistan*.

Kanji Dwarkadas's interview with Shahabuddin Desnavi in the latter's autobiography, *Deeda O Shuneeda*.

Diwan Chaman Lal's account of Jinnah leaving Delhi for Ruttie's funeral, from his article in the *Pakistan Times*, and reproduced in *Tributes to Quaid-i-Azam*.

B.A. Hashmi's reminiscence on the condolence visit, from *In Quest of Jinnah: Diary, Notes and Correspondence of Hector Bolitho*.

Padmaja Naidu's letter to M.C. Chagla dated June 1929, from the *M.C. Chagla Papers* (NMML archives).

Sarojini Naidu's letters to Padmaja dated 19, 25 and 30 March 1929; 7 April 1929; 6 May 1929; 24 July 1929; 22 and 24 August 1929; 1 September 1929; 21 October 1929; from the *Padmaja Naidu Papers*, (NMML archives).

Umar Sobhani died suddenly in August 1926 of unnatural causes that shook Sarojini very deeply.

Margaret E. Cousins, Irish suffragist and theosophist, moved to India in 1915 with her husband, James Cousins, and worked with Annie Besant. She was a teacher and author of several books, including *The Awakening of Asian Womanhood*.

Sarojini Naidu's letter to Ranadheera dated 31 March 1929, from the *Ranadheera Naidu Papers* (NMML Archives).

Dina Wadia on her grandmother as told to Ameena Saiyid in Karachi.

Leilamani Naidu's letters to Padmaja dated 9 and 15 September 1930, from the *Padmaja Naidu Papers* (NMML archives).

Letter from Frances H. Browne, The Hoo, Willingdon, Sussex, to Jinnah dated 3 September 1936, notifying him of Dina's school certificate exam results (National Archives of Pakistan, Islamabad).

Jinnah's chauffeur, Mohammad Hanif Azad's reminiscence, from *Bitter Fruit: The Very Best of Saadat Hasan Manto*, edited and translated by Khalid Hasan (New Delhi: Penguin India, 2008).